Biography of a Revolution

*The publisher and the University of California Press
Foundation gratefully acknowledge the generous support of
the Anne G. Lipow Endowment Fund in Social Justice and
Human Rights.*

Biography of a Revolution

THE FEMINIST ROOTS OF HUMAN
RIGHTS IN EGYPT

Lucia Sorbera

UNIVERSITY OF CALIFORNIA PRESS

University of California Press
Oakland, California

© 2025 by Lucia Sorbera

All rights reserved.

Library of Congress Cataloging-in-Publication Data

Names: Sorbera, Lucia, author.
Title: Biography of a revolution : the feminist roots of human rights in
Egypt / Lucia Sorbera.
Description: Oakland : University of California Press, 2025. | Includes
bibliographical references and index.
Identifiers: LCCN 2024052581 (print) | LCCN 2024052582 (ebook) |
ISBN 9780520394742 (hardback) | ISBN 9780520394759 (paperback) |
ISBN 9780520394766 (ebook)
Subjects: LCSH: Feminism—Egypt—History. | Women's rights—Egypt. |
Feminists—Egypt—Biography. | Women political activists—Egypt—
Biography. | Human rights—Egypt. | Social movements—Egypt—History. |
Revolutions—Egypt—History—21st century. | Egypt—History—Protests,
2011–2013. | LCGFT: Biographies.
Classification: LCC HQ1793 .S67 2025 (print) | LCC HQ1793 (ebook) |
DDC 305.420962—dc23/eng/20241204
LC record available at https://lccn.loc.gov/2024052581
LC ebook record available at https://lccn.loc.gov/2024052582

GPSR Authorized Representative: Easy Access System Europe, Mustamäe tee
50, 10621 Tallinn, Estonia, gpsr.requests@easproject.com

34   33   32   31   30   29   28   27   26   25
10   9   8   7   6   5   4   3   2   1

To the memory of my father, Tindaro Sorbera
For my mother, Alga Grandi
&
For my son, Francesco Marin

If you come to history, to rewrite history, history generally means his-story. We need her-story, and then, when we come to rewrite her-story, we don't want her-story narrated by the government.

NAWAL AL-SAADAWI, Cairo, October 10, 2014

If you control half of the society, it becomes easy to control society itself, all of society.

FARIDA AL-NAQQASH, Cairo, January 14, 2018

Lucia: You were telling me that your official name is Seham Abd el-Salam Muhammad, but you prefer to be called Seham Saneya Abd el-Salam. Can you tell me why?

Seham: Because this is the real story, as they say. The real history is mostly different from the official history. Saneya is my mother, Abd el-Salam is my father. Both participated in making me physically, psychologically, socially, intellectually. Why should I neglect Saneya, and acknowledge my grandfather Muhammad who I have never seen?

SEHAM SANEYA ABD EL-SALAM, Cairo, December 15, 2022

The sense that life is sort of a go-between between constant tension and confrontation and the sense that you are on the right [side], that you are fighting for something, was sort of an ongoing thing. It never ended. Some people go away, and they forget it, but you don't. You are constantly living it.

HALA SHUKRALLAH, Cairo, December 18, 2018

The revolution has perpetual life and dream. The revolution does not depend on individuals, and sooner or later, in our lifetime or that of those who will come after us, the revolution will be completed because human beings deserve better, and that ugliness no matter how it tries to beautify itself, will reveal his face.

MAHIENOUR EL-MASSRY, letter from Qanater Prison, January 24, 2016

CONTENTS

Acknowledgments ix
Note on Transliteration, Transcription, and Translation xvii

Introduction 1

PART ONE
THE LONG FEMINIST CENTURY IN EGYPT

1 · Genealogies of Women's Activism 27

2 · The Fight for Women's Bodily Rights: The FGM Task Force 50

3 · Gendered Dimensions of the Post–Cold War Order in Egypt 67

4 · Toward a Women's History of the Human Rights
Movement in Egypt 86

PART TWO
FEMINIST LIVES IN EGYPT

5 · Practicing Feminist Psychiatry as Human Rights Activism:
Aida Seif El-Dawla, Suzan Fayad, and Magda Adly 103

6 · Conceptualizing Women's Rights within the Family as
Human Rights: The Intellectual and Grassroots Work
of Azza Soliman 118

7 · Toward an Ethics of Care: The Political Journey of
Gameela Ismail 134

8 · Transgenerational Legacies in the Early 2000s Social
Movements: Mahienour El-Massry and Sana' al-Masri 155

PART THREE
TOWARD NEW WAYS OF BEING,
KNOWING, AND DOING

9 · January 25, 2011: A New Feminist Beginning 181

10 · Historicizing the Egyptian Revolution: The Politics of
Memory and Transmission 193

11 · Sexual Violence, Power, Freedom, and the Emergence
of a New Feminist Discourse 214

12 · The Twenty-First-Century Egyptian Women's
Prisons Notebooks 232

Conclusion 251

Notes 261
Bibliography 295
Index 319

ACKNOWLEDGMENTS

It takes a village . . .

. . . and the village that inhabits the pages of this book spans multiple countries, languages, and continents. It is a pleasure to thank numerous mentors, intellectual partners, and friends and families who populate this village.

There is no way I can thank all the people I am in debt to in Egypt, but I want at least to acknowledge the women without whom this book, which tells their stories, would have never been imagined, never mind written. I am indebted for their friendship, mentorship, and invaluable support to Aida Seif El-Dawla, Nawla Darwiche, Amal Abdel Hadi, Laila Soueif, Ahdaf Soueif, Hoda Elsadda, Gameela Ismail, Huda Lutfi, Mona Anis, May Telmissany, Shereen Abulnaga, Azza Soliman, Farida al-Naqqash, Safinaz Kazem, Hala Shukrallah, Lina Attalah, Mahienour El-Massry, Ragia Omran, Sally Toma, Hind Mahmoud, Yara Sallam, Yasmin El-Rifae, Laila Soliman and, last but not least, to the late Amina Rachid and Seham Saneya Abd el-Salam.

My gratitude extends to the larger community of Egyptian activists and scholars who over a decade of heavy work, high tensions, and danger for their lives gave me trust and companionship, opening their houses, providing insights and help to extend my network, always ensuring that I was safe, and sharing the most important thing a human being can share with a stranger: the stories of their lives. I will always be touched by their memories, stories, and experiences, many of them here in the pages of this book and mentioned in the bibliography, and I am particularly obliged to Wael Abdel Fattah, Nasser Amin, Hoda Abdelwahab, Sharif Abdel Kouddous, Elham Eidarous, Manal Hassan, Tarek Shalabi, Kawkab Tawfik, Malak Labib, Mozn Hassan,

Nevine El-Nossery, Basma Abdel Aziz, Nadia Naqib, Nael Eltoukhy, Pascale Ghazaleh, Mostafa Mohie, Melanie Henry, Ghasser Abdel-Razek, Naglaa Seham Younes, Helen Rizzo, Wael Iskandar, Omnia Khalil, Mai El-Mahdy, Mariam Kirollos, Dina Makram Ebeid, Randa Aboubakr, Basma Abdel Rahman, Dina Heshmat, Reem Saad, the entire *Mada Masr* team, and as importantly, the late Zakaria Ibrahim, Khalil Khalfat, and Derno Ricci.

My journey studying feminism in Egypt began in the early 2000s, when I was a graduate student under the supervision of the late Mario Nordio, to whom I will always be obliged for being an enthusiastic guide in my first steps in the field of Middle East Studies, and for providing a model of committed scholar infused with generosity, love for life, and intellectual freedom and integrity, which yet today is a source of inspiration for me.

I will never be able to express all the admiration and gratitude I feel for Margot Badran, who has been my most important guide since I began studying the history of Egyptian feminism. I have lost count of the meetings we've had since our first encounter in Venice in 2001, and the generosity of her time, insights, comments, and feedback, pushing me to question my initial assumptions, to dig deeper and to do better, has no equal. Thank you, Margot, you are inspirational in everything you do!

My scholarship is deeply influenced by the Italian tradition of feminist historiography, as developed by the Italian Society of Women Historians, where I am grateful for decades of mentorship and friendship, especially to Anna Scattigno, Elisabetta Vezzosi, Isabelle Chabot, Maria Rosaria Stabili, Giulia Calvi, Raffaella Sarti, Carlotta Sorba, Raffaella Baritiono, Silvia Salvatici, Enrica Asquer, and Elisabetta Bini.

The research that led to this book was financially supported by grants from the Faculty of Arts and Social Sciences and the School of Languages and Cultures at the University of Sydney, where I also benefited from three semesters of research leave, which I have spent in Cairo (2014 and 2017) and in New York City (2023). I am grateful to the then-director of Netherlands-Flemish Institute in Cairo, the late Rudolf de Jong, who hosted me as a research fellow, and to Tine Lavent and Ifdal Elsaket, who organized a seminar where I could workshop some preliminary ideas for this book with international students based in Egypt and with Egyptian scholars. In New York, I should thank Philip Kasinitz, the director of the Advanced Research Collaborative at CUNY Graduate Center, where I was a research fellow, and the ARC administrator, Kay Powell, as well my fellow scholars, for creating a nourishing and vibrant space of intellectual exchange, especially Jillian

Schwedler, Francesca Decimo, and the Egypt reading group with Beth Baron and Maria Frederica Malström, all of whom I am lucky to count among my friends. I wrote this manuscript during a series of research fellowships: the Kathleen Fitzpatrick research fellowship in the Laureate Program Women and the International at the University of Sydney (2017) led by Glenda Sluga, to whom I am grateful for many years of mentorship and friendship; the Fernand Braudel Senior Research Fellowship at the European University Institute in Florence (2022), where I benefited from intellectual exchange with colleagues and students in the Department of History, and the Institute for Advanced Studies in Bologna (2023), for which I thank also the Department of Modern Languages and Cultures, especially the director, my dear friend Paola Scrolavezza.

My research benefited greatly from the generous help of many librarians: primarily Ola Essam at the Women and Memory Forum in Cairo, who over the years became also a good friend, as well as the librarians of the Special and Rare Collections at the American University in Cairo and the Fisher Library at the University of Sydney.

I have conducted all the interviews for this book, and I am grateful to my research assistants for their help transcribing and translating them: Estella Carpi (now a colleague), Ella Tolponicki, Jen McLean, Rafeeq Abdel Rahman, and Hossam Hoss. I also would like to thank for profound intellectual exchange the graduate students I have supervised and mentored over the years: Rosemary Hancock, Shima Shahbazi, Zainab Abdulnabi, and Alice Loda (also now colleagues), and Paul Esber, Ahlam Abu Khoti, Amro Ali, Enise Şeida Kapusuz, Margherita Picchi, Marta Bellingreri, Martina Biondi, Ehsan Golhamar, Alia Ardon, Izabella Antoniou, Eva Boleti, and Alessandra Carnevale. They are all developing their own independent and diverse career paths, and I am proud to count them among my intellectual partners and friends.

Over the past ten years, I have benefited from the generosity of colleagues who arranged for me guest lectures and public talks at their universities and hosted me as a visiting scholar or research fellow, allowing me to refine some of the ideas that are developed in this book: Anna Loretoni at Scuola Superiore Sant'Anna di Pisa; Arturo Marzano at Pisa University; Maria Elena Paniconi and Mariangela Masullo at University of Macerata; Serena Tolino at the Department of History and Culture of the Middle East at the University of Hamburg and the University of Bern Institute for Islamic and Middle East Studies; Na'eem Jenna at the Afro Middle East

Center in Johannesburg; Shashy Jayakumar at Nanyang Technological University in Singapore; John Enry at the Baptist University of Hong Khong; Rosita di Peri at the University of Torino; Sara Roy at the Harvard Center for Middle East Studies; and Andrew Simon at the Dartmouth University Middle Eastern Studies program. Thank you for your generosity and insights!

I have the habit of sharing preliminary findings of my research and early drafts of my writing with my students at the University of Sydney. They are my first readers and advisers. Thanks to all of you for your thoughtful comments, and for your curiosity about the world, which keeps me motivated to learn and write!

Earlier fruits of this labor have appeared in three books and numerous articles and book chapters I published during the past ten years, throughout which I have valued collaborative work, learning from my coauthors, coeditors, and research partners: Maria Elena Paniconi, Lorenzo Casini, Leila El Houssi, Serena Tolino, Aymon Kreil, Bronwyn Winter, Stephanie Hemelryk Donald, Kaya Davies Hayon, Silvia Bruzzi, Jakelin Troy, Janelle Evans, Paul Donnelly, Melanie Pitkin, Bahia Shehab, Tamar Shirinian, Michael Dagostino, Michael McDonnell, Niro Kandashami, and Victor Ehikhamenor.

Numerous colleagues and friends over the years have given feedback and hospitality during the research that led to this book: Gennaro Gervasio, Lea Nocera, Sherine Hafez, Soha Bayoumi, Nicola Pratt, Hind Mahmoud, Michelle Pace, Matteo Legrenzi, Francesca Biancani, Mattia Guidetti, Francesca Prevedello, Paola Rivetti, Marina Calculli, Elisabetta Brighi, Andrea Teti, Luca Anceschi, Ashraf Hassan, Linda Martín Alcoff, Daniela Melfa, Mirella Cassarino, Daniela Pioppi, Sara Borrillo, Elisabetta Benigni, Fabio Giomi, Setrak Manoucian, Alessandro Cancian, Isabella Camera D'Afflitto, Dina Makram Obeid, Alessandra Marchi, John Chalcraft, Julie Gervais, Jonathan Shannon, Iman Mersal, Patrizia Manduchi, Larbi Sadiki, Cat Moir, Amr Hamzaoui, Hadeel Abdelhameed, Armando Salvatore, Adina Barbaro, Monica Ruocco, Naglaa Waly, Ruba Salih, Alessandro Mezzadra, and Martina Censi.

I received generous and thoughtful feedback on the first drafts of the manuscript by two reviewers and a member of the University of California Press advisory committee, for which I am extremely grateful. I was also fortunate to have several colleagues who invested time in reading and commenting on part of or even the entire manuscript: Margot Badran, miriam cooke, Beth Baron, Samah Selim, Frances Hasso, Maria Frederica Malström,

Zachary Lockman, Catherine Rottenberg, Maria Elena Paniconi, Francesca Biancani, Benoit Challand, Luisa Passerini, Angela Joya, and Dirk Moses. Thank you all for your care! I have taken on board all the recommendations I was able to, and any inaccuracy or mistake remains my own responsibility.

My family is an ongoing source of support, starting from my late father Tindaro Sorbera, my mother Alga Grandi, my sisters Paola and Valentina, and my cousins, especially Teodora and Carmelina Buzzanca. We come from a genealogy of generous and hard-working women—our late grandmothers, Lucia Penserini and Carmela Lena, and our late aunties, Laura Grandi and Pasqualina Sorbera. There is not a day I dedicate to my work that I don't feel inspired by thinking of their work, and I hope they can feel my gratitude for all the love, the care, and the strength I received from them and which I hope I will be able to pass to my own nieces: Sofia Sole Marin, Diana Soldera, and Arianna Soldera. This book accompanied the upbringing of my son, Francesco Marin, who is the apple of my eye, and whose witty sense of humor keeps me grounded. I could not have afforded the intensity of travel, study, and work I have invested in this book if I was not supported by his wonderful father, Marco Marin, and his caring grandparents, Elisa Fugaro and Martino Marin. Marco, Elisa and Martino, you have all my gratitude and love.

To my closest friends, Veronica Neri, Ermete Mariani, Cécile Bresc, Alana Lentin, Ronit Lentin, Partho Sen-Gupta, Ilaria Vanni, Michelle Verelikian, Elia Voieux, Mariam Farida, Nesrine Basheer, Antonella Beconi, Alberto Solfrini, Rebecca Servadio, Sinan Antoon, Annamaria Testa, Cristina Marogna, Francesco Borghesi, Valentina Gambelli, Sabina Santarini, Kara Niles, Cristiana Molfese, Francesca Vianello, Susy Fiocco, Benedetta Zatti, Marta Capuzzo, Francesca Brambilla, Safdar Ahmed, Daria Marlia, Massimo Francioni, Lucia Crociani, and Hani al-Husseini: thank you for always having my back, for enduring my long absences, and for enriching every single day with your presence, even at a distance.

A special thought goes to the little Italian community of Cairo-based scholars and artists with whom I have shared the dream of the Revolution between 2011 and 2016, and those from other parts of the world who shared the same moment and were close to us: Gennaro Gervasio, Enrico De Angelis, Laura Cappon, Margherita Picchi, Costanza Spocci, Marianna Ghiglia, Matteo Valle, Giovanni Piazzese, Alessandro Accorsi, Giulia Bertoluzzi, Lucia Carminati, Carmine Cartolano, Stefania Angarano, Claudia Ruta, Azzurra Sarnataro, Ahmed Samy, Aurora Sottimano, Cettina Di Natale, Mohammed Farag, Flavia Malusardi, Maria Neubert, Marta

Agosti, Jakob Lindfors, Noémi Kahn, and Giangina Orsini. The grief for Giulio Regeni will always stay with us, and we will always be living in gratitude and admiration for his family, who are carrying the load of the battle to obtain truth and justice for Giulio.

I extend my gratitude to my Italian community in Brooklyn, especially Mario Costa, Elisabetta La Tanza, and Riccardo Mazzei, and in Sydney, especially the colleagues in the Department of Italian Studies and the Powerful Stories Research Network at the University of Sydney; the comrades of the University of Sydney Branch of the National Tertiary Education Union; the National Italian-Australian Women Association; the Federation of Italian Migrants and Their Families; and the broader community gathering around the Italian Institute of Culture in Sydney and their staff, led by three directors who hosted my talks over the years and with whom I became friends: Alessandra Bertini Malgarini, Donatella Cannova, and Lillo Guarnieri and their families. Thanks also for treasured intellectual exchange to my colleagues in the School of Languages and Cultures and my Head of School, Yixu Lu; to the colleagues of the Sydney Feminist History Network; to Chicoco Music and Radio in Port Harcourt with Ana Bonaldo and Michael Uwemedimo; to Dawar Art in Ezbet Khairallah in Cairo with Ben Rivers, Ahmad Mounir, and Menna Mourad; to Arab Theatre Studio in Sydney with Maissa Alameddine, Alissar Chidiak, and Paula Abood; to Andalus Arabic Choir in Sydney with Ghada Daher-Elmowy; to the crew of Salone Internazionale del Libro di Torino, led by Nicola Lagioia; and to Biblioteca Amilcar Cabral in Bologna, with Head Librarian Simona Brighetti.

I would like to express special appreciation to my development editor, Carolyn Bond, who helped me to define the structure of this book, and my editor at University of California Press, Niels Hooper, as well as Nora Becker, Julie Van Pelt, Theresa Winchell, and all the production team for their invaluable support throughout all the phases that led to finalizing this book, from my first pitch to Niels to final editing and production. They all went above and beyond their duties, and I could have never dreamed of a better team! Thanks to Huda Lutfi for gracing the cover of this book with one of her artworks, and to Hossam el-Hamalawy and the Women and Memory Forum Library for allowing me to include some of their photos in this book.

Finally, I would like to express my gratitude to Mark LeVine for sharing an important segment of this intellectual, intimate, and political journey, for his friendship and love. Thank you so much, dear.

This book was written on stolen Aboriginal land. I acknowledge the Traditional Owners and Custodians of the lands on which I wrote this book and pay my respects to Indigenous Elders past, present, and emerging. Sovereignty has never been ceded. It always was, and always will be, Aboriginal land.

NOTE ON TRANSLITERATION, TRANSCRIPTION, AND TRANSLATION

It is my hope that the stories narrated in this book will reach also to nonspecialist readers and non-Arabic speakers. For this reason, in the transliteration of Arabic names I have privileged the criteria of expediency over philological accuracy. I have mostly referred to a simplified version of the *International Journal of Middle East Studies*' style sheet, and all diacritical marks have been omitted except for the *'ayn* (') and the *hamza* ('). To reflect the oral history methodology adopted in the research, many names are transliterated, taking into consideration peculiarities of pronunciation of Egyptian Arabic and spellings of common English language in the Egyptian media, including vocalization. For instance, the *jim* (*j*) in Egyptian Arabic is pronounced *g* (*ganubiyya* instead of *janubiya*) and what in standard Arabic sounds like *u* is pronounced as *o* in Egyptian (*horra* instead of *hurra*). Whenever the source is oral, I have followed the Egyptian pronunciation. Arabic words in common usage in English, such as *Nasser* and *Cairo*, remain in their anglicized form. The English spelling of names of public figures (political and military leaders, journalists, lawyers, activists, academics, and public intellectuals) follows the English-language version of their names used in public documents or the way these figures spell their own names in publications and documents, including social media. For instance: I have used Doria Shafik, not Durreya Shafik. In the references, the names of authors who have been published in multiple languages and people who are mentioned in archival documents can have alternate spellings, depending on the original source. The interviews have been conducted in English and in Arabic. I have quoted them as they are, and only occasionally I have slightly edited the transcript for clarity.

When not otherwise indicated, all the translations in this book are mine.

xvii

Introduction

REFRAMING THE FEMINIST CANON

The uprisings that began in Tunisia on December 17, 2010, and exploded into global consciousness with Egypt's eighteen-day January 25, 2011, Revolution did not occur in a vacuum. They were preceded at the start of the new millennium by the 2000–2005 al-Aqsa Intifada in Palestine, the regional protests against the 2003 US invasion of Iraq, Lebanon's 2005 Cedar Revolution, and the Iranian Green Wave of 2009. The revolutionary era continued through the summer of 2013, when the military coup in Egypt, the crushing of the Gezi Park protests, and the worsening civil wars in Syria, Yemen, and Libya tempered its momentum. But after a three-year counterrevolutionary interlude, when upgraded authoritarian regimes reasserted authority through well-honed combinations of intense violence and co-optation, protests ignited again in Morocco, Algeria, Sudan, and Iran beginning in late 2016. They continue to the present day, through crests and crescendos of varying intensity, most recently punctuated by the Israeli genocidal response to the unprecedented Hamas attack in October 2023.

From the start, all these eruptions of grassroots political activism were defined visually, aurally, and narratively by women. Women's participation at all levels and stages of the protest led to renewed media focus on the evolving and still highly contested roles of gender and sexuality in the region's intersecting private, public, and political spheres. Yet, women's long-standing representation as either heroines and/or victims persisted, contributing to the ongoing prevalence of stereotypical orientalist images of Egyptian and Arab women more broadly.[1]

Since the seventies, feminist Middle East Studies scholars have critically addressed both mainstream media and academic discourses that silence, romanticize, victimize, and too often still erase women from crucial political moments in the Southwest Asia and North Africa region (SWANA), and they have shed new light on the gendered nature of colonialism, nationalism, and the processes of postcolonial state-building. Expanding on this well-established tradition, a stream of research that incorporates women as political subjects, and gender as an analytical category, into the analysis of the Arab uprisings and revolutions started taking shape, soon producing some of the most innovative analyses of the politics, spaces, and concepts produced during this era.[2]

Notwithstanding the impact of their scholarship, however, the discursive arena in which the narratives of the 2011 Egyptian Revolution developed shows that the ongoing impact of feminist scholars cannot be taken for granted. Their work needs not only to be continued and expanded but can be felicitously and powerfully placed into dialogue with the critical insights of decolonial and Indigenous epistemologies, as well as engage with notions of embodied knowledge, positionality, episteme of experience, borderlands, intersubjectivity, and solidarity.[3]

Honoring the tradition of the historiography of feminisms in Egypt, Asia, and Africa,[4] *Biography of a Revolution* also engages with contemporary decolonial and Indigenous feminist theories, and, by historicizing women's contribution to the human rights movement and the 2011 Revolution in Egypt, it argues that global feminism has much to learn from the practices and theories developed by Egyptian women political activists from the seventies, and before that, during the colonial period, until today. In so doing, *Biography of a Revolution* raises a new question: *What if it was not the revolution that opened new spaces for women's political activism but rather the long history of women's and feminist activism that helped create the space for the explosion of the 2011 Revolution and its evolution into a women's revolutionary decade?*

This question shifts the focus from space (the Square, both in its utopian and dystopic meaning, as an epitome of the 2011 Revolution) to time, especially the longue durée—more than a century—of women's political activism in Egypt. To address this shift, I gather a series of interrelated intimate and relational stories, charting the entanglements between women's personal and political aspirations across a century of politics and friendships in Egypt. In conversation with SWANA feminist scholarship, I argue that feminism, culture, and women's rights need to be understood in their multiple historical and even linguistic expressions.

2 · INTRODUCTION

Biography of a Revolution reads as a curational as much as a creational and an authorial work that intervenes both in the global feminist historiographical debates about women's role in political movements and in the debates surrounding Egypt's January 25 *thawra* (the Arabic word for "revolution," which Egyptians use in reference to the January 2011 events). It situates women's political activism during this period not only at the center of the analysis but also into historical perspective. Specifically, it explores Egyptian contemporary political history through women's experiences of protests, campaigns, negotiations, victories, and downfalls.

My focus on women's experiences, their political biographies, and their narratives of political history, does not offer a supplemental narrative of the history of the last century. Rather, it shifts the epistemic paradigm for understanding Egyptian political history, enabling an innovative interpretation and periodization of the 2011 uprisings and the decade that followed. It liberates the historical narrative from the questions that have haunted scholarship on Egypt since 2011: Was it a revolution? Was it an uprising? A failed revolution? A coup? A "Spring" followed by a "Long Winter"? Did it last only eighteen days? A few months? Three years? When precisely did it end, or is it, if only below the surface, continuing still?

The conversations I have had with Egyptian women political activists and intellectuals while researching and then writing this book led me to decenter these questions. In fact, the chronology of women's revolution spans a much longer period, one where events that mattered on the (inter)national scale were associated with crucial passages in their own lives: memories of the participations in the seventies' student movement are mixed with joyful love stories and painful breakups, of being arrested with their partners on political charges and recalling the sorrow at leaving their child parentless, along with the pride in fighting for a worthy cause.

Recently, the award-winning journalist Lina Attalah, cofounder and chief editor of *Mada Masr,*[5] wrote about the reverberations of political activism in family life, which for her generation of activists became clear during the 2003 American invasion of Iraq: "The first time I saw a policeman brutally beat protesters during the 2003 demonstrations against the Iraq War in Cairo, I found that I didn't want to go back to my parents' house. I wanted to remain outdoors, as the street and the protesters felt like a home and family I had chosen."[6]

The writers and activists across multiple generations whom I have interviewed link the evolution of family relationships to the contentious politics of different opposition movements that developed in Egypt in the second half of the twentieth century and the first decade of the twenty-first, all suggesting a tangible, mutual impact between the national, international, and regional politics and personal life, what in this book I name "a politics of intimacy." The above examples and others stories I narrate in this book demonstrate that this link connects the experiences of multiple generations of women who have all been fighting from different positionalities and on multiple and intertwining fronts, the private and the public, the national and the international, the cultural, the social, and the political, emerging in a powerful way in 2011. Many of the young women I interviewed in November 2011 cheerfully remembered the 28th of January 2011, the "Friday of Rage," as the first time in their lives they "disobeyed" their parents to join the protests. The women I interviewed over the years and the stories I have read in their memoirs prove that the entanglement, indeed the bond, between the public and the private, too often neglected in narratives of political history, is as significant as it is deep. Yes, scholars have long understood that politics influences what happens in the private sphere as much as attitudes assumed in the private sphere affect state and even international politics. Yet the gendered dynamics of the resulting politics of intimacy in countries governed by authoritarian regimes deserve more attention.

This book's intervention into historiographical debate is grounded in an eclectic array of sources that include sixty-four oral histories I've collected between 2011 and 2023 and a broad collection of written documents, including memoirs, clippings, journal and newspapers articles, photographs, and flyers, combined with participant observation of feminist meetings and workshops, and digital ethnographies, including my own correspondences with Egyptian women activists and intellectuals. I am focusing on the women who played a crucial yet not adequately documented and acknowledged role in building the human rights movement, which lay at the roots of the January 25 Revolution and was brutally targeted by the new Egyptian regime that took power in 2013.

Historicizing women's contribution to the culture of human rights and protest in Egypt is essential not only to liberate the analyses of the 2011 Revolution from essentialist, orientalist, and other disempowering assumptions about women, but also to understand its multiple and often intersecting genealogies and, in so doing, to better appreciate its significance in the broader context of global history.

This leads me to offer a few words about the title of this book. *Biography of a Revolution* is polysemic. The genre of "biography" has a well-established tradition in both classical and modern literature. One of the words to allude to biography in classical Arabic is *tarjama,* which would come to mean "translation" but which originally encompassed three different ideas: "that of explanation or interpretation, that of transformation into a different medium, and that of clarification by means of division into sections and labeling."[7] *Tarjama's* classical meaning best describes the role that women's biographies play in this book: they are "translations" of opportunities, possibilities, examples that in dark times inspire hope through their actions and their writings.

The title of this book alludes both to the deep roots of the 2011 Revolution, which I locate in one century of feminist activism in Egypt, and to the lived stories of the women political activists foregrounded here. Together, they comprise a collective biography. It also reflects a research methodology grounded in feminist historiography that emphasizes the networks, solidarity, and friendship. In the oral history that I have recorded, individual lives are displayed as intersubjectivity, and this is reflected in my writing, which narrates them in relation to each other, trying to compose a collective self.[8] I chart some of the most important passages in contemporary Egyptian history through the memories of women who took part in these events or wrote about them. Belonging to different generations, social classes, and religious or political affiliations, all the women I have included in this collection of stories—which, together, compose a history—identify themselves as both Egyptian and as political activists. The ways they conceive feminism and position themselves in the political field as feminists change at different points in history, and sometimes even different stages in their lives, but they all share a project of liberation that is collective more than individual, and inclusive—that is, aiming at involving both women and men from diverse social classes and religious backgrounds.

One of the key concepts around which the book is written is that of "feminist lives," a notion meaning (per philosopher Sara Ahmed) that as both a discourse and an arena of praxis, feminism is a laboratory for political change that is neither easily detected nor occurring only or even largely in public.[9] The accounts of feminist lives in this book contribute both to building a living archive of feminist memories and to the cultural debate regarding the interplay among gender, culture, and politics in Egyptian contemporary history. The notion of feminist lives and their relationality allows me to reconceptualize the notion of biography and its relationship with historiography as a collective experience.

Throughout the pages that follow, I trace the tight network of transgenerational, personal, intellectual, and professional connections, overlaps and divergences among women who, in different capacities and from different positionalities, have been part of political life in twentieth- and twentieth-first-century Egypt. The methodology of collective biography allows me to include personal perspectives of the past and to shed light on the entanglements between formal politics and the politics of personal life, and to historicize the multiple meanings of gendered identities, concepts of family, citizenship, women's role in the public sphere, and revolution. "Revolution" in the title of this book refers primarily but not only to 2011—"the Revolution *par excellence*" in Egyptian contemporary history—but also to "century-long women's revolution" that is feminist activism in Egypt.[10] The stories narrated here demonstrate that feminist political activists were crucial actors in creating, nourishing, and transmitting more than a century an Egyptian spirit of dissent that made the January 25 Revolution not merely possible but an inspirational moment for people around the world. What remains of that spirit continues bearing fruit in the feminist groups that grew during the revolution and continued to develop during the decade that followed it and even more. Feminism, in all its different manifestations, is what has allowed what has remained of the revolutionary spirit to resist the repression implemented by the counterrevolutionary forces.

My analysis places Egyptian feminist experiences at the center of global feminist theory and intellectual history, offering a key to comprehend why the 2011 Egyptian Revolution had transnational and long-term effects even after it had been violently countered at home, including the need to reconceptualize what revolution is more broadly: the emergence of new subjectivities and the opening of new public spaces, where new conceptualizations of being a community are produced. This is what I name "a revolution,"[11] and this is the revolutionary space where the legacy of feminism is visible.

QUESTIONING THE EPISTEMOLOGY
OF FEMINIST FAILURE

Feminist analyses of the last decade in Egypt tend to agree that women opened new spaces for and of feminist activism throughout the revolutionary period of 2011–2013. During more than a decade of fieldwork visits in Cairo and other Egyptian cities (Alexandria, Aswan, and Port Said) between 2011 and 2024, I experienced these spaces rhythmically opening and closing at multiple levels, in line with broader political developments. It is safe to say that between 2011 and 2013 a feminism "embedded in the revolution"[12] permeated different types and levels of public and private space, from university lecture halls to the Queer-friendly café in al-Bustan Street in downtown Cairo, from cultural festivals and new feminist offline and online collectives to political parties and street demonstrations throughout the country. Even though between 2011 and 2013–14 feminist and human rights organizations reported increased violence against women demonstrators, women's political activism found multiple expressions across the political spectrum, from the liberal to the Islamist and leftist orientations. Simultaneously, controversies about women and gender emerged at multiple phases and in multiple settings, especially—but not only—in the context of rewriting the Egyptian Constitution. Women intellectuals remained vigilant throughout that process, ultimately succeeding in realizing some of their core demands, particularly with the insertion of Article 11 into the 2014 Constitution.[13] This article committed the state to five core goals: to achieve equality between men and women in all civil, political, economic, social and cultural rights; to ensure fair representation of women in the Parliament; to end hiring discrimination against women in the senior government positions, including the judiciary; to protect women against all forms of violence; and to guarantee women's ability to reconcile work and family duties (but not men and family duties or obligations).[14] These commitments were not embedded in the Constitution spontaneously or as concessions to women's demands; these were a result of a century of women's political activism.

It is true that the revolutionary period increased the challenges women faced both in daily and public life; yet it was also a moment of creativity and hope. Writers such as Ahdaf Soueif, May Telmissany, Mona Prince, and Basma Abdel Aziz not only produced some of the most significative memoirs and works of fiction about the revolution and its aftermath, but they were also active on the pages of newspapers, leading campaigns, and petitioning for political prisoners both in Egypt and abroad, translating into powerful essays the emotions and the desires of Egyptian people to the world.

University campuses revived their historically established revolutionary stance, with students and academics not only taking part in demonstrations but continuing the discussion about the meaning of revolution in research seminars and conferences and in the suddenly relatively free press and social media.[15] A significant amount of the revolutionary street art that vitalized the cities between 2011 and 2014 represented women not as victims of violence but as fierce participants in the fight; much of it was produced by

INTRODUCTION · 7

FIGURE 1. Graffiti in downtown Cairo, "In the clashes I will have your back." Photo by Lucia Sorbera, November 19, 2013.

women artists such as Hend Kheera and Bahia Shehab, whose works are featured in several studies about women's art-activism.[16]

In 2013–2014, as a new and far more repressive political order solidified, most of the revolutionary graffiti around Tahrir was removed and street performances that had regularly occurred between 2011 and 2013 were prohibited, while at the same time, echoing the last decades of the Mubarak Era, the military-led government tried to appropriate women's political agendas. Specifically, the Sisi presidency launched initiatives such as the Year of Women in 2017 and the National Women's Empowerment Strategy (2017–2030), while at the same time targeting high-profile feminist activists and organizations whose work was associated with the 2011 Revolution.

More than a decade since the fall of the Mubarak regime, the gap between Egypt's constitutional framework, in which women's rights are guaranteed, and the reality on the ground marked both by a Personal Status Law, which still disadvantages women, and huge socioeconomic disparities among women of different class backgrounds, continue to make the agenda of feminist activists and organizations equally relevant and fraught with obstacles. It is clear, however, that the creative spirit that flowered from the seeds of a century of Egyptian women's political activism and animated women's protests during the two-year revolutionary period is a high political stake in Egypt today.

Beyond the Egyptian or even Arab context, the experience of Egyptian feminists can help scholars reassess how the relationship between feminism and revolution has been traditionally explained by feminist historians, literary critics, and political philosophers. In fact, almost every major political revolt, from the 1789 French Revolution to the 1848 uprisings across Europe, the 1917 Bolshevik Revolution in Russia, the civil rights movement in the United States, the 1968 global student movements, and the Iranian 1979 Revolution (among others), has been interrogated by feminist scholars who challenge male-centered narratives of history, often suggesting that because these revolutions happened within political and theoretical frameworks conceived by men, they therefore failed women.[17]

There is a tradition of feminist historians' skepticism about the emancipatory potential of revolution, which has been extended to the so-called Arab Spring uprisings and revolutions. This reflects what I term an "epistemology of feminist failure," a phrase with which I allude to a generalized perception of women's defeat. As Geneviève Fraisse commented in 2012: "The issue of women's rights in the Arab revolutions echoed the history of Western democracy, which has little inclination to synchronize gender equality with revolutionary dynamics."[18]

Once the optimism of the eighteen days started fading, an epistemology of feminist failure appeared also in some of the feminist narratives of the Egyptian Revolution. An example is the 2012 essay by the Egyptian-American journalist Mona Eltahawy in *Foreign Policy*, where she argued that the revolution in the Middle East would not be completed until a substantial change in gender relationships is achieved.[19] The essay was very well received in international feminist spaces (where the episteme of feminist failure in relation to revolutions has a long history, one that can be traced back to the French Revolution), but far less so in Egypt, where women revolutionary activists did not want to be represented as victims of violence but rather as fierce agents against it. This determination to assert their power was also reflected in the blossoming popular culture at that time, where graffiti represented women as warriors and where women-authored graphic novels portrayed women superheroes inspired by Japanese manga. It is true that women were raising strong concerns about the outcome of the revolution for them, but as noted by feminist historians and scholars of Egypt,[20] this was the enduring

INTRODUCTION · 9

tension between patriarchy, revolution, and women's rights that, rather than making women feel defeated, it encouraged them to become even more defiant.

Already in 2011, many activists faced a violent backlash from the military as they attempted to link the revolution to women's agenda. As an example (which I discuss at length in part 3 of this book), on March 9, 2011, less than one month after the fall of Mubarak, the International Women's Day march in Cairo was brutally attacked by *baltaghiyya* (thugs acting as paid agents of state security forces). Yet during the same period that women's marches were attacked, women political activists were organizing against being marginalized from political decision-making during the ostensible "transition period" toward democracy. A coalition of feminist organizations was established: Majmu'at an-nisa' wal dustur (the Group of Women and the Constitution)[21] and two feminist groups, one led by Nawal al-Saadawi and the other by Hoda Badran, gathered under the name of the historic Egyptian Feminist Union, each one claiming with that name the legacy of the first feminist organization ever established in Egypt, in 1923.[22] Some leftist feminists joined the Socialist Popular Alliance Party in March 2011.[23] Young women organized feminist collectives, study groups, and self-defense initiatives against sexual assaults during demonstrations, and they did not give up their revolutionary imagination. In the words of the gender studies scholar Dina Wahba: "So many years after the revolution, some claim that we failed. Failed to do what? To bring a truly democratic regime to power? Maybe. To democratize society and promote a culture of diversity and human rights? Probably. My revolution didn't fail. I might be deeply disillusioned, but, for purely selfish reasons, I don't regret it. This is the most significant experience in my life."[24]

Wahba's words express a sentiment that recurs often in the testimonies I have collected among Egyptian women who experienced the 2011 Revolution, including those who are paying for their political commitment with exile or imprisonment of themselves or their close relatives.

The opportunity I had to observe the various ways of organizing what women experienced in the months and indeed the years following the eighteen days in January and February 2011, and even the vitality of the internal debate about the effectiveness of organizing within a feminist framework by Egyptian women activists, led me to question the consolidated epistemology of failure or incompleteness that has long dominated European feminist analyses since the French Revolution of the relationship between women, feminism, and revolution.

Studying these testimonies and my close interaction with feminist activists in Egypt (including those in exile since the 2013 military coup) have led me to shift focus from letdowns and failures, such as unequal political participation and high incidence of violence against women that continue to haunt those on the frontlines of the struggles for change, to the achievements that inspire hope by adopting a longer view of these processes. Tracing the genealogy of contemporary revolutionary activism to women's political activism in the early 1970s—which is in turn rooted in the experiences of women's intellectual and political activism in the late nineteenth and early twentieth centuries (although they are not always ideologically aligned)—and looking at the new trajectories developed by Egyptian feminists during and after the 2011 Revolution reveals that the advances they achieved are much more significant than the setbacks.

It is true that the spaces for activism opened during the 2011 Revolution gradually closed after the 2013 "revolutionary coup" (as one of my interlocutors described it with a bitter smile) that brought in the oppressive El-Sisi regime, while the level of political repression rapidly escalated, making continuing engagement by feminist activists in politics and even in social science research in Egypt unsafe. During the decade following 2013, I continued to travel regularly to Egypt, and during those visits it became clear that if institutionalized politics was indeed agonizing and public space was increasingly militarized and dominated by a socially constructed and heteropatriarchal form of maleness—what Raewyn Connell terms "hegemonic masculinity"[25]—feminism and women's activism in Egypt remained quite robust and lively.[26] While they became less visible, even the feminist and feminist-oriented and women-led organizations most severely targeted by the regime continued to function.

The Center for Egyptian Women's Legal Assistance (CEWLA), Nazra for Feminist Studies (hereafter: Nazra), and El-Nadeem Center for the Psychological Treatment and Rehabilitation of Victims of Violence and Torture (hereafter: El-Nadeem) have all seen their financial assets frozen since 2016, their headquarters sealed (for El-Nadeem), and their directors subjected to years of travel bans and pending investigations.[27] Yet despite the constant harassment, these organizations never stopped supporting women, especially poor women. Mu'assasa al-Mar'a al-Gadida (New Woman Foundation [NWF])[28] remains to this day a point of reference for several generations of feminist activists. Meanwhile, new women's groups emerged after the January 25 Revolution and continue to do so through the present day, as I discuss in detail in part 3 of this book.

INTRODUCTION · 11

Last but not least, following a tradition that goes back to the late nineteenth century,[29] journalism remains a crucial field where women continue to cultivate the tradition of feminism and to challenge the norm that journalism is mostly a male job.[30] Interestingly, it is in the newsroom of *Mada Masr* that a feminist leadership, characterized by the capacity to create community, favoring social justice and active democracy, emerges. In her writing, *Mada Masr*'s chief editor, Lina Attalah, acknowledges the inspiring role that other women's leadership style had on her: "I had been working there [at *Egypt Independent*] since 2009, when the newspaper was led by a woman named Fatemah Farag, whose leadership was truly inspiring."[31] Other women journalists of the new generation have also emerged in the context of the 2011 Revolution.

Significantly—besides this flourishing of independent feminist initiatives—human rights, environmental, and labor organizations in Egypt, with the help of feminist scholars, have made gender a core area of work. However, it would be a mistake to interpret the influence of feminism on human rights, environmental, and labor movements as a recent phenomenon. In fact, feminism is an integral part of the history of these three movements, as I discuss in part 1 of this book. Even in the darkest days of the crackdown against the civil society that intensified around 2016, during which time human rights organizations counting more than sixty-thousand political prisoners with uncountable thousands more *mukhtafeen* (disappeared) and a generation of young activists in exile, women's groups continue to produce new critical knowledge in the most urgent areas of political economy, health, human rights, and environment, and their contribution is acknowledged.

In November 2022, the world could see Egyptian women and gender activists at work during the COP27 conference at Sharm el-Sheikh, where Egyptian civil society, and especially the human rights movement, dominated the stage. The performance of Egyptian human rights activists at COP27 demonstrated the inextricable link between environmental justice, socioeconomic rights, women/gender rights, and human rights. During COP27, Egyptian human rights activists were successful in attracting the attention of the world to the human rights crisis in Egypt. As the CEWLA researcher Nada Deom stated at the conference: "There cannot be an agenda to protect the environment in Egypt unless the current human rights crisis is addressed, and unless spaces for grassroots activism are open."[32]

Women made savvy use of international networks and media (a competence developed by Egyptian feminists since the early twentieth century) to make their voices heard beyond the national borders.[33] A prime example is the efforts of Mona and Sana Seif, sisters of Alaa Abd El-Fattah, to publicize the plight of their brother, Egypt's most famous political prisoner, who has been confined in cruel conditions for most of the last decade. In the lead-up to COP27, the major newspapers in the world published the photo of Greta Thunberg joining Sana and Mona Seif's sit-in in front of the foreign office in London, asking for the liberation of Alaa (a British citizen on his mother's side) and reporting that she would not travel to COP27 in protest against the violations of human rights in Egypt.[34]

The high-profile activism at COP27 is the most internationally visible, but by no means the only, contemporary women's activism worthy of mention. Equally important, though away from the media's spotlight, is the women's work occurring in Ezbet Khairallah, one of Cairo's largest *ashawiyyat* (informal settlements). Situated between Giza and Maadi, for well over a decade it has been at the center of conflicts between the state authorities, who are trying to impose "requalification" programs of the area, and the inhabitants, who resist the evictions that these programs would imply. In this neighborhood, women are inspiring and organizing social and cultural activities, ranging from theater workshops, after-school care, art programs with high-profile artists training young children from the neighborhood, and a kitchen that employs both long-term residents in the neighborhood and recent Syrian refugees, to create community bonds and resilience in the face of otherwise unchecked and seemingly inexorable state power.

Observing these spaces, where women are not just the target of sociocultural projects but lead them, inspired my research about language and the ideas of feminism in its diverse forms, and how they permeate the practices and theories of all the spaces where culture is produced, from universities, where women and gender studies programs are well developed, to the international political summits, to the small cultural centers in the shantytowns of Cairo.

As I was making these empirical observations, I could not but wonder how this feminist vitality was possible, given the diminished spaces of freedom that people experience under the Sisi regime. I began to understand that this capacity to organize under the most difficult circumstances—in particular, the lack of freedom of expression—was not a recent experience but rather has been cemented in the collective memory of generations of women political activists. Indeed, my years of being present in feminist meetings in Cairo, Alexandria, and Aswan; reading Egyptian feminist historiography, literature, and documents; discussing politics with Egyptian women intellectuals and activists from different generations, ranging from those who participated in the seventies student movement to those who were teenagers in 2011; and reading the works produced by Egyptian women intellectuals since the late nineteenth century and the historiography about them, suggest to me that the praxes developed by Egyptian feminists over a century of activism in diverse forms (social, political, intellectual, and artistic) are at the core of the development of the human rights movement in Egypt, and of the political culture that led to the 2011 Revolution. Therefore, in this book I shift the usual scholarly and media focus on the role of women in the revolution, their spaces, and the effects of the revolution on women to women's capacity to have inspired the revolution. This is the meaning of my argument for the feminist roots of human rights and the 2011 Revolution in Egypt.

WRITING WOMEN'S HISTORY IN EGYPT AS FEMINIST ACTIVISM

The then-emerging field of feminist studies and the critical analysis of Arab societies were brought together in the seventies by three North African women scholars: Egyptian physician, writer, and activist Nawal al-Saadawi; Moroccan feminist and sociologist Fatima Mernissi; and Algerian novelist and filmmaker Assia Djebar.[35] Widely diverse in their approaches, aesthetics, themes developed, and politics, the works of these three major twentieth- and twenty-first-century writers represent three pillars of feminist intellectual production across the Arab world, situating women's experiences, sexuality, and desire for liberation at the center of their sociocultural and historical analyses.

In that same period, feminist scholarship in the United States, Lebanon, and Egypt stirred a new turn in the field of Middle East Studies.[36] Anthologies of Middle Eastern and Muslim women,[37] and research centers and chairs dedicated to women studies, as well as groundbreaking multidisciplinary studies that situated women at the core of their research, enriched the understanding of the processes of political and cultural change that took place in Muslim-majority countries between the end of the nineteenth century and the first half of the twentieth century. Scholars like Margot Badran, who gained access to the private archives of Saiza Nabarawi and other first-generation Egyptian feminists and produced what remains the preeminent collective biography of

Egyptian feminism with Huda Shaʿarawi and the Egyptian Feminist Union at the center of her narrative,[38] as well as miriam cooke's work on women's writings about war and Islamic feminism,[39] Hatem Mervat's innovative political-anthropological analyses of patriarchy in Egypt,[40] and Judith Tucker's highly original use of archives of Islamic courts in Egypt, Syria, and Ottoman Palestine,[41] offered new methodologies to recover ordinary women from the silences of history.

Middle East Studies feminist scholars worked to overcome the essentialist vision of Muslim women as a homogeneous group, and contributed to the feminist critique of Orientalism through a profound historicization of Islam and Muslim societies, as evidenced most powerfully in the works of Leila Ahmed, Nikkie Keddie, Beth Baron, Marnia Lazreg, and Deniz Kandiyoti.[42]

Together, these scholars revealed the organic relationship between feminist movements and feminist scholarship, confirming that writing women's history is integral to feminist activism. They also encouraged the rediscovery of women writers of the *nahda* (the nineteenth-century Arab Renaissance).[43]

This broad corpus of scholarship stands as a collective effort not only to write women into the record of Middle Eastern history but to produce an epistemic shift. Writing women's history allowed historians to develop a nuanced analysis of the blurred boundaries between the private and the public spheres, the transition from the colonial to the postcolonial order, and the ambivalent effects of the passage to modernity on marginal subjects.[44]

The capacity of feminist approaches to produce a contrapuntal narrative of history soon influenced the Egyptian cultural and artistic sphere at large. For instance, one of the first critical accounts about the postcolonial Egyptian state is the 1997 documentary *Four Women of Egypt,* directed by Egyptian-Canadian filmmaker Tahani Rached.[45]

The film traces the experience of politics and friendship among four Egyptian women political activists prominent on the public scene since the late sixties: Amina Rachid, professor of comparative literature at Cairo University and Marxist activist and intellectual; Safinaz Kazem, a writer, theater critic, journalist, and Islamic activist; Shahenda Meqlad, a leader of the peasant movement; and Wedad Mitri, a journalist and a leading figure of the union of journalists. Others were inspired by Rashid's effort. Filmmaker Nadia Kamel did oral history for ten years with her mother, the communist activist Mary Ely Rosenthal, who was born in Cairo to a Jewish father of Turkish-Ukrainian origin and an Italian mother and changed her name to

FIGURE 2. Left to right: Safinaz Kazem, Wedad Mitri, Amina Rachid, and Shahenda Meqlad at Shahenda Meqlad's house, 1998. They are celebrating the prize awarded to the film *Four Women of Egypt* about their lives, political activism, and long-lasting friendship. Courtesy of Women and Memory Forum Library.

Nayela Kamel after she married the communist activist Saad Kamel. Kamel turned her mother's oral history into a documentary and a memoir.[46]

These two works, while centered on the biography of women and their families, also provide a lively documentation of the history of Egyptian Jews and communists, and how the politics of Nasser and Sadat affected their lives. More recently, Iman Mersal's novel *Fi Athar Enayat al-Zayyat* (*Traces of Enayat*)[47] narrates the biography of this long-forgotten Egyptian writer (Enayat al-Zayyat) and its tragic epilogue, contributing to deconstruct nostalgic myths of the fifties and the sixties in Egypt.

The effort in artistic and the literary fields to reassess the first decades of Egypt's republican age by shifting the focus to women's personal experiences during the Nasser and Sadat periods is accompanied by a growing attention to the entanglements between social and cultural history in women's historiography, especially the works by Laura Bier and Hanan Hammad.[48] These works are a sampling of the critical reappraisal of contemporary Egyptian history produced by Egyptian women intellectuals from the nineties onward. While the 1990s were a period when women's independent political activism was hampered by the regime, it was also an extraordinary period of creativity by Egyptian women.

During that decade, Egyptian feminist historiography further developed, thanks to the efforts of a group of women academics who created Multaqa al-Mar'a wa al-Dhakira (Women and Memory Forum [WMF]), soon registered as an NGO devoted to the documentation and study of history from the women's perspective. The artist Huda Lutfi (whose artwork graces the cover of this book), herself a feminist historian, also became well-known on the Egyptian and international artistic scene in the 1990s, and she situates women's bodies and gender history at the core of her representations of contemporary society.[49] Significantly, the works of the most prolific and successful women writers belonging to the so-called *jil al-tis'inat* (the generation of the nineties)[50] are all marked by an intimate reappraisal of Egyptian contemporary history.

Biography of a Revolution builds on these previous scholars, artists, and activists whose works laid the foundation for the current debate about decolonizing feminist scholarship and epistemologies in Egypt and more broadly the SWANA region. Decolonial feminist scholarship, pioneered by Latin American and Chicana philosophers, particularly Linda Martín Alcoff, Gloria Anzaldúa, and Teresa de Lauretis, argues that women's fights for gender equality and justice take different trajectories according to their sociopolitical context. The debate about decolonizing feminist scholarship not only questions the Eurocentric paradigms of women's liberation but also claims what Brazilian philosopher Djamila Ribeiro has named "the place of speech" (*lugar de fala*) for each and every one of us, which she describes as an ethical posture that requires taking responsibility for the position we occupy as a way to reject traditional historiography and the hierarchy of knowledge that is a consequence of the social hierarchy.[51]

Situating *Biography of a Revolution* at the crossroads of postcolonial and decolonial feminist epistemologies has led me to reflect on my own "place of speech." My intellectual and personal engagement with feminism in Egypt is that of an intimate outsider, dating back to the early 2000s, when I was a PhD student, and continuing over the past two decades up to my most recent fieldwork to complete the research for this book in June 2024. In many ways, I have been more deeply socialized to feminist ideas and literature in Egypt than any other country in which I have lived, including my native country, Italy, and my country of migration, Australia. The stories narrated in this book trace very much the history of my own encounter with feminist activism and scholarship, and the process of becoming a transnational feminist historian, dwelling in between physical, metaphorical, and intellectual spaces of transition.

INTRODUCTION • 17

To interrogate my positionality in this research, I found inspiration in the work of three feminist historians—Luisa Passerini, Maria Rosaria Stabili, and Margot Badran—who theorize the interview process as intersubjectivity. The production of Passerini is characterized by the theorization of memory as a mobile process that is affected by the interlocutors' circumstances.[52] Equally insightful for me is Stabili, when she explains that her interviews with Chilean women were not just a collection of "testimonies" but joint reflections between her (the historian) and the subjects she studied about the meaning of the events and the matters they were discussing.[53] In the context of the 2011 Egyptian Revolution, Margot Badran has theorized oral history as autobiography, stressing the profound meditation on the self that the dual relationship between the agenda of the interviewer and the interested collaboration of the interviewee engenders.[54] The Egyptian Revolution inspired feminist scholars in Egypt and across the Arab world to deepen their engagement with oral history, and WMF in Cairo was at the forefront of this commitment, organizing conferences, workshops, and publications that discussed the opportunities and the challenges of oral history to build alternative archives.[55] In light of this scholarship, I use the interview not simply as a record of history but as a process through which I contribute to the creation of historical subjects and their personal "archive." Oral history interviews are not only composed of words. Narratives are seldom linear and coherent; instead, they are inhabited by omissions, silences, pauses, changes in tone of voice, sobs, glances, and smiles. The stories collected through the interviews are intense, but even if they mostly refer to traumatic or sad events, they are not all made of sorrow. Some of them are even hilarious and joyful. Interviews are embodied and gendered, like the historical subjects they contribute to create.

I interviewed Egyptian women across a range of ages, from university students to octogenarians, and listened to the oral histories collected by other scholars.[56] I did not conduct formal interviews with the many women intellectuals I am close to in Egypt. With some of them the friendship became too close, which would have not allowed what I felt was the right distance to conduct a good oral history interview, but the long-lasting intellectual exchange we developed over the years informs my understanding of Egyptian political history and the space occupied by feminism within it. Although the number of women I have interviewed over the years is substantial, not all the stories I have gathered have been included in the resulting collective biography. I made editorial decisions based on the themes I determined it was important to cover. Among the many life stories I listened to, I have deepened those that allow a broader reflection about theorization of the multiple manifestations of feminism in Egypt, its significance to global feminisms, and the relationship between women and revolution.

My analysis is transgenerational and biographical, allowing me to trace feminist legacies across generations of women intellectuals and activists. I use oral history not just to fill gaps in the traditional archives.[57] Yes, women's archives are scattered, women's memoirs are seldom recorded in traditional and institutional archives, and the women themselves have tended not to keep a written record of their work. But my use of oral history is primarily due to my interest in how memory relates to the present, and this is something I can only retrieve through the flows of oral history as a relational process.

CURATING THE DEEP HISTORIES OF THE 2011 EGYPTIAN REVOLUTION

Temporality is also important. The interviews are situated in a specific time, and the spirit of that time influences the flow of memory. I have found it inspirational to refer to the notions of "everywhen or still and yet and for all times," as theorized and practiced by my Aboriginal colleagues in Australia. Wiradjuri woman, poet, historian, academic, and teacher Jeanine Leane explains that in all First Nations languages there is a word to express the idea that "all times are inseparable; that no time is ever over; and all times are unfinished."[58] In Aboriginal philosophy and cosmology, history is not located wholly in the past, and "story" may be a more important concept than history. As discussed in a recent book curated by Ann McGrath, Laura Rademaker, and Jakelin Troy, story "is in part something larger, continuous and ongoing. Story can be about any and every time; it persists in and outside time, with time itself refused to be pinned down."[59] The Australian Indigenous notion of deep history challenges the linearity of historical chronologies and standard practices of archiving: "For many Aboriginal people time is neither exclusively linear nor cyclical but is 'always.' In other words, Australian practices for knowing, remembering, and re-enacting the past find embodiment in the present, blurring the distinctions of linear time and in some sense understanding the past as represented in a continuous now."[60]

Unlike Australia, Egypt is not a settler colony and Egyptians do not refer to themselves as "Indigenous"; therefore, vis-à-vis European colonialism, one could question the choice to honor the tradition of Indigenous epistemologies to study contemporary Egyptian history. However, Indigenous scholars argue that their Indigenous historicities can and should inform every historiography.[61] As I wrote a large part of this book on stolen Aboriginal land, I had access to Indigenous scholars, activists, and literature I might well have otherwise not encountered. Thus, their context and my situatedness in the Indigenous history within Australia, with all the experiences of marginalization, resistance, and resilience that define it, have also shaped this book. I have taken the invitation of my Aboriginal colleagues to engage with their epistemologies, and I have found that the concept of "everywhen" can inspire the development of a deeper understanding of the personal narratives of traumatic experiences, which I have found are quite frequent in the accounts produced by women political activists. Remembering a traumatic moment brings the experience right to the present, in a continuing time. The notion of everywhen also liberated my writing this book from the quest for linearity, an objective that not only was unachievable but would have taken away a lot from the stories I was gifted by my interlocutors. In that regard, multiple temporalities overlap in the stories I have collected in this book. I have listened to, transcribed, and curated my interlocutors' family memories going back to the 1919 anti-British Revolution. Rather than guiding the accounts I was listening to, according to my research agenda, the interviews followed their own, sometimes unexpected paths.

The women I have interviewed are themselves gatherers; as Jeanine Leane writes with reference to the women of her family, they are "the great gatherers of many things: food, of course, but also stories and inner strength."[62] Based on Leane's writings, and her focus on storytelling as a political enterprise, my narrative of women's discourses and practices, as well as my own active listening of their stories that form my practices of research, reflects a politics of care that, hopefully, I have learned in the process and is reflected in my writing this book.

Researching and writing about the nineties in Egypt led me to understand that the crucial themes for women's activism at that time were the effect of poverty on women's well-being and family life, the impact of female circumcision not only on their health but also on their overall safety and status, and the impact of the religious (especially Muslim but to a certain extent also the Coptic) discourse about women on the gender policies of the state. Whereas later when I worked with women who had been active in the demonstrations after 2011, the focus was on sexual violence and repression of the revolution by the state apparatus. I did my best to focus on my interlocutors' concerns and to balance them with my own needs both as a feminist historian and an intimate outsider who shares some of their apprehensions. At any given time, speaking with different women (secular and religious, socialist, or liberal, younger, or older) will result in different and potentially contradictory understandings of or focus on various sets of important issues, leading one potentially to overstate what was more important at a given moment. This also required my authorial voice to intervene and historicize the testimonies. The very notions of "Egyptian women" and "patriarchy" need to be historically as well as anthropologically and culturally contextualized.[63] Patriarchy is not a permanent and unchangeable category in Egypt or any other society, but it has been experienced in different ways by multiple subjects (colonial, postcolonial, neocolonial, European, Indigenous, secular, and religious) over the twentieth and twenty-first centuries. The stories narrated in this book similarly interrogate the relationship of mutual/reciprocal legitimacy/validation between cultural patriarchy and political authoritarianism. Gender, alongside class, race, and generation, informs power's relationships, and gender narratives are extremely important in the study of the Egyptian 2011 Revolution and the counterrevolutionary process that began after Mubarak stepped down from power. In particular, the stories narrated in this book challenge and deconstruct the notion of the Egyptian woman as a monolithic entity, mostly defined through the category of oppression and narrated through stories of misery. By rewriting them as a collective biography, which I name the *Biography of a Revolution*, this book wishes to contribute to the collective Middle East feminist's scholarship endeavor of providing a contrapuntal narrative of Egyptian contemporary history.

THE CONTENTS OF THE BOOK

Part 1 of *Biography of a Revolution* comprises four chapters covering the deep historiographical background to understand contemporary Egyptian feminism, supporting one of the overarching theses of the book: feminism is a major and essential intellectual root of the human rights movement in Egypt and, therefore, of the ideologies and the social movements that made the 2011 Revolution possible. Chapter 1 analyses women intellectuals' interventions about some of the themes that characterized the public discussion from the late nineteenth century until the early 1980s, which I call "the long feminist century." Chapter 2 focuses on one of the largest grassroots campaigns that Egyptian women led in the republican age, which was for the elimination of *khitan* (literally "cutting" and referring to women's circumcision). I have read the research produced by some of the Egyptian women who had been part of the FGM Task Force and interviewed them about their experiences. Chapter 3 explores women intellectuals' critiques of the political economy of the State from the eighties to 2011, ranging from liberal to Islamist to Marxist, including women's plural positionalities toward NGOs and transnational feminist activism. Chapter 4 sheds light on the contribution of women to the development of the human rights movement in Egypt, which is at the core of the movements that inspired the 2011 Revolution.

Part 2 of the book is composed of four chapters, each one dedicated to a specific feminist figure and to a theme that has been central in Egyptian politics. My choice of subjects was guided mostly by my capacity to connect with certain women and build with them long-standing and balanced relationships (not too close and not too distant) that by forming a collective biography, enabled a depth of analysis impossible with a single interview. Chapter 5 traces the biography of the cofounders of the organization El-Nadeem: Aida Seif El-Dawla, Suzan Fayad, and Magda Adly, who were all part of the student movement in the seventies. Chapter 6 deals with the biography of the feminist lawyer Azza Soliman, who is an expert in the Personal Status Law in Egypt, and it gives me the opportunity to discuss the evolution and the problems related to that law. Chapter 7 narrates the political biography of the journalist and politician Gameela Ismail, laying the background for a broader discussion about women and political leadership. Chapter 8 moves to a younger generation, with the political biography of the human rights lawyer Mahienour El-Massry and the rise of the social movements of the early 2000s.

Part 3 focuses on the revolutionary decade that began in January 2011, which, considering parts 1 and 2, can now be seen as simply the most recent phase in a century-long revolution in women's political subjectivity and agency. In this part I argue that among the most important changes that occurred with the 2011 Revolution is the development of a new chapter in the long history of Egyptian feminism. This perspective is articulated across four chapters. Chapter 9 narrates the emergence of new forms of women's online and offline activism in Egypt in the immediate years before the revolution and during the eighteen days of the revolution itself. Chapter 10 analyses a selection of women's narratives and their practices of memorialization of the

22 · INTRODUCTION

eighteen days. Chapter 11 focuses on the new feminist discourse about sexual violence in Egypt and the actions led by women not only to fight sexual assaults but also to change the terms of the debate about sexual violence. Chapter 12 documents the plague of imprisonment of women political activists and women's activism to support these political prisoners by relating the political biography of the human rights lawyer and former political prisoner Yara Sallam and situating it in the twentieth-century historical context of women's activism for political prisoners and women's imprisonment for political reasons.

The conclusion brings all these multiple threads together to contribute to the ongoing discussions about the nature and parameters of social and cultural as well as political revolutions in global intellectual history.

PART ONE

The Long Feminist Century in Egypt

ONE

Genealogies of Women's Activism

IN OCTOBER 2014, I attended the premiere of the play *Hawa al-Horreya* (*Whims of Freedom*) by Egyptian feminist documentary theater director Laila Soliman, an interdisciplinary theater-maker whose work is renowned for exploring the relationship between collective memories and personal stories.[1] Confirming Soliman's long-standing commitment questioning official narratives of history with accounts of the more intimate, individual experiences, *Hawa al-Horreya* engages in an intense meditation about two crucial moments in Egyptian contemporary history: 1917–19 and 2011–13.

The performance took place at the Egyptian Centre for Culture and Arts–Makan, located near the Mausoleum in memory of Saʿd Zaghlul, the nationalist leader and founder of the Liberal Constitutional Party (Wafd). His exile in 1919 along with several other members of a delegation (*wafd*) of Egyptian notables who attempted to join the Paris Peace Conference led to the eruption of a popular uprising in March of that year. The 1919 *thawra*, like 2011, was a mass national movement, a chaotic revolutionary time when social conventions were suspended, and women broke the rules of gender segregation and engaged in political militancy. Although it was violently repressed, the 1919 Revolution led to the uniliteral granting of Egyptian independence by the British in 1922 and its memorialization—including the glorification of women's participation in it—is part of Egypt's cultural imaginary.[2] In the wake of the 2011 Revolution, the memory of 1919 was not just repurposed by revolutionary forces, it was revamped in both popular and high-brow cultural productions.

By chance, on the same day I attended *Hawa al-Horreya,* I visited the Bayt al-Ummah (House of the Nation), the name by which the home of Saʿd Zaghlul and his wife, Safiyya, now a state museum, has been known ever since. Margot Badran documented that in 1919 Safiyya Zaghlul continued to use their home for Wafdists' meetings while her husband was in exile.[3] Her role in maintaining the young party's existence no doubt accounted for the fact that even two years later British intelligence ordered she was to be "closely watched."[4] Safiyya Zaghlul signed the women's petition to European consuls demanding Egyptian independence in 1919 and, although she has been largely neglected by the historiography about the Egyptian nationalist movement (but not the feminist one), she was a political figure who crafted her own public image as "Umm al-Misriyyin" (Mother of the Egyptians), linking her public role in the nationalist movement to the symbol of motherhood.[5]

This history constitutes the background of *Whims of Freedom,* but it is not its focus. By reading the papers of the Milner Commission, which arrived in Egypt in December 1919 to investigate the causes of the anticolonial uprising, the play brings to the stage the story of a young woman who reported a case of rape during the Revolution—significantly, like numerous young women did in the wake of the 2011 Revolution, ninety-five years after the events of 1919. Inspired by their involvement in the 2011 events, Soliman and her coauthors Alia Mosallam, Mustafa Said, Zeinab Magdy, and Nanda Mohamed initiated a conversation with a new generation of historians interested in working-class Egyptians who after WWI were imprisoned, tortured, raped, and killed for taking part in anticolonial protests.[6] The play's narrative builds what literary scholar Dina Heshmat has describes as a "counter-archive," a process of not simply adding previously erased stories but a method of interrogating the same logic of archiving.[7]

The combination of the two experiences on the same day, the visit to the Zaghlul museum and the play, inspired me to think more deeply about the "counter-archive" constituted by what in the Introduction to this book I have named the long feminist century in Egypt, and within it about the four picks of women's revolutionary activism (the 1919 Revolution, the student and workers' movement in the 1940s and the 1970s, and the January 25 *thawra*) unravelling along multiple, long-lasting, and underlooked genealogies of women's political activism. "Archives are collective, like collective memory, and just like memory has holes, archives also have holes," declares the lecturer played in *Whims of Freedom* by Zainab Magdy.[8]

Meeting with Soliman, we discussed the historical questions her play inspired. What are the "holes" in Egyptian popular memory of revolution and women's experience of it the play helps us see, if not fill? By opening with the excerpt of a letter by political prisoner Alaa Abd El-Fattah to his friend

Alia Mosallam, and intersecting it with Soliman's homage to two female artists and entrepreneurs of the early-twentieth-century artistic scene (Munira al-Mahdiyya and Naʿima al-Masriyya), and with the tribute to the courage of the countryside women who denounced their rape by British soldiers in 1919, the play weaves a transgenerational thread of memories made of hope, joy, and grief that unravels along a century of political activism in Egypt, where every political transition is marked by the visibility of women, from the 1919 anticolonial revolution, throughout the multiple phases of the postcolonial process of state-building, to the 2011 January Revolution.

Analyzing the oral histories I have recorded with Soliman and with other women activists of the generations who animated political opposition in the second half of the twentieth century through the 2011 Revolution, particularly, the 1970s student movement, I found confirmation that this thread is not linear; it is patchily documented at best, but it is powerful.

A few months after meeting with Soliman, I visited Professor Laila Soueif, a longtime human rights defender, founding member of the March 9 Movement for the Autonomy of Egyptian Universities (in 2004),[9] and mother of Alaa Abd El-Fattah, at her Cairo University office. The stories she told me about her youth in the early seventies reminded her of the early days of the 2011 Revolution: "One of the first things I said the first night we spent in Tahrir, I told Sanaa [her youngest daughter]: 'This is what I did. I was just about the same age as you.' Sanaa replied: 'Let's hope it doesn't take as long!'"[10]

Together, the stories collected in this chapter untangle a thread of memory, investigating the complex questions surrounding the concepts of a feminist tradition and genealogies of Egyptian feminism over the twenty century and the first decades of the twenty-first. In so doing, it offers a contrapuntal history of the process of modernization in Egypt, its entanglements with colonial capitalism, the desire for social justice that animated the militancy of women in the Marxist organizations in the 1940s, the ambivalent experiences of women in the student and leftist movements of the 1970s, and the continuities of colonial and patriarchal practices in the postcolonial nation-state and their impact on women.

WOMEN'S MODERN POLITICAL WRITING

Egyptian women's political militancy evolved in conjunction with the increasingly disadvantageous reorientation of Egypt's economy within the burgeoning global capitalist system in the second half of the nineteenth century, a trend that was marked by the accentuation of already-existing class and gender inequalities, altering the structures of the family and the society.

The period surrounding the start of British occupation in 1882 marked the beginning of a feminist literary consciousness in Egypt. Women's texts combined the writers' revendication of a feminine authorial voice with the political request of women's legitimate presence in the public space. By positioning themselves as what today would easily be termed as public intellectuals, women writers not only shaped their struggle for equality, but they also influenced all cultural and political debates from these early days until the battles in Tahrir Square.

At this time, Egypt was still a province of the Ottoman Empire, although it had become a semi-autonomous state under the regency of the Macedonian-Albanian military commander-turned-viceroy, Muhammad 'Ali Pasha (reign 1805–1849), whose dynasty lasted until 1952.[11] Egypt had greatly benefited from the outbreak of the American Civil War, which put a stop to the export of cotton from the southern states to Britain, as its role as a major producer of raw cotton for the British textiles industries helped the economy to flourish.[12] This led to loans from European banks to develop its ambitious infrastructure program, including the expansion of the railway (Africa's first, established in 1834) and the Suez Canal, which was inaugurated with elaborate festivities in 1869. But already at the end of the American Civil War and the resumption of cotton exports, the global price of cotton declined, a situation aggravated by the global financial crisis of 1873. Khedive Isma'il was forced to suspend the payment of the country's international debts and to agree on the establishment of the Public Debt Fund (Caisse de la Dette Publique) in 1876, controlled by the United Kingdom and France.[13] Rather than forestalling greater European control, in 1882 the British took advantage of the Khedive's request to support his repression of the 'Urabi revolt (the revolt by lower-ranking soldiers led by Colonel Ahmed 'Urabi against the increasing Circassian elite and European control over Egypt)[14] and invaded, occupied, and governed Egypt more or less directly for the next four decades.

Historians Hanan Hammad and Liat Kozma have documented the intersections between capitalist structures and patriarchal culture as Egyptian women entered the industrial workforce.[15] Hammad underlines that women's contribution to the textile industry in the second half of the nineteenth century was crucial, not only as workers but also as investors.[16] The transition to the modern economy had ambivalent consequences for women: it empowered those who were participating as investors and patrons, but it also exposed most working-class women to exploitation and poor working conditions. The analysis of these precarious lives led Hammad to question the relationship between modernization and emancipation for the working-class industrial culture: "More than the feminist discourse, their experience proved the relevance of Egyptian women to national productivity and modernism."[17]

In the rapidly changing context of the early twentieth century, women intellectuals were observing the consequences of economic transformations within the family, and they were questioning traditional family institutions, especially polygamy, voicing their views on the society in both the generalist press and the emerging women's journals, as well as in literary salons and narrative writings.[18] This growing literary awareness was paralleled by social and political activism, especially with the creation of philanthropy, social services, and intellectual societies run by women.[19]

This economic and intellectual effervescence was a harbinger of women's activism in the 1919 anti-British Revolution. British intelligence followed their joining the uprising, especially the Egyptian Ladies' Demonstration,[20] with concern. But there were not just upper-class ladies demonstrating. On March 14, Hamidah Khalil, "a woman of the people," became the first woman martyr, shot by the British Army in front of the Husain Mosque in the old, medieval heart of the city.[21] This marked the intensification of women's militancy in the nationalist movement; however, once independence was achieved, women were not acknowledged political rights. In protest with this exclusion, the head of the Lajnat al-Wafd al-Markaziyah lil-Sayyidat (Wafdist Women's Central Committee [WWCC]), Huda Sha'rawi, left the WWCC she had led in creating and, on March 16, 1923, she called her comrades to her house on Qasr el-Nil Street, where they founded al-Ittihad al-Nisa' al-Misri (Egyptian Feminist Union [EFU]), whose agenda encompassed women's social, economic, cultural, and political emancipation, as well as international issues. The EFU became one of the first and the most vocal feminist organizations in the world. Twenty years later, the feminist journalist Doria Shafik wrote about the importance of this date in the Egyptian women's cultural imaginary: "This day marks an unforgettable date, not only in the history of women's progress, but in the whole of the history of Egypt: this is the date of women claiming their rights. This claim came from women themselves, and in these lays its strong originality."[22] In her writings, Shafik articulated a powerful critique of the problematic positionality of male modern politicians and intellectuals toward women, anticipating many of the themes that have remained at the core of women's critique for the decades to follow. Whatever new forms of knowledge and ideas were circulating among educated male Egyptians, modernity bestowed androcentric heteronormative thought with powerful tools to limit female activity to the domestic sphere. The ideas about gender and sexuality of male politicians and intellectuals were developing in a hybrid ideological space, where the myth of women's domesticity—which was a product of modernity—was associated with an alleged "tradition" and codes of honor, while, in fact, it reflected the lifestyle to which the modern urban elites were aspiring. Differently, women's writing provides unconventional insights into the relationship between tradition and modernity, as the incongruous, almost paradoxical positionality of these women, at the top of intellectual intelligentsia and at the bottom of the juridical hierarchy, allows them to observe and to narrate the world from a new perspective, what bell hooks names a "strategic marginality."[23] As explained by the journalist Labiba Hashim, in an early twentieth-century essay, "Men write about women the way they know and think; women write about themselves the way they believe and feel. . . . [Women] are more cognizant of the condition of women, their weak points and how to win over . . . generations of women and take them to what is best for the country and of benefit to themselves."[24]

The link between intellectual production and political engagement by modern women intellectuals is demonstrated both by their writings and the connections they all had with the EFU. The pioneer in women's education Nabawiyya Musa (1886–1951), who was part of the second cohort of students graduated from the Saniyya School, the first Egyptian woman to be appointed school principal, and a member of the EFU, published in 1920 a book titled *al-Mar'a wa al-'Amal* (*Woman and Work*).[25] Musa, the orphan of an official of the Egyptian Army who participated in the 'Urabi revolt, and a pioneer in the field of women's education, was particularly concerned about educated, urban, and professional middle-class women.[26] A more openly political solidarity by women middle-class activists for working-class women emerged in the thirties, specifically in the writings of the Islamic intellectual 'Aisha 'Abd al-Rahman (Bint Shati), who wrote a book titled *Al-Rif al-Misr* (*The Egyptian Countryside*, 1936) and later, in the aftermath of the WWII, the activism of communist women (who, with few exceptions, such as Inji Aflatun, did not identify as feminists), to become more embedded with feminism in the seventies and eighties, when women's activism intersected the workers and the student movements.

Another major area of concern was women's education, on which they worked both in the public and private Egyptian schools, and by supporting some women students to perfect their training abroad. Among them were Doria Shafik (1908–1975), the first Egyptian woman to obtain a Sorbonne degree, with a doctorate thesis on the history of Egyptian women (1940), and Kawkab Hifni Nasif (Bahithat al-Badiya's younger sister), who specialized in gynecology in Ireland. They both returned to Egypt upon finishing their studies, Kawkab to work as a women's doctor and Doria to create her own feminist magazine, *Bint al-Nil,* in 1945, the *Bint al-Nil Union* (1948), and the homonymous political party in 1953.

It is important to notice that the feminist movement has never been a monolithic bloc. There were pluralist visions about politics, and especially about women's suffrage. Some figures, like Sha'rawi, who had an aristocratic family background, had a gradualist approach, prioritizing women's education as a political strategy; others, such as Doria Shafik and Munira Thabit, who were from the new generation of middle-class activists, considered political rights a priority.[27] Class and generational differences among women influence different political agendas, however blurred. Over the twentieth century, women from different class backgrounds, generations, and even political orientations have combined forces to address specific issues and launch joint campaigns.

Women continued to mobilize especially in the forties through the creation of political parties such as the Hezb al-Nisa' (The Women's Party, 1945) led by Fatma Rashid; the Ittihad Bint al-Nil (Union of the Daughter of the Nile), led by Doria Shafik; and the League of Women University and College Students (1945), led by the expressionist painter and communist feminist intellectual Inji Aflatun.[28] Women were also active in the Communist Party and some of them were incarcerated for their political activism, as was Aflatun. The geopolitical realignment after the end of the WWII and the sociopolitical turmoil with the workers and student movements would have opened new opportunities alongside new challenges for Egyptian women political activists.

POLITICS, STATE-BUILDING, AND WOMEN'S WORK IN THE MID-TWENTIETH CENTURY

Egypt was a battlefield during WWII, and when the war ended, it was extremely impoverished. Poverty instigated a new wave of mobilization of the political movements from all the streams: leftists and Islamists, students, women, and workers; they were all mobilized in these years at different levels and in different spaces.[29]

Some of the visions of a new generation of women leftist activists are reflected in the report submitted by the delegation of the Egyptian Women Students at the first Congress of the Women's International Democratic Federation, held in Paris in 1945. Inji Aflatun, who was a high-profile member of the Egyptian delegation, did not hesitate to label her home country as a "semi-feudal country oppressed by imperialism, under the cover of a semi-independence."[30] In an extensive report presented by the delegation, the first point addressed was women's and children's exploitation in the factories:

> They work thirteen hours a day, seven days a week for a famine's salary. If they get injured, they can only rely on the generosity of the patron. There is no organization to protect them. Women's salaries are one-quarter of the men's. One cannot describe the insalubrity of the workplaces. There are laws, that are ignored. It is the reign of arbitrium favored by the government: the delegates of the government are at the sold of the patrons and they make the law, and they crack down on those who manifest vague desire of resistance. The only authorized syndicates are those created by the same patrons.[31]

If the situation of industrial workers, in particular women, was grave, the condition of peasants was in some ways worse. The report denounced high rates of illiteracy and linked the deplorable situation of the population to the lack of acknowledgment of women's constitutional rights. In fact, they explained, if the Constitution of 1923 did not formally exclude women from political rights, the electoral law did not allow it. They argued that Egypt's overcoming of feudalism and its democratization would be attained only through the full acknowledgment of women's political, civil, and economic rights. While it was prepared by a group of radical university students, other sources produced by women intellectuals suggest that the report reflected a generalized sentiment of disaffection among the Egyptian people for their national state. In an essay published in the 1990s, the communist writer and literary critic Latifa al-Zayyat also remembers the 1940s as a crucial turning point for her activism: "I personally actively contributed to this revolutionary moment. As a student, I was one of three officers of the National Council for Students and Workers that led the struggle of the Egyptian people in 1946. In the street, I was a fully joined human being, with all my intellectual, emotional, and existential faculties. In the street, I was—we were—re-producing our society. I was us, which was me, and we were crafting tomorrow, feeling it as it took shape and came into being."[32]

Similarly, Amina Rachid (1938–2021), who later became a professor of French and comparative literature at Cairo University and a major figure in the Egyptian cultural field of the second half of the twentieth century, evokes the contrast she perceived as a young girl between the comfortable life enjoyed by her family (who were aristocratic landowners) and the rest of the population, which suffered from widespread poverty. Her writings highlight how the gap between rich and poor was reflected in the tensions existing within the women's movement, which was increasingly composed of women with diverse social backgrounds and personal attitudes. Some of them, like Rachid's mother and aunties, continued to conceive women's upper classes' contribution to the society in terms of charity work; others, Rachid herself, questioned the entire class structure of the society and committed their entire lives to dismantle it.[33]

With the passing of Huda Sha'rawi in 1947, the Egyptian women's movement was reorganizing, and so was the political system at large. Rachid could sense this as a young child: "One day, it was in '47, a little girl threw stones at me, because my grandfather Isma'il Sidqi had just signed the Sidqi-Bevin treaty, which seemed to link Egypt more to the English. . . . It was for me a shock from which I never recovered, that is to say that it was the first shock where I understood that I was being attacked, but that the one who attacked me was right."[34]

Rachid's intellectual trajectory reflects that of a small vanguard of upper-class women of her generation who developed an early awareness of social injustice and joined the students and the communist organizations that, after having been repressed during WWII, were coming back to the surface.

Some of the EFU founding members, such as Saiza Nabarawi, who was among Sha'rawi's closest friends and the editor of *L'Egyptienne* (the French-language journal of the EFU), progressively turned their activism toward leftist, internationalist, and pacifist networks, working with organizations such as the Women's International Democratic Federation, the Harakat Ansar al-Salam (The Partisans of Peace Movement, 1950),[35] and the Lajnat al-Nisa'i lil Muqawama al-Sha'biyya (Women's Committee for Popular Resistance), which organized relief for people in Ismailia during the 1956 tripartite aggression.

Inji Aflatun and Saiza Nabarawi were the two intellectuals who, beginning in the late 1940s and early 1950s, articulated a critique of gender inequalities in relation to imperialism, which they saw as interconnected forms of exploitation.[36] In so doing, they were a vanguard and distinguished themselves from other high-profile Marxist writers and intellectuals, such as Latifa al-Zayyat and Radwa Ashour, whose work revealed a more orthodox approach to Marxism that subordinated women's liberation to class struggle and anti-imperialism. But these alignments shouldn't be read as fixed and impermeable. The biographies of women activists reveal that the way they understood politics, feminism, and gender changed over the course of their lives.

Women's political activism continued to evolve along multiple ideological streams (liberal, communist, and Islamist) till the 1952 Revolution and the advent of Nasser both altered the power balance among social classes and soon enough closed the spaces for independent political activism. In January 1952 Amina Rachid observed the Cairo fires from her family's luxurious apartment in Zamalek: "I started to follow the news, but from a distance. Reading still occupied all my leisure time. I made it a refuge that protected me against the tensions of the outside and the pressures of the inside. Outside, the national struggle and the class conflict were spreading, and inside, anxiety was mounting at the inevitability of the change that was to come."[37] Over the next few years, Rachid decided to stand on the side of the poor people and, in her own words "to adopt communism as a system of life and a path to revolution."[38]

Nasser granted suffrage to women in 1956, and the corporatist state he established opened opportunities for generalized equal education and for public employment for all university graduates, including women. However, it also shut down all independent political organizations, including women's organizations. In 1956, all political parties, including the Women's Party, were dissolved. The Ittihad al-Nisa' al-Qawmi (National Feminist Union) was denied a permit to register in 1956. The EFU was dissolved and the Huda Sha'rawi Association created in its place focused mostly on social work. Inji Aflatun spent four years in prison for her political activism (1957–1961), a period during which she documented, both in her memoirs and her (now celebrated at the Museum of Modern Art in Cairo) paintings, the sufferings of working-class women raising their children in prison. Alongside other communist activists, the liberal and humanist feminist Doria Shafik was under house arrest since February 1957 for organizing a hunger strike at the Indian Embassy, demanding the end of dictatorship in Egypt and the withdrawal of Israel from Egypt's soil.[39] A few months later, her journals and her organization were shut. Her name was officially banned from the press. Shafik continued to campaign for human rights, but she never recovered from the trauma of being banned from public life. Even if the advent of Sadat in 1970 led to her (and other political activists') liberation, she now self-secluded herself and felt into a deep depression, which led her to tragically commit suicide in September 1975.[40]

Overall, the age of Nasser was a contentious time for women. Retrospectively, even the women of the generation who somehow benefited from the reforms introduced by the Nasser's regime acknowledge its shades. The journalist Farida al-Naqqash gives him credit for the plan to industrialize the country (a plan that, according to political economists, had a lot of failures)[41] and the larger impact this had on the opportunities offered to women in the fields of education and of the professions, while also underscoring that the shortcomings around women's rights reveal its authoritarian disposition:

> It was good and bad, at the time. It was good because Nasser had a very large plan to industrialize Egypt. To industrialize the country, you need not only working men, but working women. To have qualified working women, you have to enlarge the base of education. Education became free. Ways for women to work were open. So, both work and education were maintained. In 1956, the new constitution of Egypt gave women the right to vote and to be elected. At that time, two women were members of the parliament. . . . Still, the family law is, until now, a law against the freedom of women. Nasser's regime refused to change it, and my view is that they use this family law to oppress women, to control the movement of women for liberation. If you control half of the society, it becomes easy to control the society itself: all the society. This is the easiest way.[42]

In the three decades between the mid-fifties and the mid-eighties—that is, between the moment the independent and explicitly feminist organizations were closed and when feminism became visible again—women political activists continued to face the multiple challenges that characterize their lives throughout the twentieth century and the early twenty-first. On one side, the state engaged in what Hatem Mervat has described as the "state feminism," a series of programs aimed at mobilizing women as a productive force within the framework of postcolonial state-building.[43] On the other, they lost their independent spaces for political activism. The state continued to closely watch women's political activists, and even when they were keeping a low profile, they were safe only to a certain extent.[44] In fact, many of them ended up in prison, during the multiple waves of arrests of political activists that characterized Egyptian republican history, and self-censorship was frequent as an act of self-care.

"THE ROSES" OF THE STUDENT MOVEMENT

Since Egyptian universities were established in the early twenty century, there have always been student movements, although their strength, vibrancy, and political impact have varied over time. Trying to learn about the long-lasting legacy of women's participation in it led me to discuss Egyptian politics of the sixties, seventies, and eighties with women of two generations: those who entered universities in the 1950s, the period where women benefited from the generalization of education and of inclusion of women in the workforce under Nasser, beginning their careers in the early 1960s,[45] and those who were at universities throughout the seventies.[46]

The first time I met Farida al-Naqqash was in 2018. She received me in the professional space where she deployed most her career: the headquarters of the Hezb al-Tagammu' al-Watani al-Taqadomi al-Wahdawi (National Progressive Unionist Party, hereafter Tagammu'), and the journal *al-Hilal* (of which she has been a chief editor from 2006 to 2014, when she was replaced by her sister Amina),[47] where she is still very popular among the younger generations. I later met Farida again in her home in Maadi, in 2022, for a follow-up interview.

Over our two meetings, al-Naqqash gave me a vivid memory of how the students' perception of Nasser evolved in the decade from the mid-fifties to the late sixties. As a high school student, in the late fifties, she was a member of the Arab Socialist Union: "I was enthusiastic for Nasser's political foreign policy, and his social aspirations since he nationalized the Suez Canal Company. At that time, I was not yet at the university, I was at the secondary school, but I supported what he did very much."[48]

When I asked more about the intellectual spaces that contributed to shaping her personality, she told me that the years at university were marked more by cultural than political activism because the regime was not allowing any independent political activity. In Egypt, women first entered university in the late twenties (the first cohort of women graduated in 1930 from King Fu'ad University); therefore, at the time when al-Naqqash was a student, young women could already rely on women mentors. Among them, al-

Naqqash remembers two professors who left a mark on her upbringing: Fatma Mousa (a founder of the Department of English Literature at Cairo University), and Latifa al-Zayyat: "We were not only exchanging knowledge, but also friendship... I mean she was not only my professor, but she was also a friend."[49]

This fragment of memory from al-Naqqash expresses a shared feeling among the women I interviewed over the years: mentorship connections, often at the junction between politics and friendship, characterize their "feminist lives," meaning with it lives deeply marked by being in an intense relationship of knowledge production and transmission. Untangling the threads of these relationships gives access to a deeper understanding of Egyptian political history, where the solidarity among activists (often prosecuted by different regimes) allowed carrying on practices of activism that, generation after generation, enabled expressions of dissent to reemerge from the underground. Another recurrent element in the stories is that the activists' perception of the regimes and their politics changes over time. This evolution emerged in the life narrative I have recorded with Farida al-Naqqash.

As soon as she graduated, in 1962, al-Naqqash received multiple offers of work. There were new educational and professional opportunities open for educated women at that time: "I had the option to work in many places... I mean there was no unemployment crisis, especially for educated people. They were desired in the labor market, then I joined *al-Akhbar* newspaper, and after I joined *al-Jumhuriyya* newspaper ... I contributed to establishing Tagammu' Party later, and *al-Ahaly* newspaper, and I became the first woman editor-in-chief for it, for some years."[50]

Al-Naqqash married the journalist Hussein Abdel Razik in 1964, after which they spent three years in Algeria, invited by a colleague when he learned that, for their criticism of the Nasser regime, they had been banned from writing in Egypt. There, they contributed to the postcolonial shift from French to Arabic of the *al-Moudjahid* and *al-Sha'ab* newspapers for the Algerian Liberation Front. Once returned to Egypt, she resumed her work at *al-Ahaly,* covering, among other things, the 1967 War, where she paid specific attention to the issue of the refugees. In her memories, this moment marks a change in her own perception of the regime:

> I discovered many wrong practices in the relationship between the regime and the people. The one-party regime and its restrictions on freedom and liberties ... there was no free press, no right to unionize, and all the syndicates belonged to the government. These were the causes of the set-back of

the regime in '67. People were supposed to support, not to criticize any of the practices of the regime of Nasser and his colleagues. Later, after '67, after the set-back and the defeat—the very famous defeat of '67—I started to think that there was something wrong with Nasser's regime.[51]

The student movement grew over the years following the 1967 defeat, and by February 1972 all the universities in Egypt were on fire:

> In the university, there was what I can call a "huge outburst" because there is a desire to express and discuss the country's situation. And when the 1967 defeat occurred, it dropped all the illusions that Gamal Abdel Nasser and his regime were promoting. For instance, there was that known slogan: "The Egyptian Army is the most powerful and striking force in the Middle East." However, we found that it had been defeated by a tiny country like Israel in six days! So, it was a very complicated mental, military, and economic process indeed ... and the whole Egyptian people were mobilized to retaliate.[52]

The change of perspective following 1967 also recurs in multiple narratives I have collected from the women who were little more than teenagers at that time, and who would become the driving force of the feminist and the human rights movement in the following decades.

The sixties and the seventies were a period during which Egypt was in the middle of a process of economic development that implied increased urbanization, broader access to public education, and an overall transformation of the urban middle-classes lifestyles. These developments occurred on the heels of the participation by women who were then in their early twenties during the global wave of student movements that pushed for a cultural revolution. I discussed this at length with Amal Abdel Hadi, who studied medicine at Ain Shams University in the seventies, when she was part of the student movement and later of the underground communist movement, known as the Egyptian Workers Communist Party.

I met her in the winter of 2018, a few days before the seventh anniversary of the 2011 Revolution, in a café of al-Mohandessin, a lively and prestigious district in Greater Giza: "My political inclinations started in the second half of the sixties. I entered the university in 1965–66 and [after a while] I joined Monazzamat al-Shabab. I think I joined them in '66 or early '67. I was one of those who were shocked [about the defeat]. We were just two blocks from Tel Aviv, according to our media, and we destroyed their airplanes and so on ... so. ... It was a shock, a real shock."[53]

The conflicting sentiments remembered by Abdel Hadi are not individual feelings; they reveal both class and generational visions. Abdel Hadi admired Nasser's social policies, which had a direct and positive impact on her own life. Being one of five children of an employee at the Ministry of Education, she was aware that her ability to access free university education was a result of Nasser's politics. As documented by Tahani Rached in the documentary *Four Women of Egypt* and by Laura Bier in *Revolutionary Womanhood*, acknowledging the benefit generated by the state policies of women's generalized access to public higher education and to the formal waged labor was common sense.[54] But as a young member of the above-mentioned Monazzamat al-Shabab al-Ishtiraki (Socialist Youth Organization), Abdel Hadi had also been socialized to new ideas about politics. In fact, the Socialist Youth Organization, which had been established in 1966 by Gamal Abdel Nasser with the aim to prepare a new generation of young nationalist socialist leaders in Egypt, and which was formally independent,[55] soon became a space where young people experimented new forms of socialization and became acculturated to new political ideas and even literary genres. Influenced by Leninist and postcolonial intellectuals, Abdel Hadi and her comrades became more and more critical of the regime: "I was reading, reading, reading Lenin, and reading Frantz Fanon. It's that kind of reading about what the national bourgeois class is doing. Not a real independence; they did not want to cut [all ties with the ancien régime], but to take hold of the power for themselves. So, they are not really taking a radical position toward all the imperialist powers."

The tension caused by the contrast between the apparent change and underlying continuity from the colonial to the postcolonial order powerfully emerges in Abdel Hadi's narrative of Nasser's funeral, where, famously, an oceanic mass of people accompanied the corpse of the leader: "I was weeping, but at the same time I was saying, 'You can't just die, you can't just die and leave it like that.' Because I felt that the system needs to be really judged about what they have done to this country, and what they have done to us. So, that was a hot beginning."[56]

After the 1968 defeat, the Socialist Youth Organization, differently from its patrons' expectations, became the nest of the new radical left in the student movement, which continued to operate partially open air and partially underground during the presidency of Anwar Sadat, calling for the war against Israel to liberate Sinai: "There was a lot of university activism during that time, a lot. With wallpapers on the corridors and the discussions and so on."[57]

The leftist students soon realized that Sadat was trying to contain the Muslim Brotherhood by offering a few concessions, and in this period the tensions between the two oppositional factions (the leftists and the *ikhwan*) increased,[58] at least until they all suffered for a new wave of repression by the regime. Most of the women I interviewed were arrested; some of them, like Farida al-Naqqash, Nawal al-Saadawi, and Safinaz Kazem, wrote political memoirs about their experience, where they underline how being a political prisoner was doubly challenging for women because their morality and even their ability to be a good mother was questioned.

Al-Naqqash was arrested twice with her husband, also a communist activist: first in 1979, when she was imprisoned for two months on accusations of membership in the banned Communist Party; second in 1981–1982, for eleven months. When I spoke to her, nearly forty years later, she was processing through sociological lenses the painful memory of leaving her children, with both parents in prison at the same time:

> It's because you live in a society which is still traditional. I don't want to use the word "reactionary," but "traditional." This attitude towards women . . . I remember when I was arrested for the first time in '79, and I went to one of my doctors. The man who received us, [the doctor's] office boy said to me, "Why are you going to prison? This is the work of men." At the time, I was reporting for one of the Beirut newspapers and the police got what I wrote. I was not writing under my name, but they got what I wrote, and then they came to arrest me and to find out whether it was my handwriting or not. And when I went to the doctor, the man said to me, "This is not your work. To change Egypt is the work of men. Why do you leave your children?" As if I choose to go to prison, and I enjoy it!
> This is how the traditional society looks to politicized women.[59]

The experience of prison for women political activists in the seventies and eighties was multifaceted. It was certainly frustrating for most of them, especially for those who were separated from their kids, but also a moment when women experienced mutual solidarity: "Life in prison . . . well, of course, the prison is solitary, with closed gates and a hard life without communication with the outside world . . . but as we were staying for some time we were circumventing [the adversity]. I mean I stayed for almost a year . . . so, there was always a way to make friendships with the women guards, and officers and we were smuggling and receiving letters from our families . . . it was a hard life but survivable."[60]

Forty years later, Safinaz Kazem remembers with amusement songs she composed to tease her fellow inmates in Qanater women's prison, when she was detained for the second time, in 1981 (the first time was in 1973): "Anyway, in that jail we were close, and I used to sing and make everybody laugh. . . . I made a song for every one of them, Nawal's [al-Saadawi] song was 'Me, me, me, me. My name is Nawal, I love myself, I adore myself.' About Amina Rachid: 'My name is Amina, I am wise, I love myself in secret.' And about Latifa al-Zayyat: 'I am a Marxist, if Marx lived, he would love me.' Everyone loved the songs about them except Nawal."[61]

Others, those who were young and were detained for shorter periods, experienced prison more as a moment when they liberated themselves from family expectations and judgments. Abdel Hadi remembers how even the relationship between her parents changed because of her political activism: "After the movement and demonstrations and me being jailed, I remember that my mother, who was the typical obedient wife, began to discuss with him [my father], and he was . . . like, 'Who's this woman?' [laughs] This is not my wife!"[62]

Abdel Hadi's father was working in Algeria at the time and was seldom at home with the family. This is why, she remembers, he was treated "as a guest":

> He really didn't live the changes that happened to me, how I developed as a person. He was shocked that we never told him about [my] and my brother's imprisonment. We never told him. Why make him worry? He's coming here to spend a few weeks, and he's working like hell in that terrible place so . . . poor man. And we knew he was doing that for us, so we didn't actually. . . . It was a courtesy.
>
> But when he returned and stayed, then he began to see all that we'd endured, because he finished by '72, '73, something like that. I was kicked out of the house. I returned one day after midnight, and he just opened it like this: "Go where you have been." Astonishingly, my whole family, some of them are just [very simple people]. My uncle is a farmer. But he moved to Cairo and was living in the suburbs of Cairo, and he was fascinated by me. He lived in Qanater where the women's prison is, and he used to facilitate things for me through his neighbors who were working in prison, sending me messages and whatever. He was very proud that his niece is that strong woman in the movement. Everybody was supportive of the student movement.[63]

Abdel Hadi spent six months away from her parents' house, and when she came back, she realized that the relationship with her father had changed. "I apologized out of courtesy, but I knew at that point he has no control on me anymore. And he also knew he had not control on me. He knew that. And that was heartbreaking for him. So, c'est la vie."[64]

GENEALOGIES OF WOMEN'S ACTIVISM · 43

Breaking social conventions implied taking some risks but also discovering a sense of comradery among women that gave them strength, pride, and happiness. All these emotions came back to the surface while they narrated their stories:

> In the sixties at the Faculty of Medicine at Ain Shams University there was no cafeteria. There was a long corridor like this, which ends in a big hall, in a big room, and ... I just want you to see it. ... This is a corridor; this is a big room, and here is where they make the coffee and tea and so on. Young women would never go there. They [the men] were even bringing cannabis and so on. It was a boys club. As we are political activists, we began to sit in the corridor. We asked the man to put a table for us, and we were sitting men and women, and this was new for the Faculty of Medicine at Ain Shams University. This was the first time women would sit in the cafeteria. Everybody would sit outside, but we began to sit there, and we were sure nobody could say [anything]. We are not ... [normal] young women and young men, [about whom] a lot of gossip [can be said]. No, not for us, [because] we were the crazy political activists! And then things opened after that. I mean, there were social and political changes ongoing.[65]

In the seventies, Egyptian women university students were pushing for a social revolution, and they were doing it spontaneously, through a politics of everyday and small acts of defiance of the conventions, without even naming this as feminism. Not even the students' and the Marxist movements of the seventies escaped these contradictions of subordinating women's issues to the class struggle. Until Nawal al-Saadawi's book *al-Mar'a wa al-Jins* (*Woman and Sex*), which was first published in 1972, became a cult book for the women in the student movement, most political activists did not consider that sexual relationships or freedom was an integral part of politics: "Not at all!" as told to me by the labor lawyer and a veteran of the student movement in the seventies, and later of the Tagammuʿ political party, Zinat al-Askary; "*Kanat Harakat Wataniyya!*" ("It was a national movement!").[66] Born in a family of industrial workers, al-Askary enrolled in the Faculty of Law at the University of Ain Shams with the enthusiasm of a young woman who was determined to make the difference in the lives of nonprivileged people. She certainly succeeded in this endeavor, and, even if from her oral narrative about her life one cannot grasp a direct influence of feminism, she later participated, as a lawyer fully engaged in the civil society movement, in the campaigns for women's rights and especially for the reform of the Personal Status Law.

FIGURE 3. Lawyer Zinat al-Askary speaking at a human rights training about the right to adequate housing in international and Egyptian law, in September 2003. Courtesy of Zinat al-Askary.

Like the large majority of the women I interviewed, she confirmed that the core issues of the 1972 student movement were political and economic—namely, the protest against Egypt's inaction to liberate Sinai and Palestine from the Israeli occupation, and the harmful impact of the neoliberal capitalist economy on large and poor segments of the population: *"Sayed Bey, Ya Sayed Bey, Kilu Lahme Ba'a Ginee!"* ("Sir Sayed, Sir Sayed, a kilo of meat now costs a guinea!"), women and men students chanted together during demonstrations. Seham Saneya Abd el-Salam, a feminist medical doctor who was part of the student movement and later joined the FGM Task Force, remembered that socioeconomic rights were one of her main motivations to join the student movement:

> There is a disease called marasmus and there is another one called kwashiorkor. They are diseases of children because of lack of calories and protein. There is no medicine; the medicine is that they eat, but the parents cannot afford food for them. And when a child comes to me, and I tell their parents that the child needs to eat white cheese and chicken and eggs, the parents respond, "And what are the brothers going to eat?" This was my motif. I was

thinking if I must treat children with marasmus and kwashiorkor, I should revolt against the ruling regime.[67]

Women were bringing new approaches and visions to all the professional fields they were entering, but the leadership of the Marxist movements did not really grasp their implications. Retrospectively, the problematic attitude of the Marxists toward women and gender was also acknowledged by one of their major intellectuals, Hani Shukrallah, who in the seventies was a leader in the student movement and the outlawed Egyptian Workers Communist Party. He explained:

> Oh yes [we were talking about gender], but of course this is always the theory, and then there is the practice, and they don't march together that easily. In theory, we were a bit backwards in the sense that the assumption of equality involved, in some way, a neglect of the fact that there is something called a women's issue, [purporting that] women are equal to men, that there is no difference . . . because we are Marxist. We did not really have a feminist outlook or a feminist program: this would come a lot later. . . . It's women who forced this awareness on the men. But again, we had no problem in having women in leadership positions in the party.[68]

In general, if their presence on university campuses and their political activism were considered not only acceptable but to be encouraged as part of the broader project of women's participation in the public life, the private and intimate sphere (which is not less political than the public sphere) remained deeply marked by inequalities and taboos.

Abdel Hadi remembers the gender gap in the Egyptian Workers Communist Party, which she was part of as a young woman, and looking back to her life forty years later, she poses a critical yet caring look at her younger self:

> During that time, I wasn't at all a feminist. I wasn't, I was a political activist, I never really reflected on gender aspects, we were working like hell, but the leadership was mainly men. . . . I remember that we were a group of young women, Suzan Fayad, from El-Nadeem Center, was one of them, for example, and she was also my schoolmate. We were doing all that activism, and we never thought that we should be leaders. We were leading, in reality, we were leading, but those who will get into the central committee of our party, for example, our underground party, were not women. There was just one woman there, although we were all very, very active. . . . Yes, there were many women but how many in the decision-making positions is something else. . . . Now you understand that at that time I was just happy, when they told me I am

46 · GENEALOGIES OF WOMEN'S ACTIVISM

a member. I am just walking in the street jumping. I want to tell everybody. Wanted my mother to read about the dialect[ical], and historical materialism and so, I was very happy to be just part of that.[69]

The birth of the first child was also a recurring turning point in the relationship of companionship developed by women political activists with their political and love partners:

> For feminism I think my eye opener was the preparations for Nairobi, I wasn't at all into all the politics of it, but I began to understand there is something about women that our activism, political activism didn't take into consideration. But also, on a personal level, you marry your comrade, we all married our comrades [laughs]. We were together in the prisons, and together in the underground [movements], and together in everything. And then, we discovered that there is still, there is a lip service about equality, but it's not real . . . I was married to a wonderful man who was helping, but he was HELPING.[70]

This gap between their public and private lives allowed women to develop a more definite awareness that they also need a space of their own to pursue their feminist politics. Through their professional (many of them are medical doctors and lawyers) and personal experiences (they are young mothers, some of them experience domestic violence), they start to think critically about Marxism and their Marxist comrades and decide to open new spaces for critical reflection about women, culture, and politics. This is how they narrated to me the experience of starting the New Woman Foundation in 1984 and the work they did in it.

> You were asking me, at the beginning, why I joined. I am also from political origins, and some of our founders here, our founding members, are also from political origins, all from the left. This also explains our choices. . . . My father was a communist and a workers' lawyer, but I am talking about my political origins. I was a member of underground parties and things like this for years. In the end, however, I found that in all political parties, women are treated as secretaries, and I didn't like this. It was also after the fall of the Soviet Union. It was corrupt, and showed that, really, the experience wasn't the good one.[71]

The Marxist-Leninist Egyptian Communist Workers Party (ECWP) is remembered as one of the underground political formations that was the most open to women's participation in the eighties. Nawla Darwiche, Laila Soueif, Suzan Fayad, Magda Adly, and the late Siham Sabri, Afef Marai, and Arwa Saleh were all admired by their women comrades: "She was called the rose of the student movement," Aida Seif El-Dawla told me about Siham

Sabri. "I was so shy and was looking at her leading chants at the demonstrations, and she was so powerful!"[72] Most of the women who are today high-profile human rights activists, like El-Dawla, tend to underplay their past leadership role in their oral history narratives, and they seldom provide detailed narratives about their activism, preferring to remember the impressions their comrades made on them. Relationality is embedded into the construction of the self.

To understand the continuity of women's struggle against these multiple levels of discursive oppression and their strategies to overcome them, a linear interpretation of history is insufficient. This is a history that reads more as a spiral of memories and legacies, and maybe the text that more than any other represents the passing of the torch from the generation of the seventies to that of the nineties, but also the continuities between the two, is the memoir by a leader of the student movement and a member of the ECWP, Arwa Saleh (1951–1997), significantly titled *al-Mubtasirun* (*The Stillborn*).[73] In this memoir, the author contemplated the legacy of the student movement and its failures, especially in dealing with socioeconomic and gender issues.

At the core of Saleh's controversial critique, there was the sexism experienced by women in the communist movements, which she directly lived through,[74] and that led her to ask a tearing question: Can a revolutionary movement succeed without a feminist radical critique? Linking the class critique to the gender critique and by revealing that even the left had gendered the intellectual as a male and therefore could be situated into a patriarchal order, Saleh's book was dismissed for a long time by her comrades but was also destined to speak to the future generations, a desire she explicitly expressed in its first pages. Saleh, who suffered from severe depression and committed suicide in 1997, has an afterlife following the 2011 Revolution. To the new generations, this story became an invitation to transcend ideologies while still remaining committed to politics by positioning gender at the core of the revolutionary thought.

Women political activists who had a background in the student movements of the seventies, then the underground Marxist movements of the eighties, and then the feminist organizations that emerged across the eighties and the nineties were motivated to move away from the ideological grand narratives and to act in order to force a change from the grassroots at multiple levels of society. If the movements of the seventies were infused with (largely) Marxist theories, women's movements in the eighties and the nineties embedded theory in multiple praxes. What is important to note here is, first, that the enchantment with Marxist/Socialist theories in the seventies among the rising generation of activists occurred at the very moment that the Egyptian state began its transformation away from a socialist to a neoliberal political economy; and second, that the memories of the movements that emerged in this period (e.g., students, workers, communists) and their formative ideologies continued to haunt women activists into the period that began with the fall of communism and the end of the Cold War, and this haunting would be reflected in a conflict within the feminist field between those who engaged with the neoliberal turn and the gender policies of the (Mubarak) state as part of its "authoritarian bargain" and those activists who maintained a more independent posture toward the government and whose political commitments revealed the liberatory specter of their youthful dreams.[75]

In the seventies feminists established the foundations of what would become in the nineties a multifaceted and intersectional women's movement that would take many directions: from intellectual and academic activism to human rights organizations, NGOs, and international forums. I realized how important this cultural and political work was, when I was interviewing younger women about the nineties, the human rights movements, and their experience in the context of the NGOs and the international conferences on women. They were constantly referring to women of the previous generations and the impact they had on their formation, which to me was clear evidence that there is a genealogy of feminist thinking and practices that needs to be read through the lenses of intellectual history. This is the background that led women in the eighties and nineties to write a new page in the history of Egyptian feminism.

TWO

The Fight for Women's Bodily Rights

THE FGM TASK FORCE

I made a study and I found that one of the areas that was very highly neglected and very much needed [to be developed] was the situation of women's health.... I had come from a family and atmosphere where FGM is part of our tradition, and even many of my friends were telling me this is not an issue, but more and more I became clear. It is not [just] FGM; it is all that we are saying about the status of women, or rights, or human rights or dignity, it's how can I deal with family planning or literacy of girls and let these girls be cut.[1]

These words belong to Marie Bassili Assaad (1922–2018, hereafter Marie Assaad), a pioneer in social work and environmentalism in Egypt, a leader both in Egyptian women's activism and in several international Christian networks.

I never met Assaad, but her figure towers in all the stories I have heard about the experience of the Quwat al-'Amal li-Munahaddat li-Khitan al-Banat (Task Force to Fight the Circumcision of Girls, known in English as the FGM Task Force), which she created and led for five years (1994–1999), until—with much regret of its members—its functions were assumed by the National Council for Childhood and Motherhood and it was closed. Many of the feminists I interviewed and who had been part of the student movement and the Marxist underground organizations in the eighties had also joined the task force. In December 2018, WMF organized a conference at the American University in Cairo to celebrate her life.[2] At the time, many of the feminist organizations that had been at the core of the 2011 Revolution and on the front lines defending women's rights had their financial assets frozen, and their directors were under investigation and travel ban. In this context, the act of remembering Assaad's life, and her long-lasting independence from the government, seemed a subtle act of defiance by feminist historians against

50

FIGURE 4. Marie Assaad (left) running a grassroots literacy program with women garbage collectors in Cairo. Courtesy of Women and Memory Forum Library.

a government that had closed every avenue of direct political expression. After the conference, I consulted the WMF archive to retrieve some testimonies about Assaad's work in the 1990s and the early 2000s.

Born in Cairo to a Coptic Orthodox family that she defined as "Egyptian middle class" and "matriarchal," Marie Assaad has been an activist from a young age when she was a student at the Cairo American College for Girls on Ramsis Street in Zamalek and became involved in the Youth Women's Christian Association (YWCA). In 1951, she was one of the Egyptian delegates to the first conference that the YWCA organized in Ramallah, Palestine. The photos of her youth are full of joy, always portraying her in her school uniform surrounded by friends. Those of her mature age keep the same open and welcoming smile, revealing a fulfilling and generous life.

In a 2014 oral history she did with Hoda Elsadda, Assaad explains that she had her first feminist—her own words in English—experience during the sixteen months she spent in Geneva between 1952 and 1953 when, against her mother's will, she accepted an appointment to serve on the World YWCA as a program assistant in the Youth Department. "It was an intensive, liberating experience ... living away from the family," she explained, revealing her inclination toward expanding her cultural horizons and being independent. By 1954 she was the first woman ever nominated secretary general of the organization, and she dedicated her role to advance women's rights within it. She later became a member of the Board of the World Council of Churches, and notwithstanding the difficulties of being a woman in a male-dominated space, she ascended through the hierarchy until, in 1980, she became the deputy secretary general of the Council—once again, the first woman (and noncleric) to occupy this post.[3]

In Egyptian feminist circles, Assaad is remembered specifically for her work to erase the *khitan,* the practice commonly known in English as either female genital cutting or female genital mutilation (FGM) and which, as witnessed in numerous ethnographies, is widespread both among Muslim and Christian communities in Egypt.

Assaad published one of the first studies on this topic in 1970 when she was working at the Center for Social Research at the American University in Cairo. Her approach was holistic, bringing together medical, anthropological, historical, sociological, and even legal and religious studies research that was developed by Egyptian scholars throughout the sixties and the seventies. She appeared convinced that education would have played a crucial role toward the eradication of *khitan* and that the Egyptian government's policies needed to be oriented toward supporting people's education.

Regarding the contentious issue of how best to define the practice, Assaad explained: "Most writers seem to agree on the definition of female circumcision, excision, or clitoridectomy, which is called *khafd* (reduction) in classical Arabic and is more popularly known by the term *tahara* (purity).... It is the partial or complete removal of the external female genitalia, varying from removal of the prepuce of the clitoris only to the full excision of the clitoris, the labia minora, and the labia maiora."[4] For their part, feminist activists who were part of the FGM Task Force in the nineties alternate the terms "circumcision" with "cutting" and "FGM," depending on the context.[5]

I asked the Egyptian medical doctor, anthropologist, and a member of the FGM Task Force Seham Saneya Abd el-Salam what the preferred Arabic term is. Seham (whom I refer to by her first name, which she preferred) was well-known for her work in the Egyptian feminist movement. The daughter of a teacher of sewing and embroidery (her mother Saneya) and a graduate from al-Azhar who worked as a teacher of Arabic and Religion (Muhammad), she grew up in a Cairene, middle-class, and polygamous family, something she remembered as a painful experience not only for her mother, but also for herself and her siblings. Seham enrolled in the Faculty of Medicine of Ain Shams University in 1967, and she graduated in 1972, in the pick year of the student movement, in which she took part with enthusiasm. After graduating, she worked as a house officer in Aswan, and there she had patients who were infibulated or children coming with bleeding after the circumcision. This reinforced her already negative opinion about the practice and her desire to work toward its eradication, which she pursued primarily through her grassroots work. As she explains it, "People call it *tahara* ... purity. ... So, when I speak to them, I use their language, and at the very end I try to discuss the thing and I say: 'So, is this *tahara*, after all you said?' They say, 'NO!' 'So, what is it?' 'It is torture, it is mutilation.' I don't start speaking about genital mutilation, no, no! In classic[al] Arabic it is *khitan,* which is from a root that refers to being married, because they think that a person cannot marry without being circumcised, and this is why they circumcise boys and girls."[6]

Seham's testimony focuses on the non-neutrality of the choice of concepts. The term *FGM* is not indigenous. It was introduced by the international organizations in the early eighties in the context of programs for socioeconomic development and of programs to eradicate female circumcision. Social scientists note that the choice of the term to refer to the practice is politicized.[7] Ethnographies document how the multiple and often ambivalent perceptions of the practice vary according to numerous factors, especially generation and the level of education and income, tending to be more widespread among lower-income women, who also tend to believe that it is intimately connected to historical Islamic practice—a belief that is as widespread as it is unsupported by historical evidence.[8] In fact, both Christians and Muslims in Egypt circumcise girls, and it seems that the practice predates both Christianity and Islam. The Islamic religious texts do not provide unequivocal instructions about it (like many other issues), and the exegesis of the texts, largely shaped by male and elite scholars, changes over time and tends to intersect ideological positionalities and political interests. Margot Badran noted that in the nineties, and especially in the lead-up to the International Conference on Population and Development (ICPD), there was a "re-Islamization" of the debate about FGM, with divergences of opinions between the Islamists (who were claiming *khitan* to be an Islamic practice), and the (state-appointed) Grand Mufti, Muhammad Sayyid al-Tantawi, issuing a fatwa where it was proclaimed anti-Islamic.[9] Geopolitics and international relations also played a role in the way the discourse about *khitan*/FGM was articulated in Egypt in the nineties. As international developmentalist organizations and both international and

THE FIGHT FOR WOMEN'S BODILY RIGHTS · 53

Egyptian feminist activists were promoting programs to eradicate FGM, the United States with their European and Arab allies were attempting to create and stabilize the neoliberally grounded "New World Order," which played out through a series of wars and occupations, as well as by continuing support for the secular authoritarian regimes of Egypt, Tunisia, and Jordan, and the Israeli occupation of Palestine. In Egypt, this resulted in a discursive (and empirical) short circuit: on one side, the Mubarak regime was supporting and somehow also promoting the institutionalization of feminist work (the FGM Task Force, the Council for Motherhood and Childhood, the National Council for Women, etc.) in the name of women's rights as human rights; on the other side, the same regime was complicit in, if not directly responsible for, the most violent violations of human rights in Egypt and across the region. This contradiction had a profound impact on the perception of self and identity among Muslim people, including Egyptian women, and favored the growing politicization of gendered discourses about identity and authenticity. In this context, the governmentality of women's bodies became a very high stake.

THE PARADOXES OF MODERNITY IN RELATION TO WOMEN'S CIRCUMCISION

Among Egyptian feminists, women's circumcision is part of a broader discourse about sexual and reproductive health, and in dealing with it they necessarily had to confront the agenda of the modern state. In fact, in Egypt, women's status, gender, and sexual relationships had been at the core of politics of representation and self-representation since the advent of modernity. Since the early twentieth century, being a modern nation meant having "modern women" who could educate "modern men."[10] But in those modernist and nationalist discourses, being modern had nothing to do with women's gaining self-awareness and sexual freedom. On the contrary, women's growing mobility and presence in the public spaces (public schools, universities, workplaces, or, more trivially, the streets of the cities and public transports) generated a sort of moral panic about sexual promiscuity and the dangers that it implied for women's modesty.[11] This ambiguous relationship between modernism and gender politics continued well into the postcolonial age when, on one side, the state promoted women's participation in the postcolonial state-building project, especially through the generalization of public education and universal suffrage, while on the other, the canons of women's respectability continued to remain restrictive for women. This contradiction is reflected in both the public discourse and the legislation about *khitan*. According to Seham Saneya Abd el-Salam, the press started influencing progressive families to not practice the *khitan* since the early 1930s, and the journal *Hawwa* (*Eve*), especially through the articles authored by the feminist journalist Amina al-Said and by Rabee Gheith, played an important role in supporting the argument for the eradication.[12]

In 1959, a law was promulgated to prohibit *khitan* in public clinics and hospitals.[13] Did this prohibition result in the eradication of the practice? No, it did not. Seham, who was born in 1948 to a middle-class Cairene family remembers that her father, an Islamic scholar, was advising neighbors who were seeking his opinion not to circumcise their daughters, and that within the family there was a generational divide between her parents and grandparents: "My mother, who was circumcised, insisted not to circumcise the girls, and my father as well, and my paternal grandmother wanted us circumcised, and the issue was raised whenever one of the neighbors' daughters was circumcised. I witnessed all these debates and although I was not circumcised, I lived in fear because how should I feel safe when every now and then a girl among my friends is circumcised?"[14]

It was through collective work that women overcame the fear. By the eighties, women activists had developed the capacity to collectively work against the practice of *khitan*. The Arab Women Solidarity Association (AWSA), created by Nawal al-Saadawi, whose feminist writing was a source of inspiration for multiple generations of feminists across the Arab world and Africa, had this at the core of their agenda, intersecting it with socioeconomic and legal rights.[15]

Women's sexual health was a central theme at the UN-sponsored International Conference on Population and Development (ICPD), which was hosted in Cairo in September 1994, and which is considered a turning point in Egyptian women's political activism, as well as the beginning of a new age in the gender politics of the State. It was part of the global agenda adopted by the United Nations on development, which in the two decades from 1975 to 1995 made gender a mainstream focus in both the international and the Egyptian neoliberal agendas. For the Egyptian government, the conference was an opportunity to attract foreign investments to fuel its population and development policies. On another side, once the government agreed to host the conference, they had to include the feminist organizations in the conference preparations. The then-minister of health, in his opening address to the ICPD, declared that FGM was rare in Egypt. The next day, CNN broadcasted a video documenting the genital cutting of a thirteen-year-old girl. In fact, the practice was not rare at all. The video was highly contested not only by the supporters of female circumcision but also by the feminist abolitionists, as it was perceived as culturalist and a violation of the privacy of the girl that was filmed.[16]

The need for women working for and with women was now under everyone's eyes.

SHIFTING THE PARAMETERS OF THE DEBATE ABOUT FEMALE CIRCUMCISION

The activists and researchers involved in the conference received funding for fieldwork-based feminist research that produced multiple reports for the ICPD. Indeed, all the activists I interviewed agreed that the preparatory work for the 1994 conference provided, for the first time in decades, space for Egyptian feminist groups to engage with government policies about women, while offering feminists from different organizations and groups an opportunity to work together in relative freedom. For the first time, feminist-critical approaches on sexual and reproductive health, an approach where women's wellbeing as individuals was a value per se and not only in relation to maternity, gained centrality in public discourse. This added a new dimension to a debate which, till then, had been deployed either within the traditional religious framework(s), where, with a range of nuances, the focus was on the legitimacy of fulfilling sexual pleasure within marriage; within the framework of secular modernity, where, since the colonial age, issues related to gender, women's health, and sexuality had been subsumed under the politics of family planning and public health; or in the context of the Islamist organizations, which competed with the State (and often also among them) to accredit themselves as the custodians of "the authentic Egyptian culture," legitimizing their ideology by their capacity to provide health care services that the State was less and less able to provide. Among these services, there were of course both men and women's circumcisions. Most of the time, the public discourse had been dominated by men up to this point—in the first case, by religious accredited scholars, and in the second, by institutional actors.

Following the publication of the Egyptian Demographic Health Survey in 1999, which confirmed that 97 percent of never-married Egyptian women had been circumcised,[17] the Ministry of Health issued a decree to medicalize and hospitalize *khitan,* with the aim of reducing harm. This was obviously not considered satisfactory by feminist NGOs, especially as de facto, the medicalization often resulted in more severe cutting. Under the umbrella of the FGM Task Force, these NGOs initially gained some success, lobbying both the Ministry and the religious authorities to obtain a ban on *khitan.*[18] In response, the Islamists took the case to court, but the Ministry won on appeal. Eventually, the task force lobbying the Ministry was successful. They won the Ministry to their view, and in 1997, Law 261, which banned *khitan,* was put in force.[19]

CROSS-CULTURAL ENCOUNTERS IN THE FGM TASK FORCE

The FGM Task Force, cochaired by Marie Assaad and Aziza Hussein, included several women from different generations and political orientations, as well as both Christians and Muslims. As I discussed above, the cochair Marie Assaad had been working on *khitan* since the 1950s, both nationally and transnationally, being also a member of the YWCA. Cochair Aziza Hussein (1919–2015) was also a veteran and a pioneer of women's health activism in Egypt and internationally. The daughter of a gynecologist, whom she remembers as an enlightened and generous man, she graduated at the American College at the age of sixteen. She traveled a lot with her husband, who served as Ambassador to the United States, where she lectured about women in Egypt, and she was involved in networks for cultural exchanges between the US and Egypt. When the couple returned to Egypt, she worked with NGOs on FGM and family planning, and from 1961 to 1967 she was appointed by the government to represent Egypt at the UN, where she became the first Arab woman to chair the UN Women's Committee.

Hussein worked with Nawal al-Saadawi and Yahya Darwish in the Committee for Working Women's Affairs, and for the National Population Committee, two experiences that, in the oral history recorded by WMF, she remembers as difficult.[20] Her international experiences, especially with the International Planned Parenthood Federation (of which she was also vice president and then president, in 1977), inspired her to create the Family

Planning Association in Egypt, which from the late seventies to the early nineties worked to obtain the reform of the Personal Status Law and to eradicate FGM.

It is on the basis of this vast experience at the crossroads between her international networks, the Egyptian independent NGOs, and the governmental bodies that she was appointed the head of the National Preparatory Committee for NGO in view of the ICPD. She played a critical role in this function, especially in moving the ICPD toward a family planning agenda, prioritizing women's rights and health over traditional quota and target strategies, something that had a long-term positive impact not only in Egypt but other African countries.[21]

The above-mentioned Seham Saneya Abd el-Salam was part of the Center for Development and Population Activities and of the Cairo Institute for Human Rights Studies (CIHRS). Amal Abdel Hadi was also in the CIHRS and with Aida Seif El-Dawla and Nadia Abd El-Wahab was a member of the New Woman Foundation (NWF). Afaf Marai and Amal Sharif were part of the Coalition for Women's Issues; Marilyn Tadros was an academic; and Ragia Omran, today a high-profile human rights lawyer and a board of trustees of NWF, was at that time taking her first steps in civil society. This was the core team of the task force, which brought together representatives from more than sixty civil society organizations.

When I conducted my interviews more than twenty years after the 1997 ban was approved, the experience of the task force was history. The eldest members had passed away, others were in fragile health conditions due to their age. Among those members I could meet, some were retired. Others were feeling very much deceived by the experience of the post-2011 counterrevolution, and they were even wondering why I was so interested in "such an old story." Yet, as we went deeper in the conversation, their memories of the task force reemerged vividly.

The reality is that for many of these middle-class, high-educated, polyglot, fiercely independent, and at that time young Cairene women, the experience had been a revealing cross-cultural encounter. By "cross-cultural," I mean the fruit of exchange not only between Egyptian and international cultures but also, and perhaps even more, among the multiple cultures that shape modern Egypt: the urban, middle-class, and intellectual cultures, and rural Egyptian cultures. It was an encounter with women who were not middle class but poor, not high-educated and polyglot but illiterate or semi-illiterate, not Cairene but rural or from a peasant background. It was the discovery that women who did not receive a formal education could be competent about their own needs. In two long oral history interviews, Seham Saneya Abd el-Salam and Aida Seif El-Dawla shared with me their most vivid memory of that time.

> SEHAM: No, listen to me. This is what I discovered when we started the task force: The issue is not medical at all; it's cultural. This is why I decided to study anthropology. To understand.
>
> AIDA: I read what Nawal al-Saadawi had written about circumcision, and it was very abstract for me. I never saw an actual circumcised woman except when I graduated from medical school. And I didn't think that this was still being done until I started working in 1993 with a wonderful, wonderful elderly woman called Marie Assaad, who set up something called the Task Force against Female Genital Mutilations, and during the task force we produced papers, did trainings and workshops to address the issue of FGM. We had workshops with men, with women—several across the country—with young girls, with physicians, and with the clergy.[22]

El-Dawla's account here differs from what I have heard in both Assaad's and Saneya Abd el-Salam's accounts earlier, the first one asserting that it was part of the culture, and the latter that even if her parents did not want to circumcise the girls of the family, being surrounded by circumcised women made her feel scared. I went back to El-Dawla asking how it was possible that in a country where 97 percent of women are circumcised, she never heard about it. And she insisted: "It is just that mine was a very protective family." In this, like other interviews, the concept of "protection" of young women in the family is conveyed through the "silence" about topics that can produce harm or generate trauma.

In her account El-Dawla also emphasized the task force's independence from the government, as well as the spontaneous way in which the women of the task force had come together:

> Marie Assaad was an elderly woman who, together with Aziza Hussein [who was] a little bit older had been working with marginalized communities ever since the 1930s. They had been working mainly in Manshiyyat Nasir, close to al-Muqattam, and they addressed whatever it was that was an issue for the poor women there. And then in 1993, there was the preparation for the [1994] International Population Conference [ICPD] in Egypt. So, all the reproductive issues were on the agenda. And to produce papers for that conference, we had to do research. At the time, we were not a task force, we were just a group

meeting at Marie Assaad's house. To do this research, we did fieldwork. And the field revealed a lot that we did not know.

Like most of the feminist initiatives in Egypt that I have been able to document, the FGM Task Force started as an informal group and later assumed a formal structure. Immediately after the ICPD in 1994, the task force, under the auspices of the National NGO Commission for Population and Development and with the support of the Ford Foundation Cairo Office, shifted from grassroots activist work to become an active and efficient inter-mediator between the government and civil society.[23] This shift to political work changed the perception of the task force among its participants. Not all the core members felt comfortable with this new turn, and some of them decided to leave the group. In the context of an authoritarian regime, the dilemma that always haunted feminism in Egypt (working with the state institution to promote some change from within or maintaining full inde-pendence, both from the government and from international funding) could not find a solution.

The task force worked toward the eradication of FGM for five years. Marie Assaad was pressured by the government to close the task force as an inde-pendent entity and to accept that the campaign would be incorporated into the post-ICPD activities of the National Council for Childhood and Motherhood (NCCM), presided over by the then-First Lady Suzanne Mubarak. This was the strategy of the Mubarak regime: to subsume under government agencies the segments of the civil society that produced good results, while persecuting the independents. In 2003, the NCCM launched a national program, the FGM Free Village Model, whose projects were very much inspired by those run by independent feminist organizations for decades. By then, the task force had been closed.

THE DEBATE BETWEEN FEMINISTS, ISLAMISTS, AND THE STATE ABOUT *KHITAN*

The ongoing diplomatic effort deployed by feminists before the task force was created, during the years it operated, and after it was closed to obtain institu-tional support for eradicating *khitan* eventually led to responses from both the Islamic Egyptian authorities and the government. The sheikhs (religious scholars) of Al-Azhar University, the chief center of Islamic Sunni and Arabic

FIGURE 5. Poster of Congress against Female Circumcision, Hotel Shubra in Cairo, December 12, 1994. Courtesy of Seham Saneya Abd el-Salam.

learning in the world, published an unambiguous statement against *khitan* in 2006, and the government passed a law criminalizing it in 2008.[24] These were steps forward in the way public discourse was articulated by religious and state institutions. However, they had limited effects on the ground, given that at the time the law was passed (2008), private sector clinics and hospitals were not regulated by the law. In 2013, the debate came back to the news, when the Muslim Brotherhood, who then represented the majority in the Parliament, threatened to repeal a series of laws promulgated in the past twenty years thanks to women's lobbying activities: among them, the *khul'* (divorce) law and the penalization of *khitan*.[25] This partially explains why, according to the Egyptian Health Issue Survey published in 2015 by the Ministry of Health, the practice of *khitan* continued to be widespread,[26] and why in January 2021 the government announced legal amendments toughening the penalties for *khitan*.[27]

The debate about *khitan*/FGM, like all debates related to women's body, has always been political, but in the 1990s and early 2000s the politicization of the public discussion about it became crystal clear because it intersected the battle for power between the State and the Islamists concerning the ownership of "culture." On one hand, the State was trying to eradicate *khitan* as part of a broader project of "modernization of Egyptian culture." On the other, the Islamists were trying to Islamize a practice that, in fact, had never been related to Islam. Also, the two were operating in a broader international context, where gender issues were defining not only group identities but also geopolitical alignments.[28]

Feminists tried to change the parameters of the debate by providing a more dynamic definition of "culture" and of the relationship between traditions and religion. This included questioning the demonization of women who practice *khitan* on their daughters. In one of her research papers, El-Dawla writes: "We are constantly trying to make others understand that women who circumcise their daughters are not barbarians or vampires. We try to explain that if women are condemned for practicing circumcision, it will only create a defensive attitude in them and perhaps make them insist on circumcision, if only to spite those who do not understand and yet insist on being judgmental."[29] Indeed, during this period many NGOs working in the field were perceived as out-of-touch elites and even foreigners—*afrangi*—with little relationship to or communication with ordinary women who were at the heart of the practice.

The anthropologist Fadwa El Guindi, who has conducted ethnographic research in Nubia (Upper Egypt) since the sixties, shares El-Dawla's view by arguing that female circumcision should not be defined as a matter of men's control over women, or of violence exercised by women against women. Rather, it should be seen as a practice that, in a specific cultural-social context, women view it as a ritual of beautification and construction of femininity, a rite of passage.[30]

El-Dawla and El Guindi's comments should not be read as a justification or approval of the practice. All the feminists I interviewed, and all the feminists whose works I have read, are abolitionists regarding *khitan*. Their approach transcends the opposition between the universalism of human rights and the protection of cultural differences (which in multicultural societies can turn into cultural relativism).[31]

The Egyptian feminists' approach regarding *khitan* is based on actively listening to the women's own experiences, and it fosters change through horizontal and cooperative relations. They look at the disadvantaged communities they work with as competent regarding the problems they experience, as well as resourceful. This is why Egyptian feminist anthropologists and grassroots activists agree on the idea that the eradication of the practice can only happen through the direct involvement of women and grassroots policies, not top-down policies. This is well illustrated in the study produced by Amal Abdel Hadi on the community of Deir El Barsha, a Christian village of 2,500 households in Upper Egypt. Here, in 1991, the community leaders signed a document to cease *khitan,* which resulted in the decrease of female circumcision in that community.

Abdel Hadi uses this case study to explain that the cultural constructions of gender relations and the broader status of women in which female circumcision is embedded can, in her view, be changed through education and literacy programs, women's participation in the market, the village's and community's political leadership, and the involvement of religious authorities.[32] Thus in her writings, Abdel Hadi gives visibility to a home-grown experience of women's empowerment led by a local grassroots organization, the Coptic Evangelical Organization for Social Services, which has been operating in the area of Deir El Barsha since the fifties and which in the eighties started addressing gender issues. The success of its programs, which preceded the ICPD, and the task force of which Abdel Hadi was a member, shows the benefit of an integrated approach to female circumcision, which aims at transforming the position of women in rural communities. As Abdel Hadi explains: "These exemplary developments in Deir El Barsha demonstrate the possibility that communities can address female genital cut[ting] themselves.

Indeed, the case of this village suggests that local efforts are very effective in stopping the practice, if they arise from more fundamental shifts in value, and power relations that promote respect for women and increase women's autonomy."[33]

Abdel Hadi's analysis was the result of both her own empirical research and a collective discussion about the link between women's sexuality and politics that had been ongoing among Egyptian feminists since the seventies, the years of their participation in the student movement. In fact, similar research was produced in the nineties by Egyptian feminist activists and scholars. The scholarship produced by the psychiatrist and human rights defender Aida Seif El-Dawla provides an important example of the effort that Egyptian feminists made in this period to intersect theory and practice, with the aim of shifting the parameters of public discourse toward supporting actual change in everyday practices. In the articles that she published in the late nineties, El-Dawla highlights the complexity of the universal notion of "reproductive rights" when applied to a specific context.[34] She makes two important points. The first is that women, especially lower- and lower-middle-class women, sacrifice self-respect to comply with social norms and bargain for greater freedom elsewhere. For example, the women interviewed by El-Dawla appeared aware that certain customary practices (such as exposing a bloodstained bed sheet the day after the wedding night to show public evidence of the woman's chastity) is a humiliating practice, yet they complied with it to negotiate the social right to mobility (for instance, to work outside the household) after marriage.

Strategies of bargaining are enacted also regarding *khitan*. Some of the women interviewed by El-Dawla said that the reduction of their sexual desire diminished the power that their husbands had over them: "Being circumcised gives them a better bargaining position as the ones responsible for family honour."[35]

While El-Dawla underscores that she is against women's circumcision, she nevertheless tries to go beyond the universal condemning of the women who practice it, explaining that the perception of *khitan* changes in relation to the women's self-perception and their perception of their role in the world, and indeed with the politics around the practice.

> This is a much more complicated procedure than to be simply described as a form of male oppression. It is a form of patriarchal oppression of women, but it is so complicated, and through awareness-raising conferences and media

and messages we have all been addressing to mothers, to the women. And at one point there was this fashion of saying FGM is violence practiced by women against women, because it is women who take [the lead.... But] it's much more complicated. All you have to do is [be] surrounded with an incredible amount of ignorance, an incredible amount of sexual ignorance, that is shocking. A lot of that ignorance we got out from meetings with physicians and with men. Men are terrified of uncircumcised women. Terrified.[36]

The relationship between fear and oppression has been explored by the Moroccan feminist scholar Fatima Mernissi in one of her classic works, *Harem Politique: Le Prophete et le Femmes.* In 1975, Mernissi initiated a tradition of Muslim feminist thought that explains the relationship between gender and political power and how this relationship affects women's position (and life) in Muslim majority society. El-Dawla's comment about men's fear needs to be read alongside this tradition and refers to a fear that is ontological and that goes far deeper than the most complete circumcision. The fear of women's sexuality and desire is related to the fear of political desire, of freedom and self-determination, primarily of women, but by extension, of everyone. The postcolonial state, which continues to oppress its citizens using the modern dispositive of control inherited by the colonial rule, fears its citizens as much as men fear women.

The crucial point El-Dawla makes is that at the core of the reproductive rights of women in Egypt lies the problem of access to health care services. This approach differs from that of the international debates about reproductive rights, which in the 1990s tended to focus on women's control over their own bodies and reproductive choices. El-Dawla explains that the concept of "reproductive rights" was relatively new to Egypt and was highly contested, as it was interpreted in different ways by the different stakeholders: the state, the conservative oppositions (both Islamists and secular nationalists), the feminists, and, indeed, the ordinary women themselves who were the target of reproductive rights' policies and who, according to El-Dawla, regarded what international organizations defined as "reproductive rights" not necessarily as "rights" (i.e., something they were entitled to) but rather as "needs."

Egyptian feminists in the nineties advocated for a theory-praxis nexus, which implies thinking through doing. The scholarship produced by the feminists who were involved in the program for the eradication of *khitan* provides an excellent example of the effort that Egyptian feminists made in this period to weave theory into practice, with the aim of shifting the parameters of public discourse toward supporting actual change in everyday

THE FIGHT FOR WOMEN'S BODILY RIGHTS · 65

practices. The analyses provided by feminist activists cover the whole range of sexual and reproductive rights, from FGM to marital rape, to abortion (which is forbidden after the third month of pregnancy yet safely available to women who have the economic means to afford it), to provisions for divorce. The main thread that their various approaches have in common is that they recognize the link between sexual and reproductive rights and economic and gender justice, on the one hand, and the elimination of poverty on the other. El-Dawla explains that holding all these legal, social, economic, health-related, and emotional matters together implies also overcoming the artificial boundaries between private and public spheres.

Overall, Egyptian feminists' work in the field of sexual and reproductive rights can indeed be best understood by looking at Egyptian feminist practices as a blending of international and vernacular languages, alongside the capacity to creatively negotiate space for independent activism in a context of multiple sets of political, socioeconomic, cultural, and epistemic oppressions. This situates feminist activism at the delicate conjuncture between the national and the international spheres of action.[37] For these reasons, it is important to look also at the spaces of transnational feminist activism that, with all their limitations, represented useful fora to put forward Egyptian feminists' agendas for change.

THREE

———

Gendered Dimensions of the Post–Cold War Order in Egypt

IN THE SUMMER OF 1990, two years after the end of the Iraq-Iran war (1980–1988), Iraq invaded and annexed the neighboring Emirate of Kuwait. The United States immediately condemned the invasion, and President George H. W. Bush succeeded in persuading the international community—including post–Soviet Russia, a traditional ally of Iraq—to do the same. Nonetheless, president of Iraq Saddam Hussein ignored the UN Security Council Resolution 678 of November 28, 1990, which demanded Iraq's withdrawal from Kuwait by January 15, 1991. The largest military coalition assembled since WWII (thirty-five countries) launched Operation Desert Storm on the next day, invaded Iraq, and easily expelled Hussein's troops from the Emirate, chasing them back to Iraq in less than six weeks. In the process, the coalition destroyed much of the country's infrastructure. Egypt played a prominent role in the US-led international coalition, its 45,000 soldiers providing the coalition's largest Arab contingent and the third-largest force.

Egyptian women intellectuals vocally opposed the war in Iraq. Among them, the writer Radwa Ashour's *Granada's Trilogy* was inspired by the disdain for Desert Storm; Nawal al-Saadawi openly criticized the Egyptian government for taking part in the expulsion of Iraq from Kuwait and the invasion and destruction of much of the country; and comparative literature professor Samia Mehrez defined it as "a war of the monolingual," in reference to the incapacity of world leaders to grasp the complexity of the fin de siècle world.[1]

But women's voices were not heard by the government. If the postcolonial aspiration of a united Arab front under Egyptian leadership disappeared with the 1979 Egypt-Israel peace treaty, 1991 marked a turning—or rather, a returning—point in Egypt's regional position. The country was entering the post–Cold War world by making even more explicit than in the previous twenty years its alignment with not only the United States but with the Kingdom of Saudi Arabia and the Gulf monarchies. Joined by forces from eight other Arab countries—Saudi Arabia, Syria, Oman, Qatar, UAE, Bahrain, Kuwait, and Morocco—Egypt attacked another Arab state as part of a Western-led coalition.[2]

Such collaboration with the United States and the leader of the Arab world's conservative bloc was unprecedented and sparked a wave of popular protests not seen since the student movements of the seventies that had culminated in the 1977 bread riots. The military operation to evict Iraq from Kuwait and destroy its military capacity lasted only forty-two days, but its long-term consequences, both material and in relation to the political imaginary, shaped the geopolitics of the region into the new millennium. Specifically, a triangular and interdependent relationship between post–Cold War militarism, neoliberalism, and authoritarianism across the Middle East began when US and coalition forces crossed the Kuwait-Iraq border and invaded Iraq. The relationship between war, authoritarian politics, and neoliberal political economies directly impacted the subsequent development of feminism in Egypt to the present day, as the political, economic, and military rents that Egypt's military regime (whether Mubarak between 1981 and 2011, or the postrevolutionary regimes) drew from its role in this system enabled its greater autonomy vis-à-vis an increasingly hard-pressed Egyptian society.

The war occurred at the start of the first post–Cold War decade, when the United States and the European Union were promoting global policies aimed at supporting civil society and especially women's organizations and programs across the Global South, targeting women as a path toward a putative third wave of democracy. While rhetorically lofty, the dynamics on the ground, at both the strategic level and everyday governance, were much more ambivalent. If officially civil society organizations were encouraged to operate in Egypt, their space of action was highly constrained; in particular, they did not have any power to pressure governments to attenuate if not transform the kinds of policies that most deleteriously affected ordinary citizens.

The largely US-led wars and interventions of the 1990s and the early 2000s may have been justified in the name of a "New World Order" (in President Bush's words),[3] but the litany of violence in fact reflected an era of disillusionment for the people of Egypt and the Middle East broadly. A series of major events shaped the history of the twenty years between 1989 and 1991 and

2011: the fall of the Berlin Wall (1989); the repression of the Chinese people's revolts in Tiananmen Square (June 1989); the collapse of the Soviet Union (beginning in 1990); the war surrounding the break-up of the Socialist Federal Republic of Yugoslavia (1991–1995); the wars against Iraq in 1991 and in 2003 and against Afghanistan in 2001; the civil war in Algeria (1991–2002); the second Palestinian Intifada (2000); and last, but not least, the intra-Palestinian conflict in Gaza and the West Bank between Fatah and Hamas (2006). All these produced a web of interconnected events that had serious consequences for women, worsening their life conditions and forcing them to organize in order to overcome the problems generated by the war and the social neoconservatism that the atmosphere of war generated.[4]

The concerns of Egyptian women intellectuals anticipated what soon became readily apparent: the post–Cold War hopes and expectations for the spread of a "third wave of democracy" across the Arab world turned into two decades of war, genocide (the Muslims in Bosnia and in Chechnya), and the consolidation of the alliance between political authoritarianism and neoliberal capitalism across the Middle East. These events brought with them greater exploitation of workers, social injustice, and environmental disaster on a global scale. In response, from the cultural and intellectual sphere to political and grassroots activism, and also in the small actions of everyday life, the nineties became a decade of intense activism by women in Egypt and across the Global South.

DEBATING GENDER AT THE TURN OF THE TWENTY-FIRST CENTURY

As neoliberal policies took greater hold, Egyptians became increasingly disillusioned and disaffected during the twenty years between the second Gulf War and 2011. The dissolution of shared political imaginaries was accompanied by a worsening of socioeconomic problems. In the 1990s and the early 2000s the crisis in Egypt had economic, social, political, and intellectual dimensions, as noted by Egyptian analysts and commentators. Galal Amin, for example, focused on several decades of accrued social mobility more than the impact of Sadat's *Infitah* policies and Mubarak's more aggressive neoliberal turn, which meant that more people had access to education and consumer goods, but the gap between people's ambitions and their factual possibilities equally increased, especially in Mubarak's final decade in power.[5]

As occurred in Europe and the United States in the early post–Cold War period, Egypt experienced the opening of new spaces to renegotiate power relationships both in the public and the private spheres. This occurred during a moment of structural transformation of the international order and its attendant socioeconomic crisis that together generated multiple levels of social anxiety. This was expressed in various ways, ranging from the moral panic around the heavy metal bands that were accused of Satanism,[6] to the phenomenon of "repentant" singers, dancers, and actresses (famous artists who abandoned the scenes and adopted a pious lifestyle, including veiling),[7] their connection with the post-Islamist pious movements,[8] and, soon after, the crackdown on homosexual men epitomized by the infamous Queen Boat case in 2001.[9] Significantly, these social tendencies were contemporaneous to intellectual and political debates in Egypt about the legitimacy of using gender as an analytical category to understand the historical situatedness and social construction of femininity and masculinity.

Several women intellectuals intervened in the debate about the translation of the word "gender" in Arabic. Ferial Ghazoul, an Iraqi professor of English and comparative literature at the American University in Cairo (AUC), turned to the flexibility of Arabic language to coin a neologism, *junusa,* to signify "gender."[10] Hoda Elsadda similarly supported developing gender and women's studies within an Egyptian context, while also acknowledging the difficulties of doing so.[11] Other women scholars, especially—but not only—those closer to Islamic intellectual circles, were skeptical about the use of analytical categories such as gender, as well as about positioning themselves explicitly as feminists, even if in their intellectual practices they supported women in the professions. Among them, Heba Rauf Ezzat, then professor of Political Sciences at Cairo University, labeled gender and feminism as Western impositions,[12] while unequivocally supporting women's role in the public sphere, and offering enthusiastic support to her female students and mentees at Cairo University.

The main issue confronting Egyptian feminists of all stripes, according to Margot Badran, was not that gender is a Western category (it is not), but that the concept and the terms used to refer to and define it need to be historicized and understood in their local intellectual and political contexts.[13] Lila Abu-Lughod's work similarly questions rigid and binary concepts of culture, and suggests that notions of separate cultures might themselves be produced by the colonial encounter.[14]

The debate about gender and culture that developed in the nineties among women intellectuals and activists in Egypt (and beyond the Egyptian national borders among feminist intellectuals who were invested in the country) coincided with a new generation of women and gender studies programs (WGS, typically offered by private organizations and/or externally founded) in Egyptian and Arab universities. The Department of English Language and Literature at Cairo University was the first hub of women and gender studies in Egypt, and the founding members of Multaqa al-Mar'a wa al-Dhakira (Women and Memory Forum) in 1995 (Omaima Abubakr, Hala Kamal, and Hoda Elsadda) were professors in that department. The Cynthia Nelson Center for Gender Studies at AUC was founded in 2001. The master's program in Gender and Development was established at the Faculty of Economics and Political Science at Cairo University in 2017.[15] This ferment demonstrates that if the atmosphere of general political disillusionment hobbled women and feminists' activism, it did not weaken feminist intellectual debates or their determination to bring women's issues to the center of the national and global political agendas. Egyptian women activists had a long history of contrasting multiple discourses that aimed at silencing and disempowering them, be it colonialism with its history of exploitation, or indigenous[16] patriarchy in all its declinations, and even transnational feminism, which often did not see them as equal partners as much as subjects in need of aid and solidarity.

A FEMINIST'S CRITICISM OF CAPITALISM, RELIGIOUS FUNDAMENTALISM, AND PATRIARCHY: NAWAL AL-SAADAWI'S WRITING AND ACTIVISM

Not surprisingly, an early critique of Mubarak's neoliberal policies was produced by Egyptian feminist intellectuals who, through their grassroots work and their own experiences, found themselves on the frontline of the economic, social, and even political crises provoked by the alliance between global neoliberal capitalism and postcolonial Egyptian authoritarianism. They were building on a tradition of feminist critique of postcolonial authoritarianism. In the seventies, the medical doctor, feminist activist, and writer Nawal al-Saadawi (1931–2021) had already voiced her critique of the patriarchal alliance among the postcolonial self-proclaimed secular Arab regimes,[17] conservative religious forces, and international capital in Egypt and, more broadly, in Africa: "Religion, in particular, is a weapon often used in traditionalist societies to cut short, and even cut down, the efforts of researchers, and seekers after truth. I have come to see more and more clearly that religion is most often used in our day as an instrument in the hands of economic and political forces, as an institution utilized by those who rule to keep down those who are ruled."[18] Twenty years later, in the nineties, al-Saadawi multiplied her interventions against what she called the patriarchal alliance between capitalism and religious fundamentalism, which she considered a global problem. Addressing the Global Welfare Conference '94: Fight against Poverty and Inequality on a World Level, in Tampere, Finland, in 1994, she stated, "Commodification and trafficking of women (in the South and in the North as well) are increasing. Women are looked upon as bodies to be exploited and used to produce more profit. They must be veiled, covered physically according to religious fundamentalists, but should be undressed according to postmodern capitalists, or made to buy make-up and body conditioners. Sex is a commodity, a thriving industry. Sex shops and pornography, the commerce of sex, spread like wildfire."[19]

Nawal al-Saadawi's writing about patriarchy, capitalism, and Islamism need to be read against both her theoretical positioning and her biography. It reflected her experience as a woman activist and a writer who has always put herself on the frontline of the most difficult battles for women's freedom, and most importantly, her lived experience was an embodiment of her theoretical posture. This is what made her contribution to the women's cause exceptional and even capable of transcending the Egyptian borders: It was meaningful for women on a global scale because it raised issues—such as the perilous impact of neoliberal capitalism on middle-class and poor women—that help us understand the problems faced not only by Egyptian, Arab, and African women, but also by middle- and lower-class women in the cities of early twenty-first-century Europe and the US, including migrants and refugees. The intersection between political analysis and creative writing that characterizes her production is at the core of the transnational and long-lasting relevance of her writing, and she was aware of the power of fictional writing. When I interviewed her in 2014, al-Saadawi insisted on the profound connection between creativity and dissidence, which is also one of the main cores of her intellectual production:

> I never had a prize in Egypt. You know I had many literary prizes all over the world, not in Egypt, because of the governments. And they took my money. They fired [me] from my medical work. They obliged me to leave the country, they wanted to take my nationality from me. My Egyptian nationality.

FIGURE 6. Nawal al-Saadawi (right) at the Third World Conference to Review and Appraise the Achievements of the United Nations Decade for Women. 15–26 July 1985, Nairobi, Kenya. Courtesy of Women and Memory Forum Library.

> They wanted to divorce me by force from my third husband. I wanted to divorce him at that time but when they said "we want to divorce you," I said, "NOOO! [she laughs]. I wait until I do it with my own will, you know?" So ... when you meet a writer, in any country, not only [here], ask him or her, what's the price of creativity.[20]

The rhythm of al-Saadawi's creative and dissident political life was punctuated by a long sequence of books, intellectual controversies, and arrests and trials. It began in 1944 when she wrote her first memoir as a thirteen-year-old, *Mudhakkirat Tufla Ismaha Sua'ad* (*Memoirs of a Girl, Whose Name Is Su'ad*),[21] and continued in the late 1960s with her election to the board of the Medical Doctors Union, and leadership of the Association for Health Education. But her career as a writer really took off with the publication of her first nonfiction book, *Woman and Sex* (1972).

Censored in Egypt, the book was reprinted and distributed in Beirut, becoming a landmark of feminism in Egypt, the Arab world, and in Africa. Al-Saadawi's work had an enormous impact among women across the Arab world and Africa. Women of all the subsequent generations were inspired by her work, which linked women's mental health to sexual oppression and condemned the practice of *khitan*. But al-Saadawi's problems continued at the start of yet another decade. In 1981, she was arrested, like thousands of other dissident intellectuals across the whole spectrum of the political opposition (both Islamists and communists), for being critical of the Sadat regime, as much for its liberal turn economically as his signing the peace agreements with Israel. Yet not even the experience in prison persuaded her to stay away from political activism:

> We started the Arab Women Solidarity Association in 1982, after I came out of prison. It was banned in 1991. You remember, the Gulf, the Iraq War.... Because we stood against the American-led war in Iraq. Mubarak was furious, and they banned the Arab Women's Solidarity Association. Then, we took the government to court because they banned AWSA with no reason, with no investigation, no law. We took the government to the court, but we lost. ... We then restarted the Egyptian Women's Union, and Susanne Mubarak banned it. We were still in the nineties. Many times, we, women of the Egyptian women's movement, we came together and worked together, and tried to unite, and the government banned us. Until after the revolution. After the January revolution we said okay, let's restart the Egyptian Women's Union. And we started that in Tahrir Square. This was exactly in February 2011.[22]

In 1991, the Arab Women Solidarity Association was shut because of al-Saadawi's public criticism of Egypt's participation in the war coalition against Iraq. The government's message to women was then clear: their work on "women's issues" was tolerated, as far as they did not interfere with broader political issues. What was not clear to the regime was that the Egyptian feminists he was trying to co-opt, contain, and repress had always conceived "women's issues" as broader political issues, and there was neither intimidation nor incarceration that would have stopped them from engaging with politics.

In 1993, two years after the closure of AWSA, al-Saadawi moved to Duke University in the United States in self-imposed exile (1993–1997) to escape death threats Islamists launched against her following the publication of her novel *The Fall of the Imam* in 1988. In a forum to celebrate her memory after she passed, Professor miriam cooke, who considered al-Saadawi a mentor, remembers that al-Saadawi was as much concerned about the government guards who were sent at her door to "protect" her and who reminded her of those who had jailed her a decade earlier, as she was about the Islamists.[23] Al-Saadawi herself narrated her experience multiple times since then:

> The fanatical religious groups in Egypt who have had my name on a death list since 1988 following the publication of my novel *The Fall of the Imam* have

never read this book or any of my books. They tell the media: "We don't read heretical books." How do they know a book is heretical without reading it? It is the same as worshipping a divine book without reading it. Blind faith leads to blind fundamentalism, blind fanaticism, blind racism, blind sexism, blind hate and blind love. The person who killed the writer Farag Fouda in Cairo on 8 June 1992 was a poor illiterate fisherman who has never read a book written by the author he killed. Religious crimes or so-called honours crimes are political, economic, cultural, social, moral and historical crimes. Like religious wars, they hide behind the invisible God to rob, colonize, loot, plunder, rape, exploit and satisfy their greed and insatiable physical and material appetites. Jewish fundamentalism, Islamic fundamentalism, Christian fundamentalism and other religions are spreading widely during this twenty-first-century postmodern era for inhuman political-economic reasons and not for moral or ethical human reasons.[24]

During the three decades of the Mubarak regime (1981–2011), the ambivalent relationship between the authoritarian state and the Islamists, oscillating between alliance and competition, and mediated by capitalism, became crystal clear, and women found themselves in the eye of the storm. Both the state and the Islamists relied on the mobilization of huge capital from several sources (the remittances of Egyptian migrants in the Gulf countries and loans from the IMF, as much as less transparent flows of money from the Gulf, such as those in support of the network of welfare organizations sponsored by the Muslim Brotherhood), and both situated gender politics at the center of their public discourse. But women did not surround.

Notwithstanding attempts of intimidation, censorship, and various forms of violence, women did not withdraw from the political field, and they insisted on asserting that women's issues are everyone's issues, and they are at the core of the relationship between power and politics. In front of patriarchal authoritarianism, women activists and intellectuals reacted differently according to their ideological positioning and their personal experience, and the writings they produced in the 1990s and the early 2000s show that there is no reason to talk about "women" as a monolithic group. On the contrary, it is necessary to differentiate alongside class, ideological positioning, and political biographies.

In the nineties, Nawal al-Saadawi had good reason to feel unsafe in her own apartment and even to leave Egypt, as she was both threatened by Islamists and feared imprisonment by the government. She nevertheless continued to bear testimony of the repression of political oppositions to the Mubarak government (which at that time was considered an ally to contain Jihadism by most of the Western powers), while also denouncing the perverse effects of the policies implemented by international institutions (IMF, World Bank, and General Agreement on Tariffs and Trade) to support the neoliberal policies for "development" of the so-called Third World authoritarian regimes.[25]

Al-Saadawi is the most world-renowned Egyptian feminist. Her figure and her writing from the seventies onward bridge the passage from the first two generations of women activists (the emancipationists and nationalists who had been active between the twenties and the forties, and the women intellectuals, entrepreneurs, and laborers who had been mobilized by the state to contribute to the project of postcolonial state-building in the fifties and sixties) and the new generations that emerged in the eighties and nineties and who revamped the feminist movement after three decades when women did not have their explicitly feminist organizations to collectively mobilize for women's rights.

Her global activism spanned the second half of the twentieth century and the first two decades of the twenty-first, including the moment of collective joy inspired by the 2011 Revolution. Like most Marxist intellectuals of her generation, she did not oppose the July 2013 military coup that overthrew President Mohammed Morsi, and she never condemned the massacre of the Muslim Brotherhood supporters that followed on August 14 of the same year. This deluded the young feminists in the revolutionary field, who believe that feminism should be against both the Islamists and the military. As in earlier moments in Egyptian contemporary history, feminist activists' positionalities in front of authoritarian regimes vary according to multiple variables, and in times of political transition, transgenerational tensions are more palpable.

Notwithstanding the controversies that marked her memory after 2013, it is out of doubt that al-Saadawi's writings had a profound impact on multiple generations of women, from the seventies until today, and she is most admired for her courage. Her passing was mourned by women activists and scholars around the world, and her legacy remains unparalleled, transcending the Egyptian experience.

WOMEN'S DIVERSE STRATEGIES TO ADDRESS THE GENDERED DYNAMICS OF POVERTY AND SOCIAL INJUSTICE

The conjunction of global capitalism and its socioeconomic consequences, increasing political authoritarianism, and growing popularity of Islamism between the 1980s and the 1990s had the effect of energizing a feminism that blossomed anew in Egypt after decades of repression. The feminist discourse in Egypt in the eighties and even more in the nineties was articulated along multiple visions, but at the core of the feminists' philosophy and practice there was the idea that feminism should be conceived as an inclusive project, addressing multiple and intersecting levels of oppression. Like in other historical turning points in Egyptian history, women could build strategic alliances and negotiate profound disagreements. A major matter of disagreement among women political activists in this period was about how to interact (or refuse to interact) with governmental institutions and to accept (or not to accept) financial support from international organizations. Here, different projects and ideological positioning were palpable.

Liberal feminists—broadly defined by support for a modernist, secular, and politically pluralist vision and continued if strained faith in state-led modernization and reform—attributed the decline in women's economic situation to IMF-sponsored structural adjustment programs adopted by the state during the eighties: "Such programs have an adverse effect on the weaker segments of the population, particularly women. This may explain the increase in the number of poor women in rural Egypt from 2,135 million in 1965–1970 to 5,381 million in 1988, an increase of about 152%."[26] Liberal women tried to engage with state institutions, and they tried to draft what I read as a women-centered roadmap to address poverty: "To address women's poverty one has to deal with their participation in the labor force and the factors that affect their productivity such as education, health, nutrition, and culture. The principal asset of the poor woman is her labor."[27] As part of their agenda of working toward change from within the institutional field, some Egyptian women activists and their organizations supported the delegation that participated in the 1995 UN World Conference on Women, held in Beijing,[28] and in 2000 some of them joined the newly created National Council for Women, a consultative government body chaired by then-First Lady Suzanne Mubarak, whose function was to mediate between the women's organizations and the government while also lobbying to improve the standing of Egyptian women in law as well as the political and economic realms.

This was not an easy task, as the regime would allow some high-profile women to do good work, with the aim to show the international community its support for women's rights, but only within very strict limits. Moreover, the government and its authoritarianism were not the only burden on women's activism. The issue of foreign funding was equally divisive, as remembered by the members of the New Woman Foundation (NWF), even leading to the resignations of some of the founding members. Very important to the NWF leadership was the transmission and the continuity of feminist activism.

In the 1990s and the early 2000s the Marxist feminists who were born in the late forties and early fifties, and the then new generation (born in the sixties and early seventies) attempted to join ranks to formulate a radical epistemic critique of the ways both the Egyptian government and international organizations—even international fellow feminists—framed women's issues. They questioned the ways both governmental organizations and NGOs conceptualized the multiple problems (poverty, lack of social services, political authoritarianism, war, and social conservatism) faced by women in Egypt and, more broadly, in the postcolonial world.

In these two decades, feminists brought their themes and methodologies of research, intersecting grassroots work, and gender and political economy analysis within the human rights organizations with whom they worked. For instance, in a research project conducted in the early 2000s in the Upper Egyptian village of Deir El Barsha for the Cairo Institute for Human Rights Studies (CIHRS), Amal Abdel Hadi questioned the data regarding women's labor published by the World Bank in the mid-nineties, asserting that these data underestimated the actual contribution of women to the national economy. Two-thirds of the female respondents in Deir El Barsha did not work for money," points out Abdel Hadi, "but 34 percent of them mentioned that they perform[ed] paid work, which is higher than [the] 28 percent given in the World Bank report on female employment in Egypt. Most of the work activities that women in Deir El Barsha mentioned, such as producing food items for sale and making baskets and scuttles, are not usually listed in official statistics of labor force participation but are regarded as part of women's household duties. Nor does the 'labor' category on the official statistics include agricultural activities such as ploughing, except when women themselves declared that they worked."[29]

In October 1993, the NWF hosted an international seminar to discuss the results of the studies conducted by feminist organizations in Tunisia, Palestine, Sudan, and Egypt on women's situations in those countries. The research presented during the seminar was part of the preparation for the 1995 UN World Conference on Women, and the proceedings of the meeting were published in a book curated by Abdel Hadi and Nadia Abdel Wahab, both of whom were members of the NWF and medical doctors by training.[30]

The political-economic analysis provided by Abdel Hadi and al-Afifi takes into consideration quantitative and qualitative data including the decrease in the average annual growth rate of a working person's income (from 4.1 percent in the seventies to 2.1 percent in the eighties), and the growth of the inflation rate (from 11.9 percent in 1980 to 22.3 percent in 1991). In their analysis, Abdel Hadi and al-Afifi highlight the tension between the call by conservative political forces for the return of Egyptian women to the domestic space in the context of the economic crisis, and the actual pressures on women to earn an income, which produced a rise in women's employment in the labor force, in both the formal and the informal sectors.

It should be remembered here that the public debate about women, labor, and poverty that flourished between the eighties and the nineties had a tradition in Egyptian women's writing. Egyptian women journalists had been addressing this issue since the late nineteenth century.[31] What I want to stress here is that in the nineties, Egyptian feminists had accumulated nearly seventy years of women's intellectual production about this topic, and their knowledge and even polemical verve was transmitted generation upon generation, allowing them to develop the language and the data to systematically deconstruct the stereotypes surrounding women's lives.

As in the past, even in the nineties women were playing a crucial role in the economy of the country. In fact, according to the Central Agency of Public Mobilization and Statistics, by the mid-nineties, 22 percent of households were headed by women.[32] Furthermore, according to the experts on worker-related issues who I interviewed, such as Hala Shukrallah and Fatma Ramadan, the data was certainly underestimated, as it did not include the informal sectors, which are substantial in Egypt.[33] However, the way the political economy of the state was structured did not allow them to benefit from this contribution.

According to Abdel Hadi and al-Afifi, the negative effects of the Mubarak government's neoliberal turn also affected the achievements that had been gained by women through seventy years of political activism in the fields of labor law and political participation. In fact, even if women and men's equality at work was ensured by Egyptian law, most of the female workforce was seldom able to benefit from the provisions that law provided (including maternity leave), because informal and noncontractual work prevailed. This applied to both urban and rural spaces.[34] Their analysis acknowledged women's achievements in the labor, professional, and political fields, where decades of feminist activism and lobbying had resulted in a positive balance, but it also underscored the multiple structural inequalities that remained: economic inequalities, lack of access to social services and facilities, gender gap in the access to education, and the failure to obtain a reform of the Personal Status Law (the set of laws regulating family matters). All this allowed them to avoid framing the debate about sexual and reproductive rights within mere culturalist terms (as both the government and the international actors, including the feminists, tended to do), and developing a more articulated and multi-problematic analysis grounded on their grassroot experience, where socioeconomic conditions intersected the state policies about reproduction and the cultural narratives about it.

"WOMEN'S RIGHTS ARE HUMAN RIGHTS" . . . BUT CONTEXT MATTERS . . .

The 1990s and the first decade of 2000s were both promising and challenging years for Egyptian women. The space for independent activism and the freedom to organize, which Egyptian feminists experienced in the lead-up to the 1994 ICPD, was temporary and conditional. By the time the ICPD was over, two things were clear: first, the government was coming to understand the importance of gender-related issues to containing political dissent; and second, the dynamism of the women's groups working on gender issues both within and outside government institutions, parameters, and discourses represented an important space to challenge its power. Not surprisingly, then, the politics of the state toward feminist activism would alternately and sometimes simultaneously become one of either co-optation and/or censorship, depending on the attitude that specific feminists and their organizations were taking toward the state. This created significant uncertainty among feminists, who understood the necessity of operating within certain red lines:

> We operated within a margin that was allowed, a margin that was mostly created by the presence of international organizations and the sense of absolute security that the government felt. You must remember that Mubarak's philosophy was "Let them play." He was totally secure in the feeling that he was untouchable, and there was no way anything could happen to him. So, he did not care, really, that much. Regardless, the security forces always operated in curtailing the margin that we were allowed. As long as women's issues

are depoliticized and not seen within a broader issue of democratic and free society, we could speak about women's issues.[35]

International women and feminists' conferences had played an important role in the development of feminism since the early twentieth century, and Egyptian women have been part of them since the early 1920s.[36] But in the nineties there was a significant expansion of the transnational sphere of women's activism. Egyptian feminists used international platforms to claim women's rights and to compare the situation of Egyptian women with that of women in other parts of the world. Through their participation in international conferences, Egyptian feminist activists gained knowledge and confidence that could translate into greater power back home. They also strengthened their international networks of solidarity, which they used over the years as leverage when facing repressive or otherwise harmful Egyptian governmental policies. For instance, the senior member of the NWF, Amal Abdel Hadi, told me that in the early 2000s, when the NWF decided to register at the Ministry of Social Affairs (a legal requirement to be able to operate as an NGO), they faced obstructionism by national security and the government. Under these circumstances, the expressions of solidarity by international feminists and organizations were essential to achieve their goals:

> We went to register at the Ministry.... The law says that if you go to register, and if they don't answer you after sixty days, it's okay.... They sent us a letter after sixty-three days, saying, "We apologize for [not] registering you, because the Security opposes it." It was very good to have this letter in hand. We held a huge campaign internationally and locally, and we took legal proceedings against the government, and we won the case. It was something amazing, because the first time we went to the court, the secretary of the court called the New Woman's Centre, or something like this, and he saw all [the people in] the hall coming [up] to the judge. He was very impressed.... For us, the solidarity was something wonderful, to have the solidarity from inside the country and from outside the country. Anyway, we won our case in December 2003, and we did not receive the registration number until a very long time after. What helped us was international solidarity. The [political] adviser of President Mubarak ... called the Ministry of Social Affairs and he said, "Who is the New Woman Foundation? We are bombed with letters from everywhere asking us to register them!" So, the Ministry gave us the registration. Even if they were not very happy to give it to us, they gave it to us.[37]

While international solidarity has always been crucial for the Egyptian women's movement, the project of international sisterhood—that is, the actual solidarity among feminists across national borders—has always been difficult to achieve, a difficulty that suggests that women's organizations, although marginal, were also part of the national politics. During the colonial age, which continued under a different form well into the mid-twentieth century, the misunderstandings and disagreements between Egyptian and Western feminists had a lot to do with the different positions their respective countries of origin occupied in the system of international relations, which at that time was a colonial system.

The ambivalent if not hostile stance of the government toward independent feminist groups became evident less than a year after the ICPD, in the lead-up to the 1995 UN World Conference on Women in Beijing. When I interviewed Nawla Darwiche, a senior member of the NWF, she remembered,

> In 1993, we [the NWF] were the first organization to talk about violence against women from a holistic perspective. We were insulted by everybody, and we were considered as agents of imperialism and things like this. Even Suzanne Mubarak sent us a sort of ultimatum, because we had [done] fieldwork about the perception of women, asking, "What is violence?" We wanted to go to a conference in Beijing to present this. Somebody came and said, "The *Hanem*[38] says you are not going to Beijing to wash your dirty laundry. Even if there is violence against women everywhere in the world, it doesn't exist in Egypt." But we were able to send five girls to Beijing, and they presented the results of the findings of the work, and they were attacked by the representatives of the Ministry of Foreign Affairs.[39]

Since 1975 the UN World Conferences on Women (in Mexico City in 1975, Copenhagen in 1980, Nairobi in 1985, and Beijing in 1995) have been forums where government delegations and NGOs discuss their policies to achieve gender equality. Postcolonial feminist scholars have criticized the neoliberal framework that shines through the documents produced during these conferences by emphasizing how they foster an agenda for development grounded in ostensibly "Western" aid paradigms, neoliberal governance, and economic theories.[40] Critics of the process, most notably Gayatri Chakravorty Spivak, have labeled the UN World Conferences on Women as "global theatre," where women represent the unity of the world, a necessary mise-en-scène that serves the needs of globalization, while being disconnected from grassroots activism.[41] The development logic promoted by the UN Conferences on Women reinforces rather than challenges Arab state power, Western state interests, and transnational governance,[42] and overall what remains unchallenged is the paradigm of the Western urban and middle-class modernity as inherently emancipatory for women, even as fieldwork research in rural areas shows that the reality is far more complex.[43] Inderpal Grewal has critically named this hegemonic trend of practice and discourse "transnational feminist governmentality."[44] The topical moment of this neo-liberal feminist trend was when Hillary Clinton opened the 1995 UN World Conference on Women in Beijing by asserting that "women's rights are human rights." However, what Clinton's discourse was missing, and which becomes clear once we engage in an in-depth analysis of the Egyptian feminists' praxis, is that human rights mean different things for different women around the world, depending on the historical and present day political, economic, and cultural circumstances in which they are embedded. Human rights movements are situated in larger political, economic, and sociocultural contexts, women are not mere objects of human rights, and women's movements are crucial actors that actively contribute to shape them.

The 1995 UN World Conference on Women in Beijing was a moment when the centrality of women-related issues for international politics became more than ever evident on the global stage. The participation of heads of states, first ladies, high-profile religious leaders, and official delegations alongside the NGOs demonstrate that both the governments and the global civil societies were highly invested in it. The Beijing Declaration and Platform for Action that was produced during the conference was the outcome of decades of global women's activism, and it was characterized by a holistic approach, intersecting socioeconomic rights with sexual and reproductive rights, and human rights, all within the broader framework of global development.

In Egypt, this was the moment where the tensions among the different agendas of the international organizations, the local NGOs, and the Egyptian state emerged in a more concrete way. The Egyptian government participated with an official delegation, led by First Lady Suzanne Mubarak and including high-profile experts of women and gender issues.[45]

Parallel to the conference, the NGO Forum saw the participation of Egyptian delegates from the independent NGOs. Shereen Abouelnaga, today a professor of English and comparative literatures at Cairo University, was part of the NGO delegation and she still remembers with deep emotion the testimonies given by Chinese, Iraqi, Japanese, and Rwandan women to the tribunals on violence against women at the conference. Her narrative was still so vivid that we could feel the contrast with the atmosphere we were immersed in, on a warm spring evening in Sydney. She paused for a moment, and her voice broke when she resumed her narration: "I never imagined that there is all this violence against women all over the world.... I couldn't believe it, this tribunal, it lasted for about two or three hours, and I was there, mesmerized."[46]

The experience of the Beijing conference was both exciting and confrontational for Shereen and other young women who were part of the NGOs delegation. As she told me in the interview, she grew up in a small world of good schools (where she was a high-achieving student) and the love and care of her mother (who had been a widow since Shereen was four years old, as her father, a pilot in the Egyptian air force, died in 1970 during the "war of attrition" between Egypt and Israel). In Beijing she was exposed to the stories of women who had experienced war, abduction, and several forms of violence: "I was looking at those Kuwaiti women like, I remember saying to one of them, 'Are you serious? There are women who are abducted?' They said, 'Yeah, they have disappeared, and we don't know where they are.' It was my first time to hear of disappearance[s]."

Shereen came away with a strong sense of solidarity with the women she met and their common purpose. "We were confronting the world, the whole world, at one go."

At the Beijing conference there was a strong focus on domestic violence and on violence in contexts of war. There was, however, a big elephant in the room that was not addressed, which Shereen had the opportunity to witness when she shared part of her journey back to Cairo with Hanan, a young Palestinian woman:

> We were going back [to our respective countries] together [on] the same route. But then at some point I will go to Cairo, she will go to Amman or something. And at some point, eh, they wouldn't let her out.... They said, "You have to stay in the airport" because she didn't have a passport, she had a document, travel document. So, they wouldn't let her out. And she looked at me and she said, "Now you understand the meaning of occupation. This is the meaning." [Then] I said, "No, I'm going to stay with her, I'm not going to leave her. How could you do that?" [But] she said, "Shereen, you go. Now you understand the meaning of occupation," and I said, "Yes, I do." And that's true, that was an eye opener for me.[47]

Through her friendship with Hanan, Shereen learned something about the violence of borders, which reminded me of the borders that the Chicana feminist scholar Gloria Anzaldúa describes in her masterwork as "*una herida abierta* [an open wound] where the Third World grates against the First and bleeds."[48] It seems to me that Shereen came to understand that solidarity between women cannot but be crippled by the apparatuses of state violence, colonialism, dispossession, occupation, displacement, and racism that shape international relations. Borders are neither natural nor apolitical. Rather, borders are artificial constructions, and they govern, discipline, and oppress people who cross colonial territories, especially Indigenous people (in the case of Hanan, Palestinian people) and racialized people. Hanan's condition, as a Palestinian woman living under colonial occupation, could not be directly addressed in Beijing, because that forum was organized by the same actors that create borders and inequalities.

Shereen's memories made international politics very intimate for her, and it was from this intimate space that Shereen questioned the feminist postcolonial critique of the UN Conferences on Women put forward by leading figures such as Spivak: "You don't like the UN conferences, so . . . what do we do? You need international machinery, see? Because at least in this place the women could meet and could build alliances. . . . *Ya'ni* [I mean] we learned something in that conference."

The tension that emerges from Shereen's memories about Beijing, an experience where despite its limitations the good seemed to overwhelm the bad, would explode in 2011 when a revolutionary and far more radical generation of feminists would come to the fore, questioning not only the existence or absence of free spaces of expression but the very framework within which conversations happen. To understand the maturation of these more radical ideas, it is essential to grasp the link between the feminist and the human rights movement in Egypt, a link that not only developed in the transnational space of UN-sponsored women's conferences but that has also an equally important and powerful local, grassroots component.

FOUR

Toward a Women's History of the Human Rights Movement in Egypt

WHILE IT BECAME CENTRAL to public debates during the 1990s and the early 2000s, human rights had a long history as an issue of concern and debate in Egyptian politics. Egypt was represented on the December 10, 1948, General Assembly of the United Nations in Paris, when the Universal Declaration of Human Rights was approved; it also ratified every major human rights convention since the 1970s—albeit, as with most Muslim majority countries, with "reservations" inserted when articles were believed to contravene the values of the shariʿa, which remained a basis for law in the post-1952 republican Constitution.[1] Not surprisingly, most of the reservations concerned women and gender issues, and particularly those addressed by the Convention on the Elimination of All forms of Discrimination against Women (CEDAW), as they are the ones that tend to intersect with provisions of Islamic law.

Formal endorsement of human rights treaties has long been considered strategic for the Egyptian state, to the point that in the early nineties the Minister of Foreign Affairs had a Human Rights and Social Development Desk, which at that time was chaired by a woman, Ambassador Naila Gabr. In a paper published in *Cairo Papers in Social Sciences,* Gabr defended the work of her department, illustrating their approach as one aimed at avoiding what she referred to as "politicization and commercialization," developing "awareness and implementation," and focusing on the "third generation of human rights, including the right to development, peace, self-determination, and a healthy environment." In the same volume where Ambassador Gabr's contribution was published, one of the founding members of the Egyptian Organization for Human Rights provided a detailed documentation of the state's violations of human rights in Egypt.[2]

At least two narratives about the relationship of the state with the human rights community existed in Egypt in the nineties: the government one, clearly summarized in Ambassador Gabr's words, and that of the independent human rights organizations, which were far more critical. This should not suggest that the human rights community was separated binarily into state and nonstate actors. On the contrary, it was characterized by multiple visions and approaches to politics, and women were located at multiple critical junctures between them. As veteran activist Aida Seif El-Dawla explained to me, "There was a gap, and somehow even a fight, between those who were conceiving human rights as a tool in the struggle to achieve democracy and/ or socialism, and those who were conceiving human rights in more depoliticized terms, as not merely a purpose or end in its own terms but a profession as well."[3]

Whatever its evolving rhetoric, however, it is not an overstatement to say that the government's attitude toward the human rights community remained hostile throughout the republican era beginning in 1952, alternating waves of repression with attempts to co-opt some of its segments in the formal institutional sphere, and to neutralize their political potential. This became clear with the establishment of the National Council for Human Rights (NCHR) in 2003, an initiative that was both the result of years of lobbying by some human rights lawyers (among them the prominent feminist lawyer Mona Zulfikar), and of the strategy of the Policies Secretariat of the National Democratic Party, led by Gamal Mubarak, son of the president of the republic. Zulfikar and other human rights lawyers were trying to work within the strict margins allowed by the authoritarian state to advance human rights, while the Mubarak government was trying to represent itself as the natural patron of human rights and, as explained by the Egyptian sociologist Maha Abdelrahman, to impose a nationalist agenda on human rights, by linking human rights to the notion of "national interest."[4] The creation of the National Council for Human Rights was also part of a broader program of ostensible democratization, which included the creation of other councils (National Council for Childhood and Motherhood, 1988; and National Council for Women, 2000), and the agreement to hold contested presidential elections in 2005, which were in fact neither free nor fair, and saw Mubarak's only authentic challenger, Senator Ayman Nour, arrested and imprisoned for close to five years on fraudulent charges soon thereafter.

Among the twenty-seven counselors appointed to the NCHR, five were women: Dr. Georgette Sobhi Abdou Kellini, Dr. Zeinab Abdel-Meguid

Radwan, Dr. Lila Ibrahim Tekla, Mrs. Mona Zulfikar, and Dr. Hoda Elsadda.[5] Hoda Elsadda, a professor of English literature at Cairo University, a founding member of WMF, and later a member of the committee that wrote the 2014 Constitution, was among the high-profile feminist figures appointed to the NCHR. In the oral history interview that Nicola Pratt recorded with her, Elsadda remembered with disappointment how she, like all the other members, including Boutros Ghali, learned the news of their appointment from a newspaper: "I was furious." Elsadda recalled that all the appointed members had doubts about the national councils, and that it was a difficult decision. They nevertheless accepted, because, as Elsadda explained, they believed that the other members were a "decent ... an interesting combination."

Indeed, the government did a good job of selecting high-profile and publicly trustworthy people. Elsadda gave herself a year to see how things would evolve. However, she recalled, already on the first day she felt ill at ease in "the corridors of power"; the breaking point would come after the suicide terrorist attacks by the Gama'a al-Islamiyya (an umbrella armed organization that included Islamist militants who left the Muslim Brotherhood after it renounced violence in 1970) at the hotel in Taba, on the Red Sea, on October 7, 2004, which killed thirty-four tourists and left more than one hundred injured. The government responded with a massive arrest operation (2,400 people) in al-'Arish, the capital of the North Sinai Governorate of Egypt, alarming human rights organizations.[6] Hoda Elsadda and other members of NCHR had serious concerns, and they pressured the government to ensure that the NCHR played a role in the investigations. They presented a plan in support of the human rights NGOs who were involved and traveled to Sinai to meet the families of the men who had been arrested:

> We went on a fact finding mission, and I went, it was an experience, but the short story is that I realized that the Council was really about beautifying the image of the state, and the fact that we disappointed so many people, I mean you have no idea when we went to meet the families and basically the wives, daughters, sisters of the men who were arrested, you know they actually risked a lot to come and meet us, they went through great risks to come and talk the official National Council delegation, you know, and they really had hopes that because we were there something was going to happen, but of course we didn't do anything for them, you know we submitted a report, which I think was a fantastic report, which totally disappeared, nothing was done, and I just felt if I can't be part of this ... I mean, what's the word? It's like, it's a shame, something that is not real, so I resigned.[7]

88 · WOMEN'S HISTORY OF THE HUMAN RIGHTS MOVEMENT

The women relatives of the men who had been arrested did not give up seeking justice. In March 2004, the political economist Hala Shukrallah, a member of NWF who later (between 2014 and 2015) served for a year and a half as the head of the Dostour Party (the first woman, and a Coptic, to serve in that role), received a phone call from the headquarters of the Tagammu' Party in al-'Arish. A group of Bedouin women were holding a prolonged sit-in in front of the Tagammu' Party, protesting against the arrest of their relatives upon accusations of terrorism. Shukrallah organized a delegation of women from Cairo to travel to al-'Arish and stand in solidarity with the women: "We went by car, Nawla [Darwiche] and I. It was an incredible day! We spoke to them, and they spoke to us. It ended in an unfortunate way. The husband of one of the leading women was arrested. The police told him that they would have let him go if he could 'control' his wife. He came and dragged her by her hair. It was under everyone's eyes that this was about violence, rights, politics, all intersecting."[8]

NWF decided to stand with the women of al-'Arish and invited them to speak at the International Women's Day Conference that they (NWF) organized. There, they had a space to testify about their experience of being interrogated jointly by Egyptian and Israeli security, and about children held in prison.

The feminists who contributed to building the human rights movement in Egypt considered human rights an aim in its own right rather than a tool or even weapon in larger, more direct political struggles, which is how members of various political movements, from Communists to Islamists, deployed human rights. Egyptian feminist human rights defenders would overcome ideological divisions and support women, no matter their background. They were also trying to achieve justice for women who had very different and even opposed political positions. Specifically, what emerges from Shukrallah's and Elsadda's testimonies is a clear stand against the indiscriminate repression of Islamists following the wave of terrorist attacks that shook the country in the second half of the 1990s and the first decade of the twenty-first century.

The unique dynamic related to women's activism for human rights surrounds the difficulty of such activism. Indeed, if the environment in which human rights activists were operating was difficult broadly speaking, it was at least doubly challenging for women, who had to work under multiple layers of intersected oppression: authoritarianism, patriarchy, and classism.[9] The institutional sphere was particularly constrained, therefore most of the feminist human rights activists developed their political activities within the framework of independent organizations, which were less trusted and most targeted by the regime compared with those who were more fully within the regime orbit and even patronage.

HUMAN RIGHTS IN EGYPT: LEGAL AND POLITICAL FRAMEWORKS

Women' presence in the public sphere in the 1980s, 1990s, and early 2000s represented a complex matrix of interests, goals, and personalities whose class and social divisions extended across several eras. It encompassed both institutional forms of political participation—where some high-profile women professionals tried to navigate the difficult waters of the formal institutions under Mubarak's regime—and independent political engagement, the latter which saw women activists place their lives at risk by questioning the same structure of the regime.

The broad spectrum of women's human rights activism during these decades cannot be understood unless it is also situated in the broader context of the very limited freedom to operate that was experienced by the civil society at that time. Specifically, in the three decades that preceded the 2011 Revolution, the legislative framework was severely restricted by two laws: the emergency law (Law 162/1958) and the association law (Law 32/1964 and its later reforms). The state of emergency was first declared in Egypt by the British following the 1919 anticolonial uprisings. Since then, Egypt has always been under some sort of emergency legislation, with very few interruptions. The emergency law of 1958 has been renewed by the Egyptian parliament every three years since 1981 and, as of the fall of 2024, is still in force.[10] The law gives the president broad powers to detain, without charge or trial, individuals who are suspected to be involved in activities that are deemed harmful to the national interest. It prohibits strikes, demonstrations, and public meetings, and it also allows the censoring and the closing down of newspapers in the name of national security. In the early nineties, in response to the political violence carried on by the armed branch of the Islamist movement, the government repression against political oppositions intensified further, exemplified by the anti-terrorism law (Law 97/1992) and the routine use of military trials for civilians.[11]

The association law of 1964 imposes severe legal restrictions on the establishment of civil associations, and it gives to the government broad space to interfere in the activities of the NGOs.

There were three attempts to modify the local NGOs law, which is an extremely oppressive law, and every time we would launch a campaign against it. The first time, I think we were successful. It was a very prolonged campaign, over a year. We were meeting every week and we lobbied the Parliament; we did a lot of work on the first attempt at changing that law. Then, it was switched, and the law that actually went into the Ministry of Justice was switched, and the one that went to parliament was a very different law. Still, there was the tug of war, and we were always able to apply pressure and improve it a bit. So, there was a continuous presence of the security forces, as a force to suppress any kind of freedom, was always there. Attempts at picketing, or so on, were always confronted with violence, sometimes, but mostly one hundred people would gather and they would be surrounded by something like five thousand policemen. The main objective was to keep the people within a very small space and not allow them to integrate with the broader public, because these were the people that the regime was afraid of. These NGOs and these activists, as long as they remain within a very small space, they could be controlled.[12]

On January 22, 1995, the legislative department of the Ministry of Justice issued a ruling on the status of so-called civil companies, saying that if they failed to register under the law on associations then they would be liable to prosecution if they received foreign aid. Almost all human rights organizations were not registered.[13] Toward the end of the nineties there were attempts to reform the law, from both inside and outside the government. In 1997, the then-Minister for Social Affairs Mervat Tallawi started a process of consultation with Egyptian civil society, and in 1998 she presented a proposal to the government. The cabinet amended it and passed a reform (Law 153/1999), but it was in fact so restrictive it was never enacted and ultimately was declared unconstitutional.[14] Parallel to the government's actions, in 1988 a network of sixteen human rights organizations, three leading opposition parties, and a number of prominent academics tried to draft a new proposal.[15]

This all happened while the human rights community was systemically intimidated, as evidenced by the attempt to prosecute human rights lawyer Hafez Abu Sa'da, who was then serving as the secretary general of the Egyptian Organization for Human Rights, for having published a report about an episode of sectarian violence in the village of al-Kosheh (August 1998).[16] Eventually, a new association law was passed in 2002 (Law 84/2002), mandating all NGOs to register at the Ministry of Social Affairs. The conditions were very strict, giving power to the ministry to reject or dissolve any association threatening order or public morality.

FIGURE 7. Three generations of Egyptian women celebrating six of them at the Mubarak Public Library, Cairo, 2011. Back row, left to right: Hala Mansour (Young Women Forum), Mona Zulficar, Aziza Hussein, Soraya Adham, Aida al-Gindi, Marie Assaad, Shahenda Meqlad, Wedad Mitri, Aida Fahmi, Tahani al-Gebali, Reem Saad, and Soad Mitri. Middle row, left to right: Amal Mahmoud, Amal Abdel Hadi, Faten Gomaa (YWF), Nadera Zaki, Mervat Abu Teeg, and Hoda Elsadda. Front row, left to right: Rima el-Khoffash, Hala Shukrallah, Somaya Ibrahim, and Nawla Darwiche. Courtesy of Women and Memory Forum Library and Nawla Darwiche.

Some of the women's associations were affected by this law. For instance, it took WMF a long time to obtain their regular registration. Although founded in 1995, they only succeeded in being registered in the early 2000s. The process was not any easier for NWF, although ultimately, they, too, succeeded. These successes could not be taken for granted, however, as demonstrated by the failure the Egyptian Association to Combat Torture (cofounded by Aida Seif El-Dawla) to obtain permission to register.[17]

The restrictions imposed by the government were not the only challenge faced by civil society organizations. At that time, Islamist groups, while actively building their own civil society and NGOs networks, were posing a serious threat to freedom of expression more broadly, especially for secular public intellectuals, who were under constant intimidation to be taken to the court or even killed. The human rights community was traumatized by the assassination of the journalist Farag Fouda in June 1992, perpetrated by the militants of the Gamʿa al-Islamiyya. The assassination was not condemned by religious authorities such as Al-Azhar, and the leadership of the Muslim Brotherhood only "regretted" that it happened, with some of its senior members even testifying at the trial in favor of the assassins (who were eventually condemned to death). Between 1992 and 1993 more than two hundred people were killed in Egypt by radical Islamists. The government responded with a massive wave of arrests, also in violation of human rights, and the human rights community had to face the dilemma of defending those who were committing violence against them. Although not directly involved in armed operations, women who were close to the Gamaʿa al-Islamiyya were also the target of state repression in retaliation against their family members.

Amid all the difficulties, civil society groups tried to develop a reformist agenda. Attempting to work within the constitutional framework, they sought to influence the legislative process and, as important but quite dangerously, to stymie if not frustrate the ostensibly preordained succession of Gamal Mubarak to his father at the presidency. In this instance, the movement of the judges was crucial through the nineties, and thanks to the independence of the judiciary (especially the Supreme Constitutional Court), court litigation soon became a dominant strategy for human rights defenders in Egypt.[18]

FOR AN EXPANDED GENEALOGY OF THE HUMAN RIGHTS MOVEMENT IN EGYPT

Alongside the movement of the judges, the human rights movement was one of the most active in demanding democratic reforms throughout the 1990s and the early 2000s; however, its intellectual and ideological roots were different, as were its politics. The intellectual and ideological roots of the human rights movement in Egypt are traditionally traced back to the Marxist movements, the post-1967 leftist student activism, and liberal democratic thought. The demonstrations against the Israeli invasion of Lebanon and in solidarity with Palestinian people after the massacre of Sabra and Shatila in 1982 were a defining moment for the Egyptian (and more broadly the Arab) human rights community. In fact, already in the seventies the Marxist lawyer Nabil al-Hilali (1928–2006) stood for a human rights-driven approach to his work, defending political activists from all the political tendencies (including the Islamists, and especially those who had been tortured in jail). It was in the early eighties that the movement assumed a structure, with the establishment of the Egyptian Organization for Human Rights (1985), as a branch of the Arab Organization for Human Rights (founded in Cyprus in 1983), and with the foundation of the Ibn Khaldun Center for Development Studies (1988), chaired by Professor Saad Eddin Ibrahim.

Since then, the history of the Egyptian human rights movement has been written through the testimonies of its founders and leading figures: Nabil al-Hilali, Saad Eddin Ibrahim, Ahmed Seif al-Islam, Hisham Mubarak, Hani Shukrallah, Farag Fouda, Amir Salem, Muhammad al-Sayyed Saʿid, Bahey Eldin Hassan, Mahmud Gaber, Nasser Amin, and Mohamed Zarei were—and many of them still are—among the most prominent individuals in the movement since the mid-eighties and the most recurring names in the scholarly literature about the human rights movement in Egypt. A history that has generally been narrated as a men's history.

It is true that since the late eighties a growing group of male lawyers and male public intellectuals played a crucial role in denouncing the systemic repression and torture to which political activists were subjected by the state. However, a closer study of the history of the movement shows not only that women lawyers and political activists were closely working with men to achieve these goals, but also that the practices and the ideas developed among the circles of feminism in the eighties deeply shaped the intellectual and political trajectory of the human rights movement in Egypt. This approach does not simply add to a larger story, it complicates the very notion of human rights by positioning women as agents, not only targets, of human rights policies, and deploying a vision that encompasses and intersects political, socioeconomic, and gender rights. Women's stories and memories are testimonies of the politics of intimacy that constitutes the major thread in the experiences of the women who decided to live their lives as politics.

With the politics of intimacy, I refer to the entanglements between family, politics, and individual attitudes that translate into political activism. I discussed this at length with Hala Shukrallah. The youngest daughter in a family of political activists, Hala discovered politics at a very young age, when her brothers, Hani and Alaa, had been arrested as leaders of the student movement in the early seventies, and she found herself coordinating a network of families to support political prisoners:

> My beginning, my awareness of injustice in the public space, began when I was about seventeen years old, with the rise of a student movement, which

was, basically, a democratic nationalist movement at that time, in 1972. My brothers were in university. I wasn't. I was still in school. However, you come to a point in your life where you are suddenly aware of a world that is much wider than your little old world, wider than your family, your wants, your needs as a teenager. For me, that was when the police came to our house and wanted to arrest my brothers. At that point, when they were arrested, I was called, by others, to join the families of the arrested students, and I did. I became part of it, and I got to know my world, which was growing, and that world, which was growing, much better. I came from a much more insulated world. I was with my parents in Canada for five years. My father was in the Arab League, so I had just come back. I was still learning what Egypt was, what my country was. All of a sudden, I was made aware of this very broad world of people from different classes, different backgrounds, different educational and cultural backgrounds. For me, it created a sense of belonging. For the first time, I felt that this was something significant.

As I became part of that families' movement, I started to be an essential driving force within it. I think it was one of the first big impacts on everything that shaped me, because I went to so many houses and visited so many places that I would never have gone to. This included very poor villages and very poor slum areas. Coming from a different class, you were usually insulated from that. So, breaking that boundary was so important for me, and I think it shaped who I became later. That was a very important moment in shaping my life and my outlook on society, on people, on human beings in general. It gave me the confidence that I am able to confront. At that time, I played the role of go-between. I would go to different prisons and take messages from the window and give it to their families. I was exposed to so much, in very little time. I then entered university, and I was active at that time. I was arrested a few times, in small skirmishes, prior to entering university and afterward.[19]

Political activism always came with a high price for Egyptian women, whatever their ideological positionality. In 1975, while Hala Shukrallah's father was stationed in India, the security forces went to the family's house in Cairo. Shukrallah told me that, concerned of having her arrested while they were not in the country, her parents "forced" her to leave:

So, he got me to leave university in '75, and I stayed for a few years in England, and I visited my parents in India. However, in '77, which was the Intifada,[20] my name came in the [Egyptian] newspapers, saying that I was arrested. It was apparent that there was some report, a false report, from the agents in the universities, that filtered through to decision-making security forces. My name was put on one of the cases and I was expelled from university. At that time, I was abroad. . . . So, I had to stay for a further two years, until I became fed up and said to my father, "I am going back. Whatever happens, happens, even if they take me to the airport." They didn't take me to the airport, but it took several years for me to win the case against the university and to be reinstated. Then, I graduated in '81. The sense that life is sort of a go-between between constant tension and confrontation and the sense that you are on the right [side], that you are fighting for something, was sort of an ongoing thing. It never ended. Some people go away, and they forget it, but you don't. You are constantly living it.[21]

Activism, solidarity, arrests, and then a self-imposed exile led Hala Shukrallah to think deeply and critically about the experience of the student movement. Her way of thinking about it is not self-celebratory. There is not an inch of heroism nor nostalgia in her oral history narrative about it but rather the desire to understand what went wrong and how to build something new out of the ashes of that repressed movement. At the time I interviewed her, five years into the 2013 coup that reinstated the power of the military, her memories of the student movement explicitly related to the present and resonate with the moment we recorded the interview, linking with a subtle thread the past to the present:

> In the eighties, when I finished university, and this is similar to what is now happening, a lot of people were thinking about that experience; what was done and what could have been done. For me, it was about "How have we not made an impact on communities? How had the student movement, which was very strong at that one point, been unable to make an impact on whole communities?" That is an essential part: empowering those communities and creating space for people to express themselves. That is what is needed. It is not only that you express yourself, but you need to play a role in creating space for other voices to come in.[22]

In the early 1980s, Shukrallah got married, and she started working in the popular district of Helwan, where she contributed to opening a community center called the Helwan Community Services Center, Bashayir, which is now quite well known for its women's cooperative. "We started to reach out to working-class women through a day care center, because we recognized that women who have kids are unable to continue working, or they need more vacation time, so they are expelled from their work. So, we started with a day care center, then a cooperative and it evolved into a center that empowers victims of violence and raises awareness on the issue. So, it's a multiservice center. Also in the eighties, we established the NWF, or the New Women Center, as it was called."[23]

In the period between the mid-seventies and the early eighties it was very clear to the human rights community that first Sadat and then Mubarak were negotiating with the Muslim Brotherhood, and giving them more space to operate, to contain the democratic movement. This had consequences for women, as a discourse targeting them, especially the regarding dress code and their presence in the public space, was widespread. This attitude was visible across social classes and was in fact generalized. Women were also adapting to it, changing the way they dressed, how they behaved, as they were having the clear perception that the public space was becoming more and more aggressive toward them. This is the context where a new generation of feminist organizations emerged in Egypt, with four major organizations: First, the Arab Women Solidarity Association (1982–1991) was led by Nawal al-Saadawi and since 1989 published the magazine *Nun*. Second, the New Woman Research Foundation (NWRF) was created in Cairo in 1984 and published the newsletter *Al-Mar'a al-Gadida*. Third was the Bint al-Ard Association, first conceived in Mansoura by Hala Isma'il and Thuraya 'Abd al-Radi (both graduates of the engineering school at the University of Mansoura) and soon joined by Iman Mersal, Jihan Abu Zeid, Saniyya al-Bahhat, and other young women. Since 1984, Bint al-Ard published a feminist magazine with the same name.[24] And last but not least is the Alliance of Arab Women, created in 1987 by Huda Badran with Aida al-Gindi, Laila al-Lababidi, and Sawsan Othman. All these organizations, notwithstanding differences (and changing over time) of positionalities toward how to deal with the government and with foreign funding, framed women's rights within the framework of human rights, and all their members contributed strenuously to include women's rights within the agenda and the discourse of the human rights movement in Egypt. This was not an easy task, and the divergences within the women's movement did not facilitate it.

Shukrallah remembers that NWF was the first organization to combine a feminist and a workers' rights program by adopting a community-oriented method and trying to approach the communities by focusing on their actual needs and values: "When you talk to working-class women, or talk to people from a different viewpoint on how women should behave and act, and so on, your first topic is not going to be, Why are you wearing the hijab? It is going to be, How are you able to preserve your right to be treated as a human being, to be treated equally? You find that this is the issue that they are concerned about."[25]

An important thread linking feminist activism with the human rights movement is the participation of women in the labor movement. This is certainly a long-term consequence of the policies of economic liberalism in the seventies and eighties, which severely affected working women:

Of course, one of the things that came across, which was problematic for me, was that women during the sixties were working all the shifts; morning, noon, and evening shifts. They could pick and choose, and they could pick and choose any department, regardless of whether they were a large percentage of the working force or not. Of course, they are a much larger percentage of the working force now. Still, they were able to work in any department. Now, what happened after the mid-seventies or early eighties was that women were being relegated to specific departments; the garment department, even though they were in the spinning and weaving. They had asked not to work night shifts, because harassment had begun. The work environment was changing, and it was becoming more aggressive. So, they asked, along with the trade unionists, that women not be given the night shift. That cuts into their salary because night shifts are twice the pay. So, they were complaining about this—they recognized that this was not in their interest, but they did not know how to deal with it.

In general, what you find is that women are put in a corner where, in order to defend themselves from a bigger sort of aggression, they actually enclose themselves in a sort of prison. They imprison themselves. Part of wearing these garbs was protecting themselves from aggression. Not doing the night shifts was protecting them. They were on the defensive. A lot of women recognized that they were doing this in order to protect themselves. A lot of women recognized that and complained that their money was being taken by their husbands. Immediately, the issue of work spills into the family for women, where their husband was not working whilst they were working, and their money was being taken by the husband. That was the dilemma that they were living, in addition to a lack of support networks. So, you see a situation that in the minds of many of these women is clear but there is no solution.[26]

These were the years when the workers in the textile district of Mahalla al-Kubra had started to raise their voices in protest against low wages and poor working conditions. According to Hala Shukrallah, who at that time collected documentation about the movement for a documentary produced by NWF to which she contributed, women were starting to play a more assertive role:

> They were always the support; the women behind the men. But then they started becoming leaders in the movement, and that was very interesting. It was on the rise, but there was also much more activity and activism going on. People were speaking, the media was starting to play a role, organizations were speaking out and making conferences. I can't underline this more: with all the attempts at enforcing and prohibiting that kind of interaction, it did filter through. Mahalla was again a turning point that I think manifest the

changing roles of women in society and how they were becoming powerful and becoming leaders in their own right.[27]

Through the activity of NWF, which after the documentary organized a series of seminars targeting working-class women, feminist activism permeated into other organizations, such as the Labor Organization (then led by Kamal Abbas) and the Center for Trade Union Services, where a high-profile activist was a woman who also came from the student movement, Fatma Ramadan. The Center for Trade Union Services was established in the early 1990 and had several branches, in Mahalla, Shubra, and 6th of October, all areas where private companies were growing at the expense of state-owned companies, implying far less protection for workers.

> So, you have a very volatile situation that is going on, a strike happening, a sit-in happening, a company closing down, and two thousand workers are in the street. This was the kind of news that was going on prior to 2011. Every day there was something. It impacted on different sectors, and it definitely impacted on female workers, and Mahalla was that example. Not only Mahalla, but we started seeing it in the rise of different figures, and that was very interesting to see. You felt that you were on the brink of a change, and then 2011 happens. Everything came to a screeching halt, because what took place before the 25th of January 2011 was no longer significant, because something much bigger was happening and something else had to take its place. Other solutions, other answers and forms of organizations, other objectives had to be put in place, and everyone's roles began to be rearranged. I think it was a moment of clarity and confusion at the same time. From my point of view, we were, in the beginning, really observing, because we were not the ones (and when I say "we," I mean our generation) leading that event, although we had gone down numerous times, throughout the years, in pickets and attempts at demonstrations that were halted, but that was not our moment; the 25th of January was not of our making.
> So, we were observers, basically, at that time. We went, we participated, we stood with them, but we were not the ones leading it. I think, in time, I realized that no one was really leading it; it was very much a combination of forces.[28]

Women's sexual and reproductive rights, poverty, and working conditions were three key areas of activism for Egyptian feminists in the eighties and nineties. This activism, grounded in their experience in the student movement of the seventies, and for some of them the Marxist underground organizations in the eighties, grew-up in the broader context of the emerging human rights organizations. Women were part of these organizations since their earliest days, bringing with them their professionalism as lawyers, psychiatrists, medical doctors, and journalists. The feminist lives of these public intellectuals played a crucial but as yet too little acknowledged role in the development of the human rights movement in Egypt.

PART TWO

Feminist Lives in Egypt

FIVE

Practicing Feminist Psychiatry as Human Rights Activism

AIDA SEIF EL-DAWLA, SUZAN FAYAD,
AND MAGDA ADLY

"THE SEVENTIES, OH ... I don't want to go through any of this again. ... I was not in the leadership of anything. ... Hani will tell you about the student movement. He was in the leadership."[1]

Born in the early 1950s, an eager if today self-effacing participant in the post-1967 student movement and a graduate from the Faculty of Medicine of Ain Shams, where she is now a professor in psychiatry, Aida Seif El-Dawla is less than enthusiastic about discussing the years when the student movement spilled out from university campuses onto the streets.

When we first met, at the end of 2017, the atmosphere was gloomy. The activities of El-Nadeem Center for the Psychological Treatment and Rehabilitation of Victims of Violence and Torture[2] in Cairo had been severely reduced by the Egyptian state security. The clinic had been sealed since February 2016 by order of the Ministry of Health (a decision that El-Nadeem's doctors questioned both on substantial and procedural grounds); since then staff continued to meet with patients in various off-site locations in order to ensure providing critically needed counseling and treatment for their patients.[3] As a cofounder of El-Nadeem, Dr. Adly told me at that time: "We are like pirates!"[4] It was a critical moment; the continued existence of the center, which since 1993 had pioneered the treatment of survivors of torture and other forms of violence and abuse across the Arab world, offering free psychiatric treatment while also producing research and campaigning for human rights, was in doubt. At the time of our second meeting, in January 2018, the situation was equally bad. El-Dawla and her colleague Suzan Fayad (also a psychiatrist and cofounder of El-Nadeem) were under a travel ban, a common sanction against political activists that has also been imposed on a number of human rights defenders and lawyers.[5]

Aida appeared troubled during that afternoon, not just because of the political mood, but even more so for the future of young Egyptians, which she saw as increasingly dim. Likely because of this feeling, there was no joy, or even grudging nostalgia, in her narrative of the student movement in the seventies. I wondered if the melancholic atmosphere that understandably surrounded the community of Egyptian human rights defenders was the subtext of Aida's account. She tended to underplay her role in the student movement when we'd speak about it, and when I tried to encourage more detailed stories during this meeting, she referred me to her comrades, well-known figures such as her relative Laila Soueif, journalist (and her ex-husband and still close friend) Hani Shukrallah, his sister Hala Shukrallah, and friends Magda Adly, Amal Abdel Hadi, and Nawla Darwiche. I had already spoken to most of them, and thanks to Aida I would meet the others in the next few days. But on that day, as we sat in her living room, I was hoping to know more about the beginnings of her political activism.

Her memory returned to her ancestors: "I was brought up in a political family; from my grandfather down to today. My paternal grandfather, 'Abbas, was from Upper Egypt, and he was a sort of community leader." Indeed, throughout the interview Aida framed her political biography within her family history. In her voice I could hear the echoes of the salient moments in the national history, from the 1919 anti-British uprisings to the 1967 defeat against Israel, to the repression of the Marxist dissidents by Gamal Abdel Nasser's regime. Her narrative reminded me of the autobiographies of the Egyptian feminists who came before her, stories where family memories shape a sense of history and, in Aida's case, her approach to human rights activism. In many ways her family history incarnates the deep roots and the plural genealogies of the human rights movement in Egypt, as well as the tensions inherited by political activists from the colonial age.

The story of Aida's family took me back to a time when neither a shared international definition of human rights nor most forms of national legislation yet existed. However, at grassroots level, activists were disseminating the seeds of the ideas that half a century later would have made the notion of human rights spread relatively quickly among Egyptian political activists. As I was thinking of this longue durée historical trajectory, Aida told me more about her family, and, in so doing, she took me on a journey across a century of political activism in Egypt, one that would radically broaden and sharpen my understanding of the relationship between human rights, feminist activism, and political protest in the Arab world's most populous and politically influential country.

THE FORMATIVE YEARS

'Abbas [my grandfather], left his village, al-Badari, in Asyut, as a child, on his own. He came to Cairo and studied in Al-Azhar, where he became a *shaykh* [a senior scholar]. Then he returned to his village. He was not the official mayor, but he was the de facto mayor and led several peasant mutinies over land. . . . My mother comes from the other end of the [laughs] . . . from the other end of the country. I mean, my fathers' family were basically peasants. My mother's family is aristocracy from the Delta. Her father, Yussuf al-Guindi, is the one upon whom the street in downtown Cairo, close to the American University, is named. They lived in an area called Zifta, in the Gharbiyya governorate. It is a town through which the railways carrying cotton to be transported to Europe go through. So, this Yussuf al-Guindi in 1919 declared Zifta independent for eighteen days. They cut the railways [laughs]. They cut the railways, they set up a town orchestra, they ruled the town for eighteen days. Of course, after that he was arrested for a short time, but later he became a member of the Wafd and was nominated to be a member of the Cabinet. . . . My father was also a political activist. He was a lawyer: 'Ismat Saif al-Dawla. He was a famous lawyer, an excellent one, and he was an activist who developed his own theory, which was neither Marxist nor Trotskyist, nor Islamist, nor Nasserite. Something different, which he called the theory of the Arab revolution. And he has many followers but not in Cairo, not in Egypt. He has followers in Syria, in Iraq, Libya, in Tunis . . . who call themselves actually the Ezmatis. So, this man brought us up with stories from his family and stories of resistance, and he brought us up, basically this way. His main two principles were not to lie and not to tolerate injustice. . . . And that, within injustice, under injustice, political resistance is a must. And that there is not political resistance without a political organization; and that in a dictatorship you can't have a political organization unless this political organization is underground. So, he was telling this to me, these stories when I was fifteen, seventeen, a daughter who was not allowed out on her own from the house. For me, this was totally abstract. I remember, the first time I left the house on my own was to go to university.[6]

Gender, class, and national politics were part of the Aida's family memories. With regard to gender relationships and expectations related to being a man or a woman, somehow the family that Aida described to me appeared like many conservative middle-class families in the early sixties, not just in Cairo but in other Mediterranean cities, before the student rebellion of 1968 transformed family politics. Once women's political rights had been granted in Egypt with suffrage in 1956, the idea that women had to achieve a high level of education and then work became quite common among the middle classes as well as those of more modest origins. According to the developmentalist, nationalist ideology that permeated the then new republican state, young women's education was not just as a mean for them to access to the job market and to achieve financial independence; it was first and foremost a contribution to the project of the postcolonial nation-state construction. Many of the women I interviewed use the same words Aida proffered when they remembered the experience of being at the university: "It was absolutely natural."

Going to school and even university was what both the republican state and their families were expecting young women to do. Notwithstanding the challenges they faced in achieving leadership positions (something that was and six decades later still remains exceptional), equality in the public sphere was acknowledged by the laws of the postcolonial republican state. Yet even with these newfound freedoms, families could still exercise strict control on women's personal lives (especially adolescents and young women), as Aida's comment about not going out by herself before enrolling in the university suggests. Sexual relationships were conceived legitimate only within the context of the marriage, leading many to get married at seventeen or eighteen,[7] and limitations on personal freedom had little if anything to do with being Muslim or Christian.

As a matter of fact, the narratives of the Coptic and Muslim women I met over the years do not vary much, and intermarriage was not an exceptional experience. Moreover, most of the time religious affiliation was not a theme that came up during interviews. Control over women's bodies as a site of the family's honor was a practice that transcended both religious communities and social classes, but it was exercised in different ways by different classes. Class was not the only factor shaping women's experience, of course, but it intersected the generation alongside other variables, such as the specific family life. In the narrative produced by Aida about her life, growing up in a middle-class family whose father was a political activist, there was a protective attitude of the adults toward the children of the extended family, which played a central role in shaping her identity and inspiring her human rights activism:

> What happened was that in the last year of my school he got arrested. The patriarch. The kind, hardly democratic slash patriarch of the house got arrested. . . . He was sentenced to ten years, but he spent two years in prison. And so . . . while he was absent, I entered the university and . . . the university was . . . ON FIRE . . . there were demonstrations, for the '67 defeat, and

... lack of democracy, and hiking prices. ... But even before my father was arrested—because my father got arrested twice, once in early '71 or '72 ... I don't remember—and then again in this widespread arrest that Sadat did in 1981. Before that, I had an uncle who was a communist, and who had escaped prison. He was one of the communists who was sentenced in '59 by Nasser's regime. They were sent to al-Wahat (the Oasis) detention center. And, I had another, the cousin of my mother, who was basically killed by prison, because he died immediately after the release. So, the idea of people going to prison and out of prison and struggling an unjust regime for me was the way good people live. And, for a long time, without ... without ideology. It is not like I developed my ideology. Until now I can't describe myself as a real learned person. Ever since then, that was the drive and that's how it has been.

Aida studied in a German school and, notwithstanding her personal inclination toward English literature and political science, her mother plotted to dissuade her from such plans:

> I completed high school with very high grades, and I applied to enroll in the Faculty of Political Science. My mother was devastated. How could I have such high grades and not enter medicine? ... We used to rotate my father's visits, as I had a brother who was only two years old. So, once my mother would go with my older brother, and I stayed with the baby, and once I would go with her, and Muhammad [the eldest brother] would stay with the baby. So, she came back, and she told me: "Baba was very upset that you registered to political sciences, and he would like you to become a doctor." And of course, that was the end, I mean, that was a big burden, and ... [smiles] I changed ... of course, and it turned out to be a lie. Actually, my father would have been very happy if I'd register in political sciences ... ah ah ... [laugh] my mother was ... she had a way, and not even God could stop her!

Aida was a good student; she completed medical school with high grades, but she knew from her first day that she would not become a regular doctor. "It took six years [laughs]. Six years during which I never made an injection, I never made a stitch, I never attended an operation, I never entered the morgue. But I got excellent marks in surgery and anatomy, because I knew how to learn things well [laughs]." She decided to specialize in psychiatry because she seemed to find it easier to talk to people than to operate on their bodies. She soon would have changed her mind, realizing that, especially given the context in which she was operating, a context marked by everyday political violence, souls and bodies were inextricably intertwined.[8]

Over time Aida also realized that psychiatry was transforming her into a new human being: "I have changed a lot. Through psychiatry ... I was a terrible person . . . a terrible . . ." Then, maybe reading a shade of skepticism on my face, she insisted: "No, really . . . I mean, I entered this profession when I was still training, and I was . . . I was indoctrinated by my family, by my father especially, what is right, and what is wrong, there is only black and white, no gray zones, no excuses to make mistakes. Of course, for my father what he considered mistakes were mostly things related to moral issues. My father was . . . as progressive as he was politically, he was otherwise extremely conservative. And he was mistrustful of women."

The criticism of the various dogmatic forms of Marxism (Stalinism, Maoism, Trotskyism) that were still de rigueur in many leftist circles in the sixties and seventies was common among Aida's generation, whose approach to politics can be described as a "New Left" approach—less dogmatic and more infused by humanism, as the writings of and my conversations with the late Hani Shukrallah confirm. Indeed, the interviews I have collected show that this critical and humanistic approach to politics characterized first and foremost women human rights activists who all shared a feminist background. This is reflected particularly in Aida's narrative about her political upbringing. In fact, with reference to her young age, Aida defined her political identity along the line of continuity with a genealogy of male activists. There was a shift in her narrative when she told me about the times, when she joined the feminist reading group that would become the New Woman Research Foundation (NWF) in 1984. The NWF developed a critique of the different forms of domination and discrimination that oppress women in Egypt. They focused specifically on the interplay between the patriarchal structure of the family, the role played by the authoritarian state institutions, and the structural discrimination of women on the job market. These themes were discussed and disseminated in the NWF newsletter, booklets, and a documentary about women workers that the organization produced in the early 2000s.

This was the space where she became familiarized with Egyptian and international feminist thought, as transmitted through the archives of *L'Egyptienne,* the Egyptian Feminist Union's magazine launched in 1925, and whose copies were conserved by one of the NWF members. Aida's feminism was cultivated through a combination of grassroots work and extensive readings, especially the biographies of the modern women writers, such as Malak Hifni Nasif (known under the pen name of Bahithat al-Badiya); the nationalist feminists who created the Egyptian Feminist Union, such as Huda Sha'rawi, Nabawiyya Musa, and Saiza Nabarawi; and of course Nawal al-Saadawi. Without dismissing the intellectual roots of feminism, she points out many times during the interview that the fieldwork experience—the clinical work and the work with the task force against female genital mutilations—was what opened her eyes.

The practice of psychiatry in the clinic intersected that of feminism and it had a transformative effect on Aida's conception of politics. The experience of treating her patients—taking care of their tortured bodies and their tortured souls, and of exchanging ideas with her fellow feminists—inspired Aida to question the dogmatic values that her adored father had instilled in her and even to develop a dialectical (critical) approach to Marxism, to which she'd adhered as a university student. It should be noted that as she was developing her feminist approach to psychiatry, Aida's practice became grounded in what has been described by the social anthropologist Frances Hasso as a "multifaceted radical care politics," meaning with it a unique combination of medical practices that integrate the treatment of the individual bodies with their psyches, while also addressing violence as a broader social and political issue, and trying to change the context that normalizes it.[9] In their oral histories interviews, Aida and the other two core members of El-Nadeem, Suzan Fayad and Magda Adly, emphasize that their practice with survivors of torture was never inspired by what they'd learned at university or in medical school.[10] Rather, Aida's and other El-Nadeem psychiatrists' practice needs to be understood in the specific social and political context marked not only by political violence but equally important by resistance to it, in which it grew. Moreover, it was a context where a group of pioneering women psychiatrists found themselves at the forefront of a new way to understand and practice care.

There is a feminist stream in Egyptian psychiatry that has been inspired by the pioneering work of Nawal al-Saadawi, whose first book, *al-Mar'a wa-al-Jins* (*Woman and Sex*), first published in Arabic in 1972, was a landmark for Egyptian and Arab feminism, and deeply influenced all the future generations. The biographies of feminists who are in the medical professions, especially psychiatry, shed light on a complex interweaving of opportunities created by institutional policies (such as the generalization of free higher education and the opening of opportunities for work in hospitals for women physicians) and activists' careers anchored in a longer time frame. Such opportunities and the experiences they enabled challenge certain simplistic readings of biopolitics as largely a tool of subjectification to regulate and control people and to consolidate state power. In the experience and the life-narrative of Aida Seif El-Dawla, psychiatry was not the colonial science that pathologizes nonnormative subjects, but the practice of care, compassion, and empowerment, which can't be but politicized, and whose main aim is the care for the subjects who are treated. In her own words: "Working with people through psychiatry showed me that there was not only a gray zone, there are all colors, and all human beings are all very, very, very . . . complicated. And so . . . I became more tolerant, and more self-critical, and . . . and learned to listen a lot before I open my mouth. No, it was educational and therapeutic."

The strong link between the militancy of these women in the movements of the seventies—including their frustrations for the sexism they experienced at different levels within their own political formations—the experience of the feminist reading groups and associations in the early eighties, and the treatment of political activists contribute to make them mature an innovative and fruitful approach to psychiatry, which acknowledges the link between psychological, economic, and political liberation.

Since the early days, Aida's work was a combination of feminism, psychiatry, and democratic activism, as witnessed by her experience in the dispensary of al-'Aini:

> In 1986, I joined a small group of friends and colleagues who decided to set up a primary health care unit in al-Wayli. This neighborhood had a strong leftist presence and, of course, the community was largely conservative. It was two years before the parliamentary elections, and we wanted to set foot in the area. I joined the clinic, and I was working in the child monitoring, length, weight, development, and of course children come with their moms, and . . . and then at some point, the issue of FGM was brought up, and we decided to hold meetings with the mothers. I would have a closed meeting, where we are going to talk about FGM and its impact on women's health: physical, psychological, and sexual. . . . So, we had this meeting, and they were listening to me. I was talking about the bleeding and the infections, talking about the implications, and the difficulties in giving birth and so on, and then [laughs] I started talking about the sexual implications of women genital mutilations, and, of course, they are very polite, I am a doctor, and they have to listen [laughs], but . . . I noticed there were smiles and winks between the women, then I stopped and said: "Okay, obviously I am saying something you are not in agreement . . . so . . . what is it? What have I said wrong?" It ended up that for an hour I was sitting there and women talking about [laughs] their sexual adventures and creativity with their husbands, and what they do if their husbands don't please them. And I remember one of them saying: "*Khitan* has nothing to do with sexual pleasure. What has to do with sexual pleasure is

how he comes to you, how he approaches you in bed. That's what either leads to pleasure or does not lead to pleasure."

This experience prompted Aida to question the idea that the main argument that feminists can use against female circumcision is the control of women's pleasure. She rather suggests that the real point is the violence inflicted upon young girls. Indeed, she argues that as long as the campaigns against female circumcision focus on the theme of sexual pleasure, they remain on the same epistemic level of those who support it. In Aida's words, the decolonial and holistic approach to the campaign, encompassing medicine, anthropology and even psychology and law, cultivated by the group of women working with Marie Asaad (and of which Aida was a core member) echoes as a living memory.

The next step in Aida's trajectory as a feminist human rights defender was the creation of El-Nadeem, which, in her own words, took her to "a completely different level of understanding psychiatry and therapist-client relationship."

PRACTICING FEMINIST PSYCHIATRY AS HUMAN RIGHTS ACTIVISM: THE EXPERIENCE OF EL-NADEEM

In 1989, the Egyptian Organization for Human Rights (EOHR), of which Aida was part, supported iron and steel workers in Helwan who had been arrested for taking part in a strike. Amir Salem and Muhammad al-Sayyed Saʿid, two board members of the EOHR, published a statement demanding the release of the workers, objecting to the treatment by the government, which had violated the right to the freedom of assembly of the protestors, arbitrary detention of thousands of workers, and other violations of human rights. The government arrested them along with Hisham Mubarak and Kamal Khalil, reopening their old files on their leftist political activities. They were beaten by the police, until, upon pressure from both the national and the international community, they were released after fourteen days. This was a turning point in Aida's perception of what human rights work was needed:

> Some of our friends were arrested and were tortured. And when they came out, some of them were injured. At that time, I was working at Ain Shams hospital, Suzan was the head of psychiatry at the Palestine Hospital in

Heliopolis, and 'Abd Allah was at the Airport Hospital. Doctors in Egypt are very important. I mean, when they give orders, orders are executed. And yet, we could not have those friends of ours examined, and the one time they were examined we could not get a report of their conditions. Because, the hospitals would not give a report when they found out that they had been in prison and that they were injured in prison. So that was one reason: to set something that would provide people the reports of what happened to them.

The second thing is that because they were friends, were our friends, and when they came out, we had gatherings and we talked, we came to see an aspect of torture that we have not seen before. I had three people in my family, who were detained for a long period of time, and were very brutally tortured, during Abdel Nasser and during Sadat. But when they came out, they came out as heroes. I never heard them talk, and nobody talked about what they did to them. These tortures. With those friends, they talked. So, we saw the other side of being a hero. We saw people who are very angry, who are humiliated, who . . . some of them were angry with themselves because they didn't try to fight back, and . . . so, we saw these traumas, this effect of the trauma, and we felt that these need intervention.

At that time, Aida and her colleagues were all volunteers at the EOHR, one of the oldest civil society organizations in Egypt (it was created in 1985 and registered as an NGO in 2003). The period between 1989 and 1993 saw a rapid growth of the organization, which led on one side to a more articulated internal debate, on the other to a multiplication of the attacks against the members human rights community that were coming not only from the state but also by Islamists, and more broadly the attacks against the freedom of expression and creativity, that were coming from Al-Azhar. In June 1992 one of the most traumatic events for the human rights community was the assassination of famed journalist and human rights activist Farag Fouda, a member of the EOHR board of trustees (1986–1989). Fouda was assassinated by the Gama'a al-Islamiyya. The relationship between the leftist and liberal human rights activists and the Islamists remained tense throughout the 1990s and the early 2000s; however, the political line of the EOHR remained clear on defending all the victims of human rights violations, regardless of political affiliation.

The same human rights movement was not monolithic. There were different views about the strategies to be adopted (mass mobilization, which was supported by the Nasserists and the liberals, versus limiting the expansion, as the Marxists would have preferred), and especially the foreign funding debate.[11] International funding supported the creation of several human rights organizations in the early nineties: In 1993, Bahey Eldin Hassan founded the Cairo Institute for Human Rights Studies, and in 1994, Hisham Mubarak founded the Center for Human Rights Legal Aid, which was offering free legal representation for those who experienced human rights violations from the government and for documenting human rights violations. Nagel el-Borai headed the Group for Democratic Development. In 1995, Azza Soliman opened the Egyptian Center for Women's Legal Aid. In 1996, the Land Center for Human Rights was founded, and Mahmud Gaber was the director of the legal unit. In the same year, the Human Rights Centre for the Assistance of Prisoners was created, under the direction of Mohamed Zarei. Overall, there were about a dozen human rights organizations in Egypt at that time and many of them had international networks. They also cooperated closely with oppositional parties and professional syndicates (which also had legal aid offices), and they were active to protest against the law Concerning the Regulation and Organization of Journalism and Press Functions (Law 96/1996), which limited the press freedom, and in monitoring the People's Assembly elections.

I asked Aida and Suzan about these years. Aida told me that at first, she and her colleagues (all psychiatrists) considered establishing a center to treat the victims of torture within the framework of the EOHR, of which they were members. But they could not agree on how to deal with the privacy of the clients in the context of another organization as their sponsor, so they decided to create a new organization specializing in treatment of torture victims and other forms of (largely but not exclusively state) abuse. Aida also explains that there were also multiple visions about how to work on human rights within the EOHR. Some members believed that human rights work should be led by professionals, others—and Aida is one of them—that human rights should be developed at the level of street activism, as it happened later during the 2011 Revolution.[12] When I met Suzan, she emphasized that what brought her, Aida, and Abdallah to create El-Nadeem was the need to offer psychological support to the victims of torture, who were neglected in both private and public hospitals where they were working. As earlier mentioned by Aida, Suzan was a doctor at the Palestine hospital, which was funded by the Palestinian Authority and treated mostly Palestinians coming through Rafah: "I used to work with the victims of the violence of the Israeli occupation," explained Suzan. "I saw prisoners who had been subject to violence, sometimes we saw people who had been tortured in Egyptian police stations. Some of them were criminals [ordinary prisoners], others were political prisoners, especially Islamists in the nineties. We understood that those people need special care, special understanding, and special treatment, a long-term systematic rehabilitation not necessarily through medication."[13]

Initially, El-Nadeem focused on clinical work, but it could not but have political implications. When they started El-Nadeem, Aida and her colleagues were expecting to receive political activists who had been subject to torture. This was not the case, as the numbers were overwhelming and largely ordinary people rather than committed activists. This reality pushed them to think critically of how the human rights movement was positioned within the society: "After a year, we realized that we, the people who come from political movements, and some of us were in the political parties, and worked in human rights, we had absolutely NO IDEA of what was actually happening in the country."

The history of the human rights movement narrated through women's experiences is marked by self-reflective practices, which were developed among the feminist circles. Aida continued to tell me about the late nineties: "Because from 1993 until 2000, until the breakout of the demonstrations in solidarity with the al-Aqsa Intifada, we did not receive a single political activist as a client. Everybody we received, everybody we reached out, were people from the very low social classes, who are poor, who are marginalized, who did not have the right phone number to call when they got in trouble, and . . . and we realized that . . . people do not get tortured only to 'confess.'"

Suzan Fayad confirmed that the El-Nadeem clinic initially received survivors from Sudan who were sent to them by Amnesty International, but soon also Egyptian people, not political activists, but mostly workers who had been tortured by the state authority. She also remembered the Helwan strike as a turning point in her perception of the movement: "For instance, there was a protest by the workers of the iron and steel factory in Helwan, and the state responded with extreme brutality. Some of the protestors were imprisoned and tortured, and we found ourselves to have to do with the victims of the state violence."[14]

The nineties were also the period of the campaign against women's circumcision. The psychiatrists of El-Nadeem were prepared to deal with women who suffered from psychological consequences of *khitan:* "We found ourselves treating the victims and standing for women's rights." For Susan Fayad who, differently from Aida, did not come from a feminist background, the work with El-Nadeem was revealing. She discovered that her experience of being treated equally in the family and in her professional life was not the norm, and that women's issues were indeed very important.

FIGURE 8. Protest against torture, Cairo, June 26, 2004. In the middle of the photo: Aida Seif El-Dawla (with sunglasses and left arm holding sign). At the front: Laila Soueif (with glasses and arm folded). Courtesy of Aida Seif El-Dawla.

The work of El-Nadeem became very soon political, as Aida explained at length:

> People can get tortured just to be intimidated or to give up a piece of land, or to leave a flat that is designed for somebody up, or to teach somebody a lesson on behalf of a third party. Torture can take place for the weirdest reasons you can think of, and ... and it is happening everywhere. Wherever there are police, there is torture, or possible torture. It is in police stations, in state security headquarters, in the security offices in the universities, in the metro station, in public hospitals. Wherever there is police, maltreatment and torture can take place. When we reached that conclusion, we realized that torture is an issue that cannot be addressed only through a clinic, that people must know what is happening in the country. We also realized that the people who come to us for help because they have been tortured, or women who come to us because they were subjected to domestic violence, they are not patients in the classic sense. They are normal people who were subjected to extreme traumas, and so, the treatment is not just to listen and give advice or a prescription, the treatment has to include rehabilitation, it has to be a reformulation of this person's life, to make sense of this terrible trauma they have been subjected to. The rehabilitation needs to happen according to what this person actually needs. If it was legal aid, we refer to legal aid, if it was a campaign, we would campaign with the person, if it was publishing their real story, we did that.

El-Nadeem decided to go public with the stories they collected, using multiple channels. In 1994, Fayad published an article in a newspaper of an opposition's party, but they also used the TV talk shows. Aida told me that at the time there was a perception of more freedom on television, information that was confirmed, in a separate interview, by the TV anchorwoman and politician Gameela Ismail.[15] Aida emphasizes that one of the main challenges was to gain people's trust: "At the time nobody really believed us. . . . People who are unlikely to be subjected to torture, or who do not know people who have been tortured, they still don't believe. They either don't believe it, or they think that this happens to people who deserve it. And with the climate created after 2013, it is even worse."

By the early 2000s, the human rights movement had matured with long and often bitter experience and diversified in terms of political approaches and groups. Not coincidentally, this was the moment when state repression became even more severe. In my discussions with Aida, Suzan, and other medical professionals, they pointed to the focus in most analyses of the human rights movement in this period being on the harassment of high-profile human rights activists and organizations, such as the case of Professor Saad Eddin Ibrahim (who was arrested on June 30, 2000) and his twenty-seven colleagues of the Ibn Khaldun Center. They were brought before an Egyptian Emergency State Security Court and condemned to seven years of jail with a threefold charge: receiving foreign funding without prior government approval, propagating false information harmful to state interests, and embezzling money from the Ibn Khaldoun Center.[16] Ibrahim and his colleagues were eventually released in March 2003, but the attacks against independent human rights activism would not stop: in June 2003 the New Woman Research Center and the Legal Center for Human Rights were temporarily closed. When I asked Aida to tell me about the human rights movement in the early 2000s, she went beyond these stories of harassments that involved her fellows, and she took my attention more to the grassroots level, remembering the Queen Boat case (2001), when a police raid on a floating nightclub known as Queen Boat resulted in the arrest of over fifty men charged of debauchery, obscene behavior, and contempt of religion (which allowed the case to be judged by the security court).[17] She did not hesitate to criticize her fellow human rights activists, acknowledging that the human rights community was divided about this case. She remembers that there were human rights organizations whose directors announced that they were against homosexuality, and people who were charged never recognized their being homosexual, not even with their own lawyer. Even the human rights lawyers at that time framed the debate in a different way. While thinking retrospectively about the early 2000s, El-Dawla acknowledges a generational gap in the human rights community and that 2011 was a landmark, a moment of real change, when a new generation of human rights defenders, less ideological and more aware of the intertwine between human rights, personal and sexual rights, and political freedom, emerged.

SIX

Conceptualizing Women's Rights within the Family as Human Rights

THE INTELLECTUAL AND GRASSROOTS WORK OF AZZA SOLIMAN

I HAD BEEN FOLLOWING Azza Soliman's work as a human rights lawyer and public advocate for women's rights since I started researching the history of Egyptian feminism in the early 2000s, and I was not surprised when in 2017 she received an honorable mention for the Allard Prize for International Integrity; the next year she was the recipient of the Martine Anstett Award for Human Rights, and in 2019 she was included in a promotional calendar for Amnesty International featuring world-leading women human rights defenders. When asked about the meaning of all these acknowledgments, she commented simply: "You feel like you are not lonely."[1]

In Egypt, women's access to the legal professions has been a matter of controversy since the beginnings of the country's political and legal modernization and the introduction of French-inspired comprehensive national legislation.[2] European legal codes at the end of the nineteenth century progressively replaced the shari'a in all the penal and civil fields but not in family law. However, the cultural process of modernization implied the reform of Islamic law, including the shari'a. It involved a series of institutional reforms, among them the establishment of a system of national courts to regulate both civil and penal matters, and the codification of the Personal Status Law: a series of legal provisions to regulate family matters (especially marriage, divorce, and inheritance) and inspired by the shari'a. Azza Soliman often works on cases involving inheritance and the traditional differences in allocations between male and female heirs. As she explained to me during a wide-ranging conversation about her work and its relation to broader feminist concerns, the Muslim PSL is not applied to non-Muslims (Christians or Jews) unless they explicitly request to apply it in their own cases, as mostly happens in instances of inheritance to enable males to inherit double the amount of their female relatives. Additionally, if two parties to a case belong to the same Christian sect, one of the conflicting parties has to change their affiliation to a different sect before they can request the application of Muslim PSL in their case.[3] Needless to say, such cases comprise a significant share of her workload.

Any discussion about the access of women to the legal professions in Egypt must take place within this broader context of contestations around legal reform and changing cultural norms and practices. As discussed earlier, the process of Egyptian women entering the legal professions began in the early twentieth century and proceeded slowly. Throughout the last century, both Muslim and Christian Egyptian women wanting to become lawyers faced two levels of inequality: First, as women in a patriarchal society, they were not allowed to access all the professions that were open to men, including law. Second, as Egyptians in a colonized society, they were disadvantaged in comparison to European women residents in Egypt, who could practice (at least in theory) in the mixed courts, which were established in 1875 to deal with controversies between foreigners and natives or between foreigners of different nationalities in Egypt who did not want to utilize their consular courts.[4] In practice, Egyptian female lawyers were not admitted in the national courts until 1933, when Naʿimah al-Ayyubi became the first female Egyptian lawyer to join the bar. As for admission to the judiciary, women had to fight for this until 2003, when Tahani al-Gebali was appointed to the Constitutional Court.[5]

Margot Badran, when detailing the EFU support for both reform of PSL and access of women to the legal professions (which were documented in the pages of the journal *L'Egyptienne*), noted that several women pioneers in the profession developed an interest in societal reform and PSL.[6] In particular, reform of the law's provisions concerning the family had been a major concern of the EFU since the early 1920s, and it was a focus of study for the women who practiced the juridical professions more broadly. PSL was at the center of political discussion throughout the twentieth century and, as noted by several feminists I interviewed, it has always been a way to control not just women but the entire society. Women lawyers and feminist associations had lobbied for the reform since the early twenties, and they obtained some change (Law 25/1929; Law 77/1943; Law 260/1960, Law 100/1985, and Law 1/2000). In the late seventies, the then-first lady, Jihan Sadat (the first wife of an Egyptian president to embody the iconic American style of First Lady) pushed for a decree to protect women within the marriage and in case of divorce. She succeeded in obtaining it, and the decree has since then been known as Jihan Law. However, the Sadats' decree only lasted two years, from 1979 until 1981, when the process that had led to its approval was deemed unconstitutional and the law was repealed, which in turn had the boomerang effect of stimulating renewed mobilization by Egyptian women for their rights.[7]

Azza Karam has documented the work of a network of women lawyers in the eighties, the Group of Seven, or the Group of Women Concerned with the Affairs of the Egyptian Woman, who produced and disseminated research about laws pertaining women in Egypt, and lobbied to reform the PSL, which they obtained in June 1985, immediately before the Nairobi women's conference.[8] The network also collaborated with religious jurists to draft the New Marriage Contract, which aimed to provide for women's right to unilaterally terminate the marriage contract by repudiation (*khul'*): "This equality could only be achieved through using an indigenous language of human rights to advocate and in fact achieve this change which was intensively resisted by the prevailing patriarchal culture."[9] Advocating the Islamic concept of *khul'* was a strategy adopted by feminist Muslim lawyers to achieve equality. In 2000, the New Marriage Contract form was reissued, in implementation of Law 1/2000, allowing women to include conditions in their marriage contracts restricting the husband's right to take a second wife and permitting women to terminate marriage unilaterally by divorce rights.

Family law continues to be a controversial and highly politicized space of discussion ten years after the Egyptian Revolution. In February 2021, the Egyptian parliament presented a very regressive draft of PSL that reassessed and strengthened the power of the *wali* (the "guardian," who is the male relative who is responsible for the woman), undermining women's basic rights in relation to child's custody, freedom to travel, and even to receive medical treatment, to name just the most obvious implications. The draft sparked strong reactions by high-profile women lawyers, such as Nehad Abu Khomsa, chair of the Egyptian Center for Women's Rights (a major feminist Egyptian organization, specializing in family law), and was strongly rejected by women's organizations across the board.[10] As Azza Soliman explains, even though it included the important provision of legalizing women marrying without the presence of a *wali*, "guardian" (the father, brother, or grandfather), there are a lot of challenges in its application that prevent the realization of its empowering provisions. The continuing resistance of women lawyers against regressive laws and practices is a testimony to the social legacy of the first women who entered in the legal professions and is substantially present in Azza Soliman's political life story.

A MEETING IN BULAQ EL-DAKHRUR

I met Azza Soliman in December 2018. We met in the offices of the Center for Egyptian Women's Legal Assistance (CEWLA), the NGO she established in 1995 in Bulaq el-Dakhrur, not far from downtown Cairo.

CEWLA works at two levels: It assists low-income women from the neighborhood by offering free legal aid, support through the bureaucratic processes for issuing identity cards or obtaining birth certificates, and counseling with regard to health and sexuality issues, including female circumcision and domestic violence. It also produces research and reports documenting the negative impact that Egyptian law and socioeconomic problems have on women. In the 1990s, CEWLA was the first organization to conduct systematic research on the "honor crime," a concept which, contrary to common knowledge, comes not from the shariʿa, but from the Napoleonic Penal Code (Article 324/1810), referring to the murder of a woman by a male family member for a perceived, and sometimes merely suspected, violation of the social norms about sexuality.[11] CEWLA openly questioned the mitigation of the penalty for this kind of murder in Egypt when this topic was still taboo.

Bulaq el-Dakhrur is an ʿashawiyya (informal neighborhood, or slum). The informal—that is, illegally constructed—housing that characterizes Bulaq el-Dakhrur is the norm in Egypt, not the exception, having first emerged in the 1960s as rural Egyptians migrated to the major cities to work. In Cairo about 63 percent of the population, comprising eleven million people out of the city's total population of approximately eighteen million, lives in eighty-one informal areas.[12] In the Giza governorate, there are thirty-two slum areas, and Bulaq el-Dakhrur is one of the largest and most densely populated. Most of its inhabitants come from the rural areas of the south, known for being socially conservative.

It is rare for a feminist organization to establish its headquarters in an ʿashawiyya; among the organizations I have visited over the years, CEWLA is the only one I am aware of. When Azza Soliman established CEWLA in 1995, Bulaq el-Dakhrur was described by urban studies scholars as "characterized by profound overcrowding and physical compactness."[13] Data collected in 1995 by the German Technical Cooperation Agency and the

Governorate of Giza for Bulaq el-Dakhrur indicated a population of 650,000 inhabitants living in an area of 300 hectares (approximately 741 acres), with a density of more than two thousand inhabitants per hectare (809 per acre).[14]

Bulaq el-Dakhrur is a short car drive from downtown, yet many people who don't live there perceive it as a dangerous, dirty, and violent place. These are common prejudices about the *'ashawiyyat*. Even if one does not perceive poor areas as inherently dangerous, it is true that traveling the short car ride from a middle-class urban space to an area where most of the roads aren't paved and poverty touches every one of the senses leaves one with a sense of unease. However, my perception of the area changed dramatically after my first visit to CEWLA as I came to understand the many different levels of life in Bulaq el-Dakhrur, and in other informal neighborhoods across Cairo.

Located on the second floor of a decaying building, Azza Soliman's office was neat and tidy. It was an ordinary busy morning; she had just come back from court, and several women from the neighborhood were waiting to talk to her. Soliman greeted me and invited me into her office. She was curious about my work, and she introduced me to her team, made up of young women and men, and gave me a brief overview about the neighborhood and CEWLA's work. Then she invited me to continue the conversation at her home later in the day.

After our initial meeting, I left Soliman's office and went for a short walk along the main street, stopping to buy a couple of bananas and chat with the fruit vendor, who exclaimed, *"Kunti 'ind Dr. Azza? Dr. Azza queisa!"* ("You visited Dr. Azza? She is good!"). The woman—I could not tell her age—did not want to speak much. She did not answer my questions about the ways in which Dr. Soliman is good; she just repeated the same sentence, echoed by other customers and passersby: "She is good! She helps people!"

Late in the afternoon of the same day, Soliman and I continued our conversation at her home in Heliopolis, where she and her son, a university student at the time of the interview, welcomed me with a warm, homemade meal. Over the meal, the conversation developed quite naturally around the relationships between feminism, Islam, and the state, a theme that is prominent in classical scholarship on feminism in Egypt and other Muslim majority countries,[15] and on which I wanted her input as a high-profile law practitioner, an activist, and a scholar. I started by asking her about CEWLA and the circumstances that inspired her to establish it, and we then walked back in history to the time when she was a university student and a new turn in the spiral of Egyptian feminism was starting to emerge.

"CELWA is like my baby," Soliman began when I asked about her long involvement with the organization. Smiling just like she does in all the photos and videos I had seen of her, she continued, "I established CEWLA in 1995 with my friends, male and female, in the marginalized area of Bulaq el-Dakhrur. Our purpose was to spread legal awareness among poor women and to provide them with legal services. But after a while we decided to work also with men and to offer literacy classes. These very soon became spaces to raise awareness, as we were talking about the meaning of the Constitution, the meaning of law, the importance of justice. We started to improve and develop, and in the process, I also developed myself.... This was our beginning."[16]

Concerns about lack of women's awareness of their legal rights and consequently of engagement with politics was a major concern among Egyptian feminist lawyers in the nineties.[17] In this broader context of women lawyers' activism, what qualified Azza Soliman and CEWLA's work is that gender and women's issues need to be addressed in relation to the broader social context. In an area like Bulaq el-Dakhrur, where there is a lot of poverty, and where the population has serious problems of housing, malnutrition, and health, she emphasized the necessity to take a grassroots approach to gender issues—that is, an approach that is grounded on people's experiences, that puts them at the center of the political action, and that is inclusive in targeting both women and men as gendered subjects.

Soliman's extensive and passionate work with women and men in Bulaq el-Dakhrur developed hand in hand with her interest in the reform of PSL, an area of the jurisprudence that, as I described earlier in this chapter, has been of high interest for women since the beginning of the twentieth century, and saw further development in feminist scholarship and initiatives since the mid-eighties. Soliman links the major problems she was witnessing among women in Bulaq el-Dakhrur (domestic violence, sometimes until femicide; circumcision; and incest) and the subaltern position of women in family law. The lower the social status of women, the more they would suffer from inequality in the application of family law. This is why, according to her, reform aimed at reweighting the balance of power between the two spouses within a marriage is necessary. She also noted that, contrary to common belief, the problem in Egypt is not limited to Islamic jurisprudence; it also concerns Egypt's Coptic Christian minority, who, like Catholics, cannot remarry within the church if they obtain a civil divorce. Moreover, with specific reference to Egypt, she noted that the status of women in family law is often a battlefield (and sometimes a terrain of negotiation) between the state and the Islamists and conservative religious officials. In fact, she continued, diverse practices and laws classified as "Muslim" result from different interpretations of religious texts and the political use of religion. The right to custody of children after divorce is a typical instance where juridical interpretations can vary according to the juridical school and the social context. For this reason, women across the Muslim world consider the study of family law an important key to defending their rights.

The professional and intellectual pathway taken by Azza Soliman was conjoined with CEWLA's work, which itself was twofold, combining theory with practice: on one side, she developed projects with CEWLA where poor women were given free legal advice; on the other, she produced research about the reality on the ground. CEWLA produced detailed research about the gender-related social problems in Bulaq el-Dakhrur, and in 2002 it published the first-ever report on the so-called honor crimes in Egypt.[18] Since then, the organization has been one of the points of reference for feminist activism in Egypt; hence, its reputation across many levels, from the Bulaq el-Dakhrur to internationally based human rights organizations is not surprising.

BECOMING A FEMINIST LAWYER IN EGYPT IN THE 1990S

Born in the late 1960s, Soliman grew up in the middle of the postcolonial age, when developmentalist agendas dominated global human and gender rights discourses. She understood early on that development without human rights goes nowhere, and that women are at the very crucial intersection between the two. This became clear to her especially through her social activism:

> I was working with the Egyptian Organization for Human Rights, where in 1993 I became the executive director of a project about women. For the first time, I developed an interest in the subject, especially family law. I was like a student; everything was new to me, especially because I come from a very normal family, where I [had] never seen or experienced violence. I was free in my family, and we had a very simple life. But since I started working on this project, I saw a lot of women who were beaten and abused by men, fathers, brothers, or uncles. I was shocked.[19]

The trajectory Soliman followed to become a human rights defender, self-confident enough to sit at the table with high-profile male representatives of Christian churches and sheikhs from Al-Azhar, and question conservative and misogynist interpretations of the scriptures, developed parallel to her grassroots activism: "I have been interested in helping people, especially poor people, since I was young. For instance, I used to read for children. I studied English, and I was encouraged to become a teacher, as this was considered appropriate for women, but I did not want that. I wanted to transfer to law. I went to attend a lecture on the constitution and . . . it was amazing. I loved it, and I decided to continue in law."[20]

The faculties of law have historically been main centers of student political activism, which continued as women increasingly made their presence felt between the fifties and the eighties, including women from rural backgrounds.[21] After full-on confrontations in the seventies, when Soliman enrolled in the Faculty of Law—in the eighties—the Mubarak regime had switched to a strategy of containment vis-à-vis student activism:

> There, I met some friends from high school, and I became a member of their group, which was the Gama'at al-dirasat al-'Arabiya [Association of Arab Studies]. They were Nasserist and a bit conservative about women. The first time I was arrested it was because of them, in 1988. The police took me because they could not find them, and they thought they could find them through me. It was scary, but useful for me. First, my family supported me, and second, this broke my fear of the police. The police tried to scare me, I was very young, eighteen or nineteen, and after this I became very strong.[22]

In 1994, Soliman was arrested again for writing, under the auspices of the Egyptian Organization for Human Rights, a report about women political dissidents who were members of Islamist groups, and for disseminating the report through BBC Arabic: "I visited them [the women] in jail, and I documented the tortures, including electrocution, about which I talked at BBC Arabic. The day after, the police came and arrested me. This time I was not as scared as the first one. Also, this arrest shows that the accusations I receive from Islamic organizations of being a liberal feminist who does not care about Muslim women are wrong. The reality is that I support the rule of law for everyone."[23] During that period, she started thinking of herself as "a natural feminist," an expression with which she alludes to the fact that her feminism is inspired from a deep sense of justice and her experience of social

WOMEN'S RIGHTS IN THE FAMILY AS HUMAN RIGHTS · 125

activism. She later began to study feminism and, like other activists from her generation, volunteered in the preparatory groups for the 1994 ICPD.

In 1997, the newly founded CEWLA under Soliman's direction launched a research project on violence against women, which was followed by grassroots actions to contain and combat female circumcision. Building on the feminist practice of engaging with people on their own ground, listening to the communities, and looking to them for solutions (as they are the best experts on the problems they live with), not to dissimilar to what the FGM Task Force and other feminist groups, such as the Nawal al-Saadawi's AWSA, were doing in the same years, CEWLA adopted a positive deviance approach to the issue.[24]

They contacted families in the poor neighborhoods of Cairo who did not mutilate their girls, as well as religious leaders who were against the practice. These "positive deviants" from the norm of practicing female circumcision were then trained to talk to people, sharing their experiences and persuading them to stop the practice. The success of the campaign, which involved a broad network of NGOs, was shared in international forums by both Azza Soliman, who in 1999 participated in a workshop on women and development organized in New York by the United Nations, and her fellow feminist colleagues.[25]

The half decade between the 1995 UN World Conference on Women in Beijing and the establishment of the National Council for Women in 2000 was a crucial time in Soliman's professional development, as it saw her focus both on grassroots work and on engagement with political parties (first Tagammu' and then the Nasserists), while also becoming involved feminist research and maturing international experience. This was also the period of the institutionalization of feminism in Egypt. This institutionalization of feminism was ongoing in a context where Mubarak's regime did not tolerate political oppositions yet it could not ignore women's rights. Women and gender were internationally mainstream issues in the late 1990s and early 2000s. Given that Egypt's economic growth and geopolitical status depended heavily on international support, it was important for the regime not to disappoint the international community with regard to women and gender.

Feminism needed to be at once embraced and contained. The regime tried to domesticate and depoliticize gender, framing women's issues as primarily family issues. Women lawyers and activists used the spaces that the regime allowed to continue to pressure for women rights and they obtained some reforms. In addition to the above-mentioned *khul'* law, in 2004 they obtained

FIGURE 9. Conference celebrating International Women's Day, early 2000s. Left to right: Azza Soliman, Somaya Ibrahim, Mervat Abou Teeg, and Nawla Darwiche. Courtesy of Nawla Darwiche.

that Egyptian women could give their nationality to their children automatically and unconditionally (except for children born by a Palestinian father; these were excluded by the law). This and other successes in the field of family law (the institution of Family Courts and of special funds to pay alimony to women and children until legal action against the father was taken) was the result of a long campaign, which began in the early 1980s and was led by prominent feminist lawyers, such as Mona Zulfikar, as well as feminist associations.

This situation of ambivalence of the regime toward women's rights continued well into the first decade of the twenty-first century. The modern Egyptian state has always represented itself as secular, yet it has frequently mobilized religion to legitimize its conservative and authoritarian agenda. Clearly, women's organizations like CEWLA, which emphasized the link between women's issues and broader political and socioeconomic matters, had to navigate very difficult waters. Azza Soliman said: "In April 2010 I participated in a demonstration with Kefaya and the 6th of April movement.[26] The police attacked us, and soon after, CEWLA was refused funding for four projects. I always participated in political actions as an individual, not as chairwoman of the organization. I even resigned as executive director of CEWLA, but of course this did not help, because for the police, CEWLA is Azza Soliman."[27]

During our conversations, Soliman frequently mentioned the interplay between the politicization of religious themes, especially with reference to women and gender, and authoritarian conservatism. She remembered that when she took her first steps in feminism and family law in the mid-nineties, some feminists criticized the fact that she was trying to find religiously grounded arguments to support her feminist claims. However, she insisted on the value of her approach: "These [religious-based arguments] for me are like tools, as much as the constitution or the international laws. I do grassroots work, and I know that religion is an important factor in people's lives; that's why I take it into account."[28]

Azza Soliman's work in the field of religion and women's rights was groundbreaking in relation not only to Islam but also to Christianity in Egypt: "I also broke taboos for Christian people. When I started talking about reforming family law for Christians in 1999, nobody, neither Catholics nor Protestants, could stand to talk about that in a conference panel. Now we have them on board."[29] The dialectic between religion and feminism has been complex, and as we have seen in earlier chapters, it has been a matter of continuous negotiation, with feminists taking different positions across time—endorsing the modern reformism at the end of the nineteenth century, then shifting more toward laicism in the 1970s. Yet even within those two broad periods we can find contrasting currents of thought.

For instance, in the late nineteenth and early twentieth century, when the mainstream cultural paradigm was modernist and secular, there were women scholars such as Hind Nawfal and 'Aisha Ratib who tried to open a critical discussion about the use of religious sources to limit women's rights. And in the second half of the twentieth century, when feminism became more laicist, there were women who claimed political agency not within the feminist framework but in the context of Islamist political formations, or in the cultural Islamic revival, while others joined pious (not to be confused with Islamist) movements.[30] In the 1990s, while these various positions and views continued, the repositioning of religion in the public space prompted many feminist Muslim intellectuals to develop an Islamic feminist approach. This intellectual framework was developed by Muslim feminist scholars (mostly in the fields of law and theology, since the mid-1980s) across the Muslim world, from Iran to Pakistan, Algeria, Morocco, Sudan, Mauritius, Tanzania, and Bangladesh.

128 • WOMEN'S RIGHTS IN THE FAMILY AS HUMAN RIGHTS

This intellectual movement was inspired by the urgency to organize and campaign against the growth of global Islamism and both religious fundamentalism and military or authoritarian states, which sometimes were also allied. The core idea of Islamic feminism was to reconcile the practices of Islam with the paradigms of women and human's rights.[31] In fact, Islamic feminism, grounded on a feminist hermeneutics and exegesis of the Islamic sources and jurisprudence to promote gender equality both in the public and in the private sphere, in Egypt developed through the work by women intellectuals such as Omaima Abu Bakr (professor of English and comparative literature in the Department of English Language and Literature at Cairo University, and a founding member of the Women and Memory Forum), Margot Badran,[32] Marwa Sharafeldin[33] and Fatma Imam.[34]

In 2009, Azza Soliman participated with Egyptian feminists Marwa Sharafeldine, Amal Abdel Hadi, and Margot Badran in the first conference of Musawah, the Malaysia-based Muslim Women Network, to promote what the network refers to as "equality in the Muslim family," referring in particular to equality between spouses in family law. "I was a founding member of Musawah, which for me was an amazing experience. Since I was young, I've tried to break a lot of taboos about religion. I always thought Islam stood for justice, fairness, and equality. Musawah uses progressive Islam to support women against conservative people, or people who use Islam against women."

Why does Azza Soliman demur from identifying herself with "Islamic feminism"? As she explained to me, "I am not an Islamic feminist. What I do is just *fiqh*," meaning that she actively contributes to the construction of Islamic jurisprudence. My impression was that she was choosing to keep her feminist identity and her strategy to reform family law separate, as if labeling the strategy as "feminist" would undermine its legitimacy. Desiring to better understand her wanting to keep feminism and family law separate, something that appeared to me as a contradiction, I asked her about her intellectual points of reference. She answered that the writings of Fatima Mernissi, the Moroccan sociologist who pioneered a feminist interpretation of Islamic history and its sacred texts, occupy a special space on her bookshelves. However, her main sources of inspiration are her associations with fellow feminists. As she spoke she recalled vividly how much she learned from Aida Seif El-Dawla, Aziza Hussein, and Marie Assaad, whom she remembers as "real feminists": "From Aziza Hussein I have learned how to work together and be part of a team. It is not important who can speak, who is at the forefront. The focus should be on the work, not the individual. And she was proud about any generation. I remember all the time feeling supported and respected by her." Throughout the interview, she stressed the words "support" and "respect," two words that have stayed with me as indicating what has nourished Azza Soliman's relationship with the elder feminists and what she offers to the next generation.

FACING TRAUMA AND RESISTING STATE VIOLENCE AFTER 2011

During our conversation, Azza Soliman did not have any doubts about the positive impact of the January 25 Revolution on Egyptian women: "Yes, I think it was very important for a lot of women, and I think that even if we did not succeed on the political level, we somehow succeeded in some issues in social and cultural fields." She commented that we now find a lot of women deciding independently of anyone if they want to wear or not wear the hijab. She said that for her, the issue is not the hijab per se; she wore it when she was young, and many women in her family and her work team are still wearing it. Her main concern has always been the freedom of choice. She also commented that today we see a lot of women talking about sexual abuse and talking about freedom: "You can find a lot of movements, from young people, women and men working together. You can find a lot of initiatives supporting women to become independent. And you can find many initiatives about new interpretations, modern discourses in religion, including Christian young people who dare to criticize the church. So, you can find many things you could not even imagine before."[35]

When I asked her about her own experience during the 2011 Revolution, she explained that during the first days, she did not go to the Square: "My sons went, and the police arrested the young one. He was fifteen years old. The eldest one saved him. The 28th I was driving back from Ismailia with the late Afef Marai and with Amal Abdel Hadi. When we arrived at the 6th of October bridge, we stopped and . . . suddenly we lost each other." Then she hesitated: ". . . I don't want to talk. This is very hard for me. It is not easy."

It is not unusual that during the narration of a traumatic experience, the woman I am interviewing interrupts the flow of the narration. Sometimes the story continues, sometimes we move to a less traumatic memory. I felt that, in this instance, it was better to move to another topic, so we shifted to an analysis of contemporary politics. Azza Soliman is a convinced advocate of the secular State, which she contrasted with the illiberal policies of the Muslim Brotherhood, the major Islamic political formation in Egypt (formed in 1928, it went through multiple phases of repression and revival; the Justice and Freedom Party they formed after the 2011 Revolution won the elections in 2011–12, and both the MB and the JF Party were eventually banned after the 2013 coup). The post–2013 decade was marked by the government's determination to eradicate them. However, her most critical words were for the current El-Sisi regime: "This is the worst period," she said without hesitation.

As is true for many other Egyptian women I have interviewed over the years, Azza Soliman's experiences during the tumultuous years following the 2011 Revolution were punctuated by a number of traumatic events. As I am writing these lines, I remember the moment Soliman's iconic smile faded during the interview: "In January 2015, I was having lunch in downtown when I heard the noise of a demonstration." She went to see what was going on, only to witness the assassination of young woman political activist, ethnographer (a major expert of Egyptian folk culture), and poet Shaima' al-Sabbagh, who was shot dead while bringing flowers to Tahrir Square on the fourth anniversary of the 2011 Uprising. The violent assassination of Shaima' al-Sabbagh was narrated as a traumatic experience by many of the activists I interviewed, and the memory of this brave young woman still haunts the stories of the period subsequent to the 2013 coup today.

Azza Soliman voluntarily went to the public prosecutor's office on January 24, 2015, to give her testimony about the facts. On March 23, 2015, the Egyptian prosecutor decided that she was no longer a witness in the case but a defendant. She was accused of protesting illegally and of breaching public order and security. On May 23, 2015, Soliman was acquitted by the Qasr el-Nil Court. Less than three days later, the Qasr el-Nil Prosecution appealed the acquittal, which was then confirmed.

However, a few months later, in November 2016, as she was traveling to Jordan to participate in a training for the Musawah network, she was informed by the authorities that she was banned from traveling. This followed a judicial order enacted that same day by the investigative judge in Case 173/2011, commonly known as the "NGOs foreign funding case," which also ordered the freezing of her personal as well as her law firm's assets. On December 7, 2016, she was arrested at her home and interrogated as part of an ongoing investigation in the foreign funding case. She was released on the same day on bail, pending investigation, and eventually cleared of charges in February 2022.

WEAVING FEMINISM ACROSS GENERATIONS

In Egypt, as in other parts of the world, women have had to claim their own space in the legal professions, and the journey has not been easy. Inequalities at multiple levels remain in place today. Law scholar Radwa Elsaman points out that even if the 2014 postrevolutionary Egyptian constitution provides women with the right to appointment to judicial bodies, discrimination against Egyptian women when it comes to accessing judicial jobs continues.[36] While full equality has yet to come, there is no doubt that the presence that women gained in the legal professions through the twentieth century has had a clear impact, not only on the debate about the necessity to reform PSL—a debate that began in the early twentieth century and is still unfolding in Egypt—but also on the ways they conceive and organize their grassroots work.

There is a legacy left by women who have been involved in legal professions that continues well into the present, and this legacy emerges clearly in the political lives of contemporary activists in the field. Azza Soliman's political evolution needs to be read alongside this genealogy. Like other feminists of her generation, she joined the standard political formations in the 1980s (particularly the university students' organizations), the human rights organizations in the 1990s, and the transnational networks of Muslim feminist women in the early 2000s. Moreover, she has animated grassroots social work activities among disadvantaged communities since she was a young woman. Such multilayered experiences shape the approach to feminism that characterizes feminism in Egypt through the 1990s and early 2000s. This period was diverse and covered different areas of action, from traditional political spaces (political parties and institutions) to the cultural and intellectual sphere, grassroots and NGO work, and social movements.

A common characteristic of all these streams of feminism is the intersection of political, cultural, and socioeconomic themes. In the experience of Azza Soliman, and more broadly of women in the legal professions, the intersection between legal rights and socioeconomic rights appears clear. This intersection led organizations like CEWLA to combine grassroots social work with research and public advocacy, bridging the traditional gap between intellectual and grassroots activism, a gap for which feminists are often blamed, even if they are not the only ones who can be accused of it (Marxist male circles weren't any better in this respect).

Another key characteristic of feminism in Egypt in the 1990s and early 2000s that emerges from Azza Soliman's political biography is the continuing renegotiation of the relationship between feminism and religion. In the nineties, this process happened as religion was repositioned in public discourse from a marginal to a more central space. This occurred in the context of an authoritarian state that tried to co-opt both the religious authorities and the feminist activists, while also bargaining with the Islamists (who were not part of the religious establishment and were, obviously, averse to the feminists) by encouraging conservative practices and mentalities.

Feminist lawyers working on PSL were well equipped to engage in the public discourse about gender and religion, and to foreshadow more liberal perspectives about gender. They could do this because there was a tradition of Islamic reformism to which Egyptian women had contributed all through the twentieth century, and because there were transnational intellectual networks supporting the advancement of this kind of knowledge.

Indeed, what weaves all these threads together is the transgenerational solidarity that characterized the experiences of feminists throughout the twentieth century and that became particularly evident in the 1990s and early 2000s. This transgenerational solidarity became crucial when they faced traumatic experiences, such as the assassination of Shaima' al-Sabbagh, and as they dealt with grief, especially after the 2013 coup, which crushed their hopes for political change.

WOMEN'S RIGHTS IN THE FAMILY AS HUMAN RIGHTS · 133

SEVEN

Toward an Ethics of Care

THE POLITICAL JOURNEY OF GAMEELA ISMAIL

ON NOVEMBER 24, 2011, I joined a women's march from the Cairo Opera House to Tahrir Square. The demonstrators were protesting the violence of the army, including the use of tear gas, which had engulfed Muhammad Mahmoud Street leading into Tahrir the previous days. As I spoke to some of them, I understood that they were not veterans of the Square, let alone seasoned political activists. As one marcher explained: "[We are here] because we are against violence, what's happening. . . . I am not a political person. I would be lying if I told you that I know a lot about politics. I'm just here as a human action for all the people who have died and the use of the gases, and that's it."[1]

In the following weeks the widespread nature of the renewed political involvement since Mubarak's removal from power became clear. Ten months after the January 2011 Revolution, almost everyone in Egypt, from the academics and their students to artists and public intellectuals, small retailers, urban workers, and peasants, were not only keen to talk about politics but to go onto the streets and protest if necessary. Eighteen days in January and February 2011 had changed—at least for the time being—Egyptians' perception of politics. People once again believed they could make a difference.

After the women's demonstration ended, Mariam, among the youngest yet most experienced women demonstration leaders I'd spoken to that day,[2] invited me to join her at Café Riche, a historical café in downtown Cairo where supporters of revolutions have gathered since 1919. She introduced me to a group of young activists, among them was her friend Noor: "This is Noor, Gameela's son. You should meet his mother! She is the one whose face is on the big posters. She is great and she is running for Parliament."

Mariam was referring to Gameela Ismail, a journalist who since the early nineties had been working at Egyptian Television Network as a reporter and on-air presenter, while also being a democracy activist and politician. At that time, Gameela Ismail was running as an independent candidate for the first parliamentary elections since the fall of Mubarak. Electoral posters, her face foregrounded, were towering around the Qasr el-Nil bridge, next to the posters of her political competitors (mostly male), including the Salafi party, who represented women candidates with a rose rather than show their faces.

In the following weeks many other young revolutionary women from different political backgrounds would encourage me to talk to Gameela Ismail, and their enthusiasm sparked my curiosity. During those heady if bloody days of November and December 2011, when the revolution seemed reborn amid the renewed occupation of Tahrir and serious fighting with security forces, many activists did not consider parliamentary elections the best way forward. They did not really have a plan for the transition, but most of them believed that there should not be free elections while the Supreme Council of the Armed Forces (SCAF) governed the country. They thus called for a new constitution and an end to military trials for civilians before elections took place.

Other activists saw the elections as an opportunity to transition from military to civilian rule and thus invited people to take part in the democratic process, however flawed. Alliances and positionings in the political field were in the making and new political parties emerging. In November 2011, demonstrations became violent clashes between the revolutionaries and the armed forces in Muhammad Mahmoud Street.

It soon became clear that Gameela's popularity transcended political divides. In interviews with women across the political spectrum, from Revolutionary Socialists to liberals and Islamists, in each camp I always found someone who would refer to Gameela Ismail as an inspiring figure. I asked a young activist of the Egyptian Youth Federation (one of the many ephemeral political youth formations that emerged soon after the January 2011 Revolution) to name an inspiring political figure in the post-Mubarak period: "Gameela Ismail, for example," she responded without hesitation: "She is not even in the top of the candidates . . . and this is very bad because she was our hope. . . . Because all the others, like the Islamists, have a woman in the list just to have a woman, and say, *you see . . . we also have a woman.*"[3]

I collected many testimonies of young women who were discouraged seeing female candidates not in top positions for the elections. Retrospectively, their fear of underrepresentation proved prescient. The rate of representation

FIGURE 10. Gameela Ismail during the electoral campaign in 2011. Photo by Bassam Allam. Courtesy of Gameela Ismail.

of women in the newly elected Parliament in 2012 was less than 2 percent. But the comment of this young woman also pointed at the politics of co-optation that had traditionally characterized the electoral strategy of the Egyptian political parties with regards to women: notwithstanding a century of women's political activism, there remained a wide gender gap in the Egyptian political field. Having women among their ranks would improve the image of political parties but would seldom translate into a high percentage of women in leadership positions or promoting policies that advanced women's rights. Women political activists were of course aware of the gender gap and tried, from different positionalities and with different strategies, to make their presence in politics meaningful and effective. Others deliberately decided to abandon or not even enter the institutional political field but rather focused on professional work, aiming at influencing the reform of the Personal Status Law and the ways media depicted women- and gender-related issues (especially, but not only, violence against women) through business and corporate work. Through some successes and more failures, what became clear was that they always worked in a very hostile political and social space, carrying a double burden: authoritarianism and patriarchy.

Some were part of feminist networks, others were not, and did not foreground feminism as a framework for their political thought. This was the case with Gameela when we first met. At the time, she did not refer to herself as a feminist, despite having a long history of working on issues related to women and human rights. She was, however, a media icon; her face well known to a large share of the Egyptian public. As an activist, she carried out grassroots work with an unwavering commitment to social and economic justice. Her work gained her the respect of many radical feminists of the new generation, especially because most of them, in the first phases of the revolution, were focused on broader political activism without a specifically feminist agenda.

All these elements inspired me to expand my field of investigation beyond the traditional feminist field, trying to understand how a public figure who was not part of any of the feminist networks that populated Egyptian politics in the last three decades of the twentieth century could speak to a new generation of feminist activists in the twentieth-first century. Looking more in-depth into the biography of Gameela Ismail and following her political trajectory from her youth in the 1980s to her time as president of the Dostour Party[4] since 2022, including her participation in the National Dialogue in 2023[5] and leading the Civil Movement for Democracy in 2024,[6] also allowed me to expand my understanding of some peculiarities of women's approaches to the intersection between grassroots and institutional politics in contemporary Egypt. Lastly, over time I had the opportunity to observe both young women's and Gameela's changing visions about feminism, and about the potentials for political change that can come from exercising a horizontal feminist leadership.

ONE LINK IN A LONG CHAIN

I first met Gameela in January 2018. My initial interview with her focused on her work as a journalist. Subsequent discussions in person and by email, as well as observing her at work and interviewing other members of the Dostour Party, allowed me to deepen my understanding of the complex entanglements between her family, professional, and political lives, and how this contributed to the evolution of her political visions.

Gameela Ismail's political profile is a combination of multiple experiences: the journalist; the ex-wife of a high-profile MP of the opposition and a political prisoner under Mubarak (Ayman Nour); the mother of two young activists of the Egyptian underground metal scene in the mid-2000s and then part of the revolution (Noor Ayman Nour and Shady Nour);[7] and a politician in her own right since the early 2000s.

Her profile as a journalist is the first element of her story that requires contextualization. Here, it's important to remember two things: first, that journalism was one of the first modern professions in which women entered, since the late nineteenth century, initiating a long tradition of high-profile women journalists in Egypt, including both mainstream and state-owned and popular media, as well as editing journals dedicated to and focused on women.[8] The continuing and often high-profile presence of women in the press ensured that women's issues were constantly brought to the attention of the public debate, and the biographies of women journalists offered inspiring models for the young generations. The journalists of Gameela's generation emerged on the shoulders of a long genealogy.

At a more personal level, the figure that had a professional impact on Gameela is her mother, Egypt's trailblazer documentary filmmaker, Farida Arman. Farida was one of the few women of the first cohort of students graduated in 1959 from the journalism department at the Faculty of Literature at Cairo University. Arman's commitment to her work shaped Gameela's upbringing since she basically grew up among the cameras, the news, and the stories of the people across the country. In her biography then, the professional and the family life, the public and the private, are merged since the early years.

> I grew up with a very strong mama who was very fragile [at] the same time. She was very well known. Her name was enough to open any door and film behind it. Working for the state-owned TV, the *only* one back then, was such a big thing. Media back then meant something totally different than today. Working with the media meant no less than working at the most senior posts in the government. Maybe even more important, welcomed by everyone. She toured the country up and down, filmed and produced hundreds of films and songs and eventually won awards at many prominent festivals. Since my early childhood, I was walking hand by hand with her and around filming locations in places which she chose to film and listening to people across the country. I even took part in the films since I was five years, when I acted in "Egyptian Weddings," which she filmed in every part of Egypt. Around a crew of twenty, my mother was the only one to say "Rolling" and "Stop."[9]

Gameela's mother suffered a great tragedy when she lost her daughter Amira in a terrible accident. The two-year-old girl fell off the balcony while

Farida was engaged in an editing session at Maspero, the state TV building, a ten-minute walk from their home. Gameela was six years old: "My mother came back to find her body on the street surrounded by strangers. The baby-sitter said she was busy cooking. I was rehearsing for a school concert. My brother was studying. In the following years, she grieved. We were never able to celebrate birthdays or watch TV; grief traditions ban these in case of deaths. She must have suffered a lot of pain and guilt feelings . . . but she never stopped working. Her mother advised her to have another child. My second brother, Ismail, was born a year after in 1973."[10]

Farida continued to work intensively until the end of her life; when she died in 2018 at the age of eighty, she left behind an important audiovisual archive, including rare footage of Egyptian antiquities, communities, and areas. Gameela created a foundation named after her mother to collect and organize her artistic and intellectual legacy.

If Farida was perhaps the most influential figure in Gameela's life, her three sisters, and especially Eman, were also points of reference. Eman worked for many years in the Ministry of Education and later as a director of educational programs at Egyptian TV, traveling frequently in Egypt and abroad with her sister: "We were all the time filming, filming, filming!" she told me with enthusiastic nostalgia when I asked her about her relationship with Farida.[11]

Gameela took me to meet Eman for the first time in January 2020. A stylishly dressed woman wearing a dark headwrap opened the door to an elegant apartment in downtown Cairo. Eman appeared a bit upset when her niece showed up more than two hours later than expected, but then she couldn't hide her amusement: "This is how she is . . . she is always busy . . . she has always been like that. She keeps you waiting for hours, then she is at your door and hugs you: 'Mwah, Mwah, Mwah! I love you, auntie!' And this is it!"

In her interview, Gameela emphasized multiple times how her mother and aunties, a group of four high-achieving sisters who had all worked in media and education from the 1960s until the early 2000s, had been at once a source of inspiration and a model she wanted to differentiate herself from. With roots in Qena, in Upper Egypt, where conservative traditions dominate, Gameela well summarized the predicament all ambitious women in her family faced in their careers, and in their lives more broadly: "Women were strong in everything, academically, professionally . . . but not against traditions." In this statement, I have read a desire to also break traditions, which I have heard in other testimonies of women I interviewed and found articulated in most of their writings. I then tried to learn more about Gameela's personal trajectory in her adult life and in the context of Egyptian social and political history.

Gameela studied TV journalism at Cairo University while simultaneously interpreting (Arabic and English) at the American University in Cairo, completing her degree in 1986 at just nineteen while working as an active member of the students' union. Weeks after her graduation, she started working at the Cairo bureau of *Newsweek,* and in 1990 started working at Egyptian State Channel 3, covering the region of Greater Cairo. Her specialty was presenting street programs filmed in the disadvantaged neighborhoods in downtown Cairo, where she interviewed some of the city's most marginalized people. By 2005, she had become a well-known television presenter, to the point of exceeding her mother's fame: "People would ask her if she was 'Gameela's mum,' to which she responded with a hint of annoyance: 'No, she is Farida's daughter!'"

But already in the early nineties, Gameela's voice was considered too critical to be tolerated by the regime, especially after she married the prominent politician Ayman Noor in 1989. Together, the couple cofounded a charity association in the early 1990s, naming it after Noor, their first son:

> There was this constant passion that started back in the eighties in the university, in the scouts and guides team, to help people with their day-to-day struggles, listen to them, share with others to assist.... Later, I started through my connections as a TV journalist to accompany them to the relevant official entitled to decide to help them stay alive.... This walk in, with no appointment, to the door of the official empowered them and raised their confidence and mine as well. On the way, we would have some discussions around current affairs, their reality and some views that might have helped raise their political awareness. I was always for some reason or another a magnet. I never knew why they felt comfortable to talk and trusted the connection, the communication and moreover filming.[12]

Although she never referred to it as feminism in interviews, since her early activism in the eighties (which coincided with the implementation of more intensive neoliberal reforms by the Egyptian government), Gameela's grassroots work reminded me of what feminist philosophers have described as care:[13] an organizing principle that transcends the sphere of the private and family life to embrace the broader public sphere. Specifically, the insights of Italian philosopher Elena Pulcini on politics and emotions, and especially the importance of empathy to build an ethics of care, are useful to understand the political trajectory of Gameela and the invisible thread that links her experience to her contemporary Egyptian feminists I have been focusing on earlier in this book. There is an overarching characteristic in the work of the women who, over the twentieth and the twenty-first centuries, engaged in politics, bridging the differences across the feminist and the nonfeminist field, and across ideological political disagreements. Specifically, these actions comprise what in Pulcini's words are the tension to "care towards the unknown," which is the capacity to extend the ethics of care beyond the family and close relationships.[14]

Far from being an extension to the public sphere of the maternal function of women, the ethics of care is an idea that questions the abstract and rationalistic nature of modern ethics of justice, based on the individualistic presuppositions of rights and autonomy. This is why a politics based on care, especially care toward the "distant other" (where the idea of distance refers not only to geography but also to metaphorical distance, and even future generations) can have transformative potential for the entire society.[15] In the context of Egypt, where state institutions still function vis-à-vis citizens like the colonial administration, the ethics of care characterizes the practice of women, particularly those positioned at the margins (if not outside) the formal institutions. Gameela's personal, professional, and political trajectories, situated at the seeming margins of both institutional politics and feminist activism, provide useful insights to understand the ethics of care that shaped the broader human rights movement in Egypt, led to the 2011 Revolution, and keeps its flame lit amid the difficult circumstances imposed by the renewed and even upgraded authoritarianism of the Sisi regime.

"FEAR KILLS THE SOUL!": A LIFE FOR POLITICS

Inspired by an ethics of care rather than a concern with acceptable political discourse, Gameela's work in politics caused problems equally with her family and the authorities. Broadcast and print journalism were fine if within the margins drawn by the state, but anything that exceeded her professional activities as a TV journalist was considered by her mother as a threat to her safety and the family's. Even if Gameela could understand the roots of her mother's concerns, she could not follow her advice: "Yes, they were afraid that my life and freedom would be in danger . . . but, again, *fear kills the soul*, as Naguib Mahfouz once wrote. I think this is why I got married so early. I wanted to leave the house. To move away from any authority, even that which comes out of love. This was the only way I could leave the house."[16]

In 1987, when she became engaged to Ayman Nour, Gameela Ismail was twenty-one-years old. Ayman Nour was then a fellow journalist at *al-Wafd Daily*. The couple shared decades of pro-democracy activism, cofounding the political party al-Ghad (Tomorrow) in 2004. Ayman Nour soon became a prominent politician, the youngest person to be elected in the Egyptian Parliament. Popularity came at a high price for the family; indeed, the story of harassment endured by the Ismail-Nour family returns to the early 2000s.

The electoral success of the al-Ghad Party in the 2005 elections meant that very soon Ayman Nour came to be seen as a possible threat by the authorities, as he could possibly win if he ran for president. He was incarcerated the first time in 2004, then again from 2005 to 2010, during which he was repeatedly tortured. In this period, Gameela had to take the lead of the political party, to solo parent their two sons, and to campaign in Egypt and abroad for her husband's release. She was under the eye of the regime and not allowed on air since she staged a protest to demand the release of her husband in 2005. Constantly harassed, she was receiving anonymous phone calls in the middle of the night to let her know that they were watching her, she was being attacked by the media, and the headquarters of al-Ghad Party in downtown Cairo was even set on fire while she was inside.

Gameela never gave up. Like other women I've discussed in this book who had an indirect yet effective impact on politics—especially the wives, sisters, and mothers of political prisoners—Gameela's strenuous work eventually brought some success. At the end of 2008, she took the risk of traveling to Washington, DC, to advocate for the cause of her husband and other political prisoners at the White House. In February 2009, a few months before he would have completed his prison sentence, Ayman Nour was released, allegedly for health concerns. In August of the same year, Barack Obama met Hosni Mubarak, and the violations of human rights were on the agenda of the meeting.

The regime freed Ayman, but they did not forgive Gameela for her activism on his behalf. She was attacked by Egyptian newspapers, while rumors of her possible arrest circulated. In fact, after the fall of Mubarak's regime, she received an offer from the Ministry of Information to be the head of State Television: "So . . . you see? From being prohibited to be the head of State Television." She didn't accept this offer because she feared that this was a case of tokenism. She did not want her name to be used to crush employee protests—for example, the upward of forty thousand employees of State

Television were still being denied basic rights as employees and journalists. There were a lot of injustices, and after the revolution they also expected a change to happen. "It was a very hard decision for me, because of the family I come from. My mother used to be a senior person in television." She then smiled: "It was difficult for me with my mother. She was an institutional person and she always thought that I was meant to be 'larger than life.' She thought that this was the best chance I could ever get. To everyone, it was shocking that I said no."[17]

Her instinct against accepting the position as head of State Television proved prescient, given the wholesale repression that would return after the 2013 military coup. In the meantime, the politicization of the media continued in Egypt well after the fall of Mubarak. Under the government of the Brotherhood-aligned Freedom and Justice Party, Gameela continued to be banned from appearing on TV. Not surprisingly, the same occurred during military rule and during the rule of President El-Sisi: "Every other week, I go, and I file a new complaint. I write a new request, saying, 'I want to be back at work. I want to work.' Every month, they deposit my salary onto my debit card, and they make sure that, according to the law and the regulations, I get my money, so that I do not have anything to say apart from the fact that I'm not working. I want to work. You know, until the day before yesterday, my mother was very unhappy, because she thinks that what I'm doing is . . . it's a very simple job. She says: 'What are you doing online? Gameela Ismail online? Why? Why don't you go back?' . . . You know, she's very old, and she has these ideas that perhaps I am exaggerating. She said, 'They will tell you to stop attacking the regime. So, stop!'"

It is hard to imagine that Gameela's mother did not know her daughter well enough to be aware that she was not the kind of woman to be easily stopped. And, indeed, being banned by State Television was not enough to stop her. In 2017, she started a new project, Hekayyat Gameela (Gameela's Talks), as part of the cultural project Medinaportal, with her colleague Wael Abdel Fattah (a major cultural journalist in Egypt and a mentor for many younger journalists). With her iPhone and a small microphone, she began filming interviews with people about current affairs. When I ask her about Medinaportal, the tone of her voice reflects the creative flair that she must have had when she conceived the idea:

> What's more important for me, and makes me feel very happy, is that I am reflecting what many people in the society and especially young people feel.

TOWARD AN ETHICS OF CARE · 143

The people I meet with are people who don't find a space in mainstream television. Simple people cannot reach any of these television stations. They're not there: you can't see them. Even if you see them, what they say will be cut, and censored. So, I have them on, and they speak to me intimately. They don't have a problem speaking the truth. I listen to what they are saying, and I write my story, and I include their quotes. I get all of this to the younger generations. We are trying to fly under the radar for the time being. I don't use a direct political narrative that will make people afraid. I want people to talk to me and to watch this without sensing that it's a direct political statement. I believe that we must find and figure out new ways to survive, and to attract people back to us, away from this authoritativeness, away from this black, disgusting propaganda that's happening every day. How can we do this? It's a very difficult challenge.[18]

It is the same interest for fieldwork journalism that informs Gameela's political activism: "It depends on how you identify politicians," she told me when I asked her about women in politics, "because, you know, to me a politician is not just a person who is a member of a political party, but who is able to work with different kinds of people, within a constituency, or within an area."

Gameela underlined the importance of grassroot work for politicians, and even questioned my focus on women and gender, pointing out that we can find women parliamentarians or women members in political parties without having strong connections to the grassroots. In her view, women and gender issues need to be addressed primarily as socioeconomic issues. Interestingly, this view is like the one expressed by many Egyptian women activists across the political spectrum I have interviewed, as well as for the first generation of activists in the early twentieth century, as described in their memoirs. Women coming with different intellectual and political genealogies and from different eras, they all seem to agree on the general principle that socioeconomic issues are at heart women and gender issues because women are the most affected by them.

What Egyptian women political activists have tried to do over time, and in a more visible and explicit way in the post–Cold War era, was focus mostly on campaigns, and undertaking simultaneous and multiple actions that range from empathically connecting with people from disadvantaged socioeconomic backgrounds, trying to understand what their material needs are, and addressing them to create the conditions for democracy. This ethics of care emphasizes the importance of relationships and interdependence, and through them, the fundamental role of sentiments and emotions. The ethics of care does not fit into any neat or traditional categorization because it goes beyond any identity politics to include struggling for the conditions that would enable all people to not only live in dignity but to thrive and live meaningful lives.[19] This freedom from any orthodoxy and focus on people's experiences is what characterizes Gameela's activism, and this is what makes her particularly meaningful and close to many women of the younger generations.

THE MANY FACES OF POLITICAL VIOLENCE UNDER THE MUBARAK REGIME

The right to run for elections granted to Egyptian women alongside suffrage in 1956 did not guarantee equality in actual political representation. In fact, over the course of the second half of the twentieth century, Egypt has constantly scored very low vis-à-vis women's presence in Parliament. The political activists I interviewed have been, at different stages of their lives, involved in some sort of campaign to support women candidates, and they all expressed some level of frustration for the lack of progress with respect to equality. I have already discussed the trajectory that led to the acknowledgment of women's suffrage and the double burden carried by women politicians under the Nasser and Sadat regimes, having to face both the state's repression of independent political forces and gender inequalities. The last decade of Mubarak's regime presented a new layer of complexity with the institutionalization of neoliberal feminism and its organicity with the regime, and Gameela's experience when she ran for elections in 2001, in 2010, and in 2011 well illustrates the high level of violence sustained by independent political women activists at that time. The first time, in 2001, Gameela ran for the Shura Council (Parliament). Her main competitor was the head of the National Democratic Party: "His name was Mohamed Ragab, and he was the godfather of and the teacher of Gamal Mubarak at that time. He was a very influential guy. I think he was just over seventy years old, and I was just thirty-four years old, then. I lost against him, of course. But I think it was the first big shake from a woman candidate against one of the very strong powerful figures of the NDP then."[20]

In 2001, the Egyptian Parliament comprised less than 4 percent women, one of the lowest rates across the Arab world. In that context, Gameela's performance was quite successful, especially as her potential constituency was known to be very conservative:

In central Cairo, in poor areas, which had layers of society that started from the middle class downward, it was a shock, then, to him [she means her adversary in the elections] that even men would vote for a woman, men who were not educated or who did not belong to the intellectual class. Because, in fact, [it was] because of my experience. It wasn't a matter of men or women: it was a matter of credibility and how trust and credibility among people are built. How can you be seen, from their end, as somebody who delivers? Somebody who can quickly support them, who can understand their suffering. Even if you try with a hundred cases and you succeed with five, helping and changing their reality, the 95 percent will still remember what you have done for the 5 percent.[21]

The grassroots political work she did during her campaigns led her to interrogate herself about how to approach women, and to question the benefits of trying to design a specific agenda for women. Instead, she focused on socioeconomic issues:

In 1998 and '99, I did research in my constituency, and I found out that 80 percent of the women had been abandoned. Their husbands just left, disappeared. They have been left struggling, knowing that there was nothing else to do. These women were the victims of the continuous failure of the government to provide services for them. Can I go to one of these women, in my constituency, and talk to them about her sexual rights? Or about the difference between having sex and being raped by her husband? Could I put these kinds of feminist issues in my electoral program, for instance? No, I can't, because they want to hear completely different things. They want to hear the same things that men want to hear. They want to hear how they can solve their problems, how they will make a life; how they can save their children and find a place to live in; how to move from a temporary residence to a permanent one; how [to have a] regular income to cover their living expenses, and so on.[22]

This is an old dilemma, to which Egyptian women political activists have responded in multiple ways over a century of feminist activism, especially the intersection between Egyptian authoritarianism and global political economy. Particularly in the decade before the 2011 Revolution, the alliance between neoliberal capitalism (exploiting poor people) and the authoritarian regime (policing them) left women political activists with very few spaces for action.

This authoritarian-capitalist alliance also had direct consequences for political activists and their own understanding of their positionality. With reference to her personal experience, Gameela was ambivalent. On one hand, she argued that what made the difference for her was not just being a woman but rather being a dissident. On the other, she acknowledged that the kind of harassment she experienced for being a dissident targeted her in a specific way because she is a woman:

> It always depends on individual experiences. But, again, I'm talking about my own experience. I never thought, or felt, that operating as a woman could turn people off in politics, or in elections. It wasn't, to me, a matter of gender. It was, to me, many other issues, like whether one is pro-regime, or very supportive, or just supportive, or opposing, or attacking the regime. This is how the regime and the security organs identify you in any of the election processes. If you are very, very supportive, whether a woman or a man, you are going to win, you will be helped until the end. If you are in the middle, or if you are opposing and attacking, they will be unhappy with you, whether you are a man or a woman. But, targeting you is of course more attractive to them if you are a woman. Of course, it can hurt.[23]

During her 2001 campaign, Gameela was physically harassed by *baltagiya* (gangs of thugs in plain clothes hired by the police or the intelligence to attack regime targets) as part of government attempts to discourage potential candidates from running.

> I had a very bad experience that pushed me away from politics for several months after the elections. I was working with a program that I thought was very useful for my constituency, with women, because the police station that was in this constituency was a central point for prostitution. A woman who gets caught and convicted of prostitution, after she is released from jail, she must attend the police station every day for three years, from six o'clock in the evening until six o'clock in the morning. Of course, she gets terribly abused while she is there. Even if she has been accused unfairly, if she is facing an injustice, she is classified as a prostitute, and this has consequences on how the police deal with her. So, when I started my program, I had faith that if we can help these former prostitutes and find a way for them to live, they would be able to stop, if they wanted to. . . .
>
> So, I started this program, and I had quite good relations with them. Twenty percent of them were regular and committed to their new jobs. When the elections came six months later, unfortunately . . . the state security officer gave the women instructions to attack me in the street. So, seventeen of them, under the supervision of colonels and high-ranking policemen—who I used to deal with daily to serve the people—they used them against me. It was a terrible experience, because [an attack] on a woman coming from a woman is very different. Especially if it is coming from those whom you know, and whom you think that you were trying to help.

TOWARD AN ETHICS OF CARE · 147

But, of course, I knew that they had their reasons, and a couple of them came to me a couple of months later and told me they were very sorry: "They collected our IDs and we were supposed to do much worse than what we did. We were very, very tender with you. We were punished for three nights. We were not able to leave the police station for three nights after this incident, because they thought we were not as violent with you as we should have been." They told me that they were asked to do much worse, but they couldn't, because they always thought, "This is Gameela Ismail, who was trying to help us, who came in once to the police station when we were beaten up."

They just couldn't face the state security officer and say no. I asked them if they would like to go and testify, and of course they wouldn't. I never blamed them, really.[24]

What hurt her more than the physical violence was the psychological impact of the attack. At the time of our first interview, she was writing a memoir about that experience:

This was the first election I ran in, and because I was posing a threat to the majority leader, they wanted to do anything to break me. And they picked right, I think. I totally agree that they did "the right thing." Anything else wouldn't have broken me. I come from a very conservative family.... The hard part, the very difficult part was my family. I never dared to tell them what happened to me. I never dared to go to the prosecutor's office and make a police complaint. This is why I really respect those younger women, years later, in 2005.

Those who were attacked at the Press Syndicate. They were much stronger than me. You can be very strong in public, helping other people, but when it comes to you and to your body, this is extremely sensitive. Plus, the big difference is that I was alone, and all the cameras were left behind. And about the feminists ... here I am talking about areas they don't operate in. It's not easy for them to go there. I never thought of seeking them because they viewed me as an icon. I was the strong person. But I mean, with the Press Syndicate, on the Black Wednesday, that was different. All the cameras were there. They were all together: a lot of women together, a lot of men together. There were reporters. It was very easy to prove what happened. It wasn't easy for me to prove it, and I didn't want to prove it.

I was young, and I was very fragile, in terms of my body. Noor and Shady [my two kids] were very young. But then, of course, in 2004 and 2005, with the democratic movement, and all of the change movements I was part of, and my former husband was put in jail and I had to lead the party when he was inside, the newspaper and all of the protests and the demonstrations and the marches that I was part of and that I was leading as well. Of course, all of this made me stronger.

I still did not develop tolerance for anyone coming near my body, but I became more and more exposed to how people react. And then, when I ran for elections in 2010, in the very last elections before the revolution, I faced violence inside the polling station, from my colleagues who worked in the television building. They were supposed to be my colleagues, but they were supporting the NDP candidate, Hisham Mustafa Khalil. So, again, it was the same case: If you are supportive of the regime, you will be protected. You will be pampered. You will get protection, and so forth. But, if you are against, you will face the same fate.[25]

Gameela's detailed recounting helped me to situate in a broader context Black Wednesday, when, in 2005, a group of journalists of the Kefaya movement were sexually assaulted during a demonstration. Although the process that led them to raise the case in front of a court was not easy, there is no doubt that acting together made a difference. The activists who spoke most vociferously against the violence of Black Wednesday initiated a process that led toward a change in women's attitude about political violence, a change that then flourished during the Revolution, and which even Gameela benefited from when she ran again for Parliament in 2011, in the Qasr el-Nil district.

In 2011, it was different, because it was after the revolution. I was able to run against two very big blocs; the Ikhwan [Muslim Brotherhood], who had their candidate, and the Kutla al Mesriya, which was led by Naguib Sawiris, a very wealthy Coptic businessman, together with the Social Democratic Party, and the Masriyyn al-Ahrar, the Free Egyptians Party.[26] They decided very late in the election process to identify a candidate against me in the same constituency, even though, in the beginning, they all said they would have supported me. They wanted me to be in their party, but I wanted to run as an independent. They wanted this other candidate to face the Ikhwan, at least this was their narrative. So, I was in between....

They knew that this was my constituency, that I had run in before, and that I had popularity and so forth. Yet, they decided at the very, very end to nominate another candidate. So, I had this candidate, a candidate from the Muslim Brotherhood. They both had huge support from their parties, and a lot of money was spent.... I didn't have a big financer, or a big supporter, such a businessman, to pay [for my campaign]. They were all small contributions. And, of course, I wasn't part of the Muslim Brotherhood, the umbrella group. But, still, I was able to come in with just a very small difference, on my own. I was not with the church nor with the mosque. I had my statements against this. I had my statements against "big money" in elections, and reproducing the same old methods used before the revolution. I thought that using the old methods was a scandal for the revolution, and that we should never do this, even if we could. I did banners, I did publicity, that cost money, but I never paid for a direct vote, and I never agreed to get something that people could take home.

This was the difference. I thought, "If I do this, it would be like betraying the revolution." I had these ideas that we must live a new life in Egypt, and we must consider new, clean methods to run the elections. So, we must not get the mosque or the church involved. And we must not involve "big money," and we must not be corrupted and do the same things, even if we can, and even if we will win. To me, the path, the journey to the seat, was more important, after the revolution, than the seat itself. I wanted to set an example.[27]

Gameela did not enter the 2011 Parliament, but her campaign captured the imagination of many women revolutionaries. An activist of the NWF offered a feminist analysis of the elections' results: "Gameela's performance was impressive because she has lots of things people usually refuse. She is a woman, divorced, considered liberal and not veiled, and she is a media professional, and media professionals are seen as not moral and spreading bad values. So, it is quite impressive that she was that successful, if only the circumstances were fair and there was real democracy, she could have won and got to the Parliament."[28]

In April 2016, Gameela was invited to meet with President Hollande at the French Embassy. Both she and Khaled Ali (a founding member and a director of the party 'Aish wa Hurriyya [Bread and Freedom] and a well-known human rights lawyer) questioned the French president about France's military aid to Egypt. Following this meeting, she had to face complaints from the prosecution, from unknown lawyers and unknown people, accusing her of inciting the president of France to stop French economic aid to Egypt:

> What they did was that they sent someone. . . . I was on a beach with my dogs in a dog training camp and they took pictures of me with my swimsuit on and my dogs. This is what they did. This is how different it is with a woman. They made complaints against Khaled Ali, of course, but again, the attack against Khaled was not as strong as the attack against me. This was because, in their memory, for the final ten years of Mubarak's rule, I was, as you say, "a pain." I was not under control. I did not settle for any of the negotiations that they wanted to do with me. I was probably hostile to them. I suppose this—personal—hostility started from the day when they sent the women to attack me in 2001.[29]

Nearly one century since the birth of the feminist movement in Egypt, and more than fifty years into political equality, women's bodies continue to be a major site of political context. The attack against Gameela in 2001 was among the first (or at least, the first one being documented) to openly target a woman for her dissidence. Since then, this kind of attack multiplied, and the women's revolt in 2011 was also against this practice. Significantly, one of the major feminist fights after 2011 was against sexual violence as a tool to repress political activists.

A VICTORY FOR ONE IS A VICTORY FOR ALL, BUT ONE'S FAILURE IS EVERYONE'S FAILURE

Coming from different political spaces and having different visions about the relationship between gender and politics, women political activists all share the double burden of dealing with authoritarianism *and* patriarchy. The atmosphere of the years following the 2011 Revolution, and especially after 2013, with thousands of political prisoners, and disappeared and exiled people, could suggest that the revolution was not worth happening, but this is not how Gameela (nor anyone who was directly involved in the revolution) would see it:

> I don't want to go back to 2010. I want to move forward. The revolution happened so that we could change the reality that we lived back in 2005, 2006, 2007, 2008, 2009, and 2010. We live this narrative of, "If we can just go back to where we started, it will be best." No way! We must be innovative, and we must think of new ways, and we must work in very small groups. We must fly under the radar, and we must use very narrow underground paths.
>
> This kind of military rule, this kind of fascist rule, this kind of dictatorship, that has the full control of everything, it's not because [the regime is] intelligent or wise, or that they have wisdom. They are a failure. They just have weapons. We have a passion for change. We still have living souls inside of us. We have big ideas and small ideas. We don't want to surrender. We are perhaps trying to protect ourselves, as much as we can, from being thrown in jail or defamed more because we have been defamed for quite a long time: in the past four years, every day, by the mainstream propaganda. It is not at all bad to protect yourself, and to protect the young men and women who still have a passion. Yes, when it comes to decisions about people who would like to go to protest, the answer is no. We are not going to have more people in jail now. We are trying to properly assess our strength on the ground, and we are trying to connect with the average Egyptian citizen.[30]

Like other revolutionary activists, Gameela paid the price for 2011, but she did not surrender. On the contrary, in July 2022, she successfully ran for president of the Dostour Party. I visited her multiple times since her election, and I have observed her and her colleagues in the party working long days and well into the night, sometimes until dawn, also negotiating with the continuous fear of crossing the invisible (and constantly changing) line of what is considered legitimate and what is not by the regime. One cannot but wonder: What is this for? Why dedicate so much energy to a party that is not even running for elections (Dostour has been boycotting the elections since 2013)? Why take part in the National Dialogue, which political analysts consider a missed opportunity and a strategy of the current regime to gain some sort of legitimacy?[31]

I asked Gameela how it feels to be in this position at a time when everything seems so futile. She responded with an anecdote I had read about on social media but never heard directly from her: "In October 2022, I was invited to the economic conference organized by the government. I went to the conference opening, and I left immediately. I did not go the second day, and the third day the national TV called me. On that day we were given the certificate of the political party, after seven or eight years since we first applied."[32]

After some hesitation, since she was aware that the platform was pro-government, she eventually accepted the invitation, and on the evening of October 25 she stopped the car she was driving, answered the phone call of a TV journalist, and did an on-air interview. "I made every effort to raise the concerns that people have, to comment on the kind of narrative that the president used during the day at the conference. When they asked me about the conference, I said that Egyptians were perhaps expecting something different." When the interview concluded, she turned off her phone to join a family dinner. When she reopened it after an hour, she found hundreds of messages alerting her that President El-Sisi was angry. "Sisi spent fifty minutes responding to my seven minute interview."

At that time, the National Dialogue had just been announced but hadn't yet started. The reaction of the president to Gameela's interview made people in the party and the Civil Movement for Democracy consider how he could have potentially sat and talked with them if he could not tolerate what Gameela (or anyone else in the opposition) had to say in a short interview.

Six months later, the National Dialogue formally began: "The president attended just the opening on Zoom, and it was clear that it is not going to happen the way we expected. In the opening session, as the president of a party, I should have my slot. Then I realized I was not given a slot. I tried to take it, but they were avoiding me. I was later told that nobody wanted to take the responsibility of taking on stage Gameela Ismail talking live."

I observed a shift in Gameela's position toward an explicit feminist narrative since she was elected as Dostour's president: "When we have meetings among head[s] of political parties, I am the only woman in the room, this is not comfortable, I need to raise my voice to be heard; they are just not used to our presence . . . being in a leadership position is making me reconsidering what I told you few years ago about feminism."[33]

In September 2023, she announced on social media that she was ready to run for the forthcoming presidential elections. A few days later, two other members of the Civil Movement for Democracy announced their readiness to run: Farid Zahran, the head of the Egyptian Social Democratic Party, and Ahmed al-Tantawi, the former head of the Karama Party and a former MP for an Alexandria constituency.

The Civil movement (of which Gameela is the head) declared that each one of them would have its support. Eventually, however, none of them could obtain the necessary signatures to run and, after the elections, Ahmed al-Tantawi, the candidate who was perhaps considered the major threat for the president, was arrested, as were the leader of his presidential campaign and members of his family. I asked Gameela to comment about her experience: "With running for the presidential elections, there were people in the party who said this would be difficult, that it is going to be hard for us to cross the border with a woman president. It was hard [for me] to explain that it can be difficult this time but will be closer the next time and, in any case, nobody is going to win. If we want to do politics, we must run political elections . . . this is why a political party is there. We cannot boycott for more than ten years, and now the government [is] trying to push a law when they will deprive political parties that do not have parliamentary representation."

The margins of operation of a political party under a military regime, where the results of elections are foreseen, and every single individual who dares to even question (never mind challenge) the authority of the president is imprisoned or even disappears, are more than limited. In this disheartening scenario, Gameela continues to firmly believe that if the dream of the 2011 Revolution is fading, its values can still be translated into institutional politics. This leads her to care and mobilize for every single crisis: participating in the demonstrations in solidarity with Palestinian people that was launched in Cairo (the first one in a decade, on October 21, 2023); organizing the first convoy of aid from Cairo to Gaza (November 2023); standing in front of a police station waiting for the release of the women who in April 2024 were arrested for trying to bring a petition in solidarity with Palestinian and Sudanese women to the offices of UN Women. "This is what gives the families the best support. It might not be the reason why the people will be released, but it is telling everyone behind that even the president of a party can be waiting for the release of these women. And I was the only woman as a party president, and these are women, so I should be there and care the most, and of course appearing and being there is not everything."[34]

Gameela's political trajectory from her years of university and grassroots political work in the eighties to her work at State Television, her independent media activism, and her political activism deployed at multiple levels and in different forms. Running somehow parallel to that of the women who shaped the Egyptian feminist movement from the early eighties, they all met in Tahrir Square in January 2011, and they all have meaningful stories to tell about the eighteen days. They all opened their houses for young people who were occupying and provided supplies for the field hospitals, they all contributed to the 2011 Revolution not only by being there and putting their professional skills at the service of the people but, before the Revolution erupted, by allowing the intimate and public space for the 2011 Revolution to emerge, and now, ten years into the establishment of new regime, keeping the flame of the revolution glowing. This reflects an ethics of care that permeates feminist politics and which, even if it is not going to alter the landscape of institutional politics for the foreseeing future, can still inspire change in the ways individuals relate to each other, creating communities where caring for each other is a shared value on which a movement for the future can be built.

EIGHT

Transgenerational Legacies in the Early 2000s Social Movements

MAHIENOUR EL-MASSRY AND SANA' AL-MASRI

JANUARY 20, 2018. A young woman in a white mohair dress and braided brown hair walks through the doors of Sherazade, a popular nightclub in downtown Cairo, where *Mada Masr* is hosting its annual party.[1] My attention is drawn away from the Sudanese band on stage when I see several young people greeting the woman with joy. I recognize her face as one I'd seen many times in one of the iconic works of graffiti by the revolutionary Egyptian artist Ranya Youssef, iconic both for the image at its center and the quote aside it: "We don't like prisons, but we are not afraid of them."

The woman in question is human rights lawyer Mahienour El-Massry.

Mahienour's renown surpassed Egypt's borders in October 2014, when she flew to Florence (Italy) to collect the Ludovic Trarieux International Human Rights Prize, awarded annually to a lawyer for contributions to the defense of human rights. Nelson Mandela was its first recipient, in 1985. In her poignant acceptance speech, Mahienour celebrated the legacy of the social movements that developed in Egypt in the early 2000s and led to the 2011 January Revolution:

> I really don't feel that I deserve such honor, as all the time I was part of a bigger group, starting from being a Revolutionary Socialist, to being a volunteer lawyer at the Alexandria's protestors defense front, a member in Not to Military Trials for Civilians, Refugees Solidarity Movement, and No to the Capital Punishment, but above all, I was one of millions of Egyptians who had dreamt of justice, made a revolution that toppled two dictators and we are crossing fingers that it will topple the third. In this battle, we have won some rounds and lost others, but we are not defeated.[2]

In that speech, Mahienour also denounced the crackdown against the human rights community in Egypt, celebrated the resilience of Egyptian

155

dissidents, and asserted her professional ethic as a lawyer serving justice before the laws of an authoritarian government: "Lawyers have a great role to raise awareness, to be shield for the marginalized and voice for the voiceless."[3]

In the three years between the time she gave that speech and our first meeting at the *Mada Masr* party, Mahienour had been twice more imprisoned. The first time was from May 2015 to July 2016, after the prosecution reopened the 2013 case against her for alleged participation in the clashes that took place outside Alexandria Criminal Court in al-Mansheya district on December 2, 2012. Her second imprisonment lasted from November 2017 till January 2018 on the accusation that she violated Law 107/2013 (known colloquially as the Protest Law). The protest concerned President's El-Sisi's decision to transfer two strategic Red Sea islands, Tinar and Sanafir, to the Kingdom of Saudi Arabia, which generated significant public outrage across Egypt. Lower and high courts ruled against the sale, but Sisi could not tolerate any challenge of his foreign policy, resulting in a crackdown against high-profile political activists, including Mahienour.[4]

On January 20, 2018, newly released from prison, Mahienour came to the *Mada Masr* party to greet her friends and comrades. Witnessing the joy they shared that night I realized that even in the middle of intense repression of all forms of political activism, there could still be moments of happiness and hope. I encountered a far gloomier atmosphere six months later, in June 2019, when I met Mahienour at *Mada Masr*'s offices in the Dokki neighborhood of Cairo, just across the Nile from Zamalek. For her, it was the end of a long day of work at the Cairo criminal court, and she was visibly tired: "They [the judiciary] are now making us go on a rollercoaster. I spend hours and hours and hours and hours in court, but I'm not doing anything real because the law is not applied in Egypt. But you have to be there for your friends and comrades just to comfort them and to tell them that they are not forgotten. Having been there, I know how it feels for someone who is in prison to see people who still remember you."[5]

Frustration with the lack of respect for legal procedures was a constant and even growing theme in conversations with human rights lawyers since 2013. The situation is even worse for political detainees who don't even make it to the court but are just left languishing in jail under an endless regime of pretrial detention.[6]

Mahienour experienced the crackdown both as a lawyer and as a detainee, as she was a well-established professional (she graduated from the Faculty of

Law of the University of Alexandria in 2007), and was detained and imprisoned multiple times for her political opinions. Her political biography is emblematic of both the long arc of youth social movements from the mid-nineties through the 2011 Revolution and of their emotional, intellectual, and political connection with the generation that shaped the Marxist movements in the seventies and the eighties, however fraught they may remain. "This revolution was not an ideological revolution. It was a revolution of the heart, of the emotions. We, all of us, we were all very emotional. I mean, our emotions are what remain today and this was its [the revolution's] strength, because our emotions brought together people from different backgrounds."[7]

The idea that the 2011 Revolution transcended ideological divides is emphasized in Mahienour's and other activists' narratives about it. It comes from the activists' experiences in cross-ideological social movements in the late 1990s and early 2000s, when leftist activists initiated a dialogue with the Islamists, trying to overcome the historically rooted hostilities between the two oppositional fronts.

However, this openness was short-lived: class, cultural, and ideological divides have prevailed in the aftermath of 2011. In her conversation with me eight years after the revolution, Mahienour appeared thoughtful, acknowledging that the revolutionary front had perhaps been too idealistic, and in the revolutionary process lost sight of ordinary (and especially poor) people's needs: "At the same time, this [idealism] was also its weakness, because to move forward one needs to be practical, to give alternatives, to build roots, to formulate her or his own narrative. You know, people do not want to hear you talking all the time about people who are in prison."[8]

What led to the initial success of the 2011 Revolution was the grassroots work of mobilization in the decade that preceded it. Mahienour emphasized the necessity to exit from the "bubble" or "cloud" of a privileged social background by linking theory and praxis, being in relationship to and listening to the people, focusing on their needs, and considering them the most knowledgeable about their problems and the most resourceful to elaborate strategies to change their conditions.

> On a personal level, the revolution [has given] a lot to us and it has also taken a lot from us. You can see that in all the people that are called icons of the revolution. Their lives are not stable, they have lost years in prisons, or even if they are not in prison, they can't progress in their career. The idea of the icon comes as a burden. The only thing we know is that we want people to be happy and to live a better life, [we want] people to be equal, but we're

experimenting, so it's a load to us too, it's like a burden when someone, for example, comes and asks you: "What should we do?" Sometimes we just don't know. We're experimenting all together.[9]

This emphasis on the collective experience increased my curiosity about Mahienour's political biography. How she first experienced politics, how she developed her views, how the personal intersected with the public for her, how what was specific to her own experience was also part of her generation's coming of age. I asked her more about her upbringing, and she took me back to the nineties.

CHAINS OF TRANSMISSIONS OF POLITICAL ACTIVISM

The eldest of three sisters, Mahienour was born in 1986 in Alexandria, where she spent most of her life. Her childhood stories were a colorful sketch of the nineties, with an extended upper-middle-class family, a microcosm of the political (and apolitical) tendencies in Egypt at the time: a mix of conservative and liberal attitudes all within one family, where people who had political ideas keep them to themselves during family reunions to avoid upsetting those who preferred not to engage in politics.

> My father and my mother are ordinary Egyptians, totally apolitical. My father was an agricultural engineer, and he had been working in Saudi Arabia and Kuwait for a while, like most of the Egyptians. My mother was an accountant from a middle-upper-class background and then a housewife. But then there is the extended family that is a little bit interesting. I have an uncle who had been a member of the Gamaʿa al-Islamiyya [Islamic Society]. He is now a doctor in the US and [has] transformed into [a] milder [activist], like in the Brotherhood. He's like, "the extremist" of our family.[10]

The Gamaʿa al-Islamiyya was a radical Islamist formation, active across Egypt in the eighties and early nineties. It emerged in the mid-seventies in Minya, Upper Egypt, as a small reading group studying the works of Islamist political thinkers and soon evolved into a radical and militarized group, seeking to force the government to pass conservative laws. Similar to the Islamic Jihad (another radical Islamist formation of that period), the Gamaʿa advocated for an Islamic state, through armed struggle if necessary.

In the context of the growth of poverty as a result of neoliberal policies begun under Sadat and exacerbated under Mubarak, as well as the repression of Marxist movements, radical Islamists achieved some popularity on university campuses in the late seventies, even among student organizations. The state perceived them as a threat and tried to contain them, mostly through several waves of arrest. In 1981, the Islamic Jihad assassinated President Sadat. Later in the eighties and nineties, they launched a series of attacks against both foreign tourists and Egyptian secular intellectuals, including the writer and commentator Farag Fouda, who was assassinated in 1992; Naguib Mahfouz—the first and so far only Arab writer awarded the Nobel Prize for literature—who was stabbed in 1994; and the feminist writer Nawal al-Saadawi, who received multiple death threats, leaving Egypt for the United States with her husband, the communist writer Sherif Hetata, in 1993. Fearing an Algerian scenario, the Egyptian state adopted a hard line in the nineties against the jihadist movements.[11] To escape that repression, some of the jihadist cadres moved to Pakistan and Afghanistan, where they joined Osama bin Laden's terrorist organization, al-Qaida.[12] In Egypt, the Gama'a al-Islamiyya revised its political strategy in 1997, renouncing violence. However, radical groups continued to operate through the first two decades of the 2000s and, on a smaller scale, still operate today.[13]

Mahienour remembers her uncle as not inclined to armed militancy but as positioning himself in the socially conservative, politically right-wing field.

The Islamists were neither the only nor the majority political force that felt alienated by the economy of liberalization implemented by Sadat in the seventies and then continued by Mubarak in the eighties. Nasserists, socialists who gravitated around an illegal group called Thawra Misri (Egyptian Revolution), the Socialist Labor Party, and the National Progressive Unionist Party (NPUF), to which one of Mahienour's aunts belonged, felt equally alienated.

Mahienour explained that the political diversity of her extended family informed her approach to politics for a long time, but, more than anyone, she refers to her aunt Sana' al-Masri (1958–2000). "I had an aunt who died in 2000, when I was just fourteen [years old]. She had a huge impact on me. Her name is Sana' al-Masri. She was a communist and she wrote four important books. One about women in Islam, titled *Khalf al-hijab* (*Behind the Hijab*), and the other was about the Arab/Islamic invasion to Egypt. Of course, the same fact of naming it an invasion was controversial, as it underlined that the process that brought Egypt from Christianity to Islam was not so peaceful."[14]

Sana' al-Masri was a prolific journalist and a leading figure in the student movement of the seventies. A radical Marxist, feminist journalist, and playwright, she was an uncompromising intellectual who opposed the gradual turn of Marxist activism into NGO and professional work, as well as the normalization of relationships with Israel and the conservative social views of the Islamist movements.[15] In the nineties, when the neoliberal policies of the Mubarak government resulted in increased unemployment (especially for women) and poverty, and the Islamists adopted even more conservative gender politics, most feminist associations turned to international organizations for financial support. Al-Masri, like some of the founding members of the NWF, and with the Mansoura-based association Bint al-Ard, was against this trend, believing only financial independence could translate into freedom.[16] It is significant that she published the book *Khalf al-Hijab* (*Behind the Hijab*), where she strongly criticized the Islamist discourse about women and gender, in 1987,[17] when the Brotherhood and even other more radical Islamist organizations were at the height of their popularity in Egypt.

Young Revolutionary Socialist feminists regularly made reference to her books in our conversations, and as I developed a deeper understanding of the thread tying Mahienour to her aunt Sana', I also understood the link between the contemporary generation of leftist activists and the generation of the seventies more broadly. It is a complex interplay of continuities and fractures, the kind of transmission of ideas through practices more than words that transpire particularly through women's lineages. During the little more than two decades dividing these two generations, Egypt and even the world went through dramatic changes, yet by taking part in the revolutionary process since 2011, the youngest activists developed an awareness of the silent continuities and also the conflicts between themselves and the students of the seventies:

> She was pretty cool and funny, she used to make a lot of jokes with us, and she never treated us like kids. She used to give us books and make us act in family theater plays, which was what she was actually doing, as she had her own theater company. I think of course that her way of being an outstanding woman affected me. She was from the late-seventies generation. She participated in the 1977 movement, and later in the Hezb al-'Ummal [Workers' Party].[18] I knew all of that when I became a communist myself, but before that I didn't know anything about it. All I knew about her was that she was a journalist, that she wrote books, and that she had a theater company. We were staying in our own bubble all the time. She used to try to make us see

further than that. To take us to places, to tell us stories about workers, or farmers and, and . . . things like that, but not in a very direct way.[19]

There is a subtle thread in the transmission of memories between the generation of the seventies and Mahienour's generation. The relationship between the two is ambivalent and often contentious, if not conflictual. While Mahienour expressed unequivocal admiration for her aunt Sana', other young women I interviewed were more critical of the generation of Sana'. They blamed the generation of the seventies for what they perceived as a lack of coherence between theories and praxis. Significantly, the most critical tended to be young women, who often accused the older Marxist women of complying with the sexism of their male counterparts and of perpetuating hierarchical transgenerational relationships.

It wasn't just that Mahienour found her aunt to be an inspiring figure; by observing her, she understood the link between the personal and the political, especially in the way she related to her body and the world: "She made me feel more comfortable with myself, my body, especially that, as I told you, I lost my eye when I was really, really young, I was two years old. And so, as a very young person having one eye, I became like a bookworm, just because I wanted to be alone, more than playing with other kids. But then she made me feel very comfortable with myself, and I owe that to her. Now, many people tell me that they find me strong. I wasn't like that."

Mahienour is one of the rare feminist activists who spontaneously introduces into her narrative a reflection about the body, health, self-perception, and self-confidence. To my knowledge, this is not a theme that was directly addressed by the Egyptian feminists in the seventies, the eighties, and not even the nineties, who in their public discourse about the body privileged other themes, such as violence, bodily integrity, and sexuality. A more explicit attention to health and disability as a feminist concern is becoming more visible, both at the level of scholarship[20] and in activism.[21] Mahienour's openness in talking about the intimate conversations she had with her feminist and Marxist aunt about her body and self-perception suggests that the circulation of this new feminist scholarship as well as the practice of feminist therapists and other practitioners is producing a new level of self-reflection among women's activists. Self-awareness among feminist activists is now developing into a fully worked-out feminist philosophy, thinking of their bodies in relationship to the social space they were part of, and integrating their emotional and intellectual growth with their political trajectory, slowly from skepticism and even noninterest to a direct, open embrace of feminism.

THE NEW STUDENT MOVEMENT IN EGYPT IN THE NINETIES AND EARLY 2000S

Mahienour went to a private Muslim language school until she completed high school in 2003. She then enrolled in the English branch of Alexandria University's Faculty of Law as a "status symbol," although today she sees both the advantages and the downsides of it. In the nineties, as Egypt was reaching the peak of the neoliberal turn, middle-class families were investing in private schools for their kids, hoping that a good education would open decent professional opportunities for them. Even today, middle-class people tend not to trust public schools, where classes are overcrowded and the pedagogy is out of date, focused on mnemonic learning rather than developing critical thinking. International private schools are considered to offer a better curriculum, but, according to Mahienour, they create "bubbles" in which privileged students are confined, and they lack awareness of the world around them.[22]

This points to one of the main differences between the leftist activists of the seventies, who were part of the student movement and were often from a working-class background, and Mahienour's generation, who grew up far more protected from the reality on the ground. In the nineties, young emerging activists were noticing the gap between the urban intelligentsia and the workers, and they were wondering why the former were unable to link with the latter. Mahienour developed an early awareness of the multiple implications of class differences: "I was in a car with my father, a big car, and we were going through a *sha'abi* [popular] neighborhood. We stopped at a traffic-light and a woman sitting on the pavement asking for charity looked at me with disdain, and she told me that she would have rather gave away an eye, like me, to be in that car."

I didn't perceive any trace of resentment or self-pity in her voice. Rather, she simply used this personal story to gently lead our conversation to the intersection between the body's vulnerability and class structures in Egypt. Mahienour's story and the way she thinks of it as a moment of early awareness of social injustice echoes Professor Amina Rachid's childhood memory about her being attacked by a young girl in 1947. Like Amina Rachid in the interview by the filmmaker Tahani Rached,[23] Mahienour appeared still moved by the words of the woman. These reverberations across generations that appear like an epiphany during the interviews reveal the thread of practices, ideas, and theorizations that link feminist activists and intellectuals during the long feminist century in Egypt.

In her teens in the early 2000s, in alignment with her generation's increased political engagement, Mahienour had her first experiences in politics, notwithstanding her parents' efforts to keep her out of the political fray. Images of the second Intifada in 2000 and the invasion of Iraq in 2003 stirred spontaneous demonstrations, in which Mahienour took part.

The tradition of Egyptian women's activism in support of Palestine goes back to the 1930s, when the Egyptian Feminist Union organized in Cairo the Eastern Women Conference in Defense of Palestine (1938), and her delegates at the 1939 International Women Suffrage Alliance in Copenhagen advocated for Palestine in a feminist international forum, and it has continued through the twentieth century to today.[24] Suzan Fayad, a veteran of the seventies student movement and cofounding member of El-Nadeem, told me that it was in this context of Egyptian women's activism for Palestine in the early 2000s that she first met and then became friends with another high-profile woman activist for peasants' rights, Shahenda Meqlad: "In 2000, we knew each other during the campaign to support the Palestinian Uprising. We decided to support Palestinians with medicine by organizing relief caravans, and people started to donate after knowing about our initiative. They donated medicine and food supplies. We used to categorize the donations and sent [them] to Rafah [Egypt] and then to the Gaza Strip. These caravans lasted for two years. That's how I knew Shahenda. We also did a big protest in Tahrir Square in 2003 against the invasion of Iraq. She was a fighter and courageous person."[25]

Mahienour joined the groups for solidarity with Palestine and became impatient to start at the university and to join political groups there. She was very soon disappointed, finding that the only political group active at Alexandria University was the Muslim Brotherhood. As someone who had received an Islamic education in high school, she could not accept the conservative and strict visions promoted by the Muslim Brotherhood on campus.

> Their ideas were of course very different from mine, even if I was coming from a kind of Islamic school, and maybe that's what made me even more critical

toward their narratives. We had different views. For example, we always had those fights about the hijab, because we are part of that generation of middle-class girls who were attracted by this wave of new Islamic cool preachers like Amru Khaled ... so, when I was about fourteen or fifteen, I started seeing most of my friends wearing the hijab. That was strange for me. My mother is a *very Muslim woman* [i.e., religious, emphasis in the voice] and she wears the hijab, but she's also very liberal, and she always told me that she believes that hijab is obligatory if you think that it is obligatory, so if you don't think it is, then it is not—something like that. She had her own philosophy that made things easier for us. That's maybe why I never believed in that, though at the time I felt that I was a true Muslim, but then I felt that most of what people are doing, it doesn't have anything to do with Islam. So, I was fighting all the time the idea that hijab is obligatory in Islam, and I thought maybe that was also coming from my aunt's book, because she was saying that, and because, as I told you, even if my family is conservative, most of them don't wear the hijab.[26]

Lively discussions were happening on campus in the early 2000s between young women and men who were starting to be interested in politics. For Mahienour, as for her fellows, debating about veiling and unveiling naturally led to debating about gender equality, individual freedom, and how to interpret Islamic values. This was indeed a different world from the one where Mahienour's aunt, Sana' al-Masri, wrote her book about veiling. In the late seventies and eighties, Sana' lived in a society where a leftist young woman would have hardly worn the hijab, which in urban, middle-class, and high-educated spaces such as the universities was generally perceived of as a sign of affinity (if not belonging) to the Islamist field, and thus against freedom and equality for women. At that time, being a communist implied being secular. This does not mean that being a communist woman implied being a feminist. Most women writers and public intellectuals such as Latifa al-Zayyat (1923–1996), Radwa Ashour (1946–2014), and Amina Rachid (1938–2021) did not refer to themselves as "feminists" and did not use feminism as a significant theoretical space to frame their intellectual work. They were among the most prominent intellectuals in the Marxist field.

Mahienour's world was different. In the early 2000s, wearing the hijab had become a sign of modesty or social conformism, sometimes of piety, not necessarily of political militancy.[27] Instead, new political subjectivities—less ideological and more connected to what the sociologist Asef Bayyat has described as the politics of everyday[28]—began to emerge among young people. Even if Mahienour never wore the hijab, she, like many other middle-class and highly educated women, maintained an open mind about it. What Mahienour was the clearest about during the interview was women's freedom of choice, something she was not ready to negotiate about. This put her, and most Egyptian women, in a different position from the Muslim Brotherhood and other conservative and patriarchal political formations.

Moreover, the early 2000s was the period when the emerging generation of leftist, progressive activists opened a dialogue with the new generation of the Muslim Brotherhood to build a cross-ideological alliance against the Mubarak's regime. This did not come easily, as ideological disagreements continued to be on the table, not only between the Marxists and the Islamists but also between the Marxists and the liberals. "So, we had in 2010 something called Maktab Shabab al-Quwa al-Wataniya, which is like the Office of the National Youth Group. It was made of nine youth groups, from the very left to the very right. Like, Muslim Brotherhood was there; al-Ghad Party was there, which is the liberal; Karama, which at that time [was] still under construction, and the Revolutionary Socialists. There was a variety. We tried to work together, and we succeeded.... We organized many protests, [and] the number of the youth who were interested in politics at the time started to increase."[29]

In Alexandria the political discontent of people had grown over the years, as the city had been subjected to a great deal of financial exploitation, corruption, police violence, and manipulation of sectarian conflict. Between 2010 and 2011 the situation in Alexandria escalated. On June 6, 2010, the torture and murder under police custody of Khaled Said, a young middle-class man, raised public outrage and made known to the world what was already well-known to the Alexandrian people: "Alexandria was the capital of police torture." Six months later, the bombing of al-Qadiseen, the Coptic Two Saints Church, on New Year's Eve 2011, added to the common perception of political and sectarian violence in the city and catalyzed the already growing desire of young people for political alternatives.

This is the context in which democratic and social movements developed in Alexandria as well as across Egypt, spreading the seeds for a new political culture among the middle class and nourishing the desire for the building of a less oppressive public sphere.

WOMEN'S EXPERIENCE IN THE CROSS-IDEOLOGICAL MOVEMENTS

The years 2003 and 2004 repeatedly stand out as crucial years that deeply influenced the political trajectories of the young political activists whom I

FIGURE 11. Dr. Mohamed Abul Ghar, of the March 9 Movement for the Independence of the Universities, speaking with Mahienour El-Massry (in the middle) and other students from Cairo and Alexandria, at the conference held by the Revolutionary Socialists at Cairo's Press Syndicate, December 8, 2007, "The Struggle against the Privatisation of Higher Education." Photo by and courtesy of Hossam el-Hamalawy.

have interviewed. The year 2004 saw the rise of a protest movement calling for the end of twenty-five years of one-party rule, and the year when Egypt witnessed more demonstrations than in the twenty-five years preceding.[30] One of Mahienour's aunts, Waffa El-Massry (whom Mahienour described as a Nasserist), was part of the major movement, the Egyptian Movement for Change, known as Kefaya. The protests of Kefaya in 2004 represented a high point in the evolution of the prerevolutionary (i.e., pre-2011) social movements in Egypt. The first demonstration was on December 12, 2004:

> I heard from her that there was something called the Kefaya movement that was against Mubarak, and of course, as a young person who was born under Mubarak, I felt that this was a very important thing. Most of the people, of course, thought that the fall of Mubarak was unrealistic and not even practical. I signed up for the mailing list of Kefaya, like most people. One day I received an email that they were having their first protest in Alexandria, and I went with a friend from college and my younger sister. That's when a new whole world opened to me.... This was the first time I was part of a demonstration that concerns only Egypt. And it was so interesting to see such a huge number of police officers, like I've never seen before. There were some young people chanting, and they were inspirational for me.... After the

first protest, I saw a small group of young people, and I wanted to know who they are, so I found out that they were Shabab min Agl el-Tagheer [Youth for Change], which was the youth branch of the Kefaya movement. I contacted them, and they started to tell me about other protests. Then I was recruited.[31]

Youth for Change was the core group of Kefaya's young activists, a coalition bringing together young people from different political stands. Like other offshoots of Kefaya (Workers for Change, Journalists for Change, Doctors for Change, and Artists for Change), Youth for Change was a cross-ideological movement whose agenda was centered on promoting democracy through free elections open to multiple political parties. The political networks of the early 2000s attracted highly educated middle-class activists from different orientations, from the Karama Party (Nasserists) to the Revolutionary Socialists (Marxists), the Ghad Party (liberals), the Wasat Party (Islamists), the Labor Party, and some independent figures.[32] None of these parties were formally registered, and members of the traditional opposition's parties, such as the Tagammu', the Wafd, and the Arab Democratic Nasserist Party, were involved. The group did not have connections with the Muslim Brotherhood. For all these reasons, Kefaya is considered a post-ideological movement, whose agenda was centered on the promotion of democracy, obtaining free parliamentary elections, and rotation of power. The political scientist Rabab al-Mahdi, who has studied and has been part of the early 2000s social movements, documented that these were requests that had already been put forward by the Egyptian Labor Party in 1992, and then again by the three main opposition parties (Tagammu', Wafd, and Arab Democratic Nasserist), during the assembly of the National Democratic party in March 2004, yet they had always been rejected.[33] In February 2005, three months after the first Kefaya demonstration, Mubarak's attitude seemed to be slightly changing. He proposed a constitutional change, allowing multicandidate presidential elections. However, this change remained only on paper, and Ayman Nour, the only candidate popular enough to represent a tangible threat in the electoral race to the presidency of Egypt, was arrested and spent five years in jail for taking Mubarak at his word. The unwillingness of the regime to listen to the request for democracy coming from the people fueled the growth of the social movements.

Protests continued. Mahienour participated in Kefaya's protests, but her strong inclination toward social justice issues led her to transit soon toward a more radical leftist group, the Revolutionary Socialists. The Revolutionary Socialists were a group of students inspired by the works of the British sociologist Chris Harman. They began gathering in the late eighties as a read-ing group, and they started educating themselves, developing Trotskyist ideas. However, such ideological categories become blurred when applied to the Egyptian field. In fact, Mahienour remembered very lively discussions about them. She refrained from thinking of herself as a Trotskyist or a Leninist: "I hate the idea of labels! . . . I think revolutionary socialism as a word would be more appealing to me than to say that I'm a Trotskyist."[34]

The general atmosphere of repression that characterized the Egyptian public sphere in the nineties pushed the Revolutionary Socialists to keep a low profile and stay semi-underground. In 2000, they were among the groups who expressed solidarity with the Second Palestinian Intifada, inspiring the revival of street politics in Egypt.[35] Mahienour, who, as we have seen above, had already been part of Palestinian solidarity groups, joined the Revolutionary Socialists in 2005: "I think that truly made me who I am, because that was the time when I started to work with workers, peasants, fishermen, and I started to learn about communism more by being involved in the movements than from books."

The Revolutionary Socialists organization soon became the main pillar of the new left in the early 2000s. Differently from the Stalinism and even the Leninism of the previous generations of Egyptian Marxists, they developed a platform that was open to collaboration with the Muslim Brotherhood students on campus and whose common aim was to uphold democratic prac-tices. The scholar and Revolutionary Socialist Hossam al-Hamalawy remem-bers that when state security banned Islamist candidates from running in student union elections, and when Islamist students were expelled from school, the Revolutionary Socialists supported them.[36] However, the Revolutionary Socialists would severely criticize the Muslim Brotherhood when they made sexist or sectarian statements. These practices reflected also the teaching they learned from Harman: "Sometimes with the Islamists, never with the state," meaning that they were ready to build cross-ideological alliances, as long as they were within the spectrum of the opposition, but they were not ready to negotiate with the authoritarian regime.

The gender politics of the Revolutionary Socialists appeared egalitarian, at the point that when Mahienour and other women activists first joined them, they did not feel the need to think of themselves as feminists:

At the very beginning I didn't like to call myself a feminist, as I thought this is something that would segregate women from men. This was before reading and knowing more about feminism. So, I hated the idea of the quota for women in some groups, for example, and I felt like this [was] very degrading for women as well. In the Revolutionary Socialists, especially in Alexandria, we were mainly women. . . . I was elected in the high office of the Revolutionary Socialists [2008], and . . . even if I shouldn't say that, as we were an underground organization, so nobody is supposed to know how many we were, we were four women out of ten.[37]

During the interview, Mahienour emphasized that women were represented at the highest levels among the Revolutionary Socialists: "They wouldn't treat you as the usual type of woman, like, you shouldn't do that, or you should do that or no."

Mahienour's narrative on this point is similar to that shared by many feminists of the eighties I have interviewed. Overall, they find the younger men more respectful of their women comrades than the young men in the seventies and eighties used to be with their women comrades. This suggests that their lesson about gender equality as something that matters to everyone, not only women, but women and men together, and that has to do with power relationships at multiple levels (including the relationship between the citizens and the state authorities), has been passed not only to young women but also to young men as well. This could indicate the development of new visions about gender, politics, and culture in Egypt. However, the experiences of young women revolutionaries in Tahrir Square during the eighteen days of the revolution and the aftermath shows that this cannot be generalized. Many were sexual harassed, and even raped, and not only by the *baltagiya* (plainclothes thugs hired by state security), but also by their revolutionary comrades—a sign of just how far the achievement of gender equality has to go.[38]

The Revolutionary Socialists remained semi-underground (which means that the group was technically banned, but they were still holding public cultural events) until the 2011 Revolution. They were mostly educating themselves and discussing classical political philosophy, especially the Marxists, such as Lenin, Marx, Engels, Rosa Luxemburg, and the most recent political philosophy, like that of Chris Harman and Tony Cliff.

Mahienour appeared emotional as she related to me the times she volunteered as a translator when Chris Harman gave his last lecture at the Center for Socialist Studies in Giza, Cairo. Tragically, during that lecture Chris Harman had the heart attack that caused his premature death, on November 7, 2009: "He gave a great lecture! We were very young, and as we didn't have money, we used to volunteer to translate. There had been many young people, and I was one of the people who volunteered to translate. I think that one of the most important things that the Revolutionary Socialists have done is the literature and, like, the conferences. It was very eye-opening!"[39]

There is no doubt that the experience of the Revolutionary Socialists deeply shaped the new generation of leftists in the cities of Egypt. Mahienour recalled having been an avid reader of the *Awraq Ishtirakiya* (Socialist Papers), a "fantastic magazine" that promoted progressive ideas, and a forum that encouraged her to think about the relationship between communism and Islam as well as between communism and feminism. She found the articles on feminism valuable and innovative because they included contributions on both intellectual and grassroots feminism, filling a gap in the understanding of feminism among the leftists:

> There had been a huge sit-in [in] 2007 for the tax collectors, the real estate tax collectors and maybe half of the sit-in was women as well, so there had been interviews with them, interviews with workers in Mahalla as well. Because actually women had been very much present and at the core of the protests of Mahalla and, of course, not only Mahalla. Most of the protests anywhere, if they included women, you could see them more. I don't want to be like . . . because this may be something emotional, but they were very militant. When they join, they have nothing to lose. If they took the decision to join, then it wouldn't be like men. Men would probably join without even thinking too much, but as a woman you have to think many times, especially in a place like Egypt, where to be part of something, you know that you will pay a heavier price than men. You would be disgraced, the community would see you as someone who's immoral or impolite, just for staying the night in a sit-in with workers, with guys, for example.[40]

The first decade of the 2000s was in fact a time of high worker mobilization in Egypt. Historian Joel Beinin has recorded more than 3,400 strikes between 1998 and 2010, with over two million workers taking part.[41] The protests initially addressed the worsening of working and living conditions consequent to the implementation of the Economic Restructuring and Stabilization Program imposed on Egypt by the International Monetary Fund and in 1991 accepted by the Egyptian Trade Federation. However, as Beinin explains, since 2007 the workers' struggle was increasingly framed in a broader political context with national implications. The Misr Spinning and Weaving Company Ghazl al-Mahalla, in al-Mahalla al-Kubra, was the single largest factory complex in Egypt, employing between twenty-two thousand and twenty-seven thousand workers in the early 2000s. Since it had been nationalized, in the sixties, its wages and working conditions were typically the benchmarks for the entire public sector. For this reason, the mobilizations in al-Mahalla were very important. By the spring of 2007, there were strikes almost everywhere. The strikes were being documented by the emerging generation of bloggers, who were reaching out to a new audience and were trying to fill the gap between middle-class young people and wage workers. The intersection between feminism, industrial action, and labor is particularly evident in the blog Manala, launched by a couple of young activists who pioneered the blogosphere in Arabic, Alaa Abd El-Fattah and Manal Hassan:

> Greetings to the women of Egypt who led the sit-in with courage and awareness that men envy them for. What happened and is happening this year from the workers is a big, strong thing, even if we do not take it seriously.
> And a big salute to all those who supported them and stood by them, especially Hossam El-Hamalawy and Malek Mustafa.[42]

As I have learned from Mahienour and by the women workers I interviewed, this was not the only labor action.[43] Mahienour militated with women strikers during the hundred day sit-in at Toson, in Alexandria, where the State had planned a series of home demolitions. Women workers engaged in over a hundred protests, and they also organized a sit-in in Cairo in front of the Agricultural Ministry in Dokki: "I stayed with them for two days and it was very interesting, just to see, to see all of that, to see women in such places." The mobilization of workers and students continued in the subsequent years, and women—who in Egypt officially represent 22 percent of the working force but are actually more than 50 percent if the informal sectors are also considered—were an integral part of them, not only as a force on the ground but also as leaders and ideologues.

When I interviewed a group of women activists of the first independent syndicate in Egypt, the independent syndicate of the tax collectors, which was established in April 2009, they made very clear the key role that they played in all the phases of the fight for workers' rights. After a long meeting in the premises of the 'Aish wa Hurriyya (Bread and Freedom) Party, a leftist political formation established after 2011, Rasha Elgebaly, who when I interviewed her in 2014 was serving as the general secretary of the syndicate in Alexandria, gathered a group of women to share their stories. They explained how protests were motivated by attempts by the government to change their tax status, in response to which protests were held across all the country's governorates, followed by an eleven-day sit-in in front of the Cabinet headquarters in Cairo:

> It was in November and December 2008. It was a problem to do such a strike at Mubarak days. The security forces were surrounding us. Too many men from our side wanted to end the strike, while women were enthusiastic to continue until we have a response from the government. Eventually, the government responded to our demands, and we moved under the responsibility of the ministry of finance . . . after that we realized that this strike brought us together. Kamal Abu-Aita was our official spokesperson at that time, so we decided to organize ourselves. We realized that it's a necessity to be heard in the future by the government to be in a strong group, so we did the syndicate, which was the first independent syndicate in Egypt.[44]

The high rate of women's participation in the protests led the syndicate to put a women's quota on the board (25 percent, later raised to 30 percent). When I asked if women had specific demands, Rasha emphasized the broader role played by women in continuing the strike for everyone more than pledging for women's rights: "Women led the strike. Men wanted to end it, while women refused, until they got a response from the government." I could not refrain from asking why the women wanted to continue. The answer was as telling as it was brief: "Because women have more determination than men."[45]

MEMORIES HAUNTING THE PRESENT: THE LIFE AND ASSASSINATION OF SHAIMA' AL-SABBAGH

On July 26, 2008, Mahienour took part in the first demonstration called by the 6th of April movement in Alexandria. As she explained, "At that time, I was the only woman to be arrested, but I was released. There was also a minor and a sixteen-year-old boy who had been arrested with us. We were all released."[46]

After her arrest, Mahienour came to know better some of the activists who were already part of her circle. The atmosphere of repression that pushed many activities underground certainly contributed to this lack of mutual knowledge. Among her meetings with women activists after her first arrest, one of the most remarkable was her encounter with the ethnographer and poet Shaima' al-Sabbagh, whose face became sadly celebrated in January 2015, when the images of her, exhaling her last breath in the arms of her partner, circulated worldwide.

FIGURE 12. Om Refaʾi speaking about the struggle of Qaleʾt el-Kabsh slum residents, at the conference held by the Revolutionary Socialists at Cairo's Press Syndicate, December 9, 2007. Photo by and courtesy of Hossam el-Hamalawy.

FIGURE 13. Qaleʾt el-Kabsh slum women reading copies of *Al-Ishtiraki* (*The Socialist*) at the conference held by the Revolutionary Socialists at Cairo's Press Syndicate, December 9, 2007. Photo by and courtesy of Hossam el-Hamalawy.

FIGURE 14. Helwan University, November 10, 2008. Students protest in front of the Public Prosecutor's office against police assaults of activists on campus. Photo by and courtesy of Hossam el-Hamalawy.

FIGURE 15. Woman tax collector leading chants, April 21, 2009. Photo by and courtesy of Hossam el-Hamalawy.

Shaima' Al-Sabbagh had been shot by a policeman while she was marching from Tal'at Harb to Tahrir Square, holding in her hands flowers to commemorate the martyrs of the revolution on its fourth anniversary.

> I [knew] Shaima' al-Sabbagh from before the revolution, and from something different than politics. She was doing her studies in folk law . . . she was, she's very energetic, she's very, very energetic . . . she was all the time so funny, and I didn't know about her political position at the time, but I was enchanted by her knowledge about the folk law and the Egyptian traditions. I found out by time, when I was arrested in 2008, that she also had a political stand and she's a leftist. . . . She used to attend all the cases and the judicial hearings of the people who were arrested in 2008.[47]

Mahienour's and Shaima' al-Sabbagh's political experiences in the years between 2008 and 2011 were characterized by intense grassroots activism, especially with workers. When she remembered with me these days, ten years later, Mahienour was thoughtful about what had happened since then. Her assessment was that, paradoxically, through the experience of the revolution, the activists had lost touch with ordinary people, and in her view, this was maybe the main reason for their defeat: "When we used to work with workers, she [Shaima'] was a true and real communist. She was dedicated to workers especially so much, and she tried all the time to break the rules [that are normally imposed upon] women. Because to work with workers, you have to be either a lawyer, a journalist, or something like that. Instead, she was just the activist who comes and does poetry, or she [does] storytelling. She makes things lighter with the workers then."[48]

Mahienour suggested that maybe the social background of Shaima' facilitated her extraordinary capacity to connect to people, an aspect of her character Mahienour admired and was inspired by:

> She [Shaima'] was better than us in it [getting involved with workers]. As I told you, we, those among us who are coming from kind of the middle class, are very . . . dull, I think. We're boring, you know. . . . She wasn't like that. She was coming from a place that is a little bit poor and very warm, where everyone knows everyone, and so she was very full of life, and she was all the time practicing her ideas on a daily basis. Not like us. I think sometimes when I look at myself, I think I'm a little bit [of a] hypocrite. . . . She wasn't like that, at all. She was very active when it comes to workers.[49]

Shaima' al-Sabbagh occupies a special place in Mahienour's and other feminist memories, the memory of an unfulfilled dream. One of the letters

FIGURE 16. Poet and activist Shaima' al-Sabbagh running an art workshop for kids in Alexandria, 2014. Photo by Ihab Azazi and courtesy of Ihab Azazi and Osama Elselhi.

that Mahienour wrote from jail is dedicated to Shaima', on the anniversary of her assassination: "Oh Shaima' ... on the first anniversary of your death, carry our regards to our martyred angels... and tell them that we are still full of hope and that imprisonment and oppression have only increased our adherence to our dream and our revolution."[50]

On September 22, 2019, Mahienour El-Massry was once again arrested, while in court, in the wake of the protests against corruption and poverty that erupted in Cairo and across the country. Plainclothes security agents took her away while she was attending the hearing of a fellow lawyer at Alexandria Court. Her whereabouts were unknown for days until she appeared in front of a public prosecutor. Her incarceration has since then been renewed multiple times, and once the legal terms (one year of pretrial incarceration) were over, a new case was opened against her. During the first six months of the pandemic, like all the other prisoners, she could not receive any visitors. Like all the other prisoners, she was worried for her family.

From the prison, she wrote poignant letters, some of them smuggled out between the pages of books, others transcribed by her sister, who used her training as a theater actor to learn them by heart during her visits. In all

Mahienour's letters, the theme of socioeconomic rights is a central concern. "Prison is a microcosm of society," Mahienour wrote from the Damanhour women's prison in 2014:

> Those who are slightly more privileged than others find ways to get all they need inside, while the underprivileged are forced to work to meet their basic needs. Prison is a microcosm of society. Prisoners discuss what is happening in the country. You can find the whole political spectrum here. . . . Here they speak of this classist society and dream of social justice without complex theories. We should never lose sight of our main objective in the midst of this battle, in which we have lost friends and comrades every other day. We should not turn into people demanding the freedom of this or that person, while forgetting the wider needs and anxieties of the Egyptian people, who merely want to survive hand to mouth. . . . If we have to hold up the slogan, "Free this or that person," then let the slogan be, "Free Sayeda," "Free Heba," and "Free Fatima"—the three girls I met at the Security Directorate accused of being members of the Muslim Brotherhood and of committing murder among other things. They were randomly arrested and have been incarcerated since January without trial. Freedom for Umm Ahmed, who hasn't seen her children for eight years. Freedom for Umm Dina, who is the sole provider of her family. Freedom for Niamah, who agreed to go to prison instead of someone else in return for money to feed her children. Freedom for Farhah, Wafaa, Kawthar, Sanaa, Dawlat, Samia, Iman, Amal and Mervat. Our pains compared to theirs are nothing, as we know that there are those who will remember us, say our names from time to time, proudly mentioning how they know us. Instead, these women, who deserve to be proudly remembered, will only be mentioned at most in family gatherings. Down with this classist society, something we will never accomplish if we forget those who have truly suffered injustice.[51]

Mahienour was released on July 22, 2022, and she immediately went back to work. "It is normal," she told me in a phone call: "They have taken years of my life. I can't allow them to take it all. This would be a double victory for them!"[52] During her long incarceration, her words of hope were evoked on a number of social media pages by young Egyptian activists, and they have been a source of inspiration for people of her generation: "The revolution is the perpetual life and the dream, and that the revolution does not depend on individuals, and sooner or later, in our lifetime or that of those who will come after us, the revolution will be completed because human beings deserve better, and that ugliness no matter how it tries to beautify itself will reveal his face."[53]

PART THREE

Toward New Ways of Being, Knowing, and Doing

NINE

January 25, 2011

A NEW FEMINIST BEGINNING

THE MULTIPLE AND INTERTWINED SOCIAL mobilizations during the first decade of the 2000s—for democratization, for workers' rights, for international solidarity (especially with Iraqi and Palestinian people), for the reform of the Personal Status Law, and against sexual violence—brought together women from different generations toward a renewed interest in politics. That doesn't mean their visions or strategies were unified; feminists of different generations were engaging with politics at different levels and in different ways from each other, resulting in plural and sometimes conflicting conceptualizations of feminist activism. Indeed, diverse positionalities toward state institutions have troubled transgenerational relationships among feminists since this time. If 2011 was the highest point of at least two decades of underground social activism, it was also an event that expressed a strong tension between the old and the new, continuity and its disruption—what Hannah Arendt termed "a new beginning."[1] In the Egyptian case, this new beginning had at its core a profound awareness among the women who inspired, participated in, and carried on the spirit of the revolution of the inextricable relationship between gender and power in Egyptian society.

This tension sometimes resulted in a further evolution of feminist practice and ideas. For instance, feminist visions about violence against women in the public space did not simply acquire a renewed relevance in the Egyptian feminist discourse after 2011; they acquired new vocabulary and were framed according to new analytical categories that marked what I argue is a new turn in Egyptian feminist political thought and activism. In the lead-up to the January 2011 Revolution, its explosion and its aftermath, a new generation of activists became visible through their participation in the planning and leadership of the protests, taking care of wounded protesters, claiming their rights to take back public spaces not only through physical occupation but also through their care (cleaning of the streets) and decoration (graffiti). Young women joined ranks with their male counterparts to overthrow Mubarak's regime and, later, to face the deep state and the consequences of doing so. As occurred in every critical conjunction in modern Egyptian history, women found themselves at the core of political contestations, which since 2011 was marked by growing violence.

WOMEN ON THE FRONTLINES: FROM THE SOCIAL MOVEMENTS TO THE JANUARY 25 REVOLUTION

At least four of the major movements responsible for the January 25 Revolution—the 6th of April Youth Movement, We Are All Khaled Said, Kefaya, and the Revolutionary Socialists, were all characterized by a strong presence of women. The 6th of April Youth Movement was born in 2008 to support the strike of the workers. A then thirty-year-old blogger, Esraa Abdel Fattah, created a Facebook group that supported the workers to organize the strike. The Mubarak regime tried to repress the movement; in fact, soon after the 6th of April protests—the strike itself was prevented from taking place—Esraa Abdel Fattah was placed under arrest for two weeks. This was only the beginning of a decade of high-profile activism for her, as someone who actively took part in the 2011 Revolution (and continued to embrace its ideas of freedom, dignity, and social justice in the years that followed), was a founding member of the Dostour Party (April 2012), and was a democracy and human rights media activist.[2] All these activities earned her a nomination for the Nobel Peace Prize in 2011, but at the cost of a decade of juridical harassment, including a travel ban (since January 2015), investigation for foreign funding, prosecution for "joining an illegal organization," "defamation," "spreading of false news," and "misuse of social media" and, finally, pretrial detention from September 2019 until July 2021.[3]

The 6th of April movement became one of the core organizing forces leading up to the protests that began in Tahrir Square on National Police Day, January 25, 2011, which marked the beginning of the revolution. Choosing that day for protests was an act of defiance against the everyday violence and torture by the police experienced not only by political activists but equally by poor Egyptians who would end up abused, arrested, and imprisoned for the most trivial of reasons, if any at all.

Esraa Abdel Fattah was part of a small and influential vanguard of women bloggers who contributed to change the power dynamic in the blogosphere as part of the larger participation of women at the core of the 1990s and early 2000s protest movements. Some in this new generation of women activists grew up in politically active families, others developed their ideas in conversation with their peers and mentors. I discussed this with a pioneer of the Arabic blogosphere who took part in the 2011 Revolution, Manal Hassan, who explained her precocious awareness of the link between feminism and technology in very personal terms: "It's related to how I was brought up. I was brought up in a family of human rights defenders, a feminist family. Both my mother and my father help in tasks around the house, and even when I have my cousins at home, everyone is expected to help with preparing the table, the dishes and stuff like that—not just the girls, like in some of our extended family's [houses]. No, boys and girls would do the same jobs. And I was brought up to the notion that girls and women can do anything they want."

I interviewed Manal around the same time I interviewed her mother, Amal Abdel Hadi; perhaps it is this coincidence that allowed me to hear in the narrative of the daughter an echo of the mother's words, revealing the thread uniting them but also the looser strings where their experiences depart from each other.[4] Like other women of her generation, social class, level of education, and political inclination, Abdel Hadi carried a heavy burden to live a feminist life. As I narrated in part 1 of this book, she was in the leadership of the student movement in the seventies, was arrested for her political activism, and became part of the feminist wing of the human rights movement in Egypt in the eighties as a founder of the NWF. Yet, as she recalled in her interview, since giving birth to Manal, she experienced a tension between her obligations as a mother and her career, as opposed to Manal's father, who was not expected to prioritize parenting over professional duties.

Not surprisingly, for Abdel Hadi caregiving and raising her daughter was equally a feminist act; she was determined to raise Manal according to "her own values," not those of the grandparents or the broader conservative mainstream society. In this, my interviews document, Abdel Hadi's experience was neither unique nor isolated but were instead shared by many feminist activists of her generation, who often recount the need to slow down their professional and political commitments to prioritize family and caregiver duties, and the importance of doing so without giving up their activism. Children were regularly brought by their mothers to feminist meetings, growing up together in this shared space of women's activism, exposed to a community of women who witnessed all the phases of their lives and supported each other in politics and friendship.

Now young women and men, in 2011 the children of this generation of feminist activists, together attempted to fulfill their mothers' projects, pushing back against the patriarchal structures and rules upon which the postcolonial Egyptian state had been built. As a young revolutionary man promptly replied when I asked him about the motivations that inspired his militancy against sexual violence, "I am my mother's son!"[5]

This raises another question: Is growing up in a family of activists and with a feminist mother necessary to become a revolutionary, or is it in itself sufficient to take up such a struggle? It does not seem so on either count. I discussed this with a number of younger women activists and found that not all of them came from families of political activists. The feminist activist and scholar Hind Mahmoud explained to me that for some young women of her generation (she was born in the seventies), being part of the Muntada al-Shabbat (the youth forum of NWF) was extremely formative and shaped their feminism. Hala Shukrallah and Nawla Darwiche (both founding members of NWF) confirm their commitment in creating the space for a new generation of feminists.[6] Together, their testimonies corroborate what has been long theorized by feminist scholarship, particularly by Audre Lorde, bell hooks, and Sara Ahmed: living a feminist life requires a space that is larger than the family, or that allows one to rethink the family; it requires an elective community of peers, which Manal found among her fellow techies, while other women of her generation found it in the Muntada al-Shabbat and, later, other feminist organizations that were created in the *fin de millennium,* such as Nazra for Feminist Studies (2003).

But it was not only tech-savvy, often English-speaking younger activists who were the backbone of the emerging generation of women's activism, as became evident a week before the planned Police Day demonstration, when a young, headscarfed, and until then publicly unknown woman, Asmaa Mahfouz, recorded and posted to YouTube a call from an anonymous Cairo apartment to Egyptian people to join the planned protests: "If you consider yourself a man, come with me on January 25. Instead of saying that women should not come, because they will be beaten, let's show a bit of honor, be men, come with me on January 25."[7]

Esraa Abdel Fattah, Manal Hassan, and Asmaa Mahfouz, along with bloggers like Nawara Nejm, who emerged in the early 2000s, were not exceptions in the landscape of Egyptian activism. They belonged to the galaxy of post-ideological activists who grew up in the nineties and came of age with the 2011 Revolution. Like other groups that were emerging in the early 2000s (especially the Revolutionary Socialist Movement, We Are All Khaled Said, and the 6th of April Youth Movement), these women turned to blogs and social media to circumvent censorship and persecution by the national security apparatus and to introduce women's perspectives to the emerging activist sphere. These spaces, which emerged in the early 2000s when the internet was liberalized across the Arab world,[8] seemed to allow anonymity and fluidity in communication, young political activists perceived them as relatively safe spaces, and even less politicized young people were influenced by them.[9]

But even in this context of growing online and offline activism, what Asmaa Mahfouz did was unusual and risky. To begin with, her video was not anonymous, and her face was uncovered and recognizable. She presented herself as an ordinary, young Egyptian woman, speaking in vernacular Egyptian, wearing the headscarf (a conventional sign of modesty),[10] and steadily looking at the camera. This was an extraordinarily brave stance to take, and, given the precedents (including what had happened to Esraa Abdel Fattah), she must have been aware of the risk of imprisonment or worse before her.

A young woman armed with only a video camera and an internet connection, Asmaa Mahfouz broke the wall of fear that for many years had inhibited Egyptian people from rebelling. What I want to emphasize here is that Mahfouz was not alone, not an exception; she was part of a vanguard, a group of young (and not only young) radical (and not only radical) people advocating for political reform and social and cultural change in Egypt. Women intellectuals from the generation of the nineties were also part of this broad movement for change. They were inspired by many intersecting causes, including the multiple attacks against churches in Egypt that went unpunished for years.[11]

All these themes were present in Mahfouz's eloquent speech, including keywords of the revolution that would begin days later such as *karama* (dignity) and *'adala ijtima'iyya* (social justice). Mahfouz also used the term *kefaya*, "enough" in colloquial Egyptian. Kefaya was also the name of the social movement which, since 2004, had been used by Egyptian democratic activists to express their discontent with the policies of the Mubarak regime.[12] Most importantly, she invited men not to ask women to stay away from the streets in order to be safe, but to join her in protest and show some "honor" and "manhood" by protecting women from violence. Women activists' discourse about "protection" evolved further over the years, but what Asmaa Mahfouz did was a step in a new direction: she linked the January 25 demonstrations to the expectation that ordinary Egyptian women like herself would be in the Square, and that it was their right to experience that space as a safe one. Given the recurrent violence experienced by women (especially political activists, but also ordinary women) in the previous decades, this was an ambitious expectation. The anti-sexual harassment groups (one of them led by women) that developed in the following months and years have pushed this expectation even further.

But Mahfouz's speech was demanding much more than safety. By reappropriating and re-signifying the words at the core of Egyptian patriarchy ("honor" and "protection"), she deconstructed the gendered binary between normative femininity and masculinity upon which the modern nation-state was founded. In fact, as Beth Baron has illustrated in her study about the connections between gendered images of the nation in Egypt and the politics of Egyptian women nationalists, this rhetoric goes back to the late nineteenth century and was absorbed by the women's movement as well.[13] By claiming their right as young and modest Egyptian women to join in the protest (among other significations, headscarves are worn as a sign of modesty), the women of the 6th of April movement challenged the gender binary that is at the foundational core of not only Egyptian nationalism but also late nineteenth- and early twentieth-century feminism.

It seems to me that Mahfouz's brave and powerful act exposed an existing tension between continuity and fracture also within the century-long history of the Egyptian feminist movement. The continuity was reflected in the participation of Egyptian women in the 2011 Revolution. This was the most recent in a long trajectory of women's political activism, yet as in other revolutionary moments in Egyptian (and indeed world) history, women's demands were considered as secondary if not subordinated to more general political demands. This trajectory reached back to the early twentieth century, when Egyptian women joined male nationalists to challenge the British colonial authorities, only to find themselves subject to a constitutional monarchy where political rights were not granted to them. It continued well into the first decade of the 2000s, when the women of the workers' movements joined the sit-ins and occupations of factories, defying the prejudice that it was shameful for Muslim women strikers to sleep in the streets, yet again saw their specific demands for women workers rights such as maternity leave and childcare treated as secondary to more "general" workers' rights.[14]

The fracture that occurred with their participation in the January 25 Revolution involved the challenge by revolutionary women to the gender roles and binaries constructed by the modern nationalist discourse in all its forms, both the male-dominated (secular as well as religious) and the feminist versions. Nobody could tell, yet, where it would head to, but it was clear since day one that this was a new turn.

A NEW TURN IN THE HISTORY OF FEMINISM IN EGYPT

My conversations with women of multiple generations, ranging from those who had been part of the student movement in the seventies to those who came of age in 2011 within the revolutionary spaces, reveal that 2011 marked a new turn in the history of feminism in Egypt—a turn that in part builds upon the work of previous generations but also takes new directions. The new generation of revolutionaries questions normative discourses about gender and sexuality, and it critically engages with notions such as gender fluidity. I discussed this with activists of Nazra, or the collective Ikhtiyar for a Feminist Choice, and Ganubiyya Hurra, but also with young women activists who are not affiliated to any specific group yet identify themselves as feminists, meaning with it as activists for gender equality.

In 2014, I interviewed a member of Bidaya, an LGBTQ group created in 2010 that at the time of the interview also had a branch in Sudan, and their main activities were research, media communication, and offering medical and legal support to LGBTQ people.[15] The Bidaya's activist, who asked me not to reveal their name for security reasons, reflected about what changed in relation to LGBTQ people during the 2011 Revolution, and they suggested that solidarity (by other feminist groups) and visibility (of the LGBTQ people) were the most significant changes: "Even transgender were in Tahrir Square, we were all there, we were all participating in this movement.... There was a very good solidarity going on in the Square and that's why we started gaining the trust of the liberal activists in Egypt after the revolution, because they saw us fighting there. Before that, I believe that they thought that we only care about sex, that's all we want. But now seeing us fighting for the same principles they're fighting for, I think it was a great help for us."[16]

The 2011 Revolution produced a change in the perception of LGBTQ rights, which since then has become an explicit part of feminist and human rights agendas in Egypt. This was a new development, which can be compared with the hesitance shown by members of the feminist and human rights movements to support defendants in the Queen Boat case in 2001, when a police raid on a floating disco on the Nile frequented by gay men led to intense media and public vilification and prosecution for "habitual debauchery."[17]

The nexus between the Egyptian government's attack on the LGBTQ community in the post-2013, counterrevolutionary phase equaled if not exceeded the hope for a change in public and state attitudes inspired by the revolution. In fact, LGBTQ people soon became a major target of the post-2013 regime. Many migrated, seeking relief from the mix of social pressure and security threats they were feeling. The Queer activist Sarah Hegazi, who in 2017 was arrested, tortured, and forced to exile, a trauma that eventually led her to commit suicide in 2020, just for raising the rainbow flag at a concert, well-articulated in her writings the link she sees between sexual and political repression in counterrevolutionary Egypt: "Whoever differs, whoever is not a male Sunni Muslim heterosexual who supports the ruling regime is considered persecuted, untouchable, or dead."[18] Hegazi's writings weave together themes of class, gender, and religion as intersecting factors that determine one's inclusion in or exclusion from what is generally considered the normative Egyptian identity. The new generation of feminist activists embraced LGBTQ rights demands, including an overall reconceptualization of gender and sexuality in their work, which went through multiple phases. Between 2011 and 2013 they tried to develop their work in less formal structures, which seldom took the form of NGOs registered at the Ministry of Social Affairs but most of the time were informal groups, kept together by common intents as well as friendship bonds among the members. Many of these initiatives emerged from the feminist schools organized across Egypt by Nazra for Feminist Studies after 2011. In 2013, there were about fifty-five groups across Egypt, but not all of them continued to operate in the following years.[19] Among those that continued were Ganubiyya Hurra (Free South), created in 2011 in Aswan, which linked the feminist issue to race and specifically Nubian issues; Durik (Your Role), Ikhtiyar for a Feminist Choice, and Barah (Safe Space) were created in Cairo between 2012 and 2013. Women's groups have also been active beyond the cities in the rural areas: Bint al-Nil (Daughter of the Nile) works on child marriage, domestic violence, and education for girls in the villages of Baheira. Untha (Female) is also based in Baheira and in Damanhour and has produced research about girls' dropout rates from school. In Ismailia, Radio Banat Offline talks about women's issues, and all the operators are young women from Ismailia. The women's scene blossomed also online: Thawrat el-Banat (The Girls Revolution) and Femi-hub operate as solidarity groups for young women who choose to live alone and who face multiple challenges (especially violence). There are artists groups like Bussy (Look), a theater company that originated in the Department of Arts at the American University in Cairo and then developed independently, that produces storytelling about gender-related topics (especially masculinity, femininity, gender stereotypes, and sexual violence), and Banat Masarwa (Daughters of the Egyptians), a Cairo-based musical group that produces songs inspired by the stories they collect from workshops in different parts of Egypt.

These emerging feminist groups initiated a long-lasting (and still ongoing) process of dismantling the foundations of a national ideology about gender that, while it had over the years accepted the arguments of the "gender mainstream" (as a young feminist intellectual once told me: "You would hardly find in Egypt someone who openly tells you that she/he is not for women's rights"), still imposed a number of restrictions on women's political action and did not ensure women's safety in the public space.

The limited ideological and political space for feminism, never mind fully recognizing the equality of women, was part of a conservative culture that permeated both the secular and the religious fields, influencing activists across the political spectrum—liberals, Marxists, and Islamists, although at different degrees and from different perspectives. The common thread among these different streams of gender conservative thought was that they all built upon the mutually constitutive relationship between heteronormative colonial patriarchy and heteronormative anticolonial nationalism. For these reasons it seems to me that to draw from Queer decolonial and Indigenous theories—specifically, on the notions first introduced by the Chicana feminist philosopher Gloria Anzaldúa of the New Mestiza and the Neplantera, or threshold people, with reference to a subject that allows for contradictions, that lives on the borderlands and accepts multiple identities, challenging the status quo and embracing ambiguity—can be productive to understand this new turn in the spiral of Egyptian feminism.

If it is true—and I argue it is—that feminism represents a challenge to the patriarchal order (that is, a challenge to power relationships based upon the prevalence of men over women, and of older generations over the younger), then the feminism that inspired the 2011 Egyptian Revolution and then evolved into something new through that experience, infused a cultural and social change into Egypt. This change builds on the long history of Egyptian feminism, but it also introduces new practices to address women and gender issues (such as those experimented with by the groups fighting sexual violence), new themes (such as LGBTQ rights), and a new language (such as the shift from "victims" to "survivors" in relation to sexual violence). This means that the era that started in 2011 is the most recent chapter in the history of women's century-long and still ongoing revolution in Egypt.

THE 2011 FEMINIST REVOLUTION

From the start, gender was on the agenda of women revolutionaries, and soon its relevance became obvious to many revolutionary men as well. I discussed this with several young women I met at a demonstration toward the end of 2011, in the feminist associations I have been visiting over the years, in research workshops I attended with them, and in the newsroom of *Mada Masr*, whose journalists had all been part of the revolution.

In the initial period of the revolution, from the eighteen days through March 2011, the tension around women's bodies and their activism in the Square encouraged women organizers to assert their presence in the revolutionary space as equal to men, and to redefine the same meaning of feminism:

> [The revolution] started with men and women, young and old people, and all these tendencies to focus on certain groups [as the ones who started the revolution] didn't get it right for me.... All I can say is that, not as women but as Egyptians that are activists, human rights people, both men and women had a great role in this revolution.[20]

> I prefer to believe in the human rights issue [more] than in the feminist issue. And for me it [feminism] is not a priority because it is a bit ... I see it as a human issue instead, and not specifically women.... I know there are lots of them who suffered a lot, lack of education and so on, but it is the whole system that needs to be changed.[21]

These quotes express the feeling of a specific moment in the revolution and, although they need to be recorded—they are indeed a constitutive part of how the discourse evolved—they cannot be essentialized. As I discussed earlier in this book, women issues and human rights have never been separated issues, not only because women's rights are human rights but even most importantly because women were crucial actors in both influencing the government policies and defining the grassroots activism about human rights in Egypt. The human rights movement in Egypt has been profoundly shaped by the presence of feminist activists in it. Yet, among many of the young women I interviewed, a small yet qualitatively significant sample (they were all well-known among the activists' scene) were hesitant to identify themselves as feminists. As I dug deeper, talking more to them and to other feminists with more experience, I realized this expressed a desire to take a distance not from feminism per se but from the feminism they'd grown up with—that of the increasingly neoliberal, depoliticized women's activism epitomized by the NGO sector and "civil society" *à l'américaine* that had been seeded by Western donors in the nineties with the end of the Cold War (few places more powerfully than in Egypt). For the millennial generation, especially those trained in critical humanities and social sciences' programs in Egyptian universities where postcolonial feminist critique of liberal civil society paradigms was increasingly ubiquitous, this kind of women's activism lacked political strength. Beyond this critique yet clearly related to it, the "Tahrir generation" of young women activists also wanted to differentiate themselves from the elitist and governmental policies on women that had characterized the last decade of the Mubarak's government, which in the collective imaginary of young people was therefore associated with its authoritarianism and corruption. As the pre- and postmillennial generations interacted, the women of the eighties and the nineties, who had developed professional expertise and skills in the area of women and development programs and worked in international organizations for children and women's rights, fighting to produce change both within and from the margins of the system, did not agree with the younger generation's viewpoint.

For them, the younger women's critiques smacked of the *damnatio memoriae* that is all too common in the dissemination of feminist history—the problem of transgenerational memories according to which each generation thinks of itself as pioneering a field and building exclusive memories. But being in Egypt multiple times over many years allowed me to observe that this intergenerational relationship further evolved. As Egyptian women revolutionaries of the younger generation went through a long series of traumatic experiences, such as sexual assault, rape, and imprisonment, they became increasingly aware of the need to create a group memory and to overcome the ongoing transgenerational tension among feminists, acknowledging that there are different feminisms for different times and different bodies. Moreover, three simultaneous factors have led these younger women to develop a renewed interest in feminism: first, the danger of women's marginalization from institutional politics (the first parliamentary elections after the 2011 Revolution, which saw only three women elected, equivalent to less than 2 percent, and women's exclusion from the first constitutional committee were two important wake-up calls for women that the fight for substantial political rights was still ongoing); second, the generalized experiences of sexual violence and orchestrated assaults during protests demonstrations; and, third, the growing perception that women, gender, and sexuality-related issues continue to be mobilized by politicians in search of legitimacy every time there is a political crisis. These experiences encouraged women political activists to consider how feminism can contribute not only to shift the public discourse about women and their place in society but also to a holistic social change that involves all the segments of the society and that produces new conceptions of power relationships.

I have documented and analyzed these processes, including the major challenges faced by the women since 2011, the strategies they activated to overcome them, and how the difficulty in archiving and transmitting history has both historiographical and political implications. This analysis shows that since day one of the 2011 Revolution, the young revolutionary women were not rejecting feminism per se. Rather, they were trying to move away from the well-consolidated modernist episteme of women's rights and freedom. The new generation of Egyptian feminists takes a step back from the ideological legacy of twentieth-century nationalist ideologies, which continue to permeate the anticolonial and postcolonial spaces in favor of a decolonial and Queer feminist epistemology where identities are fluid and borders are blurred. Thus, we see that, over time, Egyptian feminism has reflected different ways of being, knowing, and doing.

TEN

Historicizing the Egyptian Revolution

THE POLITICS OF MEMORY AND TRANSMISSION

IN HER WRITINGS ON SEXUAL violence, Panamanian philosopher Linda Martín Alcoff conceptualizes the relationship between experience, testimony, and memory. Alcoff explains that when talking about women's experience, and especially when their experiences and memories of, and testimonies about, violence are reported to state institutions such as hospitals, the police, and the courts, their truth is always questioned and their experiences as a form of valid knowledge are challenged. Alcoff uses the reality of how women's experiences of violence are ignored, degraded, and erased to explore the intersection of phenomenological and epistemological groundings of truth claims and the importance of developing new frameworks, grounded on women's testimonies rather than men's power to evaluate and judge them, within which to build our knowledge.[1] Alcoff and other feminists' focus on experience, testimony, and transgenerational memory allows for an investigation of how power shapes the construction of historical memory, contributing to a reformulation of historical questions and in so doing playing a crucial role in the recovery from trauma of survivors of violence.[2]

Alcoff's decolonial notion of "testimonial episteme" can be productively related to the specific context of the 2011 Revolution. Here we deal with competing political forces claiming the legitimacy of the revolution and, especially since 2013, when the military came back to power, the crackdown against human rights activists, academics, intellectuals, and journalists revealed that there is a concerted effort to rewrite (one could say "erase") the collective memory of 2011.

Multiple coexisting narratives about the eighteen days developed in the subsequent months and years, alternating utopian and dystopian visions, depending on the specific moment, some of them focusing on the joy of being part of a special moment, others on the violence experienced by women. They do not exclude each other; they coexist as they express different conditions and even different needs at different moments, highlighting the tension between violence and care during the eighteen days. On one side, numerous accidents of violence happened; on the other, and sometimes simultaneously, people assumed control of the public space primarily by taking care of it and trying to ensure that everyone was safe. In the narratives of the young women I interviewed, what remained unforgettable was the management of the Square through direct participation and the inclusivity of the movement, which also allowed them to cross class barriers. Lobna Darwish, one of the young women who interrupted her graduate studies abroad to join the revolution, and who was part of the collective Mosireen (a group of activists who filmed and gathered videos to bear testimony to the revolution and contrast the narratives of the military), remembers this crosspassing as a highlight of the revolutionary experience:

> It was the only time we got to meet each other outside of forced class ... gender ... and political relations. It's sad to say, but in a country that's very class-divided, [like in] Egypt, you don't meet the taxi driver unless your relationship to him is as a taxi driver, you don't sit on the *qahwa* (café) and have a shisha with him. It's not how things are in Egypt, sadly, because [the] class system is very [rigid].... There was really a moment where people got to deal with each other outside of the forced relationships, which was exciting, and I think for both sides was exciting.... And I think it's something very exceptional, and sadly very short.[3]

In her interview, Darwish emphasized that class and gender go hand in hand, and there cannot be feminism without broader social justice. This positioning echoes the tradition of the feminist left (especially the NWF and their commitment to women workers' rights, which I had the opportunity to discuss with senior members of the organization), while at the same time it takes it one step ahead, because here, in the experience of the revolution as narrated by Darwish, people from different social classes, men and women, operate on an equal level and toward the same aim, which is everyone's liberation.

Others of my interlocutors underline that there were no leaders,[4] and decisions were taken collectively. Order was maintained in the public space through a distribution of tasks. The street children of Wust al-Balad (downtown Cairo) had poured into the Square, where they found people who took care of them, fed them, clothed them, and offered them a tent in which to sleep. Medical doctors were operating in camp clinics to treat the injured in the clashes with the army, and overall women felt safe, to the point that some of them refer to the Square as "the safest place in Egypt they have ever experienced":

> Those eighteen days were just a utopia, I have to say, everything was just perfect, women were treated in an equal way. Also, my friend had issues with harassment during the demonstration, not during the eighteen days. I have to tell you that before the revolution, the idea of harassment was everywhere, and it wasn't just harassment by the people, but harassment by the state.[5]

> Actually, I think that in those eighteen days there was a Tahrir country inside Egypt. I think I can call it that way because it had its own food and security and no leaders ... it was like a big complex that they had to protect, the way people were dealing with each other in Tahrir must be in the whole country, that's what I think. No sexual harassment or stolen things whatever ... no violence except the police against the protesters ... it was just amazing ... I don't know how people talked about sexual harassment inside the Square.[6]

Prominent women intellectuals, such as the writer Ahdaf Soueif, who reported for the *Guardian* and was interviewed by numerous media, and Nawal al-Saadawi, who was commenting on the pages of *al-Masry al-Youm*, narrated to the world this experience of Tahrir Square in the eighteen days as a "reclaim of the spirit of Egypt,"[7] an inclusive and safe space, which they juxtaposed to the practices of repression, co-optation, and violence of Mubarak's regime.[8]

The aim of the utopian narratives about the eighteen days was not necessarily to mirror reality, not even as the events were unfolding: it was rather a conscious revolutionary act, aimed at shaping a new future. In its genuine optimism, spontaneity, and enthusiasm, this narrative was strategic. Against a mainstream representation of the public space as unsafe and violent for women, it presented the icon of an inclusive and peaceful Square, occupied by "the peaceful people" as opposed to "the violent regime." However, taking this hopeful, if not positive, narrative as the unique narrative of women in the revolution risks silencing the voices of those who have been attacked, and in so doing, to perpetuate the trauma. This was a recurrent critique among the young feminist activists I interviewed, who were interpreting the silencing of women who experienced sexual violence as a sign of the growing masculinization of the public space, involving at different levels both in the military field and the revolutionary fields.[9]

HISTORICIZING THE EGYPTIAN REVOLUTION · 195

FIGURE 17. Novelist Ahdaf Soueif and her son, writer Omar Robert Hamilton, in Tahrir Square, Cairo, February 3, 2011. Photo by and courtesy of Hossam el-Hamalawy.

Building on Alcoff's decolonial feminist episteme of testimony and memory, it is possible to acknowledge the credibility of these memories without falling in the trap of asserting that the revolution was largely nonviolent, particularly on the part of the regime. Some of the feminists I interviewed in fact provided a more troubled account of those days: "It was beautiful. I still think that this is not the end. There is something that has changed inside the people. There was a feeling of solidarity between people. For example, I don't remember any case of sexual harassment during the eighteen days. But the day that Mubarak stepped down, we again went to Tahrir, my daughter and I, and we were almost raped. It was as if all the bad instincts were coming out."[10]

Both international and local organizations and media documented innumerable violations by regime forces, and protesters used force as well until Tahrir was secured. Violence also occurred across the country. Amnesty International reported that during the eighteen days "at least 840 people were killed, and 6,467 others were injured, according to Ministry of Health and Population sources, and thousands were detained, many of them tortured."[11]

In an attempt to prohibit the activists from solidifying their tenuous hold on Tahrir, on the January 28 the regime disrupted mobile and internet communications as well as violently attacked protesters (in what quickly became known as the "day of anger"), only to achieve the opposite effect: "I think that the most stupid thing the regime has done is cutting off the internet [on February 28], and the connection between people, because that's when people start going down to the street to look for their friends and their relatives and everything. They wanted to know what's going on, on the ground, ah, and the more they go out, the more people die."[12]

Not even the dispatching of camels and horses on February 2, during the "Battle of the Camels,"[13] could stop the wave of popular rage. On that day, two of Egypt's founding coders and bloggers, the couple Manal Hassan and Alaa Abd El-Fattah (who as of mid-2024 has been imprisoned for most of the last decade), returned from South Africa, where they lived, and joined the protests, along with other young Egyptians living abroad. Manal Hassan evoked these days when I interviewed her in January 2018, while Alaa, her then-husband and the father of their six-year-old son, was becoming one of the world's most famous prisoners of conscience:

> On the first of February, we saw the first Million [person] March, and we just couldn't stay out. We booked our tickets, and we flew the same day. We arrived the next day, on the day of the Camel Battle.... We were flying over night, and it was such a different state from the Million March that we saw when we decided to take the flight back to Egypt, to the arrival at the Camel Battle. It was a tough day because we didn't know what was happening. My mother's house was very close, ten to fifteen minutes' walk from Tahrir Square, so we decided that we would go to her place directly. She came and picked me up from the airport with Alaa's mum. Alaa went with his mum directly to the Square and I went with my mum just to drop the bags and to walk back to the Square. And in those few minutes, Alaa was in the Square, the Camel Battle started, and we started getting news about what was happening and advice that no one was to go there, and that the Square was surrounded by thugs, groups of thugs, and that it was very.... So, the whole Square was surrounded with groups of thugs and Alaa and I got separated.
>
> Alaa was in the Square and I couldn't go to him and it took the whole day until I was able to get in the Square and it was very dangerous. People who wanted to go there were advised to go to the Hisham Mubarak Centre and that from there we could go in groups, instead of going on our own. I went with one of the groups late at night with medical aid and food. We were stopped so many times by these neighborhood committees. At one point one of these committees took the food from us because they said they had

enough of these protests in Tahrir and, that, if we take food to people then we help them stay longer. The last one got very violent: it turned into a mob very quickly and it was one of the most dangerous things that happened. An angry mob surrounded us and jumped over the car. I don't know . . . it was a miracle that we got out of that.[14]

The regime's various forces didn't only utilize beatings, shootings, and other forms of physical attack on protesters. Sexual harassment, assault, and rape were also far more common during the eighteen days than is generally realized. This was difficult to discuss, even among the most radical components of the revolutionary forces. Lobna Darwish told me that at the beginning nobody would admit that sexual assaults were happening in the Square because they wanted to protect its image: "A very long fight took place for people to admit that this was happening. And then another fight took place to basically take responsibility and act on it. And then a third fight took place for women to be part of this action, and then another fight took place for this discourse not to be about protection of women but basically allowing everybody to be safe and in a space that we think is like a revolution space."[15]

Darwish emphasizes that the continuing pressure exercised by the revolutionary activists allowed feminist ideas to permeate everything, from chants to graffiti, influencing young women's determination not to remain silent in the face of sexual violence. A decade has passed since I discussed this with Darwish, who since then gained further experience as a human rights defender.[16] Yet the crimes against women protesters Darwish was among the first to denounce have not been punished nor has the survivors' right to compensation been recognized.

Not only that, but these crimes, and the traumatic experiences that came with them, would certainly be erased by the collective memory if it was not for a conscious effort to document and to narrate undertaken by feminist activists. Despite their often-heroic efforts, multiple layers of silence continue to surround sexual violence; besides the hostility of the state institutions, which tend to blame women, many women revolutionaries also remain silent because of the deep trauma they've experienced without even a hope for justice or recognition by the government or most of their fellow Egyptians (including, often, their own families).

Under these circumstances, documenting became vital, not to merely interrogate the representation of the revolution as an inclusive and women-friendly space nor to question if it relates to the reality on the field. Feminist organizations deployed huge efforts to document and denounce. Nazra gathered a series of blog posts where survivors of sexual assaults were narrating their terrifying experiences, and published a series of joint statements with other feminist and human rights Egyptian organizations to denounce mob sexual assaults and gang rapes that occurred between 2011 and 2014,[17] while El-Nadeem collected hundreds of testimonies from January 2011 to 2013 in a comprehensive and painful-to-read report.[18]

According to Magda Adly, the psychiatrist and human rights defender who curated the El-Nadeem report, publishing the testimonies of the survivors helps them in the process of recovery by contrasting widespread narratives that blame women for participating in demonstrations, and affirming that sexual crimes should not be a shame for the victims but for the perpetrators. By shaming the perpetrators, it contributes to stopping sexual crimes, which at time she wrote, went largely unpunished. Finally, it allows people to study the techniques used to attack women and learn how to contrast them. Dr. Adly affirms that publishing is at once a form of resistance against the violence, of solidarity with the victims, and a call to the State to assume the responsibility to stop sexual assaults.[19]

The 2011 Revolution was a moment where historical feminist narratives about public space, with requests of safety for women and other vulnerable subjects, came to surface. But these were violently opposed by counterrevolutionary forces: the SCAF, the Muslim Brotherhood, and the military, which disseminated a disempowering counternarrative of Tahrir Square as a hypermasculine space of mob assaults and licentiousness, against which only the army could restore order. This narrative diminishes women political activists to the victims of violence, neglecting their agency and silencing their voices. This was paralleled by a significant shrinking of the space for women's political action, and men's political action generally.

The narrative about the squares as safe spaces is a counternarrative to the one produced by the Mubarak, the SCAF, the Brotherhood, and the El-Sisi regimes, which not only described the public spaces as unfit for women and as crossed by intersecting gendered and class barriers but also organized sexualized assault and terrorizing of women activists.[20] On the other hand, acknowledging that violence during the eighteen days did not only come from the regime but involved the protesters against each other (and especially against women) allows us to recuperate a critical view on the revolution. Gender violence crosses political divides and requires an even deeper "human revolution"[21] to change the order of things. It highlights the deep link between

FIGURE 18. "Down with Mubarak," Cairo, February 2, 2011. Photo by and courtesy of Hossam el-Hamalawy.

FIGURE 19. Independent trade union demonstration in front of the headquarters of the state-backed Egyptian Federation of Trade Unions, Cairo, February 14, 2011. Photo by and courtesy of Hossam el-Hamalawy

FIGURE 20. Striking doctors, Cairo, September 22, 2011. Photo by and courtesy of Hossam el-Hamalawy.

authoritarianism, militarism, and violence against women—a link that is embedded in the history of the modern Egyptian state and its colonial military structure, that permeates also the political cultures of the (male-dominated) oppositions. The line of continuity of sexual violence against women displayed along the feminist century by multiple regimes reflects, more than a "cultural" attitude (as simplistic culturalist approaches would suggest), a political structure of power relationships that are gendered and that oppress not only women (and more than everyone, women who are opponents of the regime), but whoever does not conform to the standard of hegemonic masculinity.[22] As such, it can be dismantled only through radical political interventions at discursive, grassroots, and policy levels. Women activists have put in place discursive and practical dispositives to engage at all the three levels.

ARCHIVES OF FEELINGS AND FEMINIST PRACTICES OF COUNTER-MEMORIALIZATION

March is an important month in Egyptian women's memory, because on March 16, 1919, women organized an anti-British demonstration, whose images became iconic.[23] Beth Baron has shown how women's participation in the nationalist movement has been celebrated, mostly through the iconic photos of the women demonstrations (which were published in a special issue of *al-Musawwar* to celebrate the fiftieth anniversary of the revolution).[24] Most notably, the iconization of Huda Shaʿrawi started as early as in 1945, when she was conferred the Nishan al-Kamal award (Order of the Virtues), and continued throughout the republican age. Nasser issued a postage stamp commemorating Huda Shaʿrawi and a street in downtown Cairo (and others around Egypt) was named after her,[25] and the Arabic version of her memories was issued by the General Authority for Egyptian Cultural Palaces as part of the Memory of Writing series.

However, this memorialization was not always conducive to historicization. In fact, the testimonies I have collected from the feminist historians who pioneered the effort of writing the history of Egyptian feminism show that their most important contribution was to write history from scattered and private archives, relying on oral histories from women's activists and on women's networks, because neither official governing nor educational institutions had any interest in enabling women's history to be collected, preserved, or publicized.[26] In the late seventies, Egypt, like many other countries around the world, responded to the invitation of the United Nations to celebrate March 8 as International Women's Day. Since then (1977), public events have been organized to celebrate women's activism during the week of March 8–16. However, governmental institutions, especially the Egyptian Council for Women since 2000, tended to monopolize the celebrations without involving independent women's organizations, and the general atmosphere of repression in the late Mubarak age did not allow public women's demonstrations.

Empowered by the experience of the eighteen days, in March 2011 for the first time in years Egyptian feminists felt motivated by the desire to celebrate International Women's Day. The rally was brutally attacked by men in plain clothes—most likely a combination of security personnel and thugs (*baltagiya*), as they occurred with the indifference (one could even say the tacit approval) of the police, who did not intervene against the attackers.

> If you've seen the demonstration on March 8 of the women, they have been attacked, and I was there, and there was the TV and everything, and some girls were harassed, some girls were beaten by men that were there ... [they were] not a lot, around five hundred, one thousand maximum. But there were a lot of international media there, and that's why lots of people said, "Those women are foreigners, they are not Egyptians." It was not organized

in a correct way, the march started at 3:00 p.m., 4:00 p.m., and the attack started at 5:00 p.m. At the beginning, it was just strong arguments, and then it really happened in a very strong way, and someone got harassed and also some friends of mine. . . . There was a woman that came there and asked me if I was able to cook, and [she also] said, "Are you kidding me? It is not allowed for a woman to become a president, this is *haram,* this is forbidden, this is taboo," and they even got me some other women saying, "This is the woman that is in Egypt, you are not Egyptian." I don't have anything Egyptian? I am totally Egyptian, Black and brown ... and so they told me, "But you are a cultural woman from a high class and you don't represent the majority of the Egyptian women."[27]

Hala Shukrallah was among the participants at the demonstration; she immediately published her testimony in *Al-Ahram Weekly,* emphasizing the political weight of the women's march:

The women's march started from in front of the Press Syndicate and ended in Tahrir Square, where they were joined by independent participants from different walks of life: university professors, students and artists, as well as men who had joined the march in solidarity with the demands of women for their fully participation as citizens and as a reflection of the revolution's slogan of freedom, democracy and social justice. Statement and leaflets called for a revision of discriminatory laws, including the promulgation of laws against sexual harassment, the formulation of a new constitution along with a participatory process as well as the postponement of parliamentary elections.[28]

For an experienced activist such as Shukrallah it was not difficult to detect the correlation between the social conservatism of most Egyptians and the orchestration of attacks by the secret police and the thugs of the National Democratic Party (Mubarak's party). Her analysis highlights the combination of anti-Coptic and anti-women propaganda disguised as religious teaching that had characterized the strategy of containment of democratic political movements in Egypt during the Mubarak era.

The gendered nature of the sectarian and authoritarian policy promoted by the SCAF after Mubarak's downfall, and their attempts to neglect and to attack women political activists, was commented on painfully by young women also on social media:

Today is a very sad day in Egypt, Misogyny showed its ugly face in Tahrir today and women are treated as less than 2nd class citizens on the International Women's Day.

That is very sad . . . I thought this change would actually bring about change . . . what does it take?

Are the women at all organized into a lobbying group or are they split along socio-economic lines? Are there any female candidates for office?[29]

Often ephemeral sources such as tweets, Facebook, other social media posts, and graffiti constitute what I call an "archive of feelings," which, if adequately collected and assessed, can support feminist historians to enable antinormative experiences and counter-memorialize the days of the revolution, questioning the heteropatriarchal narratives that confirm gender norms. A typical example of the importance of this practice are the reports about what happened the day after the women's march, on March 9, 2011, when seventeen activists were arrested, held in the Egyptian Museum, and those who were unmarried among them were forced to take a so-called virginity test.

I think the virginity tests incident was a very, very moving and important event for most of us. First of all, having to deal with [it], just hearing the testimony all of a sudden in a press conference without knowing beforehand. [Until then] we thought just arrests and torture [were happening], and we didn't know that there was anything [specific] happening to the women. Just hearing it on stage, and then trying to make sure [verify] it's true, and trying to get any of the women to come out and talk about it, because some of them said, yes this happened but I cannot talk about it. And just watching Samira [Ibrahim] being that brave, and the whole campaign . . . it was a very interesting experience because, especially with virginity tests, nobody wanted to believe the story because it was too violent. And it was something very important, and now when we talk about the crimes of the military with anybody from the revolution, I'm sure they would list the virginity tests as one of them and one of the strongest ones. On one level, it's very masculine because, you know, protecting the honor and everything, but also because all of the sudden women become at the core of things and become the victims of army and police brutality and it's not something that happens most of the time or it's not as public as well.[30]

At that time, Amnesty International reported the comment of a general—who later was revealed to be then Field Marshal Abdel Fattah El-Sisi—on the incident, which exposes the SCAF's attitude toward women revolutionary activists: "The girls who were detained were not like your daughter or mine. These were girls who had camped out in tents with male protesters in Tahrir Square, and we found in the tents Molotov cocktails and drugs. We didn't want them to say we had sexually assaulted or raped them, so we wanted to prove that they weren't virgins in the first place. None of them were."[31]

He was lying, but what is more important here is the heteropatriarchal epistemological violence of this statement, which pairs the fragmented tones of women's testimonies about the accident. The virginity test became a collective trauma because there was neither acknowledgment nor reparation for it. In the quote from the general above, there is no focus on the crime (the rape), and the morality of the survivors is questioned. The survivors are not considered reliable, they are not trusted, their testimonies are delegitimized, and their rebel voices silenced by patriarchal speech, which echoes colonial narratives. Shifting the focus from the sources produced by the authorities to those that constitute the "archives of feelings" produced by women can flip the narrative, as exemplified by the story of Samira Ibrahim, the only one of the seventeen women who lodged a lawsuit when she was released after March 9, 2011.

Lobna Darwish explained to me that Samira Ibrahim, who was not part of any feminist group, inspired overwhelming admiration and solidarity from her peers and from women's associations: "She is probably twenty-three … I don't know what to say about her. I mean, she is like an average Egyptian, she is poised and veiled, not very flashy, like a typical Egyptian. But I think she is very strong, amazing, and inspiring. No one would have expected her to do that as it takes lots of courage."[32]

Further, a woman from the Committee to Defend the Revolution, an informal group of young activists that emerged in January 2011, told me that among the reasons for this widespread solidarity there was the fact that she appeared as an "ordinary young woman": a student from Upper Egypt, wearing the scarf, non-English-speaking.[33] As she was sharing with me these thoughts, a young, veiled woman entered Café Groppi, where we were sitting, and my interlocutor, enthusiastic, jumped on her chair: "This is Samira! I am sorry, I need to go and greet her!"

Samira's rebellion to the sexual violence she experienced while arrested shows that after one century of women's activism, feminist ideas had also permeated the mentalities of women who were not directly connected to feminist groups. Samira's courage inspired another woman to testify and gained the support of the community of feminist activists in Egypt. The journalist Heba Afify followed her case throughout its deployment; Human Rights Watch researcher Heba Morayef, cofounder of Not to Military Trials for Civilians Mona Seif, and journalist Shahira Amin testified at the court that "they were informed by three different members of the Supreme Council of the Armed Forces that virginity tests are performed as a routine measure on female prisoners in military prisons to avoid accusations of women being violated while in custody."[34] As soon as the acquittal of the military doctor accused in the "virginity test" case was proclaimed, a group of sixteen Egyptian women's organizations (among them the Alliance of Women's Organizations, which, alone, includes fourteen women's groups) issued a pledge to continue the pursuit of all involved in the crime.[35] By then, this was no longer Samira's story but a collective cause, becoming emblematic of women's collective resistance. It was among those narrated on Cairo's walls, where feminist graffiti denounced the neglect of Samira's case by the international media, which instead covered the story of the American journalist Laura Logan, who was assaulted in Tahrir, and the story of Aliaa Elmahdy, an Academy of Arts student and blogger who posted a self-portrait of herself naked, wearing glittery red shoes and a red ribbon to protest sexism and violence in Egyptian society in November 2011. In the following years, Samira left the activist scene and withdrew to private life. Aliaa was bullied and threatened with so many death threats that she was forced into exile. She joined the Femen collective for a short period and continued to blog about women and gender issues until 2021.[36]

Walking in downtown Cairo in 2012, my attention was taken by a graffiti work that brought Samira and Alia into visual conversation, with this caption:

> Samira Ibrahim: 25 years old. She was stripped and forcefully given a virginity test in front of military officers and soldiers. She vowed not to stay silent and pursued legal action against them. No attention, no public interest, no media coverage, no one cares. Aliaa Elmahdy. 20 years old. Stripped and revealed her whole body of her own free will, the media and public went crazy, her nude photo was viewed almost 3 million times and no less than 50 articles and several TV shows about her.
>
> A salute of respect to Samira Ibrahim, daughter of Upper Egypt.[37]

The experiences of the two young women were perceived in two different ways by most activists on the ground. The first one as a brave act to restore collective honor, the second one as an individualist act, which expressed lack of sensibility for the local culture. In a context of high tension between a delegitimized patriarchal authoritarianism and emerging new feminist movements, a moral panic seemed to prevail, and transgressions against social and visual norms were still considered unacceptable by many if not the majority of activists at this point. But attitudes evolved from this point during the ensuing decade. Already in 2013, Lobna Darwish shared with me a critical view about this graffiti, pointing out the implicit moralism of its message:

> There was a ... horrible campaign comparing them to each other, saying that Samira was a good example of a virtuous [girl] ... and the other is a bad example of what revolutions are about.... The issue is that the graffiti was comparing them without any critical thinking of whether comparing them makes sense or not. I think this would happen differently now, and reaction to [such facile comparisons] would be stronger. I think someone would take the graffiti down or paint on it at least. Maybe I am wrong, and everything would be the same, but I hope not.[38]

The debate occurring among feminists was articulated along different positions as time progressed during the revolutionary decade, but it must be remembered that women political activists, whatever their positionality was about the standards of morality, were all navigating very difficult waters. That the environment was hostile to women, even when they conformed to the standards of modesty (like Samira did), is shown by the fact that the doctor who violated the women at the Egyptian Museum was eventually acquitted by a military court.[39] The anthropologist Sherine Hafez's close analysis of the public scene of the early years of the revolution points to the importance of women being willing to speak about violence and sexuality publicly and "to transgress the limits placed on their bodies."[40] But the reaction to any kind of challenge to authority by women, whether normatively clothed or transgressively naked, produced the same results: the continued power of male-centric epistemology of justice and the realization that the counterrevolution was already there from the start. Nevertheless, women activists were determined to continue their battle to make their narratives prevail, if not in the court, at least in the broader public space.

A FEMINIST EPISTEME OF MEMORIES AND TESTIMONIES

I was in Cairo in December 2011, and Heba, a young woman who back then was part of the Civil Society Popular Committee, walked me through the sit-in that for six weeks occupied the space between the Cabinet and the Parliament in Cairo. The space was populated with tents and little food kiosks, but what was immediately attracting the attention of the passersby was the street art, which Heba proudly illustrated to me:

> There is this memorial [made] of plastic food plates with all people expressing themselves with prayers, chants, demands, anything, so . . . this is [saying] "kill me, torture me, blind me, I will still defend my country," and this "I am breathing freedom in the Square," and this one is a joke about Tantawi, and there is a guy asking "if Mubarak gives you the chair with the glue," so he is not going to give the chair, it means . . . and what else . . . this one is calling the Nile (*"ya nahr el Nil"*). And this one says: "Christians + Muslims = life in Egypt," and this one is "We are here in the Square, until every coward is down!" and this A.C.A.B. you can see it all over downtown."[41]

The atmosphere was joyful, but also tense. After the clashes of November-December 2011 in Muhammad Mahmoud Street (just a few hundred meters away from the Cabinet sit-in), where protests against having parliamentary elections under military rule led to the killing of over forty people by security services,[42] there were a lot of uncertainties:

> Now people are afraid, as we had no freedom before, and we've changed three governments in four months just by sitting in Tahrir. But people are more powerful now and they believe in themselves. So, if there is something they don't want now, people go and ask. But this is really happening: the government is having a hard time controlling all these strikes and demands from the bottom, from workers, from everyone. . . . So, they know their rights now. And if the government starts talking about hijab and not addressing the economic issues, it will go down in a minute.[43]

There were several new political parties emerging from the revolution. The alliance of left-leaning parties Tahalluf al-thawra mustamirra (Alliance of the Continuing Revolution), also known as Istikmal al-thawra (Completion of the Revolution), which built on the famous slogan *"al-thawra mustamirra"* ("the revolution continues"), expressed the wishful thinking of the revolutionary youth:

> Because they don't want the revolution to stop by the way . . . we want a decent and proper life and distribution of resources, as there has been economic growth for years but the rich are getting richer and the poor poorer in this country. And we want the choice to elect who should rule us or not, and Mubarak instead had started ruling the country since four years before

I was born! It is a long time ... and we don't want another military dictatorship, the military has been ruling for fifty years since Nasser, we want a civil state now. We triggered a new spirit in the country, and corruption is not the norm anymore at least, and before it used to be a system. Now you can see the women of Egypt speaking out; before we didn't use to talk of that that much, not even in the media. Now people take initiative.[44]

Police violence continued throughout the period of the parliamentary elections. In December 2011, a weeks-long sit-in at the Cabinet Office was attacked by security forces and the *abaya* (cloak) of one of the young women taking part in the sit-in was ripped off, revealing her torso and a bright blue bra. The picture of her anonymous semi-naked body became one of the visual icons of the Egyptian Revolution. The story was extensively covered by the international media, which, eager to condemn this brutal act, displayed their whole paraphernalia of orientalist derogatory stereotypes against the alleged intrinsic misogyny of Arab men.

Most, however, missed the main point: that the "blue bra incident" revealed the gendered nature of state violence. They also failed to report that Egyptian women reacted immediately and forcefully: a large demonstration was organized in the days following the incident, and women political activists' outrage at the attack found a voice at multiple levels. In a private email correspondence, a young woman scholar I first met in November 2011 in Cairo and who was at the demonstration described it as "a TRUE demonstration, made by ordinary women. It was not organized by any movement or feminist group. Cairo, 21 December 2011."[45] Prominent feminist creative artists and intellectuals—including Bahia Shehab, Mona Abaza, Ahdaf Soueif, and Laila Soliman—also publicly shared their rage about the attack.

Specifically, Ahdaf Soueif, who is also the author of an ardent memoir on the 2011 Revolution, suggested a correlation between the exercise of gender violence under the Mubarak's regime and during rule of the SCAF:

> Six years ago, when popular protests started to hit the streets of Egypt as Hosni Mubarak's gang worked at rigging the 2005 parliamentary elections, the regime hit back—not just with the traditional Central Security conscripts—but with an innovation: militias of strong, trained, thugs. They beat up men, but they grabbed women, tore their clothes off and beat them, groping them at the same time. The idea was to insinuate that females who took part in street protests wanted to be groped.
>
> But, a symbiotic relationship springs up between behaviors. Mubarak and Omar Suleiman turn Egypt into the US's favorite location for the torture

of "terror suspects" and torture becomes endemic in police stations. The regime's thugs molest women as a form of political bullying—and harassment of women in the streets rises to epidemic levels.

Until 25 January. The Revolution happened and with it came the Age of Chivalry. One of the most noted aspects of behavior in the streets and squares of the 18 days of the Egyptian Revolution was the total absence of harassment. Women were suddenly free; free to walk alone, to talk to strangers, to cover or uncover, to smoke, to laugh, to cry, to sleep. And the job of every single male present was to facilitate, to protect, to help. The Ethics of the Square, we called it.

Now our revolution is in an endgame struggle with the old regime and the military. The young woman is part of this.[46]

Soueif explained that the use of sexual violence against political protesters was not a new phenomenon in Egypt, pointing out how it represented continuity with the darkest face of the republican regime going back to its earliest days. Indeed, feminist historians have shown that violence against women in the context of political struggle is rooted even more deeply, in Egypt's colonial experience. As Margot Badran elaborates it, during the 1919 Revolution "women of the people" were beaten and killed when they took part in demonstrations, and she suggested that if today we are aware of their martyrdom, it is because the intellectual and upper-class early feminists paid homage to their working-class sisters' sacrifice. "Sha'rawi and other women collected the names of the dead and wounded and visited their families."[47]

During the years of the 2011 Revolution, there was a general feeling that memory should not remain neatly compiled and curated in libraries and formal archives but rather engraved onto the walls of the city, and in placards and posters. Returning to Cairo in November 2012, a year after the so-called blue bra incident, I saw such an ephemeral archive of the revolution taking shape on Cairo's walls in the form of political graffiti,[48] in which the image of the "blue bra" was a key signifier, standing for women's opposition against gender violence and against new forms of authoritarianism. The art historian and artist Bahia Shehab stenciled the Arabic word "*La*" ("No") above her image of the blue bra on the walls of Cairo. In the Ted Lecture the artist gave a few months later, she explained: "'La' is for 'no!' to stripping the people. And the blue bra is to remind us that it is a shame for our nation that we allow a veiled woman to be stripped and beaten in the street. And the footprint says: "long life and peace with revolution" because we will never retaliate with violence."[49]

Blue bras became also quite popular in the street market in Cairo, and both Egyptian and international women bought them to express solidarity with the unnamed woman who was attacked.

A couple of years later, I discussed the events with the feminist psychiatrist and activist Sally Toma, who emphasized women's courage at that stage:

> It's actually women who think better in this revolution. The first protests that came really big against the military council in general were women's protests, because it's women who are affected by what happened in the Cabinet sit-in and said you're not allowed to touch women this way or treat women in this manner and we've gone out in protests of thousands of women and we showed that we are capable of continuing.... Starting then you found a lot of women in marches. Even though the numbers increased, it is like a response. You are trying to oppress us, so here we go. And also, with the sexual harassment, there is an increase in the sexual harassment, but there is also an increase in the number of women coming out and protesting against anti-sexual harassment. We are not scared, we are defiant.[50]

At the Cabinet sit-in, Sally Toma was beaten, and the reaction of the police when she tried to file a report against the army led her to conclude that this was the moment to escalate the level of the protest:

> I filed a report against the army in the police station that day, and they were joking and laughing at me because.... Are you coming to file a report against the army? I said, yes, it's the army that dispersed the sit-in. Usually, I come to file a report against you, but today I'm filing it against the army.
>
> No one ever called me for this report.
>
> On that same night, they launched a new initiative called Kadhibun [Liars]: We thought the media was now not allowing us to say anything against the military, and people were buying the propaganda of the military that they are here to protect the revolution.... So, we thought we have to do the alternative media and show people the truth and that's what Kadhibun did.[51]

Kadhibun organized screenings all over Egypt where they combined the sound of an officer commenting on something that happened with a video contrasting his narrative. The idea was to create a cognitive dissonance through the juxtaposition of contrasting and incompatible words and the images, with the aim of encouraging people to seek the truth by themselves.

The violence experienced by women in 2011 led an emerging generation of artists and intellectuals to discuss the relationship between sexual harassment, rape, and political power in their works. Most importantly, one

FIGURE 21. Women marching against the Supreme Council of the Armed Forces, Cairo, January 20, 2012. Photo by and courtesy of Hossam el-Hamalawy.

century of women's activism contributed to creating the space for imagining that a revolution was not only possible, but necessary. The next step, undertaken by Egyptian women intellectuals and artists, was to write contrapuntal narratives about women's experiences in the revolution and to change the terms within which the discourse about sexual violence—especially, but not only, against women—was articulated.

2011 and 2012 were years of continuous mobilization, and women activists challenged the legitimacy of military rule. The chant of January 25, *Yaskut, yaskut ya Mubarak!* (Down, down, to Mubarak!), became *Yaskut yaskut hukm al-askari* (Down, down with military rule!) and new oppositional practices took shape. Violence escalated, and confrontations between different components of the revolutionary front, the supporters of the Muslim Brotherhood, and the security forces became more intense.

The situation worsened until 2013, when some members of the Shura Council (at that time dominated by the Muslim Brotherhood and Salafis) called for separating men and women during protests to prevent sexual harassment, blamed women for mingling with men during protests, and represented men protesters as "thugs and street inhabitants," adopting a narrative that aimed at restoring class- and gender-normative boundaries. The fact that in all these circumstances there were women activists challenging the legitimacy of political authority in office was completely wiped from the political debate.

In the context of growing state violence and exclusion, new forms of resistance were generated, and new political discourses about gender and political legitimacy were produced. Women activists rejected the idea of victimization, and they produced their own narratives of these days. *Words of Women from the Egyptian Revolution*, a series of video interviews published on YouTube featuring women activists from across the political spectrum, provided an effective counternarrative to the official ones. Even the words used by women activists to describe their experience shaped a new discourse. For instance, all the documents produced by Nazra for Feminist Studies and by the Egyptian Initiative for Personal Rights (EIPR) refer to women who experienced sexual violence and rape as *survivors* rather than *victims,* while it is evident that the political space becomes more and more oppressive.

These practices of narrating a story of empowerment rather than victimization, of celebrating memories and creating legacies to contrast neglect and oblivion, of filling the gaps in the official archives with the archives of feelings—all these characterize and define women's activism in the 2011 Revolution and the following decade, a revolutionary decade. Despite political setbacks and the reassertion of authoritarian control, when viewed through a feminist lens the 2010s can and should be considered not as a counterrevolutionary but a revolutionary decade, marked by ongoing and in important ways increasingly powerful mobilization by and for women.

ELEVEN

Sexual Violence, Power, Freedom, and the Emergence of a New Feminist Discourse

WOMEN FIGHTING BACK AGAINST STATE VIOLENCE IN THE EARLY 2000S

The fight against violence and in particular against sexual violence was a crucial theme during the 2011 evolution and the revolutionary decade that followed, as new initiatives and theorizations about such violence began to appear. However, the power of these new contemporary feminist discourses to confront sexual violence, and its immediate capacity to connect to other transnational campaigns (such as the #MeToo, of which Egypt was an important hub in the global south), cannot be adequately understood without proper historicization of the movement.

As I discussed in part 1 of this book, Egyptian feminists, and especially the activists of the NWF, AWSA, CEWLA and El-Nadeem, produced extensive and in-depth research throughout the eighties, nineties, and early 2000s documenting violence against women. Their findings informed their grassroots activities, particularly their linking of the struggle against sexual violence to issues of socioeconomic inequalities and the rights of women workers, and their lobbying efforts with the Egyptian government to issue laws that protect women from violence. The preparatory works for the ICPD conference (Cairo 1994) and the UN World Conference on Women (Beijing 1995) were particularly productive in this regard.

Improvements did not always come through legislation; in previous periods it was often through judicial rulings. For instance, in 1950, the Criminal Chamber of the Court of Cassation ruled that to make an accusation of sexual assault "there is no need to prove that the offender had complete sexual intercourse with the victim against the victim's will. It is sufficient for the offender to touch the victim with their hands, reproductive organs, or device against the victim's will."[1] Yet it was only in the early 2000s that the Egyptian government intensified its attempts to include feminist themes in its agenda. In 2000, the National Council for Women was established: a consultative body directly affiliated to the Presidency of Egypt and chaired by First Lady Suzanne Mubarak, its mandate was to ensure that equality between women and men was reflected in law, the economy, and the culture of the country. The same year, the *khul'* law was approved, allowing Muslim women to initiate a lawful divorce without the husband willing or even permitting her to do so. However, due to the husband not being found "guilty" for the divorce, the wife has to give up all her financial legal rights and restores to him the dower he gave her.[2] In 2004, a woman judge, Tahani al-Gebali, was nominated to the Constitutional Court for the first time in Egyptian history, and in 2009 the law concerning the Egyptian People's Assembly (Lower House) was amended to allocate sixty-four new seats to women.[3]

All these measures were the long-term results of decades of women's political activism and certainly marked important improvements in women's lives, freedoms, and protection. However, looking at the broader picture and with a focus on how the discussion about sexual violence evolved in this period, there are notable contradictions, many concerning the ambivalence of Mubarak's state gender policies, and as such they uncover its broader conception of political power. In fact, the 1990s and early 2000s witnessed serious incidents of sexual harassment that reasserted the political centrality of women's bodies and the control of their political expression by the same state machine that changed its rules.

MEMORIES OF BLACK WEDNESDAY AND THE HEROISM OF NAWAL ALI

No one can forget the tragedy of 25th of May, 2005, when security forces cleared the way for "thugs" and their men, donning civilian clothes, to violate women in front of Sa'd Zaghlul's memorial and the Press Syndicate. We cannot forget the words of a policeman to a female protester on that day explaining the violence used against female protesters, "so you would stop taking part in demonstrations again."[4]

It is significant that in 2013, when attacks against women protesters were at their peak, Dr. Magda Adly, psychiatrist and cofounder of El-Nadeem, referred to "Black Wednesday" (this is the name under which the attack against the women journalists of Kefaya was generally known) to introduce a powerful as much as painful collection of testimonies about sexual torture that occurred during the 2011 Revolution. In the memories of women human rights defenders, Black Wednesday had been a revealing moment which showed that in the early 2000s, the sexual violence long documented by feminist organizations was not merely endemic but also openly politicized.

Women did not remain silent in front of these abuses. The journalist Nawal Ali (one of the women attacked on Black Wednesday) filed a report to the public prosecutor's office against the NDP thugs who assaulted her. In a touching testimony collected by the Egyptian Initiative for Personal Rights (EIPR), she reported:

> Their hands were messing with my chest, harassing all the sensitive areas of my body, ripped my clothes off and assaulted me with their hands.... I fell in my face on the ground, and I was surprised by a large number of these thugs on top of me, harassing me again and messing with all my sensitive areas. I started screaming for help and I kept screaming until I passed out. They weren't trying to hit me, but they were sexually assaulting me, and they were tearing my clothes apart. And I ended up almost naked as a result.... They pulled me down the stairs, hacked the security ring, threw me on the sidewalk in front of all the officers (then Ismail El-Shaer, the head of the Cairo investigator) and everyone standing there. Hussein Metwally took off his shirt and covered me with it. And we left before the assault was repeated.[5]

The signs of violence on Nawal Ali's body and her torn clothes were not enough for the investigators, however. They refused to register eyewitness testimony by those who were present during the assault. Instead, Nawal Ali and her family were threatened to such an extent that she was fired from her job and divorced by her husband. She then decided to bring her story to the media, even as the systematic campaign of defamation against her continued. Attorney General Abdul Majeed Mahmoud archived the case in December 2005 "for not identifying the actor." Nawal Ali, alongside other women journalists assaulted on the same day (Abir Al-Guindy, Shaima Abu Khair, and Eman Taha), then went to the EIPR to seek assistance. They also submitted a complaint to the African Commission on Human and People's Rights, in Banjul, Gambia, which was filed on May 18, 2006.

In the years that followed, and until she died of cancer in 2009, Nawal Ali bravely continued her activism; her courage inspired many women activists after her. Activists from EIPR describe how Nawal Ali remained traumatized by her experience of assault, yet fearlessly persisted in her search for justice: "Nawal continued to go down the street. After the incident, she decided to join the Kefaya movement . . . wear[ing] more layers of clothes that are hard to tear. Sometimes she was shaking and whispering to her colleagues at the demonstration: 'I am ready to be locked up and beaten up or anything, but not to be naked on the street again.'"[6]

The practice of wearing multiple layers of clothes, sometimes even a bathing suit, to avoid being stripped of their clothes during the street assaults, including gang rapes, became a common practice among the Egyptian women activists after the 2011 Revolution, and their denunciations of attacks became increasingly vocal. In the context of the 2011 Revolution and the multiple episodes of extreme violence against women that occurred during demonstrations, the memorialization of Nawal Ali's brave resistance against the attempts to silence her testimony and, with her, that of other women survivors, infused courage into younger women. Memorializing women's experiences of resistance in the past and finding connections across time gives strength to the contemporary movements and helps participants heal from the collective, individual, and even vicarious trauma of sexual violence. On their own side, feminist groups did not give up denouncing the structural violence endured by Egyptian women; they noted the inefficacy of the state institutions, including the National Council for Women, to effectively address it; and they tried to organize independently, also using the IT competences among the young generations. In 2005, the Egyptian Center for Women's Rights (ECWR) launched a campaign named Safe Streets for Everyone. In October 2005, the blogger Manal Hassan published a testimony about her own experience of sexual harassment, this one not on the streets but on an airplane.[7] In 2007, the NWRF published a detailed paper with guidelines to draft a law against sexual harassment and rape, but the government did not take it on board.

Despite these efforts, following Black Wednesday serious episodes of violence against women intensified the streets of the cities of Egypt in the first decade of the 2000s, in particular during the celebrations for 'Eid in 2006 and 'Eid al-Fitr in 2008. These are moments when people from everywhere in Cairo, particularly from the popular suburbs, come to downtown to celebrate. In this context, it was not difficult for the regime's propaganda machine to blame young working-class men for the sexual mobs against women that occurred in the streets. The same state that had censored the feminist organizations when they were trying to raise collective awareness of the systemic state violence that characterized that period, and that had sent thugs in plain clothes to assault the women journalists on Black Wednesday, to attack women voters and candidates who were against the regime at the pull stations, or that threatened of rape the women family members of men suspected of being part of Islamist terrorist organizations in Sinai, used the incidents of the ʿEid to criminalize working-class men and, under the rhetoric of "protecting women," to police the entire population.[8] This narrative, however, was strongly rejected by activists, and particularly in the burgeoning blogosphere, who were the first to denounce the paradox of the securitization of the public space in Egypt: "This time the question of policing was brought to the front, downtown Cairo is where most political protests happen it's common to see thousands upon thousands of police officers and anti-riot soldiers attacking a few hundred (and sometimes a dozen) protesters yet on a day like the first day of el Eid they failed to show up and protect the women," wrote the then nineteen-year-old Alaa Abd El-Fattah on his blog.[9]

The gravity of the situation was also illustrated in a detailed study produced by the ECWR in 2008 titled *Clouds in Egypt's Sky*, according to which 83 percent of Egyptian women reported exposure to harassment, while 98 percent of foreign women stated they had been sexually harassed while in Egypt.[10] The dissemination of this study opened a new phase in the way the problem was publicly discussed. In 2008, Egyptian feminists and human rights organizations joined the ranks to create the Task Force against Sexual Harassment, drafting the proposal of a bill to emend the penal code.[11] In 2010, three young women with IT and gender-studies expertise (Engy Ghozlan, Rebecca Chao, and Ebaʾa al-Tamami) designed and cofounded Harrassmap, a digital platform to monitor, document, and denounce sexual harassment in Egypt. Then, in December 2010, on the eve of the 2011 Revolution, the film *Cairo 678* was released. Based on the ECWR's research and inspired by the story of the filmmaker Noha Rushdi, who in 2008 filed a police report against a man who sexually harassed her at a bus station (and the man was eventually condemned), the film openly addressed the plague of sexual harassment in public spaces from a feminist intersectional perspective, while also illustrating problematic class dynamics and representations. At the vigil of the January 2011 Revolution, thirty-eight years after the first publication of al-Saadawi's iconic *Woman and Sex*, and seventeen years after the ICPD in Cairo, thanks to the long-lasting work of the Egyptian feminist activists the public debates about sexual violence and human rights were at a turning point.

WOMEN FIGHT BACK: SEXUAL VIOLENCE DURING THE REVOLUTIONARY DECADE

In the words of the young revolutionaries, the 2011 January Revolution was an attempt to dismantle an entire system of domination, which was authoritarian, patriarchal, and classist. Looking at it retrospectively, one could say that it changed a lot of things; the use of sexual violence to intimidate women, and more broadly the high level of violence against women that permeates the society, certainly continues, yet there has certainly been a qualitative shift in the way the discourse about sexual harassment is addressed.

Notwithstanding the positive narratives about the public space promoted by the revolutionaries, the multiplication of streets demonstrations and the growing of women's presence in them augmented the opportunities of assault and gang rapes. Moreover, the growing awareness by women that sexual harassment and rape were not something to feel ashamed of and to hide but something to report produced an increase in the statistics. What is sure is that years of pressure exercised by the feminist organizations, combined with the mushrooming of spontaneous feminist initiatives and informal groups after the revolution, changed the way the problem was discussed and perceived.

Women mobilized at multiple levels, with artists on the front line. The street artist Hend Kheera emphasizes the importance of blogging and tweeting but also of creating graffiti against sexual harassment: "The first time I was making one, two men stopped there and asked 'What are you saying?' and I answered 'I am saying don't touch, castration awaits you' (in Arabic, *'mamnu' al-lamas, al-khasi fi intizarak'*), and they responded, 'We are in Ramadan, no one will touch you during Ramadan.' And I was like, 'No, they are touching me even in Ramadan!'"[12]

The gallery of feminist graffiti that exploded in the cities of Egypt between 2011 and 2013 was eclectic and inspired by numerous themes, including references to the Pharaonic heritage and the celebration of the mothers of the martyrs (especially the mother of Khaled Said), as well as the revolutionary women who died during the demonstrations. But there were also works of street art that directly denounced sexual harassment and produced a counternarrative that saw women as "rescuers" of the revolution rather than victims. These works reflected the action on the ground, where a new feminist revolutionary culture was emerging, bringing together feminist women and men to challenge normative visions of gender and of security.

To protect themselves against sexual mobs during the demonstrations, the feminists set up their own unarmed security groups: Tahrir Bodyguard, Quwwa dud al-Taharrush/Opantish (Operation Anti-Sexual Harassment), and Basma were created out of emergency to face violent sexual mobs in 2012. In this context, the State was perceived as sponsoring sexual harassment to intimidate and delegitimize political activists, or at least covering it by its complicity.[13]

A discussion also developed among revolutionary activists about the best approach to take with regard to sexual harassment. Some were afraid that denouncing the episodes would have discredited the Square and undermined the revolution. Others had a different view, and they believed that denouncing sexual violence in the Square should be an integral part of the revolutionary commitment. The feminists who were involved in the revolution and the human rights movement considered it as part of a broader political issue, as Lubna Darwish explained to me: "Sexual violence has been used systematically by the army to terrorize people and to harass and to arrest them. But there was no separate campaign, it is seen as part of the whole thing, for example with the virginity test there was torture, and sexual harassment was part of the rape. So, this is the way we face the issue."[14]

Already in the late 2011, following a series of traumatic events—especially the attacks against the women's march on International Women's Day and the virginity tests on the day after, the massacre of Coptic demonstrators in front of the Maspero Television building on October 10 and 11, the attack to the Cabinet's sit-in, and the Muhammad Mahmoud Street clashes—the revolutionary narrative of the public spaces as safe spaces evolved into new representations, where the public spaces became areas that could be perceived as safe only through continuous revolutionary actions, with women and men equally committed to contrast violence. In these days at the end of 2011, the most recurrent carillon call was *"al-thawra mustamirra"* ("the revolution continues") and women were asking for the end of street violence, without knowing that more violence was about to come.

PROTECTING EACH OTHER AND HEALING TOGETHER: CREATING AND REMEMBERING OPANTISH

That the state security apparatus used violence against women to attack the protests during and in the aftermath of the 2011 January Revolution is undeniable. However, one cannot deny that multiple actors participated in these acts, at multiple levels. A young activist of the groups Mosireen and Opantish noticed how the perception that women and men had of each other's changed during the revolution: "I mean there was something, a moment when I remember in the eighteen days and the few months after, many men talked to me saying I've never in my life dealt with a woman in that context."[15] Here my interlocutor alludes to the experience of young men who were educated in boys-only schools and, apparently, even at university did not have much interaction with women besides the family. "So, it was very different for them to see women on the front line and deal with her as a person of like, equal in everything and she's doing the same thing and I think a lot of people felt it was very, it was very moving for a lot of people to kind of rediscover each other."

The kind of equality young women and men experienced in the days of the January 2011 Revolution was not only in the demonstration but also in a broader reappropriation and resignification of the public space. My interlocutor remembers playing soccer in the street for the first time with unknown young men, an experience that for a middle-class young woman would have been unthinkable just few months before:

> My first time playing soccer with people I don't know, men I don't know, in my life was actually because of the revolution. We were in the Square and some kids were playing soccer and I decided to go play with them and they were very intimidated by a woman being there and trying not to touch them, and trying not to approach and then like the game took on and we became like ... and, I mean, never in my life would I have had in Egypt the chance of playing with normal people on the street soccer without the context of having the public space that's reclaimed and collectively. We were equals and we had to interact with each other as equals, and I think it's something that forced on all of us this kind of dealing with people they usually avoid in the street. [Normally], there is like kind of very classist and very racist attitude that we all have, that there is a kind of kids when you see in the street, you avoid them and just walk away from them because you're expecting sexual harassment and you're expecting comments and you're expecting everything and these kids are the kids we go on front lines with now, and you get to deal with them on a very close level. ... We kind of like, a moment of difference or like out of context, we were being completely put out of context and we were building a new relationship. So, on a personal level, I think we were all going through something very, very intense, kind of like revising all of our ideas and expectations from people.[16]

If the outcomes of the political revolutions were uncertain (leading political scientists to talk about an aborted or failed revolution), a human revolution, a change in the ways women and men were perceiving each other, was ongoing, but change would come at a very high price for women, and first and foremost for women political activists. A year after the fall of Mubarak, Egypt was under the government of the Brotherhood-dominated Freedom and Justice Party, which gained the majority of the parliament seats with the 2011–12 elections, and then saw Mohammed Morsi elected president in June 2012. One day in November 2012, a woman who was working for EIPR was attacked by a man on her way to work, and when she yelled and tried to get people to help, she found that the crowd around her wasn't being very helpful. This made her very angry. She realized that even the organization she was working with, EIPR, that at that time was dealing with police brutality at protests, had no plan for how to deal with sexual violence. She decided to do something, trying to involve the most revolutionary among her friends, especially from the Mosireen collective. The group was immediately active on the ground, organizing a security service to protect women during the demonstrations, but they were also discussing among themselves the strategies to move forward. The founding members were keen to initiate a dialogue with the juridical institutions, but more radical members of the team refused this idea, and eventually—most likely, also given the circumstances on the ground, which rapidly deteriorated—they prevailed.

The atmosphere was very tense in November of 2012. There were a lot of demonstrations against the government, and the Brotherhood, now in power, was doing its best to undermine their legitimacy by alluding to the sexual assaults that were happening there, remarking that these kinds of assaults never happened at the Brotherhood protests. My interlocutors noted that this was the same narrative previously used by both the Mubarak and the SCAF regimes, but since October 2012, attacking women during demonstrations had become a pattern, at which point women began posting their testimonies online. "So . . . you started to see testimonies from women online and in the media saying that this had happened, or they had seen this happening to someone else. At some point it was clear that it was becoming more and more frequent. That's what triggered the mobilization of Opantish, and also Opantish started, and it started to really begin to take off when it was people reacting to the fact that their friends had been attacked."[17]

Opantish initially developed as an informal network of people who knew each other and organized to prevent violent attacks, until January 25, 2013, on the second anniversary of the Revolution, the level of violence became so high and unexpected that it shocked everyone, deeply. "The 25th of January 2013. It was a horrifying day, it was a very, was a horrible day. It was a day of sexual assault that does not stop. A small number of people trying to intervene but failing or succeeding, but it doesn't matter, because the assaults were very bad, including women being raped with knives, and it was horrible."[18]

On January 27, 2013, Opantish published a press release, where they denounced both the escalation of the violence against women in Tahrir Square and the indifference of revolutionary groups to it. Opantish received nineteen reports of group sexual assaults against women in the area, some of them involving life-threatening violence. Opantish intervened to rescue women and to escort them to safe houses or hospitals.[19] From that point, the group grew a lot stronger and a lot more organized, and it was able to recruit a lot more volunteers. That's when they started to really see a structure emerging made of different teams specializing in different tasks—some intervention teams on the ground, safety teams, people in the operations room, people working with lawyers and doctors:

> When I looked back recently, it was like three or four hundred people, I mean it was big. The team of core organizers was mostly women, and then when it came to the people who were volunteering to be part of the intervention team on the ground, so the most kind of physical, dangerous work, was definitely mostly men, but about at least a third women. So, two-thirds men and one-third women. And then the rest of the staff was probably a mix of half-half, or maybe mostly women again. It was usually people in their twenties and thirties, mostly Egyptians.[20]

Other anti–sexual harassment and assault groups emerged in the same period, such as Tahrir Bodyguards and Basma. Even if they shared the same general mission, they differed in terms of strategies: "Tahrir Bodyguard is very different, you know, it was these huge guys and like fluorescent vests and carrying sticks and it was much more kind of muscle and macho and they didn't have women on the ground at first with them, and it didn't necessarily have this thing of seeing itself as part of the revolution, which Opantish did.... For Opantish, it very much wanted to place itself as part of the revolution."[21]

As for Basma, over time it specialized on LGBTQ rights, one of the areas that became more targeted, and therefore more dangerous after 2013, forcing the group to keep a very low profile in the subsequent years.[22] At popular

FIGURE 22. Anti-Sexual Harassment March in Cairo, February 6, 2013. Photo by and courtesy of Hossam el-Hamalawy.

level, the discontent about the government of the Muslim Brotherhood grew to the point that a large campaign to dismiss them was launched in the spring of 2013, with the name of Tamarod. Hundreds of thousands of signatures to support the campaign were collected and on June 30, 2013, the streets of Cairo and other cities in Egypt were once again full of people, perhaps even more so than during the eighteen days of the January 25 Revolution. People were asking for, once again, the fall of a regime, but this time it was not Mubarak but rather the Muslim Brotherhood government of Mohammed Morsi. Some were invoking the intervention of the army by chanting *"al-sha'b wa-l jaish ieed wahda"* ("The people and the army are one hand"). Many among the revolutionaries did not feel comfortable in this opposition between the Brotherhood and the army, which did not leave space for what they termed a "the third square," that is, the democratic activists who wanted a secular and democratic nonmilitary state. The army launched an ultimatum to President Mohammed Morsi: either resign or be removed by force. The second scenario happened on July 3 when the army took power and a new phase in the revolutionary decade started.

Women of all political persuasions paid an extremely high price for the coup. Noha Mohamed, a young woman from Alexandria who went to

FIGURE 23. Graffiti in downtown Cairo, "No to Harassment," November 19, 2013. Photo by Lucia Sorbera.

celebrate on July 3, driving around with the logo of Tamarod on the car, was attacked by young Brotherhood supporters in the Sidi Gaber neighborhood of Alexandria who pulled her out of her car, tore her clothes, and stabbed her 116 times, killing her. There are no accurate figures about the sexual assaults that happened during these days, but activists talk of at least two hundred female protestors brutally sexually assaulted (mass group harassment, individual harassment, and rape) between June 30 and July 3. The seriousness of the assaults ranged from mob sexual harassment and assault, to raping female protestors using knives and sharp objects. The escalation of violence left even the revolutionaries uncertain about what to do. There was not unanimous consensus about how to deal with it. Broad components of the movements wanted to keep a low profile about sexual violence, fearing that talking too much about it would undermine the protests.

Women I spoke to lament that many of their male comrades were either in denial—in order to keep the revolution as pure as possible—or accusing the Brotherhood of planning such attacks. It was indeed very traumatic for revolutionary women to soon realize that harassment and rape was also happening within the revolutionary field, but this did not refrain them from opening an important debate within it, with young women (and some men) radical revolutionaries courageously standing up for their comrades and calling for a radical change in the narratives about sexual harassment and rape. Some of them noted that this was an eye-opening moment for many men:

> I think for a lot of men seeing how horrendous things are, they haven't seen how bad sexual assaults are and I think for many of our friends, I think they were as surprised as women, because for the first time in their lives they're seeing how violent things can become. Because usually they're happening in the privacy of, you know, interaction on the street or in the home or whatever, or the workplace. But all of a sudden it became very public where you see three hundred men surrounding a woman and you see the whole thing and you see the woman afterward. And I think for most of the men it made them question things about masculinity and, and the public space and the presence in the public space and all that stuff. And even being more careful about the way they talk or joke about things. So, on that level I think Opantish or the events of mob sexual harassment and intervening in them was very helpful. It made people think again about things.[23]

What women revolutionaries were calling for was a new way of talking about sexual violence, shifting the focus (and the blame) from the survivors to the perpetrator of the attacks, and trying to liberate women from the responsibility of carrying the honor of the revolutionary field, a burden that women have been carrying since the 1919 Revolution. They were responding to the activists who were concerned about the revolution, that sexual harassment, rape, and assault was actually something that was threatening the revolution itself. It was not something that could be postponed or ignored by any of the political groups who claimed to be part of the revolution. Interestingly, these were the years when the memoir by Arwa Saleh, *al-Mubtasirun* (*The Stillborn*)—by then available also in English, thanks to the translation by Samah Selim—came to a new life, circulating and being broadly discussed by the new generations. As the country was falling into a new autocracy, the level of sexual violence against women activists increased, making self-evident what Arwa Saleh had dared to write thirty years before: a revolution can't be successful unless it is also about gender and sexuality.

A change was needed, and it was happening, however fitfully. "For a long time, people would say, you know, we'll deal with women's issues later, things like this. I think there was also just a kind of disbelief, there was a really a bit of a sort of it can't be that bad, this kind of thing. It can't possibly be that bad, even if there's like, videos of the mob and whatever, how badly are they harassing her, so it was only when really the violence got so bad and the documentation of it was good enough that it could, it was like undeniable that this was happening, and that it was also life threatening. I mean there were people who went, people who were raped with knives, like this was, you know, someone could have died, it wasn't just groping, you know. So, yeah. So yeah, definitely one of the things that we were trying to do was sort of push the issue."[24]

This renewed women's activism against sexual violence was successful, and it also opened the opportunity to discuss other taboo issues, such as sexual assault when in custody and how it concerned both women and men. The activists I interviewed underline that for many men who had been in prison, it was possible to talk about other kinds of torture, but not sexual ones, but now they were coming out, some of them even on television.[25]

All the testimonies I have collected from Opantish activists emphasize their rebellion about the way sexual violence is discussed in Egypt at all levels, from the state to mainstream media, to street culture. There is a lot of victims blaming in the public discourse, and journalists do not respect the privacy of survivors. Women who denounce sexual harassment and assaults receive emotional and psychological pressure from the harasser's families to drop charges, and sometimes even by institutional figures (policemen, doctors), warning them that taking the man to the court can "ruin his life." Opantish tried to dismantle these narratives, first by making it clear that these were women who were being attacked regardless of what they were wearing, and then shifting the language away from the binary between victimhood and victims blaming and turning away from machismo and the rhetoric of men saving women.

THE EMERGENCE OF A NEW FEMINIST DISCOURSE • 227

The binary narratives that characterized the discourse about sexual violence was reflected in the public discussion about the broader political situation in Egypt, especially in the days leading to July 3 coup:

> We were out on the Square every day late into night, it was hundreds of cases. We were much more organized so we were able to intervene much more efficiently, and I think the overall level of violence wasn't as high as before but it was extraordinarily tiring and everyone was just completely exhausted and burnt out and nerve wracked by the time it was over, and then it was like, oh, let's now figure, you know, for me at least I was a bit like, well, let's try and understand what's happening and of course the media was just kind of like rushing to label what had happened, was it a popular change, was it a military coup, and it was both, ultimately, but the debate was stuck in this binary for weeks. It was really very beside the point.[26]

The nature of what was going on became clear on August 3 when the Egyptian army cleared the sit-ins of the Muslim Brotherhood supporters in Rabaa al-Adawiya Square and in al-Nahda Square. The number of deaths remains to date officially unknown, but according to humanitarian organizations in the field, this was among the major massacres in contemporary history, and the worst ever in Egypt, with consequences that impacted everyone in the activists' field:

> Rabaa was when it was like, this kind of, you know, yeah, being sort of just so, so stunned and shocked at the level, the level of violence that they were willing to use against ultimately families. . . . Then of course you had curfew and it was all very bleak and new status quo that I think was very difficult for people to adjust to, and I think, part of what I remember feeling at the time was that it was very strange that the circumstances had changed and so we [Opantish] stopped working and so we never really processed or talked about what we had been through or what we had done together, because everything was this abrupt stop and we didn't quite realize that that was it, it was like done, and then by the time that we realized it, it was Rabaa and it was so over and everyone just went home to deal with their traumas. You get yanked from one sort of intense thing to another, but you go from being part of a collective to then being on your own, so I think a lot of people struggled, with trauma and PTSD and depression and anxiety and it was in the years after that that people started to get sick from everything they'd seen, everything they'd done.[27]

In this somber atmosphere, it is not surprising that feminists were rather aloof when the amendment to the penal code to punish sexual harassment that was passed in June 2013. In their comments, they underline that the amendment was the result of the long struggle of the women's NGOs and the grassroots initiatives they undertook for decades. The same fact that the word "harassment" was for the first time part of the legislation and there was a penalty for the crime was considered a success. However, many flaws remained. First, it touched only one article, while the rest of the legislation regarding rape still maintained ambiguous language, referring generally to "immoral assaults." Plus, the amendment was not enough to solve what they considered "a societal illness":

> There are other reforms and restructure that has to be done, you can't talk about combating sexual violence without addressing more pressing issues like restructuring the Ministry of Interior, because there is huge corruption in this entity and this corruption and this impunity actually helped them in perpetrating sexual violence crimes and getting away with it, and you can't talk about the police being more responsive to men, or to women, or having experience to deal with sexual violence crimes if they still have this mentality that they are using sexual violence to penalize men and women in detention centers, they have the liberty to harass women in the street etc. etc. And at the same time, there are other reforms in the field of education, the field of health, and in media and all of these had to be incorporated to be able actually to make progress in this problem.[28]

The major problem that feminist activists find in this law is that the penal code focuses more on the punishment for the crime than the resources to support the survivor. Many find that the way the judiciary deals with the cases is very problematic because it forces women to bring the evidence of the crime, and it does not substantially trust them. The same critical view is expressed by women revolutionary activists about the national strategy to combat sexual violence, an initiative taken by the president of the Republic after one of his supporters was attacked during the celebrations of his inauguration, in June 2014.

Opantish was part of a broader network, which included other feminist and human rights organizations, especially Nazra for Feminist Studies, EIPR, and El-Nadeem. Most of the activists in these groups were already connected with each other, and the collaboration came naturally. However, there were also differences of vision and strategy with other feminist groups, which my interlocutors defined as "traditional feminists." Generational and political discrepancies of vision about what should be considered part of a feminist program and action, as well as strategies to implement, emerged clearly after

2013. The old dilemma that feminists had to tackle since the republican state decided to include women in its modernist and authoritarian project of development (cooperating with the state institutions, fighting them or finding ways in between the binary) became even more lacerating after the 2013 coup because the state became, at all effects, a military state, and the space for political activism shrunk. Notwithstanding that, in the subsequent years women continued to mobilize against sexual violence in many ways. Following their one-century consolidated tradition, they mobilized on multiple levels, intersecting the cultural and artistic scene with the more explicitly political. Among the major artistic projects was the photo exhibition *Sidewalk Stories: Women in Cairo's Public Spaces,* curated in 2015 by Maria Newbird (at that time a university student in Germany and resident in Cairo). Featuring the works by Egyptian photographer Sarah Seliman, the exhibition illustrates the experiences of sexual harassment of seventeen women (both Egyptian and foreigners), and by narrating the stories, it tries to encourage women to come out and seek support. Projects to contain and to contrast sexual harassment were also launched in the main university campuses, and Nazra continued to publish well-documented research on the topic.[29]

The progressive closure of the public space that happened since 2013 and made demonstrations almost impossible produced a shift in the spaces where sexual violence happens and necessitated a change of strategy by women's groups to address it. The units that had been acting in the streets and the squares between 2011 and 2013 progressively left space for new initiatives, many of them online, that building on their effort to change the narrative about sexual violence, supported women who wanted to denounce their experiences. The insistence of women's groups, including artists, intellectuals, and activists, on the theme of sexual violence and the inadequacy of the state's provisions to address the problem was proven well founded in the following years, in particular between 2019 and 2022 when a series of high-profile cases was brought to the public attention, revamping the discussion. This time, women used social media to come out collectively, (mostly) anonymously, and denounce the assaults. According to feminist activists, all the institutions that had the responsibility to deal with the cases—from the general prosecution to the universities, to the film industry, and even to the syndicate of journalists—failed to do so. In an article that analyzes the larger issue, Elham Eidarous explained: "Everyone is asking for verification, investigation and justice, but no one has the responsibility to create these justice tools and mechanisms and make them safe and acceptable to complainants."[30]

As violence was reemerging in new forms and women were reorganizing to face it, the urgency of elaborating the traumatic memories of the revolution became more apparent. In November 2022, Yasmin el-Rifae, one of the founders of Opantish, presented her memoir about the experience of feminist revolution at a bookshop in Brooklyn, which in the past ten years has become one of the major hubs of a new Egyptian diaspora—in fact, exile—community. The bookshop was packed with young Egyptians, many of them former activists of Opantish, and in the same days in which the global human rights community was holding desperately, waiting for word about Alaa Abd El-Fattah, who was on a long and life-threatening hunger strike, the book talk became a cathartic moment of shared memories. At least for a moment, the Opantish community of 2011 could overcome the loneliness of the exile.

It could be fair to assert that the intensity of that moment indicates that the violence experienced by women in the decade that followed 2011 is part of a broader wave of political violence that has sought to annihilate the idea and the momentum of the 2011 Revolution, erase its memories, and mortify the bodies of the revolutionary activists through women's assaults and rape during demonstrations, confinement in prison of political opponents, torture, and exile. The level of violence experienced by women political activists over the decade profoundly traumatized an entire generation and made clear their physical and psychological vulnerability against the full power of state violence. Yet the deep and invisible link between gender, sexuality, and power became more and more apparent as the decade progressed, inspiring new ways of thinking about feminism and new forms of activism, which are at once the long-lasting legacy of previous generations and new ways of thinking and acting. The directions that this new activism is taking remains to be studied.

TWELVE

———

The Twenty-First-Century Egyptian Women's Prisons Notebooks

Sept 1, 1922

To his excellency. The Field Marshal Lord Allenby, Bacos, Ramleh

Dear Sir,

Since yesterday I have had the occasion to communicate with Madame Wasif Bey Ghali who has been to visit her husband in prison. She has written [to] me a letter in French, which I enclose here, with the details of the life our prisoners are living. Her husband was three days in his cell, after which he was removed to the infirmary on account of failure of health. Thinking perhaps, that the condition of the prisoners was altered after that, I also met Mr. Albert Khayatt, who has been to see his father George Bey, and he seconded Mme Ghali's report.

I am sure your Excellency can imagine the condition of this gentleman locked-up during 22 hours of the day in a two-metre cell in the Cairo August weather, both in light and in darkness undergoing all sorts of discomfort, ennui and indignity, sharing the private life and being in daily contact with criminals of the worst character.

. . .

Huda Shaarawi Pasha[1]

March 13, 2011

Lawyers at military prosecution now. We hope to find out the status of the protesters. Pray for Freedom and Justice. We found out that the protesters were interrogated after midnight on March 10th without any human rights lawyers.

Ragia Omran[2]

January 18, 2018

My beginning, my awareness of injustice in the public space, began when I was about seventeen years old, with the rise of a student movement, which was,

FIGURE 24. Protest against the protest law after 2013. Courtesy of Aida Seif El-Dawla.

basically, a democratic nationalist movement. It was in 1972. My brothers were in university. I wasn't. I was still in school. However, you come to a point in your life where you are suddenly aware of a world that is much wider than your old little world, wider than your family, your wants, your needs as a teenager. For me, that was when the police came to our house and wanted to arrest my brothers. At that point, when they were arrested, I was called, by others, to join the families of the arrested students, and I did. I became part of it, and I got to know my world, which was growing, and that world, which was growing, much better.

Hala Shukrallah[3]

February 10, 2019

So, this afternoon, after 5 days of waiting at Tora Prison gates, Laila Soueif and Mona Seif were allowed to go in and see Alaa Abd El-Fattah. We are grateful for that, and he is fine and well. However:

The visit took place—not in the prison Alaa is held in, Tora Agriculture Ward, but in Tora 2 Maximum Security.

The visit was in a small room divided by a glass panel. They had to speak to Alaa through handsets from behind the glass.

Several security personnel were present on both sides of the glass throughout the visit. Alaa had been kept in ignorance about why his family had not been to see him on Tuesday or any of the following days.

When Laila had gone to visit on Tuesday, she had taken him the usual things: food, clean laundry, books, vitamins, etc. The prison had refused to receive them. But on Wednesday (as the prison authorities negotiated with her to go away with a promise that she would visit Thursday) they agreed to take the things and give them to Alaa. We thought this would help him understand that there was an administrative problem preventing the visit, nothing worse. Today it turned out that the authorities had not delivered the things to him despite their promise.

Anyway, Alaa is fine and in good spirits and counting the days—36 now—till his release. We hope these days pass without further incident.

We are totally aware that other families are going through what we've just gone through—some for as long as 4 years. We hold them in our thoughts and continue to hope that truth and justice will win out.

Your solidarity and support mean the world to us. Thank you.

Ahdaf Soueif[4]

"I AM THE MOTHER OF POLITICAL PRISONERS!": THE LONG HISTORY OF WOMEN'S ACTIVISM AGAINST POLITICAL IMPRISONMENT

One hundred years separate the first document above from the last one. Four generations span between the women who participated in the 1919 Revolution, advocated for the political prisoners, and then gave birth to one of the first feminist organization in the Arab world (the Egyptian Feminist Union [EFU], 1923–1956), and the women who took to the streets to participate and even lead the demonstrations in January 2011, initiating a new phase in the history of Egyptian feminism.

The first one is a letter by Huda Sha'rawi, the leader of the EFU, archived at the British Foreign Office Archives, in London. The latter three are part of my own archive, a collection comprising the ephemeral sources (photos of graffiti, photos, songs, newspaper articles, and social media's posts), oral histories, and the fieldwork notes I have collected during the past fourteen years as part of my own efforts to contribute to the collective feminist endeavor of documenting women's experiences in the 2011 Revolution. Among these is the testimony of Hala Shukrallah, a feminist community activist and the first Egyptian (and Coptic) woman to serve as president of a political party in Egypt (Dostour, February 2014–April 2015). Her testimony is perhaps one of those that more than anything helped me to understand the transformative effect that the imprisonment of political activists has not only on them, but also on their close friends and families, who, as Shukrallah explained to me, find themselves entering a new world:

> The most important thing I discovered was a word I had no knowledge of, and it became part of my own identity. I was entering the houses of these women who were mothers of political prisoners, and they became my mothers.
>
> We went to meet the speaker of the Majlis al-Sha'b, the lower house of the Parliament. At that time, political prisoners had protests inside the prison, and they released the police force to beat them up.
>
> We, the *harakat al-ummat*, the "movement of the mothers," went to the Parliament to protest.
>
> We all sat down and initiated the protest, until we were asked to send a spokesperson to talk to the Parliament, and the other women, who were all much older than me, wanted me to go and talk.
>
> I got up and said: "We are the mothers of the political prisoners!"
>
> The spokesperson of the Parliament laughed and said: "You are a mother? I know your father!"
>
> I was seventeen. I responded: "I am not here to talk about my father!"
>
> The *harakat al-'ummat* were pushing me to speak. I was affected. It gave me an insight into people's life in the community.
>
> If you enter people's life, you are part of it, and you become responsible of how they live.
>
> It is also emotional engagement that can inform your politics.
>
> . . .
>
> I was arrested a few times. But once we went to the court because we used to go to the hearings with the mothers.
>
> We went to the hearings and by chance one girl was arrested in front of us. We then said: we are not going to leave until you release her.
>
> Then they took me. The mothers tried to take me back. They took them all [into] a small anteroom between the court and the prison and they started to put us in a police van.
>
> My mum was with me, and she lost her shoes [laugh].
>
> When we came back home, we found my father, who was desperate: "Everyone is gone!" he was saying . . . [smile].
>
> My mum was very brave. I identify a lot with her.
>
> Today it is worse. We never went through the hell they are going through today. The student movement was a picnic.[5]

The plague of the prisoners of conscience is certainly not an exclusive prerogative of the post-2011 Revolution. Repression of political dissent has been a common practice of most modern states. However, the fierceness of the post-2013 Sisi regime against its opponents is particularly noteworthy, especially in the context of its strategic alliance with Western democracies. As I am writing

the last lines of this chapter, in June 2024, there remains no accurate account-
ing of the number of political prisoners currently detained in Egypt. Egyptian
human rights organizations talk about close to one hundred thousand people.
What is certain is that the Egyptian state has built sixty new prisons between
2011 and 2022.[6] Among the prisoners are thousands of women, some of them
well known. Others do not make the news, and the only documentation we
have about them is the letters to their families that their lawyers manage to
smuggle from the prison, or the lawyers' reports. Many of the political prisoners are in a regime of pretrial detention. The families who are protesting against
their illegal detention are intimidated with violence, notwithstanding their age
or status. The mother of Alaa Abd El-Fattah (Laila Soueif), her sister Ahdaf
Soueif, Alaa's sister Mona, and Professor Rabab al-Mahdi have all been arrested
(and then released) for protesting against illegal detentions of political opponents during the COVID-19 crisis. Neama Hisham, the wife of Abd El-Fattah's
lawyer, Mohamed El-Baqer, was also detained for protesting his maltreatment
in April 2023.

As spaces for demonstrating political dissent are shrinking, dissent takes
new forms and activists relocate to continuing their activism. This is the case
of the Soueif sisters, who, after their British citizenship was confirmed,
moved to London in order to expand the international campaign to liberate
their brother.

If the fight for equality in the public sphere (especially education, work,
and political representation) marked the first decades of Egyptian feminism
(1923–1956), the fight for bodily integrity and sexual and reproductive rights
alongside socioeconomic rights was dominant in the eighties and nineties,
and the fight against sexual violence was a major theme in 2011 and during
the revolutionary decade. While all these fights were continuing and intersecting with others during the long feminist century, it seems to me not exag-
geration to assert that today, the fight to support political prisoners is a cen-
terpiece of feminist political activism in Egypt, with an increasingly
prominent thread developing since 2011 around the idea of prison abolition-
ism. Like all the struggles that I have illustrated in the earlier chapters, this
also is rooted in a century of women's political activism, achieving an important peak during the 2011 Revolution. The experience of women in the initiative Not to Military Trials for Civilians and the political biography of high-
profile human rights defender and former political prisoner Yara Sallam,
from whose testimony a link with previous generations of political prisoners
emerges, illustrate this deep historical thread.

NO TO MILITARY TRIALS OF CIVILIANS:
A WOMEN-LED INITIATIVE

The attempt of the Egyptian military to repress the 2011 Revolution began already during the eighteen days, with the use of military courts (a colonial heritage from the British during the 1919 revolution) to prosecute civilians,[7] one of the first tools deployed to break the movement. An official number of military trials against civilians, or those imprisoned by them, has never been made public, but between January and July 2011 alone, more than ten thousand young activists were imprisoned.[8]

Political activists, especially women, did not wait to act against this practice. The memory of their century-long activism to support political prisoners came to the surface in this period, and they quickly organized a network, No to Military Trials for Civilians (NMTC), to spearhead their efforts. I first learned of NMTC toward the end of 2011. A young woman psychiatrist, Basma Abdel Rahman, told me about the initiative, emphasizing that it was run by women: "You know after the revolution the army went to the streets and people got arrested and underwent military trials. So, this initiative was done for the rights of the people undergoing trials in courts and following up the prisoners during the revolution and until now ... they are still working on this. And this initiative became bigger and bigger, and attracted more people, but it started with few activist women like Mona Seif and Rasha 'Azza."[9]

The initiative started in March 2011, when thousands of violations happened and the numbers of people who were arrested, tortured, and sentenced with no access to lawyers became evident. At the beginning, the group was formed by about twenty people, mostly young women and activists: "For some reason, we never see the men, the fathers, but just the sisters or the mothers going everywhere after their kids went to prison, and protesting and having sit-ins, doing hunger strikes, and doing amazing work. And then you see people that were very poor, and the revolution was not even that important for them, and the problem is how they could participate, and on the other side kids instead were joining the group and supporting the protests and so on. It was amazing and inspiring."[10]

All the testimonies I have collected confirm that a large share of activists against military trials were women. They started by trying to collect the names of every single person that had been arrested, and to campaign for each one of them, in order to get them free or, at least, sentenced through legal procedures. This proved to be a very difficult task, as most of the time the military did not give access to the names of the arrested people. Another important issue they raised, besides the respect for legal procedures, was the conditions in prison and torture. They found out that people were kept in horrible conditions, sometimes even one hundred people in a small space, with no water and no food for days. Sexual assault was the norm, and for women, "virginity tests" were routine: "This was done to punish people that made the revolution. And then what happened was highly political, it wasn't just an issue of human rights, but an issue of the revolution, and which sides are going to win," a member of the network NMTC explained to me.[11]

NMTC mobilized to get the attention of Egyptian and international media, recurring also to sit-in and hunger strikes, as explained to me by Laila Soueif. Many of the young activists I interviewed between 2011 and 2014 (when protests were forbidden) were part of multiple and intersecting networks, each one with its own specificity but also with overlapping aims: "It depends on what's taking place" explained me Lobna Darwish, who was part of Mosireen, NMTC, and Opantish:

> It depends on what's taking place. If people are arrested, you go to the prosecution office and stand there waiting for them. If there's protests, you go to protests. If there's something to prepare for the No To Military Trial or Opantish, you deal with this. So, it depends on the day, but things are very, very linked together I think, because a lot of people are coming between all these things. It's something we do collectively, and we don't see kind of the boundaries between groups, but we see them as like, work or something to do, something we must finish.[12]

Over the years since 2011, the commitment of women to the freedom and rights of political prisoners has been multilayered, as in the long tradition of women's activism. Besides protests and media campaigns, which sometimes themselves led to imprisonment, they used their professional expertise to support political prisoners. On the front line in this field were psychiatrists and lawyers. The psychiatrist Sally Toma wrote about the trauma endured by children she treated after imprisonment, denouncing their torture and voicing her desperation about the possibility to treat them: "I have one guy now this is his fourth detention, you know? And he's been detained now for three months, and he was raped before three times and, you know, like I'm expecting him to come out totally lost, gone forever, no treatment will even work. . . .

He's nineteen now, he started getting arrested when he was sixteen. He got raped when he was sixteen."[13]

El-Nadeem systematically collected testimonies of political prisoners since 2011, trying to break the silence around them. El-Nadeem paid its commitment to the cause with a long period of censure (its clinic was sealed by the authorities, its bank account frozen, and its board under investigation and travel bans). Other women human rights defenders, such as the translators Marwa Arafa and Khoulud Said Amer, ended up in jail for being suspected of raising funds for the families of political prisoners. While Amer has eventually been released, at the time of writing Arafa is still in prison. The lawyer Hoda Abdelwahab, a leading defender of political prisoners, has been under a travel ban since 2016, but this intimidating measure does not stop her from doing her work with extreme dedication. She works relentlessly, and although she is well aware that the large picture is gloomy, she celebrates the release of every single one of her defendants on her social media platform. I see here traces of what I called "a politics of radical care" performed in their everyday lives by Egyptian women over the twentieth and the twenty-first century: although well aware that big, structural changes are hard to achieve, at least in the span of a lifetime, the celebration of small achievements empowers the community and it instills hope among them.

Women are very much paying attention to the intersection between political, socioeconomic, and gender rights in Egypt, and some of them try to break the traditional binary between political prisoners and common criminals: "Not just the political prisoners," the feminist human rights lawyer Yara Sallam, who served fifteen months in Qanater (the women's prison made famous by the paintings of Inji Aflatun, detained there 1959–1963, and the memoir of Nawal al-Saadawi, imprisoned there during the 1981 wave of arrests of political dissidents), told me. "No one speaks about women's prison conditions. No one speaks about bodily rights, like how they are being searched, the vaginal search. No one speaks about anything related to that, apart from the very progressive organizations, such as the Egyptian Initiative for Personal Rights."[14] A few months after my interview with Yara Sallam, I found out that the EIPR had launched a campaign called Periods in Prison, which calls on prison authorities to provide cotton-based sanitary pads to female prisoners free of charge.[15] In July 2023, the journalist and former political prisoner, today living in exile, Solafa Magdi, published a report denouncing the poor conditions of women's detention in Egypt and the lack of awareness about them.[16] An explicit feminist agenda seems to be an integral part of the activism to liberate political prisoners, and not only to ameliorate the conditions of detention but to abolish it. In this context, the story of Yara Sallam sheds light on the longue durée continuity among generations of women political activists who experienced their own or their family members' imprisonment.

EVEN THE FINEST OF WARRIORS . . . YARA SALLAM

I had been familiar with Yara Sallam's cheerful as much as defiant smile since the autumn of 2014, when her photos were among those of young political prisoners appearing on big panels in the streets of the central districts in Cairo, with the warning sentence: "They are celebrating 'Eid in prison." This was a campaign launched by No to Military Trials for Civilians to raise public awareness about the detention of young political activists.

The campaign for the release of Yara Sallam lasted the fifteen months she had been detained, from June 21, 2014, until she was released with a presidential pardon on September 23, 2015. Two days after granting the pardon to a small number of political prisoners, President El-Sisi flew to the United Nations Summit for the Adoption of the Post-2015 Development Agenda (September 25–27, 2015), where he presented Egypt's agenda for sustainable economic development, social justice, and the struggle against terrorism.[17]

A couple of months later, I was in Cairo, and I could sense a growing skepticism among NGOs professionals and activists. The economy was not flourishing and the spaces for political activism were shrinking. I tried to contact Yara, but she was not ready to meet. I sensed that she was still processing the experience of detention, a period that many former political prisoners narrate not as a parenthesis in their lives but a transformative one. A couple of years later I found an explicit testimony by Yara about that passage: "In March 2017, I wrote that I still had not recovered from my prison experience; now I feel a distance from the word 'recovery,' and no longer imagine a return to how I was before passing through that wooden gate. I no longer want to go back to who I was before. It's enough that I've come to know myself better in recent years and called up enough acceptance and maturity to understand and accept the changes in myself."[18]

I waited till June 2018, when Yara gave me an appointment in the Garden City offices of the Egyptian Initiative for Personal Rights, the NGO where she had been working in several capacities since 2007.[19] At time of the interview, Yara was thirty-two years old, a couple of which were spent between the US and The Gambia, and more than a year (fifteen months) at Qanater.

A graduate from the Francophone section of the Law School at Cairo University, Yara specialized in international human rights law in the US, and her LLM degree took her to work as professional legal assistant at the African Commission on Human and Peoples' Rights (ACHPR) in Banjul (The Gambia). When the revolution started, Yara was still in Banjul, and, initially, she did not grasp the size of the event and decided to stay and fulfill her contract obligations. She later regretted that decision, which led her "to miss the revolution."[20] "I came back in March 2011. I remember, I came back a few days before the first protest against military trials for civilians. I remember going with a friend. It was the first time I participated in such a protest. She passed by me, and we went there. Military Prosecution is in Nasser city, so we went there and saw another friend, and then we just stood there, inside the gates of the prosecution's building. No one could enter inside. There were more than fifteen or twenty people."

Between 2011 and 2013, Egypt was in turmoil. All the activists I met during these years were talking and writing about "the continuing revolution," and women, especially young women, were at the core of the struggle, and the counterrevolutionary forces increasingly recurred to sexual harassment and gang rape to intimidate demonstrators and delegitimize the revolutionary movement. Again, the harassment of women political activists was not new; it is documented in the studies about Marxist (especially radical) women in the 1940s,[21] and in the testimonies I collected from democratic women in the 1990s and early 2000s. The Black Wednesday attack on May 25, 2005, marked an important milestone in violations and sexual violence against women protesters. But many women I spoke to over the years agree that the level of brutality experienced since 2012 is unparalleled.

Yara's narrative about the demonstrations reflects women's political allegiance at this difficult juncture. She remembered participating in the demonstration of June 2011 at the Ministry of Interior to commemorate the torture and death under police custody of Khaled Said: "Right now, you can't even get close, but back then there were people drawing graffiti on the walls on the Ministry of Interior, of Khaled Saeed's face." Like many of the young women I interviewed at the end of 2011, she had vivid memories of the July 2011 sit-in, the Maspero massacre in October 2011, the Muhammad

Mahmoud clashes in November 2011, and the Cabinet clashes in December 2011. These were life-changing experiences for all of them.

At the end of 2011, Yara decided to contribute to the revolution through her professional skills and to attend as a lawyer the investigations with detainees: "I went to one of the investigations in the Muhammad Mahmoud case, a case where they gathered a lot of protesters." She moved from her mother's house in Heliopolis to downtown, as it was easier both to go to work at Nazra for Feminist Studies, where she served as Women Human Rights Defenders Program manager, and to participate in the ongoing protests centered around Tahrir Square:

> We were in the street almost all day. Even now, I don't remember how many days the clashes lasted. I remember that my birthday was in the middle. I remember starting on the 19th of November [2011]. I think I was getting calls for my birthday when I was running from something, but I do not remember how many days. We were very close to home, so we would just go in the morning and see what was happening, then go back, take a shower, and come back again. There were continuous clashes. Sometimes we would need to bring water or napkins or whatever it was. We would see what we needed and then we would get it from the pharmacy and come back. Participating in demonstrations has always been dangerous, especially for women, but since the end of 2012, gang rapes were happening all the time: I remember when the protests started happening against Morsi, I used to march from Mohandessin to the end of Qasr el-Nil Bridge and go somewhere else. Ever since June 2012, I stopped going into Tahrir Square. That was the peak period of gang rapes, it was too dangerous.

On June 21, 2014, twenty-three people were arrested, seven of them women: Sanaa Seif, Hanan al-Tahan, Salwa Mehrez, Samar Ibrahim, Nahed al-Sherif, Rania al-Sheikh, and Yara.

"I was arrested almost a week or ten days after Sisi took power," Yara told me. "It was a protest calling for the release of political detainees. It was almost over. I was going, with my cousin, to just have a look at the police tanks, and then, in the blink of an eye, two police officers came out of the blue and they got both of us. Then, they let him out, and they kept me." This was the first protest since El-Sisi was elected president of the Republic and it was about political prisoners, she emphasizes, "but this one was for all political detainees, not only the left, which was a good point to make."

This specification is important, as it points to the self-reflectivity of the young revolutionary women after the massacre of Muslim Brotherhood supporters in August 2013. In all the testimonies I collected in 2014, they offer a narrative that goes beyond the ideological and traditional divide between leftists and Islamists, reminding me that if part of the left did not stand in solidarity with the victims of Rabaa, many did.

"For sure I was not supportive of the military intervention, nor the massacre," Yara Sallam explained. When I asked what the charges against them were, Yara couldn't help but laugh, as if, four years on, it still seems surreal: "Thuggery, being a part of illegal protests, of course, destroying public property and attacking citizens, carrying a Molotov, and things like that." Yara's colleagues and even her mother, the translator and artist Rawia Sadek, whom I met few months later (January 2018), suggest that she was arrested and detained because of her professional affiliation to a human rights organization. It is undeniable that human rights defenders have been under the eyes of the military since the early days of the counterrevolution: in February 2011, the Hisham Mubarak Law Center was raided and staff members were arrested. In March 2011, security personnel raided the headquarters of multiple foreign NGOs. Following prosecution in June 2013 (Case 173/2011), forty-three Egyptian and non-Egyptian civil society workers, including sixteen Americans, were sentenced to between one and five years in prison on charges of illegally receiving foreign funds and operating without a license. Upon strong pressure coming from the international communities (both civil society and governments), they were all acquitted in December 2018.[22]

The harassment of human rights defenders continued in 2013 and 2014, with raids at the Egyptian Center for Economic and Social Rights, whose files and computers were seized and staff members detained. Mohamed Lotfy, the executive director of the Egyptian Commission for Rights and Freedoms, was banned from travel to Germany on June 2, 2015, to attend a roundtable organized by the Green Party at the German Parliament. In May 2018, his wife, Amal Fathi, was arrested after she posted a video where she denounced sexual harassment. She was then accused of being part of the outlawed 6th of April group and condemned to two years, but both her husband and members of the group denied the affiliation.[23] Meanwhile, the director of the Cairo Institute for Human Rights, Bahey Eldin Hassan, and the board members were forced into exile in 2014.

In August 2014, two months after Yara was arrested, the government gave NGOs a November 10 deadline to register under the law on associations (Law 84/2002), which empowers the government to reject registration applications without reasoning, shut down any group virtually at will, freeze its assets, confiscate its property, reject nominees to its governing board, block its funding, and deny requests to affiliate with international organizations. A new, even more restrictive law on NGOs was ratified by President El-Sisi in April 2017 (Law 70/2017), making it virtually impossible for NGOs to operate in Egypt. Notwithstanding numerous appeals launched by Egyptian and international human rights organizations,[24] the crackdown escalated, leaving these groups with very marginal space to operate. In light of this context, it seems more than plausible that Yara Sallam was arrested for her association with human rights activism. That she decided to resume her work after her release tells a lot about her determination.

What stroke a chord with me about Yara's memories from the prison was her strenuous daily effort to make every single moment of her fifteen months in prison meaningful by engaging with her roommates and other prisoners' stories:

> We were altogether in one cell. Each cell in prison is headed by a woman prisoner with a long prison sentence; fifteen or twenty-five years. She is responsible for keeping order in the cell and informing the administration of anything going on inside the cell. We were eight: the seven of us and that woman. She was older than us and apparently convicted for something related to her business . . . then . . . you never know in jail . . . what the real story is. Sometimes people tell stories just to ensure that they are not labeled. There is always this kind of hierarchy between crimes and between each crime, inside of it, there are more layers. I really liked her; she was a really nice woman.[25]

As she was remembering her imprisonment and her charges, Yara smiled, and her smile suddenly brought to the front of my own memories of that period the photos of her and the other women that were popping up on my social media newsfeed during the fifteen months of their detention. A small group of women in their twenties, some of them even younger, wearing the white *galabeyya* of the prisoners—a garment on which Yara wrote powerful words to talk about class differences in prison—and . . . all smiling. I was wondering how that was possible. "Yes, we were smiling in that photo because that was the first time we could see our friends! They came in, some friends, and we were just joking with them, because we knew it was a joke. It wasn't a real trial: you wouldn't respect such a trial, it was a camouflage!"

This was not the first case in which a group of leftist secular women were arrested and then condemned since the 2011 Revolution. The Cabinet clashes had women convicted in the case, like Hend Nafea². In November 2013 a group of women (among them Salma Said, Nazly Hussein, Mona Seif, and

Rasha 'Azza) had been arrested and released before the trials, literally abandoned in the middle of the desert. Back then, it was considered detrimental to the image of the regime to detain young secular women, and mostly women from the Muslim Brotherhood were detained for political reasons. This was not the case anymore in 2014, a clear sign of the escalation of the repression.

For Yara Sallam, the prison was a new world, a prism through which she experienced injustice and socioeconomic differences on a whole different level. At the same time, it was a time that reconnected her to her family's history. In fact, Yara's narratives about prison and her family's history inform each other. On one hand, her memory of the family's history revolves around prison experiences; on the other, her family background allows her a critical perspective on the replication and amplification of class differences in jail.

Yara does not describe her parents as directly involved in politics: "My father is originally from a village in the countryside and his parents were not politicized. His parents were just like many other Egyptians. He was politically active during university, like many at the time. When he became a journalist, he used to take part in the sit-ins and the protests in the Press Syndicate. I remember in the late eighties or beginning of the nineties, being with him at one of the sit-ins. I remember when the Press Syndicate had a garden, and they were just sitting there, striking. But neither of my parents really encouraged me to go into a political party as opposed to being independent and saying what one's conscience tells them to say."

The experience of approaching politics through informal networks and the mistrust for political parties is emblematic of Yara's generation, and it informs the revolutionary activism of her peers, whose political prerevolutionary work happened in informal spaces and has been defined as post-ideological. At the same time, there is clearly a long-lasting legacy of political activism coming from the families, which is transmitted generation upon generation, sometimes even through silences. As she moves to the mother's side of her family, I can hear how her approach to politics was informed by the stories she heard—and even more, those that she did not hear—in family's history. The complex interweave between words and silences reflects a pattern in the controversial genealogies of political activism in Egypt and beyond.

"My grandmother's name is Dina Hamawi, and my grandfather's name is Ahmad Sadiq Sa'ad. These are their names after they converted to Islam under Nasser. The rest of the family migrated to France." Yara's family's history is clearer in the broader context of the history of what Beinin described

EGYPTIAN WOMEN'S PRISONS NOTEBOOKS · 245

"a heterogenous community of cosmopolitan hybrids,"[26] and for their class, cultural backgrounds, and European connections, they were a core component of the communist movements in Egypt, even if their loyalty was often questioned by the nationalist wings of the movements. Beinin writes that Ahmad Sadiq Saʿad (Yara's grandfather) was, together with Yusef Darwiche and Rymond Douek, one of the founders of the magazine *al-Fajr al-Jadid* (*New Dawn*), which was established as a formal organization in 1946.[27] *Al-Fajr* dealt with the controversial issue of the status of Jews, Greeks, and other *mutamassirun* (minorities) by a theory they called "the corridor" (*al-mamarr*): "Those who mastered Arabic and identified with Egypt passed through the corridor, were considered *cent pour cent* Egyptian, and were admitted to the organization; those who did not were excluded."[28] Beinin also explains that, while workers in the movement were satisfied with the procedure, intellectuals continued to nourish concerns about the Jewish origins of Darwiche, Saʿad, and Douek, even after they converted to Islam. The question of the allegiance of Jews to the Communist Party became even more controversial after the proclamation of Israel and the first Arab-Israeli War. It was discussed in the early 1950s, in the Egyptian Workers and Peasants Communist Party (Hezb al-ʿUmmal wa al-Fallahin ash-Shiuʿi al-Masri), of which Saʿad was a board member.[29] When the Communist Party of Egypt was established (January 8, 1958), Jews were included in the central committee, except for those emigrated to Paris (the Rome group, led by Henri Curiel). Beinin writes that Darwiche, Saʿad and Douek supported this decision, mostly because they considered Curiel too sympathetic to Zionism.[30] Being nationalists and loyal to the postcolonial political project did not spare communists from jail. Ahmad Sadiq Saʿad was arrested twice. Only fragments of this story can be retrieved from Yara's memories: "I don't remember where he was the second time, but I remember that during Nasser's time he was for five years in Wahat detention camp and was tortured."

In 1959, there was a big wave of arrests of communists, and in her narrative about her grandfather, Yara refers to it:

> I don't remember seeing him: I was around three years old when he died. My grandmother died when I was older, but she never spoke about her political activism, to the point that I was not even aware of it. I think she hated it because they paid a high price ... no one appreciated my grandfather's work, and when he was detained, no one took care of her. She raised three kids on her own, borrowing money from a lot of people. I think she never spoke about that period because she hated it. I was surprised and amazed when my former

mother-in-law told me that my grandmother's story was narrated in a book on women in the Egyptian Communist Movement. I spoke to my mum about my grandmother's activism, and she confirmed it. I then learned that my grandmother was from the poor Jewish community, and my grandfather was from the rich Jewish community. So, when they were both arrested, she was detained in a bad place [where] she almost died, while he was detained in a very nice place and well respected, because . . . he spoke Italian. Class mattered.[31]

The memory of the generations of communists who were in jail under the Nasser regime lurks in the family memories of many revolutionary contemporary activists. There is certainly a gap in intergenerational transmission of history and knowledge. In an interview the journalist Hani Shukrallah, a leading figure in the seventies students' movement, gave me in 2018, he critically reflected upon the position of his generation toward their fathers; he defined their critical attitude toward the decision to officially dissolve themselves and being co-opted by Nasser as "too harsh" and oblivious of the context they were operating in.[32]

The curse of memory (and of the lack of its transmission) adds to the other limits of Egyptian Marxism, especially the incapacity to mobilize the masses, and the prevalence of nationalism, with a dangerous overlapping between Marxism and pan-Arabism.[33] From a feminist perspective one could add the incapacity to address the issue of women's equality (even within the movement) and more broadly a moralistic attitude toward sexuality, which characterizes the communist movements in the second half of the twentieth century. Of particular interest in this respect is the testimony of Latifa al-Zayyat collected by Selma Botman in 1980, when the communist militant and intellectual defined feminism "a luxury."[34]

What is interesting from an oral history perspective is how memory plays into the construction of the present. In Yara's oral history, the scattered family memories about her grandparents led us to talk about her own experience in prison, how that period led her to think critically about the intersection between class and gender and how, in her view, Egyptian feminism has not yet developed a satisfactory approach to it. The conversation about what feminism is brought us back to reflect upon Yara's feminist education. She started by pointing out that for her this did not come primarily from books but from her family:

> I have been raised in a feminist family. It is the same when someone asks me if I am leftist, or not: I didn't know what "left" is, I just knew that everyone has the right to education and health care. Everyone should be equal. If this

is called "leftist," then I am a leftist. I have always been aware of equality because we lived in a house where there was equality. That was life for me. It wasn't something that I learned in books. Neither my political affiliation nor my ideas as a feminist came from books. I started reading about feminism later, after I graduated from law school.

It would perhaps be fair to suggest that her academic education, where she explored the canons of both liberal feminist theories and classical Arab feminism (such as Fatima Mernissi and her critique of Orientalism), allowed Yara to name what she instinctively already knew, enabling her to develop a fruitful conversation with her peers, especially within feminist circles in Egypt. Yara's approach to feminism is hence informed by numerous experiences and sources, taking her to deconstruct the false binary between universalism of rights and cultural relativism, the global dimension of violence against women, a violence that is not only physical and psychological but also epistemic when it does not acknowledge the dialectic between universalism of rights and cultural specificities of women's struggles around the world. It comes across very clearly from Yara, as it does from many other activists of her generation, whose focus is on the link between socioeconomic and gender inequalities. The experience of prison and reading about other women's theories about it informs Yara's feminism. When she left prison, Yara started reading the works of an activist and scholar whose books I have found in many of the libraries of young revolutionary feminists, and whose popularity continues to grow as I am writing these pages: Angela Davis.[35] For Yara, reading Davis was eye-opening and helped her to envision a renewed feminism that pushes the boundaries of the critical issues feminists need to address collectively. When she refers to women in prison, she notes that sex workers and women who have been imprisoned for crimes related to drugs are invisible in the Egyptian feminist discourses, somehow replicating the moral standards set by the dominating patriarchal culture, including a systemic critique of prisons as patriarchal institutions:

> No one speaks about how prison is a patriarchal institution, how we should refuse the criminal system in its totality, how this system is not the solution, but it is part of the problem. No one speaks about controversial issues, such as sex work. You hear about it, but when you enter in jail, and you see sex workers and people who run the business together, in one cell, and then you see women who are using drugs in the same cell as people who are selling drugs, you realize that the whole system does not really make sense. We should engage structurally with the whole system of how we are putting people in jail.

Like other women of her generation, Yara underlines that she does not perceive the presence of a solid, unified feminist movement in Egypt, but there are NGOs she considers more progressive, as they are working on the right to abortion, LGBT issues, transgender issues, and sexual violence, and others that she considers as mainstream, traditional women's rights organizations that work on the right to work, et cetera: "It's not over," she exclaims.

> The battle for equal working rights is not over. Sexual violence is not over. Abortion is not even allowed yet. But I still think that there is a need for . . . someone who challenges the state structure, who cares about women in jail, not just the political prisoners. There needs to be someone who talks about them. The state uses these women, who are in jail, who are not being able to pay the money for their fridge or washing machine, or whatever, for its own propaganda, and nobody speaks about women's prison conditions. No one speaks about bodily rights, like how they are being searched, the vaginal search. There is no intervention in the criminal system. The only people who push for the ceiling are the ones who talk about personal rights, because they are personally involved, such as sexual, reproductive, and bodily rights, anything related to the LGBT community, anything related to abortion. Individuals speak more about these issues, but there is not a progressive debate about general issues that involve the state. No one is questioning why, in cases of sexual violence, why do we want more prison time?

Yara's intersectional philosophy is reflected in her writings about prison, where she gives voice to the victims of the state's violence. Particularly poignant are her testimonies about women on death row[36] and her meeting Aya Hegazy, a woman human rights defender who was arrested upon false accusation of exploiting children in May 2014. The two women knew each other since 2007, when they took part in a university student activity (artistic workshop) for Palestinian children. They then met again in Qanater Prison: "I had not seen her at all between the summers of 2007 and 2014, a period long enough for the birth and murder of hope," writes Sallam. It is a piece about hope and a call to remembering political prisoners: "while in prison you always fear that you will be forgotten at some point."[37]

During her interview, Yara discussed how her conception of prison and politics changed over time:

> I think that before, I thought that if there is one cause that I would have make me accept, would make me accept the fact that I would go to jail for, that was for political prisoners, which I actually believed in. That is why I don't regret having gone to that protest, and I don't regret serving time for this cause.

Perhaps Sanaa [Seif] and I helped in increasing the attention around political prisoners' stories, because we were both high profile, but with this number of people in prison and this kind of strategies of the regime, it is not useful for anyone to be in prison right now. I like Mahienour's sentence when she says, "We don't like prisons, but we are not afraid of them." I feel the same way. I wouldn't do something extra risky if I didn't think of it as worth losing my days and going through a pretty [difficult time] for not only me but also my family, because I come from a fairly leftist political family. My mum used to tell me, "If you are participating in one thing, make sure that you know its consequences. If you are ready for the consequences, just do it."

In fact, when I interviewed Yara's mother, she told me with pride that Yara's braveness and determination reminded her of her father, Saʿad, the Marxist Jew converted to Islam who Yara didn't have the time to develop a relationship with but whose legacy she carries. But there is something very specific to her experience as a young woman in the turbulent twenty-first century: Yara is at the core of the young women's movement that after the 2011 Revolution challenged what Deniz Kandiyoti called a masculinist restoration agenda,[38] setting the foundation for a new feminism whose radical ideas are deployed through an intersectional agenda of activism. By continuing to participate in demonstrations, even when gang rape became the strategy to intimidate the revolutionaries, and by continuing to take to the streets when protests were banned, these women openly challenged the patriarchal violence of the state. By writing and talking about their experiences in prison and sexual violence, they push the boundaries of feminist action and thought, starting to draft a new feminist agenda.

Conclusion

CAIRO, JUNE 2024

The temperatures in early June 2024 have already been breaking records across Cairo; daily power outages are the rule, while Aswan recorded the highest temperature on earth on June 11. Nevertheless, the women I have come to know during the last two decades of research in Egypt, whose stories compose this book, are—as always—happy to meet and catch up on life, work, and family. News about personal life intertwines with opinions and fears about domestic and international politics, the normal rhythm of our meetings.

The city's landscape is rapidly changing. Just in time for the full force of global warming, trees that for generations have embellished Cairo's streets and mitigated the heat of the summer have been cut down to make space for new highways—"All Sisi cares about are bridges," more than one person exclaimed, noting his well-known penchant for ambitious construction projects that enable the regime and its cronies to siphon ever more of the country's wealth into private hands.

On another and perhaps less sour note, middle-class neighborhoods that used to be mostly residential have been enlivened by the growing presence of Syrian shops and Sudanese cafés. Today as a century ago, middle-class refugees from Syria, Palestine, and Sudan are electing Cairo their new home, bringing new energy and building new communities in the process. Tragically, however, the motivation for these migrations is some of the worst state-imposed violence in memory across the region.

In this changing scenery, which opens a number of questions about the new political economy of Egypt and how it relates to the global movement of capital and people, the joy of celebrating an old friend's birthday, a child's wedding, or the arrival of a newborn are shadowed by the absence of a close friend or relative, one who died inexplicably of a minor illness, another who is languishing alongside thousands prisoners of conscience in one of Egypt's notorious prisons. More pressing still is the ongoing genocide of Palestinians in Gaza. While Western media emphasize the role of Egypt as a major "negotiator" between the Israeli political leadership and Hamas, the Egyptian women political activists I've become close to while studying the relationship between the feminist and the human rights movements in Egypt do not appear optimistic. There is no trace of these criticisms in government and mainstream Egyptian media, and *Mada Masr*'s newsroom is under intense pressure for its coverage of the disastrous situation in Rafah, at the Gaza border, three hundred kilometers from Cairo, where people are starving to death and where buying a permit to get out of Gaza can cost up to eight thousand US dollars. Rafah is out of reach for Egyptians, as no one can get near without special permits the government almost never gives out; there are too few people to witness what is happening there, yet the news that trickles out is devastating.

I began the research that became this book in the wake of the hope generated by the 2011 Revolution, a moment of joy that redefined the political imaginary of all those who participated in or otherwise witnessed it. The year 2011 promised a new dawn in Egyptian and international politics, a shift away from the neoliberal development strategies initiated in the mid-1980s under the aegis of the Washington consensus-driven policies of the World Bank and IMF. The promise of 2011 was to put an end to the corrupted alliance between the military, state, and economic elites (who themselves were either part of or retired members of the military or government), and to develop a model of governance inspired by values of solidarity, dignity, and social justice. When I began this research about the feminist roots of the 2011 Egyptian Revolution, hope, determinism, and optimism—however cruel—defined the activist scene.

As I am writing the last lines of this book, the world is witnessing the genocide in Gaza, a crime that marks a twilight of international law, human rights, and, indeed, our humanity. Everything seems to be irrelevant and unimportant compared to the magnitude of the continuing Palestinian Nakba.

Yet, amid an inescapable sense of grief, the women I am meeting in Cairo continue to share stories of defiance, and I can perceive a hint of pride when they mention the unexpected return of the crowds to Tahrir Square on

October 21, 2023: "This [the demonstration] was the 21 of October 2023. The first time in Tahrir Square in ten years. It was unexpected. Across the country there were demonstrations, but Tahrir was not allowed. So first we went to Mostafa Mahmud in Mohaddessin, but then we thought: let's see what happens if we go to Tahrir Square. Part of the Square, let's say half of it, was full."[1]

A question I never dared ask during the oral history interviews I conducted over the years keeps lurking during our meetings in June 2024: "Why are you doing this? What keeps you going?" Today, like the past fourteen years, I failed to ask this question, and in the attempt to make up my own mind about it while also escaping the heat of a summer, I withdrew to one of the few places where the beautiful trees of Cairo have not been cut yet, the Gezira Club in Zamalek, and resume editing this book.

There I came to my own interpretation about the origins of this strength. The stories I have gathered in this book suggest that the power I sense when I am with these women comes from the fact that they are walking in the footsteps of their ancestors, learning from their downfalls and building on their accomplishments. Transmitting their stories of defiance, in a cycle of narration that connects different generations, is part of building this strength.

The movement of solidarity with Palestinians led by Egyptian women is documentable to the International Women Suffrage Alliance (IWSA) Congress in Copenhagen in 1939, when Huda Sha'rawi tried in vain to bring the Palestinian anticolonial revolts to the attention of the IWSA board—of which she was the vice president. She then organized the Eastern Women Conference in Defense of Palestine in Cairo two years later. It continued throughout the twentieth century, bringing relief to displaced people in Sinai and in Gaza over the multiple attacks they were subjected to, advocating for them in all the international fora Egyptian women were involved in, and contrasting the dominant Western narratives that dehumanize Palestinian people, an epistemic violence that de facto enables their genocide. This all happened while Egyptian women activists were also fighting on a double front in their own country: patriarchy in the family and the broader society, and authoritarianism in politics. Colonialism, patriarchy, and authoritarianism—in all the historical variables they have experienced in Egypt throughout the twentieth century—are all part of the same matrix of power, and over the long feminist century (within which in the chronology of this book I include the first two decades of the twenty-first), Egyptian women political activists have been fighting against the three of them together.

The longue durée of Egyptian women's activism for Palestine intersects the development of the Egyptian movement for human rights, with feminism at the core of both. As much as in the past, and perhaps even more today, every time women political activists put their bodies on the front lines to defend human rights, their mere presence questions not only social and cultural norms but the international order, and often even state practices. For Egyptian women, Palestine has always been both a feminist and a national issue, both personal and political.

It is not by chance that in 2024 the International Women's Day was marked in Egypt by events in solidarity with Palestine, including a women's march, the first one since the one that was attacked in 2011 and since protests were banned in 2013. The government allowed the events to happen, for once, but they did not allow the space for the women's initiative to turn into a larger, new movement of dissent. The lesson of the early 2000s, when the movements of solidarity with Palestinian and Iraqi people joined ranks with the workers and the Kefaya movements, resulting in the 2011 Revolution, has been well learned by the military and the upgraded authoritarian regime of Abdel Fattah El-Sisi.

On April 24, 2024, when the women's collective in solidarity with Palestine (an informal group of women journalists, lawyers, doctors, and other activists) delivered a letter to the offices of UN Women in the residential neighborhood of Maadi, their peaceful and democratic initiative was repressed by the state security. The women (about twenty) were attacked by the police, and eleven among them, including journalists and lawyers, were arrested.

Their whereabouts remained unknown for hours, leaving their friends full of anguish: "I got the news of the arrests, and my first thought was: What do I do now? All my friends have been taken!" The journalist Lina Attalah and her friend, filmmaker and former prisoner of conscience Sanaa Seif, jumped in the car and spent the night going around Cairo's police stations, looking for their friends.[2]

Following what has become a routine protocol for them, human rights lawyers started the frantic activity to obtain the women's immediate liberation, as it is easier to liberate a political prisoner before they enter the tunnel of formal detention.

The women were separated at different police stations: "God forbid us from being together and making trouble!" commented Mai El-Mahdy, one of the women who were arrested, with a hint of sarcasm.[3] Even if this was the

254 · CONCLUSION

first time for her, she had the courage and mindfulness to smuggle her iPhone into the police station, allowing the lawyers to find her and the others' whereabouts. They appeared in front of the general prosecutor, and their case was announced: Case 1567/2024. Joining a terrorist group and organizing a demonstration. The lawyers could organize the defense and eventually obtained their release on bail. A well-known script that doesn't always end so quickly or happily, but for once, did.

This was the most recent attack against women's political activism in a long series, a context that requires learning how to coexist with fear and create new praxes, as explained by Lina Attalah:

> The politics within the politics and positionality is our issue. This entire practice does not exist. We must create it by praxis. We are Hegelian in a sense, for us the truth is in the movement. For me what matters is ambition, acknowledging that there is fear, and it is okay to stay with the emotion for a bit, and what matters is dealing with it. . . . There are no red lines . . . we keep fighting with the ceiling. The ceiling is changing all the time. There is immense opportunity in a crisis all the time. *Mada* is a channel of opportunities and crisis because we see opportunities in crisis everywhere.[4]

If, to paraphrase Nelson Mandela, courage is not the absence of fear so much as acting despite it, these women's courage and bravery are undeniable. Since the July 2013 coup, many of the women who have been interviewed during research for this book have faced trial for their political activities, they have been put under travel bans, and/or have been fighting to support family members who are in prison for political reasons. Some are in exile. One, Shaima' al-Sabbagh, was shot dead at a demonstration to commemorate the January 25 Revolution. Others courageously continue their critical work in Egypt, knowing that one or another organ of the apparatus of state security could and likely will knock at their door at any time, the most likely outcome being years of imprisonment, if not worse. The doors of some of the feminist and human rights organizations I have visited over the years, some of which hosted my seminars, have been closed pending investigations on alleged violations of the restrictive NGO law. At the same time, in Egypt, as in the rest of the world, the #MeToo campaign has raised multiple storms, and the COVID-19 crisis forced Egyptian intellectuals to think critically about the multiple and continuing, changing meanings of body politics and politics of health and care. Even as Egypt remains one of the most oppressive regimes today, the stories I have gathered in this book show that it also continues to be one of the most important hubs for global feminism, where vanguard discussions about gender, sexuality, and women's rights and how they intersect socioeconomic, human, and environmental rights, as well as conversations with deeply grounded theories around the coloniality of gender and the links between colonial and gender oppression, are taking new shape.

The tension between neoliberal military authoritarianism—the success of which owes to the support of both Western democracies and Gulf monarchies—and the longue durée of women's revolutionary resistance to it, is epitomized by the war on the memory of the 2011 Revolution that has now been ongoing in Egypt for more than a decade. What is clear in the summer of 2024 is that the memory of the 2011 Revolution is fading. As one of my friends, a writer and a journalist who was part of the 2011 revolutionary movement, explained over dinner, it is not just formal regime censorship that has increased; self-censorship has increased among writers and artists as well. Laila's Soliman's *Whims of Freedom,* with whose analysis I have opened this book, was perhaps the last theater work staged in Cairo containing explicit references to the 2011 Revolution. Today, no one would dare to be so explicit.

This tension is also part of a larger struggle Egyptian historians are fighting to access the National Archives, which are becoming less and less available due to the regime's paranoia of disclosing information that can put at risk the security of the state. In this context of deliberate erasure of memory, it is of foremost importance to develop a feminist epistemology of the 2011 Revolution that can inform a renewed feminist philosophy of history, one that builds on "unauthorized" archives and that challenges authoritarian narratives about history, allowing the transmission of a revolutionary knowledge. This is in essence a living archive and an archive of and for the future.

Indeed, in this atmosphere of general hostility for history and unavailability of national archives, feminist historians are the best equipped to engage in the effort of building alternative archives and write contrapuntal narratives to mainstream and state-controlled history, precisely because—as I discussed in the first part of this book—this is what the feminist methodology of writing history is grounded on. Finally, women's political activism and intellectual production are the ideal spaces to engage in contrapuntal writing of history because, as the stories I have collected in this book show, women have a well-established tradition of keeping the flame of dissidence alight in times of repression. They have been doing it in multiple spaces: in the family, in the newsrooms, in the legal courts, and in the political parties, before they entered the Parliament, and even after, in government institutions—from the center and from the margins. There is no doubt that most women who engaged in politics from whichever positionality, within or outside the structures and institutions of the Egyptian state and government, helped achieve something for Egyptian women. The magnitude of women's work in Egypt is such that there is no book that, individually, can pay justice to it. My aim was to test a methodology—writing history as a collective biography—and to test a hypothesis about the importance of the feminist roots of the human rights movement in Egypt. But more work needs to be done—and a lot is already in the making—to expand the knowledge of one of the most significance, diverse, and documented feminist movements in the world.

Collecting women's oral and written testimonies of the Egyptian Revolution is part of a broader and collective feminist work to contrast, on the one hand, the counterrevolutionary narratives and the male-dominated militarization of political space, but perhaps more important, to contribute to reinforcing the transgenerational thread of collective memory that is necessary to heal the trauma of the physical and epistemic violence inflicted on women at different stages of modern and contemporary history. Feminist oral history does not see women's testimonies as a homogenous and coherent block, but it situates them at the intersection of class, ethnicity and gender relations, structure of power, and people's resistance to them.[5]

Genealogies are crucial to understanding contemporary feminism, as there is a new generation of activists who, on one side, continue the mission of the older generations to affirm a more just society for everyone through the multiple pathways of women's liberation, while on the other, each generation lives their own moment and even within the same generations, approaches are not homogenous. Multiple genealogies weave into and out of each other.

Some of the women who had been part of the 2011 Revolution deepened their feminist awareness in conversation with those who had been part of the 1970s student movement and the underground Marxist movements in the early 1980s. Others identify more with liberal approaches to feminism, yet others still think of feminism in conjunction with Islam (Islamic feminism), while some reject the feminist label altogether. Some remain willing to work, when relevant, within institutional and even government frameworks, convinced that every single step toward gender equality is a victory worth pursuing. Others do not see the possibility of articulating women's rights under a military dictatorship that oppresses everyone. In between these different streams there are nuances, and even during the span of a life, women can change their positionality because of the experiences they go through.

CONCLUSION · 257

Today, feminists continue to discuss and debate the dilemmas that had divided their movement since the mid-eighties, especially the correct posture to take toward the government (open opposition or being mediators between the grassroots and the government, trying to change things from within versus continued pressure from without) and how to deal with foreign funding (another divisive issue). The framework of NGO activism that prevailed since the nineties was questioned by the new generations in the first two decades of the 2000s, even if after the 2011 Revolution many decided to work within it, realizing that it was the only option available.

There are clear continuities between old and new feminisms but also fractures, disagreements, and new ways of conceiving what feminism is. Feminism, like all political ideas and movements, assumes different configurations according to the context, and priorities and strategies change over time.

After the experience of the 2011 Revolution, the feminist agenda expanded to include more issues, such as the rights of sexual minorities, and showed a growing attention to the intersection between gender and social marginality, a theme that had been raised in the previous decades by several of the feminists that built the movement but had never been foregrounded as central. One could probably assert that among the merits of the 2011 Revolution was that it made explicit the link between gender, sexuality, socioeconomic issues, political rights, and freedom of conscience and expression.

In other words, if one questions if the 2011 Revolution brought revolutionary change into the formal and institutional political realm, the biographical approach I adopted in this book sheds light on the deployment of women's feminist agency in the politics of their everyday lives—a revolution that is long-lasting and still in the making, and whose outcome has yet to be seen and written. Indeed, if it is true, as I believe it is, that feminism is present everywhere there is a need for it, in Egypt feminism must be alive and well. What matters is to engage in active listening of the voices that contribute to its continuous renewal.

I opened this book with a question about the relationship between feminism, the human rights movement, and the 2011 Revolution, and I suggested that feminism has been one of the generative spaces that allowed the 2011 Revolution to happen. After listening, reading, and writing about the lives of dozens of women who from different positionalities contributed to the political life of twentieth- and twenty-first-century Egypt, I believe the evidence presented confirms my claim. It is important to celebrate the life and the work of the women who during the longue durée of the Egyptian feminist century believed that it was worth it to put their lives on the front line to allow a new world to take shape. Memorializing the idea that 2011 happened, that it was grounded in the longue durée history of the Egyptian feminist movement, and that it was a beautiful moment of collective joy, is a small contribution to the fight that Egyptian women bravely continue to enable a better world to take shape.

NOTES

INTRODUCTION

1. Lila Abu-Lughod and Rabab El Mahdi, "Beyond the 'Woman Question' in the Egyptian Revolution," *Feminist Studies* 37, no. 3 (2011): 683–91; Nadine Naber, "Imperial Feminism, Islamophobia, and the Egyptian Revolution," *Jadaliyya,* February 11, 2011.

2. Margot Badran, "Egypt's Revolution and the New Feminism," *The Immanent Frame* (blog), March 3, 2011; Zakia Salime and Frances Hasso, *Freedom without Permission: Space and Bodies in the Arab Revolutions* (Durham, NC: Duke University Press, 2016); Nermin Allam, *Women and the Egyptian Revolution: Engagement and Activism during the 2011 Arab Uprisings* (Cambridge: Cambridge University Press, 2018); Shereen Abouelnaga, *Women in Revolutionary Egypt: Gender and the New Geographics of Identity* (Cairo: American University in Cairo Press, 2019); Sherine Hafez, *Women of the Midan: The Untold Stories of Egypt's Revolutionaries* (Bloomington: Indiana University Press, 2019); Manal Hamzeh, *Women Resisting Sexual Violence and the Egyptian Revolution: Arab Feminist Testimonies* (London: Zed Books, 2020); Nicola Pratt, *Embodying Geopolitics: Generations of Women's Activism in Egypt, Jordan, and Lebanon* (Oakland: University of California Press, 2022); Rusha Latif, *Tahrir's Youth: Leaders of a Leaderless Revolution* (Cairo: American University in Cairo Press, 2022).

3. Gloria Anzaldúa, *Borderlands/La Frontera: The New Mestiza,* 3rd ed. (San Francisco: Aunt Lute Books, 2007); Linda Martín Alcoff, "An Epistemology for the Next Revolution," *Transmodernity* 1, no. 2 (2011); Maria Lugones, "Toward a Decolonial Feminism," *Hypatia* 22, no. 1 (Winter 2007): 186–209; Raewyn Connell, *Southern Theory: The Global Dynamics of Knowledge in the Social Sciences* (Crows Nest, NSW: Allen & Unwin, 2007); Bronwyn Carlson, Madi Day, Sandy O' Sullivan, and Tristan Kennedy, eds., *The Routledge Handbook of Australian Indigenous Peoples and Futures* (London: Routledge, 2023); Jean Comaroff and John Comaroff, *Theory from the South: Or, How Euro-America Is Evolving toward Africa* (London: Routledge, 2012).

4. Margot Badran, *Feminists, Islam, and Nation: Gender and the Making of Modern Egypt* (Princeton, NJ: Princeton University Press, 1995); Beth Baron, *Egypt as a Woman: Nationalism, Gender, and Politics* (Berkeley: University of California Press, 2005); Kumari Jayawardena, *Feminism and Nationalism in the Third World* (London: Zed Books, 1986); Marnia Lazreg, *The Eloquence of Silence: Algerian Women in Question* (New York: Routledge, 1994); Elizabeth Thompson, *Colonial Citizens: Republican Rights, Paternal Privilege, and Gender in French Syria and Lebanon* (New York: Columbia University Press, 2000); Islah Jad, *Palestinian Women's Activism: Nationalism, Secularism, Islamism* (Syracuse, NY: Syracuse University Press, 2018); Zahra Ali, *Women and Gender in Iraq: Between Nation-Building and Fragmentation* (Cambridge: Cambridge University Press, 2018).

5. Independent and bilingual (Arabic and English) Egyptian online newspaper specializing in investigative journalism that was created by the journalists of *Egypt Independent* following its shutting down in April 2013. *Mada Masr* was launched on June 30, 2013, on the same day of the big popular demonstration against the Muslim Brotherhood government that turned into a military coup on July 3, 2013.

6. Lina Attalah, "On a Belated Encounter with Gender," in *Our Women on the Ground: Essays by Arab Women Reporting from the Arab World*, ed. Zahra Hankir (New York: Penguin Books, 2019), 47.

7. Dwight F. Reynolds, ed., *Interpreting the Self: Autobiography in the Arabic Literary Tradition* (Berkeley: University of California Press, 2001), 42.

8. Luisa Passerini, *Autobiography of a Generation: Italy, 1968* (Hanover, NH: University Press of New England, 1996); Barbara Caine, *Biography and History* (London: Red Globe Press, 2019); Alexis Wright, *Tracker: Stories of Tracker Tilmouth* (Artarmon, NSW: Giramondo Publishing, 2017); Maria Rosaria Stabili, *Il sentimento aristocratico: Élites cilene allo specchio (1860–1960)* (Lecce: Congedo, 1996); Krista Cowman, "Collective Biography," in *Research Methods for History*, 85–103 (Edinburgh: Edinburgh University Press, 2022).

9. Sara Ahmed, *Living a Feminist Life* (Durham, NC: Duke University Press, 2017).

10. Margot Badran used "Long Revolution" in relation to Egyptian feminism in a series of lectures in October 2013 in Australia.

11. Lucia Sorbera, "Writing Revolution: New Inspirations, New Questions," *Postcolonial Studies* 17, no. 1 (2014): 104–8.

12. Badran, "Egypt's Revolution and the New Feminism."

13. After the suspension of the Constitution of 2012, drafted by a constituent committee with an Islamist majority, a new committee was appointed and the new constitution was endorsed by 98 percent of voters in a popular referendum in January 2014, where the turnout was 38.6 percent of the fifty-three million eligible to vote. Hoda Elsadda, "Women and Justice in the Egyptian Constitution: A Reading from Within," *Al-Raida*, no. 143–44 (Fall/Winter 2014): 18–26; Serena Tolino, "Gender Equality in the Egyptian Constitution: From 1923 to 2014," *Oriente Moderno*, no. 2 (2018): 140–65.

14. Elsadda, "Women and Justice in the Egyptian Constitution."

15. Lubna Youssef and Salwa Kamel, eds., *Proceedings of the 11th International Symposium on Comparative Literature: Creativity and Revolution, 13–15 November 2012*, Department of English Language and Literature, Faculty of Arts, Cairo University, Giza, Egypt, 2014.

16. Névine El Nossery, *Arab Women's Revolutionary Art between Singularities and Multitudes* (Cham: Springer International, 2023); Walid El Hamamsy and Munira Soliman, *Popular Culture in the Middle East and North Africa: A Postcolonial Outlook* (London: Routledge, 2018).

17. Lidya Sergent, *Women and Revolution: A Discussion of the Unhappy Marriage of Marxism and Feminism* (Montreal: Black Rose Books, 1981); Sheila Rowbotham, *Women, Resistance and Revolution.* (London: Allen Lane, 1972); *Women's Liberation and Revolution: A Bibliography* (Bristol: Fallin Wall Press, 1973).

18. Geneviève Fraisse, *La fabrique du féminisme: Textes et entretiens* (Paris: Éditions le passager clandestine, 2012), 9.

19. Mona Eltahawy, "Why Do They Hate Us?," *Foreign Policy,* April 23, 2012.

20. Badran, "Egypt's Revolution and the New Feminism"; Deniz Kandiyoti, "Promise and Peril: Women and the Arab Spring," Open Democracy, March 8, 2011; and "Disquiet and Despair: The Gender Sub-Texts of the 'Arab Spring,'" Open Democracy, June 26, 2012; Andrea Khalil, "Gender Paradoxes of the Arab Spring," *Journal of North African Studies* 19, no. 2 (2014): 131–36; Elsadda, "Women and Justice in the Egyptian Constitution"; Latif, *Tahrir's Youth*, 165.

21. Elsadda, "Women and Justice in the Egyptian Constitution," 23.

22. Nawal al-Saadawi, Cairo, October 10, 2014; Elsadda, "Women and Justice in the Egyptian Constitution."

23. Carnegie Endowment for International Peace, "A Backgrounder on the Socialist Popular Alliance Party," October 19, 2011.

24. Dina Wahba, "My Revolution!," in *Women Rising: In and Beyond the Arab Spring,* ed. Rita Stephan and Mounira M. Charrad (New York: New York University Press, 2020), 318–20.

25. Using the lenses of both Gramscian and feminist theory on hegemony, gender, and power to analyze social inequalities among teenagers in high schools in Sydney, Raewyn Connell interrogates the same notion of "patriarchy," arguing that there are four different masculinities (hegemonic, complicit, subordinated, and marginalized), and that there are hierarchical relationships among them, which change across time, society, culture, and the individual. This allows Connell's formulation of the concept, which has three dimensions (as a position, a system, and an ideology), to overcome the essentialism that characterized the first wave of masculinity studies. Raewyn Connell, *Masculinities* (St. Leonards, NSW: Allen & Unwin, 1995).

26. Lucia Sorbera, "An Invisible and Enduring Presence: Women in Egyptian Politics," in *Informal Power in the Greater Middle East,* ed. Luca Anceschi, Andrea Teti, and Gennaro Gervasio (London: Routledge, 2014), 159–74.

27. In 2021, they were acquitted of the charges against them. For most of them the travel ban was only lifted in 2024.

28. It started as a reading group in 1984 named Gama'iya al-Mar'a al-Gadida. About its story, which I discuss in chapter 1: Nadje Al-Ali, *Secularism, Gender and the State in the Middle East: The Egyptian Women's Movement* (Cambridge: Cambridge University Press, 2000).

29. Beth Baron, *The Women's Awakening in Egypt: Culture, Society, and the Press* (New Haven, CT: Yale University Press, 1994).

30. Marianna Ghiglia, "Journalistes en quête d'eux-mêmes: Une socio-histoire des professionnels de l'information en Égypte (1941–nos jours)" (doctoral thesis, Aix-Marseille University, 2020), 396–414.

31. Attalah, "On a Belated Encounter with Gender," 50. Farag, who was among the funders of *Egypt Independent* (the English edition of *al-Masry al-Youm*) and then the founder and CEO of Welad El-Balad Media Services LTD (a company dedicated to community media development and media excellence in Egypt), is an internationally renowned journalist and educator, with lengthy, professional experience in both media and development programs. In 2018, she was the first Arab woman to ever join the board of the World Association of Newspapers and News Publishers (WAN-IFRA).

32. COP27 Conference, Sharm El-Sheikh, German Pavilion, November 8, 2022.

33. Sanaa Seif, "Press Conference of Global Campaign to Demand Climate Justice," Sharm El-Sheikh, German Pavilion, November 8, 2022.

34. Charley Moloney, "Climate Campaigner Greta Thunberg Pleads for Blogger Alaa Abdel Fattah's Freedom," *The Times* (UK), October 31, 2022; Siobhán O'Grady, "As Egypt Hosts COP27, Its Most Famous Political Prisoner May Die, Family Warns," *Washington Post*, November 3, 2022; Yasmen El-Rifae, "The Most Eloquent Speaker at the Climate Summit Is Alaa Abd El Fattah," *New York Times*, November 12, 2022.

35. Nawal al-Saadawi, *Al-Mar'a Wa al-Jins* (Beirut: Al-Nashirun al-'Arab, 1972); Fatima Mernissi, *Beyond the Veil: Male-Female Dynamics in Modern Muslim Society* (New York: Shenkman, 1975); Assia Djebar, dir., *La nouba des femmes du Mont-Chenoua* (New York: Women Make Movies, 1977); and *L'amour, la fantasia: Roman* (Paris, J.-C. Lattès/Enal, 1985).

36. Margot Badran, "The Institutionalization of Middle East Women's Studies in the United States," *Middle East Studies Association Bulletin* 22, no. 1 (1988: 9–18); Simona Sharoni, "Women and Gender in Middle East Studies: Trends, Prospects and Challenges," *Middle East Report*, no. 205 (1997): 27–29; Judith Tucker, "Rescued from Obscurity: Contributions and Challenges in Writing the History of Gender in the Middle East and North Africa," in *A Companion to Gender History*, ed. Teresa A. Meade and Merry E. Wiesner-Hanks (Malden, MA: Blackwell, 2004), 393–412.

37. Elizabeth Warnock Fernea and Bassima Qattan Berzigan, *Middle Eastern Muslim Women Speak* (Austin: University of Texas Press, 1977); Nikki R. Keddie and Lois Beck, *Women in the Muslim World* (Cambridge, MA: Harvard University Press, 1978).

38. Margot Badran, "Huda Sha'rawi and the Liberation of the Egyptian Woman" (PhD thesis, Oxford University, 1977). This became the basis for her book *Feminists,*

Islam, and Nation. See also Huda Shaʿrawi, *Harem Years: The Memoirs of an Egyptian Feminist (1879–1924)*, translated, curated, and introduced by Margot Badran (London: Virago, 1986). For a personal account of her feminism and becoming an Egyptian, see Margot Badran, "Foreign Bodies: Engendering Them and the US," in *The Concept of the Foreign: An Interdisciplinary Dialogue,* ed. Rebecca Saunders (New York: Lexington Books, 2003).

39. miriam cooke, "Telling Their Lives: A Hundred Years of Arab Women's Writings," *World Literature Today* 60, no. 2 (1986): 212–16; *War's Other Voices: Women Writers on the Lebanese Civil War* (London: Cambridge University Press, 1988); *Women and the War Story* (Berkeley: University of California Press, 1997); and *Women Claim Islam: Creating Islamic Feminism through Literature* (New York: Routledge, 2001).

40. Mervat Hatem, "The Politics of Sexuality and Gender in Segregated Patriarchal Systems: The Case of Eighteenth- and Nineteenth-Century Egypt," *Feminist Studies* 12, no. 2 (1986): 251–74; Hisham Sharabi, *Neopatriarchy: A Theory of Distorted Change in Arab Society* (New York: Oxford University Press, 1988).

41. Judith E. Tucker, *Women in Nineteenth-Century Egypt* (Cambridge: Cambridge University Press, 1985); and *In the House of the Law: Gender and Islamic Law in Ottoman Syria and Palestine* (Berkeley: University of California Press, 1998).

42. Leila Ahmed, *Women and Gender in Islam: Historical Roots of a Modern Debate* (New Haven, CT: Yale University Press, 1992); Nikki R. Keddie and Beth Baron, *Women in Middle Eastern History* (New Haven, CT: Yale University Press, 1992); Baron, *Women's Awakening*; Lazreg, *Eloquence of Silence*; Deniz Kandiyioti, ed., *Women, Islam and the State* (London: Palgrave Macmillan, 1991).

43. Margot Badran and miriam cooke, *Opening the Gates: A Century of Arab Feminist Writing* (Bloomington: Indiana University Press, 1990); Marilyn Booth, *May Her Likes Be Multiplied: Biography and Gender Politics in Egypt* (Berkeley: University of California Press, 2001); Marilyn Booth, "Before Qasim Amin: Writing Women's History in 1890s Egypt," in *The Long 1890s in Egypt: Colonial Quiescence, Subterranean Resistance,* ed. Marilyn Booth and Anthony Gorman (Edinburgh: Edinburgh University Press, 2014), 365–98; Mervat Fayez Hatem, *Literature, Gender, and Nation-Building in Nineteenth-Century Egypt: The Life and Works of ʿAisha Taymur* (New York: Palgrave Macmillan, 2011).

44. Lucia Sorbera, "Narrare il sé, raccontare la modernità: Ambienti, temi e forme della scrittura femminile in epoca moderna," in Lorenzo Casini, Maria Elena Paniconi, and Lucia Sorbera, *Modernità arabe: Nazione, narrazione e nuovi soggetti nel romanzo egiziano,* 245–352 (Messina: Mesogea, 2012).

45. Tahani Rached, dir., *Quatre femmes d'Egypte/Four Women of Egypt,* DVD (Montreal: National Film Board of Canada, 1997).

46. Nadia Kamel, *Al-Mawluda* (Cairo: Karma Publishing, 2018); Nadia Kamel, dir., *Salata baladi = Salade maison* (New York: Women Make Movies, 2007).

47. Iman Mersal, *Fi Athar Enayat al-Zayyat* (Cairo: al-Kotob Khan, 2019).

48. Laura Bier, *Revolutionary Womanhood: Feminisms, Modernity, and the State in Nasser's Egypt* (Stanford, CA: Stanford University Press, 2011); Hanan Hammad,

Industrial Sexuality: Gender, Urbanization, and Social Transformation in Egypt (Austin: University of Texas Press, 2016).

49. Samia Mehrez and Venetia Porter, *Huda Lutfi* (Dubai: Atlas Media, 2010); Samia Mehrez, "Huda Lutfi in Context," in *Egypt's Culture Wars* (Cairo: American University in Cairo Press, 2008); Margot Badran, "Dis/Playing Power and the Politics of Patriarchy in Revolutionary Egypt: The Creative Activism of Huda Lutfi," *Postcolonial Studies* 17, no. 1 (2014): 47–62.

50. Samia Mehrez, "Where Have All the Families Gone: Egyptian Literary Texts of the Nineties," *Arab Studies Journal* 9/10, no. 1/2 (2008): 31–49; and *Egypt's Culture Wars: Politics and Practice* (London: Routledge, 2011); Maria Elena Paniconi, *Bildungsroman and the Arab Novel: Egyptian Intersections* (Abingdon, UK: Routledge, 2023).

51. Djamila Ribeiro, *Il luogo della parola* (Alessandria: Capovolte, 2021).

52. Luisa Passerini, *Memory and Utopia: The Primacy of Intersubjectivity* (London: Equinox, 2007); *Fascism in Popular Memory: The Cultural Experience of the Turin Working Class* (Cambridge: Cambridge University Press, 1987); and *Europe in Love, Love in Europe: Imagination and Politics between the Wars* (New York: New York University Press, 1999).

53. Stabili, *Il sentimento aristocratico*, 26.

54. Margot Badran, "Theorizing Oral History as Autobiography: A Look at the Narrative of a Woman Revolutionary in Egypt," *Journal of Women's History* 25, no. 2 (2013): 161–70.

55. Hoda Elsadda, "Challenges, Opportunities, and Methodological Issues in the Creation of Oral History Archives in the Arab World," *Cairo Papers in Social Sciences* 35, no. 1 (2018).

56. WMF has a collection that is partially available. The oral histories collected by Nicola Pratt can be accessed through the SOAS Digital Collection Middle East Women's Activism.

57. Passerini pioneered criticism of the populist and positivist approaches to oral history that were dominant in the 1970s, reconceptualizing the interview as a process that "is more concerned with drawing out forms of cultural identity and shared tradition than with the actual facts of social history." Passerini, *Fascism in Popular Memory*, 8.

58. Jeanine Leane, *Guwayu—For All Times: A Collection of First Nations Poems* (Broom, Western Australia: Magabala Books, 2020), xi.

59. Ann McGrath, Laura Rademaker, and Jakelin Troy, *Everywhen: Australia and the Language of Deep History* (Lincoln: University of Nebraska Press, 2023), 4.

60. McGrath, Rademaker, and Troy, *Everywhen*, 7.

61. McGrath, Rademaker, and Troy, *Everywhen*, 25; Mark LeVine and Lucia Sorbera, "Collaborative Ontologies and the Future of Critical Theory," *Souffles Mondes: A Pan-African Journal and Platform*, no. 3 (2024).

62. Jeanine Leane, *Walk Back Over* (Calton South, Victoria: Corditebooks, 2018), xi.

63. Lila Abu-Lughod, *Remaking Women: Feminism and Modernity in the Middle East* (Princeton, NJ: Princeton University Press, 1998); and *Writing Women's*

Worlds: Bedouin Stories (Berkeley: University of California Press, 2008); Hatem Mervat, "The Politics of Sexuality and Gender in Segregated Patriarchal Systems: The Case of Eighteenth- and Nineteenth-Century Egypt," *Feminist Studies* 12, no. 2 (1986: 251–57); Nadje Sadig Al-Ali, *Secularism, Gender and the State in the Middle East: The Egyptian Women's Movement* (Cambridge: Cambridge University Press, 2000); Margot Badran, "Islam, Patriarchy, and Feminism in the Middle East," *Trends in History* 4, no. 1 (Fall 1985): 48–71.

CHAPTER ONE

1. For a broad and deep overview of Soliman's work: Dina Heshmat, *Egypt 1919: The Revolution in Literature and Film* (Edinburgh: Edinburgh University Press, 2020).

2. Baron, *Egypt as a Woman,* 107–34.

3. Badran, *Feminists, Islam, and Nation,* 81; Baron, *Egypt as a Woman,* 140–41.

4. Letter from C. F. Ryder to the Commandant of the Cairo City Police, Cairo, Ministry of the Interior, December 25, 1921, 141/511/6, PRO, FO.

5. Baron, *Egypt as a Woman,* 138–41.

6. Alia Mosallam, *Strikes, Riots and Laughter: Al-Himamiyya Village's Experience of Egypt's 1918 Peasant Insurrection,* LSE Middle East Centre Paper Series, no. 40 (2020); Kyle J. Anderson, *The Egyptian Labor Corps: Race, Space, and Place in the First World War* (Austin: University of Texas Press, 2021). Emerging research from these and others builds on the tradition of the social history of modern Egypt, particularly the works by Ellis Goldberg, John Chalcraft, Joel Beinin, Zachary Lockman, and Rheinhard Schulz about workers and peasants in early twentieth-century Egypt.

7. Heshmat, *Egypt 1919: The Revolution in Literature and Film,* 188; Dina Heshmat, "A Journey in the Archives in the Footsteps of Fikriyya Husni" (in Arabic), in *Gendering the Arab Archive* (in Arabic), ed. Laila Dakhli, Hoda Elsadda, Zahra Ali, Lamia Moghnieh, Hana Soliman, and Reem Joudi (Beirut: Arab Council for the Social Sciences, 2024).

8. *Whims of Freedom,* notes from the theater representation; Laila Soliman, Cairo, October 22, 2014.

9. Benjamin Geer, "Autonomy and Symbolic Capital in an Academic Social Movement: The March 9 Group in Egypt," *European Journal of Turkish Studies* 17 (2013).

10. Laila Soueif, Cairo, December 3, 2015.

11. Pasha was the highest official title of honor in the Ottoman Empire. It was given to high civil officials, not to men of religion, and was purely personal and not hereditary, except in nineteenth-century Egypt. About Muhammad ʿAli and his reign: Khaled Fahmi, *All the Pasha's Men: Mehmed Ali, His Army, and the Making of Modern Egypt* (Cambridge: Cambridge University Press, 1997); and *Mehmed Ali: From Ottoman Governor to Ruler of Egypt* (Oxford: Oneworld, 2009).

12. Aaron G. Jakes, *Egypt's Occupation: Colonial Economism and the Crises of Capitalism* (Stanford, CA: Stanford University Press, 2020).

13. Ehud Toledano, "Social and Economic Change in the 'Long Nineteenth Century,'" in *The Cambridge History of Egypt*, ed. M.W. Daly (Cambridge: Cambridge University Press, 1998), 252–84.

14. Juan Ricardo Cole, *Colonialism and Revolution in the Middle East: Social and Cultural Origins of Egypt's Urabi Movement* (Princeton, NJ: Princeton University Press, 1993).

15. Hanan Hammad, *Industrial Sexuality*, 81; Liat Kozma, *Policing Egyptian Women Sex, Law, and Medicine in Khedival Egypt* (Syracuse, NY: Syracuse University Press, 2011), xvi.

16. Hammad, *Industrial Sexuality*, 83–86; Joel Beinin, *Workers and Peasants in the Modern Middle East* (Cambridge: Cambridge University Press, 2001), 68–69.

17. Hammad, *Industrial Sexuality*, 105.

18. For broad and in-depth analyses of women's contribution to the *nahda*, see Marilyn Booth, "Zaynab Fawaz Al-'Amili," in *Essays in Arabic Literary Biography, 1850–1950*, ed. Roger Allen (Wiesbaden: Harrasowiz Verlag, 2010); and *May Her Likes Be Multiplied*; Baron, *Women's Awakening in Egypt*; Badran and cooke, *Opening the Gates*; Lucia Sorbera, "Narrare il sé, raccontare la modernità"; Hatem, *Literature, Gender, and Nation-Building in Nineteenth-Century Egypt*; Hoda Elsadda, "Gendered Citizenship: Discourses on Domesticity in the Second Half of the Nineteenth Century," *Hawwa* 4, no. 1 (2006): 1–28.

19. Badran, *Feminists, Islam, Nation*, 47–60.

20. *Political Views and Activities of Egyptian Women*, PRO.FO141/511/5; Baron, *Egypt as a Woman*, 107–34.

21. Badran, *Feminists, Islam, Nation*, 75.

22. Doria Shafik, *La femme nouvelle* (Cairo: E&R Shindler, 1944), 50.

23. bell hooks, *Ain't I a Woman: Black Women and Feminism* (London: Pluto Press, 1987).

24. Labiba Hashim in the introduction to *Fatat al-Sharq* (*Young Woman of the East*), no. 1 (1906), cited in Hoda Elsadda, "Egypt," in *Arab Women Writers: A Critical Reference Guide, 1873–1999*, ed. Radwa Ashour, Ferial J. Ghazoul, and Hasna Reda-Mekdashi (Cairo: American University in Cairo Press, 2008), 98.

25. Nabawiyya Musa, *Al-Mar'a wa al-'Amal* (Alexandria: Matba' al-Qawmi, 1920).

26. Nabawiyya Musa was the first Egyptian woman who published an autobiography: *Tarikhi bi qalami* (*Cairo, Women and Memory Forum*, 1999), first published in the journal *al-Fatat* (*The Young Woman*), which she founded in 1937. The autobiographical series of essays appeared between May 1938 and August 1943. See also Badran, *Feminists, Islam, and Nation*; Badran, "Expressing Feminism and Nationalism in Autobiography: The Memoirs of an Egyptian Educator," in *De/Colonizing the Subject: The Politics of Gender in Women's Autobiography*, ed. Sidonie Smith and Julia Watson (Minneapolis: University of Minnesota Press, 1992).

27. Thabit, the first woman to be elected in the Egyptian Parliament, narrated her militancy for women's political rights in a memoir: *Thawra fi-l-Burj al-'Aji: Mudhakkirati fi 'Ashrin 'Aman 'an Ma'rakat Huquq al-Mar'a al-Siyasiya (A Revolution in the Ivory Tower: My Memoirs of Twenty Years of Struggle for Women's Political Rights)* (Cairo: Dar al-Ma'arif, 1946).

28. Besides her memoirs, Aflatun published two books: *Thamanun Milyun Imra'a Ma'ana (Eighty Million Women with Us)* (1948); and *Nahnu al-Nisa' al-Misriya (We Are the Egyptian Women)* (1949).

29. Joel Beinin and Zachary Lockman, *Workers on the Nile: Nationalism, Communism, Islam and the Egyptian Working Class, 1882–1954* (London: I. B. Tauris, 1988), 399–403.

30. *Congrès international des femmes: Compte rendu des travaux du congrès qui s'est tenu à Paris du 26 novembre au 1er décembre 1945; Rapport déposé par la délégation egyptienne* (Paris: Fédération démocratique internationale des femmes, 1946), 239.

31. *Congrès international des femmes: Compte rendu,* 248. Historian Hanan Hammad has documented that the leftist press of the period published articles about the horrific condition of female workers in Mahalla. See Hammad, *Industrial Sexuality,* 94.

32. Latifa Al-Zayyat, "al-Katib Wa-l-Hurriya" (The Writer and Freedom), *al-Fusul* 11, no. 3 (Fall 1992).

33. Salma Mubarak, *Amina Rachid ou la traversée vers l'autre* (Casablanca: Centre culturel du livre, 2020), 113–14.

34. Rached, *Four Women of Egypt.* Also in Mubarak, *Amina Rachid,* 33.

35. The Harakat Ansar al-Salam was a movement associated with the World Movement for Peace, which was supported by the Soviet Union, and in Egypt it included the Socialist Party, the National Party, the Muslim Brotherhood, the communists, and the left of the Wafd. See Rami Ginat, "The Egyptian Left and the Roots of Neutralism in the Pre-Nasserite Era," *British Journal of Middle Eastern Studies* 30, no. 1 (2003): 5–24.

36. Aflatun, *Nahnu al-Nisa' al-Misriya (We Are the Egyptian Women).* Other women who were part of the Union were Hawa Idriss (the niece of Huda Sha'rawi) and Hikmat al-Ghazali, the communist sister of Zeinab al-Ghazali. See also Margot Badran, "Independent Women: More than a Century of Feminism in Egypt," in *Arab Women: Old Boundaries New Frontiers,* ed. Judith Tucker (Bloomington: Indiana University Press, 1993).

37. Amina Rachid, "Dans notre société masculine, je me sentais descendante d'une race féminine," *al-Hilal,* April 2002, in Mubarak, *Amina Rachid ou la traversée vers l'autre,* 34.

38. Mubarak, *Amina Rachid ou la traversée vers l'autre,* 35.

39. Cynthia Nelson, *Doria Shafik, Egyptian Feminist: A Woman Apart* (Gainesville: University Press of Florida, 1996), 238–52.

40. Nelson, *Doria Shafik, Egyptian Feminist,* 271–75.

41. Mahmoud Abdel Fadil, *The Political Economy of Nasserism* (Cambridge: Cambridge University Press, 1980); John Waterbury, *The Egypt of Nasser and Sadat:*

The Political Economy of Two Regimes (Princeton, NJ: Princeton University Press, 1983).

42. Farida al-Naqqash, Cairo, January 14, 2018.

43. Mervat F. Hatem, "Economic and Political Liberation in Egypt and the Demise of State Feminism," *International Journal of Middle East Studies* 24, no. 2 (1992): 231–51.

44. I interviewed Farida al-Naqqash, Nawal al-Saadawi, Safinaz Kazem, Amina Rachid, and Amina Shafik.

45. I interviewed Amal Abdel Hadi, Aida Seif El-Dawla, Laila Soueif, Nawla Darwiche, Magda Adly, Seham Saneya Abd el-Salam, Zinat al-Askary, Suzan Fayad, Rawia Sadek, and, from the younger generation, Hala Shukrallah, Hoda Elsadda, Nagwa Abbas, and Azza Matar.

46. Farida al-Naqqash was among the founders of the Tagammu' Party (1978), and since 1994 chief editor of *Al-Adab wa al-Naqd,* the cultural journal of the Tagammu'. See Marianna Ghiglia, "Journalistes en quête d'eux-mêmes: Une socio-histoire des professionnels de l'information en Égypte (1941–nos jours)" (doctoral thesis, Aix-Marseille University, 2020), 114.

47. Farida al-Naqqash, Cairo, December 16, 2022.

48. al-Naqqash, 2022.

49. al-Naqqash, 2018.

50. al-Naqqash, 2018.

51. al-Naqqash, 2022.

52. Amal Abdel Hadi, Cairo, December 18, 2018.

53. Abdel Hadi, 2018.

54. Bier, *Revolutionary Womanhood,* 180.

55. Abdul Ghaffar Shukr, *The Socialist Youth Organization: An Egyptian Experience in Leadership Preparation 1963–1976* (in Arabic) (Beirut: Center For Arab Unity Studies, 2004).

56. Abdel Hadi, 2018.

57. Abdel Hadi, 2018.

58. al-Naqqash, 2018. Farida al-Naqqash published her memoirs, titled *Al-Sijn, Dam'atain, wa wardah* (*Prison, Two Tears, and a Flower*), in 1985. Marilyn Booth translated part of it. Marilyn Booth, "Women's Prison Memoirs in Egypt and Elsewhere: Prison, Gender, Praxis," *Middle East Report,* no. 149 (1987): 35–41; Farida al-Naqqash, "Barred from Writing in Egypt," *Index on Censorship* 12, no. 3 (1983): 20–22.

59. al-Naqqash, 2022.

60. Safinaz Kazem, Cairo, January 18, 2020.

61. Kazem, 2020.

62. Abdel Hadi, 2018.

63. Abdel Hadi, 2018.

64. Abdel Hadi, 2018.

65. Abdel Hadi, 2018.

66. Zinat Al-Askary, Cairo, December 29, 2022.

67. Seham Seneya Abd el-Salam, Cairo, December 15, 2022.

68. Hani Shukrallah, Cairo, January 4, 2018.

69. Abdel Hadi, 2018.

70. Abdel Hadi, 2018.

71. Nawla Darwiche, Cairo, January 7, 2018.

72. Aida Seif El-Dawla, personal communication, Cairo, December 14, 2022.

73. *al-Mubtasirun* (1996). Arwa Saleh and Samah Selim, *The Stillborn: Notebooks of a Woman from the Student-Movement Generation in Egypt* (Chicago: Chicago University Press, 2017).

74. Hanan Hammad, "Arwa Salih's 'The Premature': Gendering the History of the Egyptian Left," *Arab Studies Journal* 24, no. 1 (2016): 118–42; Samah Selim, "Translator's Introduction," in Saleh and Selim, *The Stillborn*, vii–xxvii.

75. Jacques Derrida, *Specters of Marx: The State of the Debt, the Work of Mourning and the New International* (London: Routledge, 2006); Pamela McCallum, "Questions of Haunting: Jacques Derrida's 'Specters of Marx' and Raymond Williams's 'Modern Tragedy,'" *Mosaic* 40, no. 2 (2007): 231–44.

CHAPTER TWO

1. "Marie Assaad 1922–2018," oral history and interview by Women and Memory Forum, 2018, WMF Library.

2. AA.VV., Tribute and Memorial for Marie B. Assaad. October 16, 1922, to August 30, 2018, Conference proceedings published by the Marie Assaad Family with Women and Memory Forum in Cairo in 2019.

3. Aziza Sami, "Republished: Marie Assaad—Egypt's Gentle Warrior," Ahram Online, March 27, 2016.

4. Marie Bassili Assaad, "Female Circumcision in Egypt: Social Implications, Current Research, and Prospects for Change," *Studies in Family Planning* 11, no. 1 (January 1980): 3–16. Published by the Population Council.

5. Siham Abd el-Salam, *Female Genital Mutilation: Violation of Human Rights* (Cairo: Cairo Institute for Human Rights Studies, 1995); "Female Sexuality and the Discourse of Power: The Case of Egypt" (MA thesis, American University in Cairo, 1998); "A Comprehensive Approach for Communication about Female Genital Mutilation in Egypt," in *Female and Male Circumcisions: Medical, Legal, and Ethical Considerations in Pediatric Practice,* ed. George C. Denniston, Frederick M. Hodges, and Marilyn F. Milos (New York: Kluwer Academic and Plenum, 1999); and "Genital Mutilations. History, and Suggestions for Change," paper presented at the International Meeting on Preventing and Eliminating Female Genital Mutilation, Swedish Parliament, Foreign Ministry, Ministry of Health and Social Affairs. Stockholm, 2003.

6. Seham Saneya Abd el-Salam, Cairo, December 16, 2022.

7. Maria Frederika Malström and An Van Raemdonck, "'The Clitoris Is in the Head!' Female Circumcision and the Making of a Harmful Cultural Practice in

Egypt," in *Interrogating Harmful Cultural Practices: Gender, Culture and Coercion,* ed. Chia Longman and Bradley Tasmin (Farnham, UK: Routledge, 2015), 121–39; Lisen Dellenborg and Maria Frederika Malström, "Listening to the Real Agents of Change: Female Circumcision/Cutting, Female Genital Mutilations and Human Rights," in *Female Genital Cutting: Global North and South,* ed. Sara Johnsdotter (Malmö: Center for Sexology and Sexuality Studies, Malmö University, 2020), 159–84.

8. Maria Frederika Malmström, *The Politics of Female Circumcision in Egypt* (London: I. B. Tauris, 2016), 6, 40–41, 47.

9. Badran, "Body Politic(s): Women, Power, and Sexuality in Egypt," 181.

10. Baron, *Egypt as a Woman,* 36–39.

11. Francesca Biancani, *Sex Work in Colonial Egypt: Women, Modernity and the Global Economy* (London: I. B. Tauris, 2021), 125–150.

12. *Hawwa,* July 20, 1957, and November 1, 1958, in Abd el-Salam, *Female Genital Mutilation,* 41.

13. Malmström, *The Politics of Female Circumcision in Egypt,* 40.

14. Abd el-Salam, 2022.

15. Nahid Toubia, *Women of the Arab World: The Coming Challenge* (London: Zed Books, 1988). The book is a collection of papers presented at an international conference organized by the Women Solidarity Association in Cairo, September 1–3, 1986. Al-Saadawi remembers that 159 participants from across the Arab world attended the inaugural session (p. 4). Toubia, "Challenges Facing the Arab Women at the End of the 20th Century," in *Opening the Gates,* 366–72.

16. Malmström, *The Politics of Female Circumcision in Egypt,* 44–46.

17. Aida Seif El-Dawla, "The Political and Legal Struggle over Female Genital Mutilation in Egypt: Five Years Since the ICPD," in "Living without Children," special issue, *Reproductive Health Matters* 7, no. 13 (May 1999): 128–36.

18. The invite to refrain from practicing FGM by Islamic reformist authorities is documented since the early twentieth century; however, the jurists' opinions have never been unanimous, and in the nineties there was still space to argue for the religious legitimacy of FGM. The debate between Dar al-Ifta' and Al-Azhar has been documented in An Van Raemdonck, "Egyptian Activism against Female Genital Cutting as Catachrestic Claiming," *Religion and Gender* 3, no. 2 (2013): 235–37; and in Badran, "Body Politic(s): Women, Power, and Sexuality in Egypt."

19. The work of the Task Force and the political debates around the ban are analyzed in Amal Abdel Hadi, "Islam, Law, and Reproductive Health in Egypt," in *Islam, Reproductive Health, and Women's Rights* (Kuala Lumpur: Sisters in Islam, 2000); Badran, "Body Politic(s): Women, Power, and Sexuality in Egypt"; and Raemdonck, "Egyptian Activism against Female Genital Cutting as Catachrestic Claiming."

20. Aziza Hussein, oral history, October 9, 2020, WMF Library.

21. Bonny Lemma, "A Million Women's Movements: Reconciling Diverse Conceptions of Feminism," *Harvard International Review* 40, no. 3 (Summer 2019): 14–15.

22. Abd el-Salam, 2022; El-Dawla, 2018.

23. Raemdonck, "Egyptian Activism against Female Genital Cutting as Catachrestic Claiming," 231.

24. Raemdonck, "Egyptian Activism against Female Genital Cutting as Catachrestic Claiming," 232.

25. The woman Islamist MP 'Azza al-Gharf made the news to support the depenalization of FGM in the name of freedom. Mariz Tadros, "Mutilating Bodies: The Muslim Brotherhood's Gift to Egyptian Women," Open Democracy, May 24, 2012; Margot Badran, "Keeping FGM on the Run? Between Resolution and Constitution," *Ahram Online,* January 10, 2013.

26. El-Zanaty and Associates (Egypt), Ministry of Health and Population (Egypt), and ICF International, *Egypt Health Survey 2015* (Cairo and Rockville, MD, 2015).

27. Egyptian Streets, "Egypt Introduces 20 Years Imprisonment for Female Genital Mutilation," January 21, 2021.

28. Malström, *The Politics of Female Circumcision in Egypt,* 46–49. About the relationship between geopolitics and women's bodies with specific reference to Middle East politics in the 1990s and early 2000s, see Pratt, *Embodying Geopolitics.*

29. El-Dawla, "The Political and Legal Struggle over Female Genital Mutilation in Egypt," 134.

30. Fadwa El Guindi, "'Had This Been Your Face, Would You Leave It as Is?' Female Circumcision among the Nubians of Egypt," in *Female Circumcision: Multicultural Perspectives,* ed. Rogaia Mustafa Abusharaf (Philadelphia: University of Pennsylvania Press, 2006), 46; Maria Frederika Malmström, "The Continuous Making of Pure Womanhood among Muslim Women in Cairo: Cooking, Depilating, and Circumcising," in *Gender and Sexuality in Muslim Cultures,* ed. Gul Ozyegin (Farnham, UK: Taylor & Francis, 2016).

31. This issue was central in the feminist political philosophy debate in the 1990s and early 2000s, especially in Europe. The essay by Susan Molle Okin, "Is Multiculturalism Bad for Women," sparked a debate, and essays inspired by it were later collected in a volume: Susan Moller Okin et al., *Is Multiculturalism Bad for Women?* (Princeton, NJ: Princeton University Press, 1999).

32. Amal Abdel Hadi, "A Community of Women Empowered: The Story of Deir El Barsha," in *Female Circumcision: Multicultural Perspectives,* ed. Rogaia M. Abusharaf (Philadelphia: University of Pennsylvania Press, 2006), 123.

33. Abdel Hadi, "A Community of Women Empowered," 105.

34. Aida Seif El-Dawla, Amal Abdel Hadi, and Nadia Abd El Wahab, "Women's Wit over Men's: Tradeoffs and Strategic Accommodations in Egyptian Women's Reproductive Lives," in *Negotiating Reproductive Rights: Women's Perspectives across Countries and Cultures,* ed. Rosalind P. Petchesky and Karen Judd (London: Zed Books, 1998).

35. El-Dawla, "The Political and Legal Struggle over Female Genital Mutilation in Egypt," 130. About the nexus between desire and morality: Malmström, *The Politics of Female Circumcision in Egypt,* 102–38.

36. El-Dawla, 2018.

37. Lila Abu-Lughod, "Dialects of Women's Empowerment: The International Circuitry of the Arab Human Development Report," *International Journal of Middle East Studies* 41, no. 1 (2009): 83–103; Abu-Lughod, "Against Universals: Dialects of (Women's) Human Rights and Human Capabilities," in *Rethinking the Human,* ed. J. Michelle Molina and Donald K. Swearer (Cambridge, MA: Harvard University Press, 2010), 69–93.

CHAPTER THREE

1. Samia Mehrez, "Translation and the Postcolonial Experience: The Francophone North African Text," in *Rethinking Translation: Discourse, Subjectivity, Ideology,* ed. Laurence Venuti (London: Routledge, 1992).

2. Being part of a West and Saudi-led coalition attacking an Arab country was a big discontinuity even with previous Egyptian military interventions in the region, including Yemen in 1965.

3. Cited in Joseph S. Nye Jr., "What New World Order?," *Foreign Affairs* (Spring 1992).

4. Nadje Al-Ali and Nicola Pratt, *What Kind of Liberation? Women and the Occupation of Iraq* (Berkeley: University of California Press, 2009); Yasmin Khodary, Noha Salah, and Nada Mohsen, "Middle Eastern Women between Oppression and Resistance: Case Studies of Iraqi, Palestinian and Kurdish Women of Turkey," *Journal of International Women's Studies* 21, no. 1 (2010): 204–26.

5. Galal Amin, *Whatever Happened to the Egyptians? Changes in Egyptian Society from 1950 to Present* (Cairo: American University in Cairo Press, 2000), 7.

6. Mark LeVine, *We'll Play till We Die: Journeys across a Decade of Revolutionary Music in the Muslim World* (Oakland: University of California Press, 2022), 50.

7. Karin van Nieuwkerk, "'Repentant' Artists in Egypt: Debating Gender, Performing Arts and Religion," *Contemporary Islam* 2, no. 3 (2008): 191–210.

8. Saba Mahmoud, *Politics of Piety: The Islamic Revival and the Feminist Subject* (Princeton, NJ: Princeton University Press, 2005).

9. Nicola Pratt, "The Queen Boat Case in Egypt: Sexuality, National Security and State Sovereignty," *Review of International Studies* 33, no. 1 (2007): 129–44; and chapter 4 in this book.

10. Ferial Ghazoul, "Editorial" (in Arabic), *Alif: The Journal of Comparative Poetics* 19 (1999): 210–30.

11. Hoda Elsadda, "Women and Memory" (interview, in Arabic), *Alif: The Journal of Comparative Poetics* 19 (1999): 210–30; Heba Rauf Ezzat, "Women and Ijtihad: Toward a New Islamic Discourse" (in Arabic), *Alif: The Journal of Comparative Poetics* 19 (1999). See also interview by Margot Badran of Heba Rauf Ezzat in Badran, "Gender Activism: Feminists and Islamists in Egypt," in *Identity Politics and Women: Cultural Reassertions and Feminisms in International Perspective,* ed. Valentine M. Moghadam (London: Routledge, 1994), 202–27.

12. Rauf Ezzat, "Women and Ijtihad"; Elsadda, "Women and Memory."

13. Badran, *Feminists, Islam, and Nation*, 31–32.

14. Lila Abu-Lughod, "Introduction: Feminist Longings and Postcolonial Conditions," in *Remaking Women: Feminism and Modernity in the Middle East*, ed. Lila Abu-Lughod (Princeton, NJ: Princeton University Press, 1998), 17.

15. Hoda Elsadda, *Gender Studies in the Arab World: An NGO Phenomenon*, World Humanities Report (Consortium of Humanities Centers and Institutes, 2023), 7.

16. By "indigenous" I refer to the native inhabitants of any colonized territory, of which the subcategory of "Indigenous" would refer to those communities and groups who claim, or are recognized as having the claim, to being the first or original inhabitants of a territory and are accorded specific status as such under international law.

17. "Self-proclaimed secular Arab regimes." I am using this locution because even if they were secular from an institutional perspective, this is not how they are described by the feminists I have interviewed, and, as I have explained in the introduction, the way feminists experienced state politics is central in my methodology and my approach to political history in this book.

18. Nawal El Saadawi, *The Hidden Face of Eve: Women in the Arab World* (London: Zed Books, 1980), 3. Orig. Arabic, *al-wajha al-ʿārī lil-marʾa al-ʿarabiyya*, 1977.

19. Nawal El Saadawi, "Women and the Poor: The Challenge of Global Justice," keynote address to the Global '94 Congress, Tampere, Finland, July 3–7, 1994; *The Essential Nawal El Saadawi: A Reader*, ed. Adele Newson-Horst (London: Zed Books, 2010), 86 (earlier published in *The Nawal El Saadawi Reader* by Zed Books in 1997).

20. Nawal al-Saadawi, Cairo, October 10, 2014.

21. Alongside all her novels and essays, this was then published by al-Saadawi's Egyptian publisher, Madbouli.

22. al-Saadawi, 2014.

23. miriam cooke, "Introduction," *Journal of Middle East Women's Studies* 18, no. 1 (March 1, 2022): 147–49.

24. Nawal El Saadawi, "How to Fight against the Postmodern Slave System," Atlanta, Georgia, September 11, 2008, in *The Essential Nawal El Saadawi: A Reader*, ed. Adele Newson-Horst (London: Zed Books, 2010), 13–14.

25. El Saadawi, "Women and the Poor," 78–89.

26. Hoda Badran, *The Road to Beijing: Egyptian Women's Journey* (Cairo: UNDP Cairo and Al-Harara Publishing, 1997), 39. According to the World Bank, the Egyptian population almost doubled between 1970 (when it was 34,781,986 people) and 1988 (54,298,446). However, Badran's analysis is not only quantitative but qualitative, including education, health, and socialization practices.

27. Badran, *The Road to Beijing*.

28. The first UN conference on women was held in Mexico City in 1975 and it namely opened the UN Women's Decade, during which the United Nations set up some targets worldwide to link their agenda on development to the advancement of

women's condition, especially in what were then called "Third World countries." The next two conferences were held in Copenhagen (1980) and Nairobi (1985). The UN agenda for women has inspired a broad feminist scholarship, mostly critical of the institutional and top-down approach taken by the UN. Gayatri Chakravorty Spivak, "'Woman' as Theatre: United Nations Conference on Women, Beijing 1995," *Radical Philosophy,* no. 75 (1996); Shahhen Sardar Ali, "Women's Rights, CEDAW and International Human Rights Debates: Toward Empowerment?," in *Rethinking Empowerment,* ed. Jane L. Parpart, Shirin M. Rai, and Kathleen A. Staudt (New York: Routledge, 2002).

29. Abdel Hadi, "A Community of Women Empowered," 116.

30. Nadia Abdel Wahab Afifi and Amal Abdel Hadi, eds., *The Feminist Movement in the Arab World: Interventions and Studies from Four Countries; Egypt, Palestine, Sudan, Tunisia* (Cairo: Dal El-Mostaqbal al Arabi, 1996).

31. Baron, *The Women's Awakening in Egypt,* 144–167.

32. In Aida Seif El Dawla, "Reproductive Rights of Egyptian Women: Issues for Debate," *Reproductive Health Matters* 8, no. 16 (2000): 51.

33. Hala Shukrallah, Cairo, January 18, 2018; Fatma Ramadan, Cairo, September 23, 2014.

34. Nadia Abdel Wahab Afifi and Amal Abdel Hadi, "The Feminist Movement in Egypt," in *The Feminist Movement in the Arab World,* 15.

35. Hala Shukrallah, Cairo, December 18, 2018.

36. Badran, *Feminists, Islam and Nation*; Lucia Sorbera, "Gli esordi del femminismo egiziano tra XIX e XX secolo," *Genesis: Rivista della Società Italiana delle Storiche* 6, no. 2 (2007): 115–36; Sorbera, "Viaggiare e svelarsi alle origini del femminismo egiziano," in *Margini e confini: Studi sulla cultura delle donne nell'età contemporanea,* ed. Anna Rosa Scrittori (Venezia: Cafoscarina, 2006), 265–94; Sorbera, "Egyptian Feminist Union at the 9th Congress of International Women Suffrage Alliance (Rome, 1923)," in *Egitto oggi,* ed. Elisabetta Bartuli (Bologna: Il Ponte, 2005), 165–74.

37. Abdel Hadi, 2018.

38. Allusion to First Lady Suzanne Mubarak. "Hanem" is an Ottoman-Turkish word referring to a lady or a noble woman. In republican Egypt it is used with a sarcastic tone.

39. Nawla Darwiche, Cairo, January 7, 2018.

40. Spivak, "'Woman' as Theatre."

41. Spivak, "'Woman' as Theatre."

42. Frances Hasso, "Empowering Governmentalities rather than Women: The Arab Human Development Report 2005 and Western Development Logics," *International Journal of Middle East Women Studies* 41, no. 1 (2009): 63–82.

43. Lila Abu-Lughod, Fida J. Adeli, and Frances Hasso, "Overview: Engaging the Arab Human Development Report 2005 on Women," *International Journal of Middle East Women Studies* 41, no. 1 (2009): 59–60.

44. Inderpal Grewal, *Transnational America: Feminisms, Diasporas, Neoliberalisms* (Durham, NC: Duke University Press, 2005).

45. *Report of the Fourth World Conference on Women, Beijing, September 4–15, 1995* (New York: United Nations, 1996), 158; Badran, *The Road to Beijing.*

46. Shereen Abouelnaga, Sydney, August 26, 2019. Shereen Abouelnaga also wrote about her experience in Beijing in her book, *Women in Revolutionary Egypt,* 107.

47. Abouelnaga, Sydney, August 26, 2019.

48. Anzaldúa, *Borderlands/La Frontera,* 3.

CHAPTER FOUR

1. Egypt participated in the drafting of the International Declaration of Human Rights, and it ratified the International Convention on the Elimination of All Forms of Racial Discrimination (1967), the Convention on the Elimination of All Forms of Discrimination against Women (1981), the International Covenant on Civil and Political Rights and the International Covenant on Economic Social and Cultural Rights (1982), the African Charter on Human and People's Rights (1984), the Convention against Torture and Other Cruel, Inhuman or Degrading Treatment or Punishment (1986), and the Convention on the Rights of the Child (1990). Neil Hicks, "Transnational Human Rights Networks and Human Rights in Egypt," in *Human Rights in the Arab World,* ed. Anthony Chase and Amr Hamzawy (Philadelphia: University of Pennsylvania Press, 2013), 68, 291.

2. Mustapha Kamal Al-Sayyid, "State, Society and Violations of Human Rights in Egypt," *Cairo Papers in Social Sciences* 17, no. 3 (1994), 47–52.

3. El-Dawla, 2018.

4. Maha Abdelrahman, "The Nationalisation of the Human Rights Debate in Egypt," *Nations and Nationalism* 13, no. 2 (2007), 285–300.

5. National Council for Human Rights, Council Sessions.

6. Egyptian Organization for Human Rights, *The Situation of Human Rights in Egypt: Annual Report, 2004* (in Arabic) (Cairo, 2024), 158–59.

7. Hoda Elsadda interviewed by Nicola Pratt, SOAS Digital Collection, Middle East Women's Activism, 2014.

8. Hala Shukrallah, personal communication, June 19, 2023.

9. This particular intersectional matrix compares in very interesting ways to that first elaborated by Kimberlé Crenshaw, who created the term to account for the intersection of race, class, and gender in the American context. Kimberlé Crenshaw, "Mapping the Margins: Intersectionality, Identity Politics, and Violence against Women of Color," *Stanford Law Review* 43, no. 6 (1991): 1241–99.

10. Sadiq Reza, "Endless Emergency: The Case of Egypt," *New Criminal Law Review: An International and Interdisciplinary Journal* 10, no. 4 (Fall 2007): 532–53.

11. Hicks, "Transnational Human Rights Networks and Human rights in Egypt," 71.

12. Hala Shukrallah, Cairo, December 18, 2018.

13. Hicks, "Transnational Human Rights Networks and Human Rights in Egypt," 79.

14. Human Rights Watch, "Egypt: Margins of Repression; State Limits on Nongovernmental Organization Activism," July 3, 2005.

15. By February 1998, the draft law was presented to the People's Assembly by Ali Fateh Bab of the Labor Party, Ayman Nour and Fouad Badrawi of the Wafd Party, and Mohammed Abdel Aziz Shabban of the Tagammu' Party. Tamir Moustapha, "Got Rights? Public Interest Litigation and the Egyptian Human Rights Movement," in *Human Rights in the Arab World: Independent Voices,* ed. Anthony Tirado Chase and Amr Hamzawy (Philadelphia: University of Pennsylvania Press, 2006), 162.

16. Moustapha, "Got Rights?," 172.

17. Lina Attalah, "Human Rights in Focus," *Mada Masr,* April 16, 2015.

18. Moustapha, "Got Rights?," 159; Tamir Moustapha, *The Struggle for Constitutional Power: Law, Politics, and Economic Development in Egypt* (Cambridge: Cambridge University Press, 2007); Nathan Brown, *The Rule of Law in the Arab World: Courts in Egypt and the Gulf* (Cambridge: Cambridge University Press, 1997); Ebherard Kienle, *Grand Delusion: Democracy and Economic Reform in Egypt* (London: I. B. Tauris, 2000); Kevin Boyle and Adel Omar Sherif, eds., *Human Rights and Democracy: The Role of the Supreme Constitutional Court of Egypt* (London: Kluver, 1996).

19. Shukrallah, 2018.

20. Here Shukrallah is referring to the 1977 Bread Riots in Egypt.

21. Shukrallah, 2018.

22. Shukrallah, 2018.

23. Shukrallah, 2018.

24. Iman Mersal, personal communication, July 16, 2024; Hanan Hammad, "The Other Extremists: Marxist Feminism in Egypt, 1980–2000," *Journal of International Women's Studies* 12, no. 3 (2011): 217–33.

25. Shukrallah, 2018.

26. Shukrallah, 2018.

27. Shukrallah, 2018.

28. Shukrallah, 2018.

CHAPTER FIVE

1. Aida Seif El-Dawla, Cairo, January 4, 2018. When not otherwise indicated, quotes in this chapter are from this interview. Hani is the journalist Hani Shukrallah.

2. Markaz al-Nadim li-munahidha al-'Unf wal-Ta'dhib (Center el-Nadeem against Violence and Torture), https://elnadeem.org.

3. El-Nadeem, "Our Reply to the MOH Allegations Regarding Closure of El Nadim," press release, February 25, 2016. El-Nadeem had been previously challenged by the state authorities in 2004, but this is the longest ban they experienced until they won the appeal at the beginning of 2021.

4. Magda Adly, Cairo, January 16, 2017.

5. The charges against Mozn Hassan and Azza Soliman were dropped on October 21, 2021, whereas Aida Seif El-Dawla's appeal was dropped in April 2024.

6. El-Dawla, 2018. The biographies of 'Abbas and of 'Ismat Saif al-Dawla are featured in Alia Mosallam, *Strikes, Riots and Laughter.*

7. According to UNICEF, the median marriage age for Egyptian women is only a bit over twenty: www.unicef.org/mena/media/1796/file/MENA-CMReport -EgyptBrief.pdf.pdf.

8. About the ways Aida Seif El-Dawla and the other psychiatrists of El-Nadeem conceive the relationship between the body, the psyche, and the society as care work, see Frances Hasso, "Beyond the Treatment Room: The Psyche-Body-Society Care Politics of Cairo's El-Nadeem," *Signs: Journal of Women in Culture and Society* 49, no. 1 (Autumn 2023): 1–29.

9. Hasso, "Beyond the Treatment Room," 2.

10. El-Dawla, 2018; Magda Adly, 2017; and Suzan Fayyad, Cairo, June 23, 2019. See also Hasso, "Beyond the Treatment Room," 7–35.

11. Hicks, "Transnational Human Rights Networks and Human Rights in Egypt," 76; Nicola Pratt, "Human Rights NGOs and the 'Foreign Funding Debate' in Egypt," in *Human Rights in the Arab World,* ed. Chase Anthony and Amr Hamzawy (Philadelphia: University of Pennsylvania Press, 2013).

12. El-Dawla, 2018.

13. Fayad, 2019.

14. Fayad, 2019.

15. Gameela Ismail, Cairo, January 9, 2018.

16. Moustapha, "Got rights?," 153.

17. Pratt, "The Queen Boat Case in Egypt."

CHAPTER SIX

1. Azza Soliman, "Opening Ceremony of the International Film Festival on Human Rights," March 9, 2018, Geneva, Switzerland.

2. Nadia Sonneveld, "Khul' Divorce in Egypt: How Family Courts Are Providing a 'Dialogue' between Husband and Wife," *Anthropology of the Middle East* 5, no. 2 (2010): 100–120; Monika Lindbekk, "Women Judges in Egypt: Discourse and Practice," in Sonneveld and Lindbekk, *Women Judges in the Muslim World.*

3. The Christian laws are those of the Coptic Orthodox, Greek Orthodox, Syrian Orthodox, Armenian Orthodox, Catholic, and Protestant denominations. The Jewish laws are those of the Rabbinic and Karaite sects. Until 1955, when they were abolished, there were also separate family courts. Since 1955 the religious family laws are administered by national courts. Maurits Berger and Nadia Sonneveld, "Sharia and National Law in Egypt," in *Sharia and National Law: Comparing the Legal Systems of Twelve Islamic Countries,* ed. Jan Michiel Otto (Cairo: American University in Cairo Press, 2010), 51–89.

4. The mixed courts were closed in 1949. The notion of foreigner and native (or *indigène*, as the records of the courts are in French) was a matter of controversy in the first years of the activity of the courts. Mark S. W. Hoyle, "The Mixed Courts of Egypt, 1875–1885," *Arab Law Quarterly* 1, no. 4 (August 1986); Erwin Loewenfeld, "The Mixed Courts in Egypt as Part of the System of Capitulations after the Treaty of Montreux," *Transactions of the Grotius Society* 26 (1940): 83–123.

5. Sonneveld, "Women's Access to Legal Education and Their Appointment to the Judiciary."

6. Badran, *Feminists, Islam, and Nation*, 183.

7. Essam Fawzi, "PSL in Egypt: An Historical Overview," in *Women's Rights and Islamic Family Law: Perspectives on Reform,* ed. Lynn Welchmann (London: Zed Books, 2004), 30–44; Beger and Sonneveld, "Sharia and National Law in Egypt," 63. The impact of the repeal on mobilizing women is discussed by Hoda Elsadda in "Women and Justice in the Egyptian Constitution: A Reading from Within."

8. Azza M. Karam, *Women, Islamisms and the State: Contemporary Feminisms in Egypt* (Basingstoke: Macmillan Press, 1998), 142, 145, 146; Mona Zulfikar, ed., and the Communication Group for the Enhancement of the Status of Women in Egypt, *Legal Rights of Egyptian Women in Theory and in Practice* (Cairo: Dar El-Kutub, 1992).

9. From Mona Zulfikar, CV.

10. Nehad Abu Khomsa, "ECWR Rejects the Draft PSL," ECWR, Cairo, 2021.

11. In fact, the same provision can be found until recent times throughout Europe. On the influence of the Napoleonic codes on modern Egyptian law provisions: Sonneveld and Lindbekk, *Women Judges in the Muslim World*.

12. Gaétan Du Roy, *Les zabbālīn du Muqattam: Ethnohistoire d'une hétérotopie au Caire (979–2021)* (Leiden: Brill, 2022).

13. Claudio C. Acioly, "Can Urban Management Deliver the Sustainable City? Guided Densification in Brazil versus Informal Compactness in Cairo," in *Compact Cities: Sustainable Urban Forms for Developing Countries,* ed. Rod Burgess and Mike Jenks (London: Routledge, 2002), 129.

14. Acioly, "Can Urban Management Deliver the Sustainable City?"

15. Badran, "Competing Agendas: Feminists, Islam and the State in Nineteenth- and Twentieth-Century Egypt"; Al-Ali, *Secularism, Gender and the State in the Middle East.*

16. Azza Soliman, Cairo, December 9, 2018, and follow-up Facetime call, Sydney-Cairo, June 13, 2020.

17. Karam, *Women, Islamisms and the State,* 142.

18. Egyptian Centre for Women's Legal Rights (CEWLA), *Honour Crimes: An Analytical Perspective* (Cairo: CEWLA, 2002).

19. Soliman, 2018.

20. Soliman, 2018.

21. Sonneveld, "Women's Access to Legal Education and Their Appointment to the Judiciary," 65.

22. Soliman, 2018.

23. Soliman, 2018.

24. Fatma Khafagi, *Honour Crime in Egypt,* United Nations Expert Group Meeting, Violence against Women: Good Practices in Combating and Eliminating Violence against Women, Vienna, May 2005.

25. Khafagi, *Honour Crime in Egypt*; J. M. Masterson and J. H. Swanson, *Female Genital Cutting: Breaking the Silence, Enabling Change* (Washington, DC: International Center for Research on Women and the Center for Development and Population Activities, 2000).

26. The Egyptian Movement for Change (El-Haraka el-Masreyya men agl el-Taghyeer), better known as Kefaya ("enough" in colloquial Egyptian Arabic, from one of its slogans), had its first demonstration in December 2004. The movement advocated for the democratization of the political system; the 6th of April movement (Haraka Shabab 6 Abril) was launched in 2008 in solidarity with the workers movement.

27. Soliman, 2018.

28. Soliman, 2018.

29. Soliman, 2018.

30. It is important to remember that the two are not the same. Islamist formations aim at providing a political alternative to the secular state, whereas pious movements act more in the private sphere and the civil society, with no ambition to take over the state. On women in the Islamist movements in Egypt: Karam, *Women, Islamism and the State.* For women in the pious movements: Mahmood, *Politics of Piety.*

31. Islamic feminism is a global intellectual movement, and the literature that developed about it since the early nineties reflects its global breath. In addition to the above mentioned works by Abu Bakr, Badran, and Sharafeldin, the works by miriam cooke and Marnia Lazreg on Islamic feminism are also points of reference: miriam cooke, *Women Claim Islam: Creating Islamic Feminism through Literature* (Florence: Routledge, 2001); and *Nazira Zeineddine: A Pioneer of Islamic Feminism* (Oxford: Oneworld, 2010); Marnia Lazreg, *Islamic Feminism and the Discourse of Post-Liberation: The Cultural Turn in Algeria* (Abingdon, UK: Routledge, 2021).

32. Omaima Abu Bakr is a professor of history at Cairo University and a founding member of WMF. Among her recent publications: Omaima Abou-Bakr, "Teaching the Words of The Prophet: Women Instructors of the Hadith (Fourteenth and Fifteenth Centuries)," *Hawwa* 1, no. 3 (2003); "Rings of Memory: 'Writing Muslim Women' and the Question of Authorial Voice," *The Muslim World* 103, no. 3 (2013); and "Articulating Gender: Muslim Women Intellectuals in the Premodern Period," *Arab Studies Quarterly* 32, no. 3 (2010). Margot Badran was among the first feminist historians to engage with Islamic feminism: "Towards Islamic Feminisms," in *Hermeneutics and Honor in Islamic/ate Societies,* Harvard Middle East Monograph Series, ed. Asma Afsarrudin (Cambridge, MA: Harvard University Press, 1999); Margot Badran, *Feminism Beyond East and West: New Gender Talk and Practice in Global Islam* (New Delhi: Global Media Publications, 2007);

Margot Badran, ed., "Islamic Feminism," *Samyukta: A Journal of Gender and Culture* 2, no. 1 (2017).

33. A scholar specializing in family law, Sharafeldin graduated from the University of Oxford, UK, in 2021 with a PhD thesis titled "PSL Reform in Egypt: Women's Rights: NGOs Navigating between Islamic Law and Human Rights." She is also a feminist activist and a member of the Knowledge Building Working Group at Musawah. Among her publications: Marwa Sharafeldin, "Islamic Law Meets Human Rights: Reformulating Qiwamah and Wilayah for PSL Reform Advocacy in Egypt," *Men in Charge* (2015): 163–96; and "Challenges of Islamic Feminism in PSL Reform: Women's NGOs in Egypt between Islamic Law and International Human Rights," in *Feminist and Islamic Perspectives: New Horizons of Knowledge and Reform,* ed. Omaima Abu Bakr (Cairo: Women and Memory Forum, 2013).

34. A Nubian blogger and in 2007 one of the founders of Nazra for Feminist Studies, Fatma Emam is also part of transnational Islamic Feminist networks. Fatma Emam, Cairo, December 11, 2018.

35. Soliman, 2018, for this and the next quote.

36. Radwa Elsaman, "Egypt: Making Exceptions Doesn't End Discrimination against Women Judges," *Enheduanna, a Blog of the Middle East Women's Initiative,* May 2, 2021.

CHAPTER SEVEN

1. Nadine (a woman involved in the protest), Cairo, November 19, 2021.

2. I later learned that she started to be politically active during the January 2011 Revolution and continued to be involved in demonstrations since then.

3. Young woman activist who wishes to remain anonymous, December 1, 2011.

4. Dostour is a liberal party founded in April 2012 under the leadership of Mohamed ElBaradei declaring the aim of preserving the ideals of the revolution. Since ElBaradei left Egypt following the 2013 military coup, the party went through a prolonged leadership crisis, and the only presidents who served for long terms were two women: Hala Shukrallah (in 2014 for fourteen months) and Gameela Ismail (since 2022 and continuing).

5. The National Dialogue was an initiative that President El-Sisi announced in April 2022 and opened one year later (May 2023), ten years after the military coup. Representatives of the civil society have been invited to meet with the president and discuss government political and economic issues regarding Egypt.

6. Al-Harakah al-Madaniyah al-Dimuqratiyah is a liberal political movement formed in Egypt in 2017. It includes the Dostour Party, the Karama Party, the Socialist Popular Alliance Party, the Egyptian Social Democratic Party, and the Bread and Freedom Party.

7. The trajectory of Noor Ayman Nour and Shady Ayman Nour from their teens to early adulthood is typical of young artist activists in the late Mubarak and then revolutionary eras in Egypt, and it has been featured in the documentary *Before the*

Spring after the Fall, directed by Jed Rothstein, 2013; Mark LeVine, *We'll Play till We Die: Journey across a Decade of Revolutionary Music in the Muslim World* (Oakland: University of California Press, 2022).

8. Baron, *The Women's Awakening in Egypt*; Booth, *May Her Likes Be Multiplied*; Badran, *Feminists, Islam and Nation*; Badran and cooke, *Opening the Gates*; Irene Fenoglio Abd El-Aal, *Défense et illustration de l'Égyptienne: Aux débuts d'une expression feminine* (Cairo: CEDEJ, 1988).

9. Ismail, personal communication via email, March 1, 2021.

10. Ismail, 2021.

11. I met Eman three times, in January 2020, June 2023, and June 2024.

12. Gameela Ismail, Cairo, January 9, 2018.

13. Carol Gilligan, *In a Different Voice: Psychological Theory and Women's Development* (Cambridge, MA: Harvard University Press, 1982); Seyla Benhabib, *Situating the Self: Gender, Community, and Postmodernism in Contemporary Ethics* (New York: Routledge, 1992); Martha Craven Nussbaum, *Upheavals of Thought: The Intelligence of Emotions* (Cambridge: Cambridge University Press, 2001); Joan C. Tronto, *Moral Boundaries: A Political Argument for an Ethic of Care* (New York: Routledge, 1993).

14. Elena Pulcini, "What Emotions Motivate Care?," *Emotion Review* 9, no. 1 (2017): 64–71.

15. Sophie Bourgault and Elena Pulcini, *Emotions and Care: Interdisciplinary Perspectives* (Belgium: Peeters, 2018); Elena Pulcini, *Care of the World: Fear, Responsibility and Justice in the Global Age* (Dordrecht: Springer Netherlands, 2013).

16. Ismail, 2018.

17. Ismail, 2018, for this and quotes in the next paragraph.

18. Ismail, 2018.

19. The Care Collective, *The Care Manifesto: The Politics of Interdependence* (London: Verso Books, 2020).

20. Ismail, 2018.

21. Ismail, 2018.

22. Ismail, 2018.

23. Ismail, 2018.

24. Ismail, 2018.

25. Ismail, 2018.

26. Michele Dunne and Amr Hamzawy, *Egypt's Secular Political Parties: A Struggle for Identity and Independence* (Washington, DC: Carnegie Endowment for International Peace, 2017).

27. Ismail, 2018.

28. Ismail, 2018.

29. Ismail, 2018.

30. Ismail, 2018.

31. Hesham Sallam, "Grooming and Gaslighting in Egypt's New Republic," *Jadaliyya* (blog), July 27, 2023; Khalil Al-Anani, "Egyptian National Dialogue: A Lost Opportunity for National Salvage," Arab Center Washington DC, July 7, 2023.

32. Gameela Ismail, personal communication, June 19, 2024.

33. Gameela Ismail, personal communication, June 9, 2023.

34. Ismail, 2024.

CHAPTER EIGHT

1. In 2020, the party was canceled due to pressures by state security on the club that was hosting it. Since then, only small cultural events at *Mada*'s premises for the organization's members have been possible. The chief editor Lina Attallah and other journalists have been summoned multiple times for their investigative journalism work.

2. Mahienour El-Massry, "Discourse of Acceptance of the Ludovic Trarieux Award," October 31, 2014, www.youtube.com/watch?v=Z-uuBoiGdWM.

3. El-Massry, "Discourse of Acceptance of the Ludovic Trarieux Award."

4. In January 2018, the Constitutional Court reverted the administrative courts decisions and ruled for the two islands to legitimately be under the sovereignty of Saudi Arabia.

5. Mahienour El-Massry, Cairo, June 23, 2019.

6. There are not official numbers for political prisoners in Egypt, but Egyptian and international human rights groups estimate the number at more than 100,000. Collective Antigone, *Imprisoning and Revolution: Writings from Egypt's Incarcerated* (Oakland: University of California Press, 2024), 6.

7. El-Massry, 2019.

8. El-Massry, 2019

9. El-Massry, 2019.

10. El-Massry, 2019.

11. Political scientists have noticed how the repression of Islamist groups was also a pretext used by the government to enforce restrictive laws against all sorts of opposition. Eberhardt Kienle, *A Grand Delusion: Democracy and Economic Reform in Egypt* (London: I.B. Tauris, 2001); Jillian Schwedler and J. Clark, "Islamist-Leftist Cooperation in the Arab World," *ISIM Review* 18 (Autumn 2006): 10–11.

12. Tal'at Fu'ad Qassim, interview with Hisham Mubarak, "What Does the Gam'a al-Islamiyya Want?," in *Political Islam: Essays from Middle East Report*, ed. Joel Beinin and Joe Stork (Berkeley: University of California Press, 1987), 314–26.

13. Mohamed El Agati, ed., *Youths and Radical Groups from the Perspectives of Youth* (Cairo: Arab Forum for Alternatives and Rosa Luxemburg Foundation, 2015).

14. El-Massry, 2019.

15. Hanan Hammad, "The Other Extremists; Marxist Feminism in Egypt, 1980–2000," *Journal of International Women's Studies* 12, no. 3 (2011): 217–33.

16. Bint al-Ard has not yet been the object of a comprehensive study; the only contribution to its history I am aware of is in Hammad, "The Other Extremists: Marxist Feminism in Egypt, 1980–2000."

17. Sana' al-Masri, *Khalf al-Hijab: Mawaqif al-jama'at al-islamiyya min Qadiyyat al-Mar'a* (*Behind the Veil: The Position of the Islamist Groups towards Women's Issues*) (Cairo: Sina lil-Nasht, 1987).

18. The Hezb al-'Ummal was a Marxist-Leninist political formation to which several women who later became part of the feminist and the human rights movement belonged.

19. El-Massry, 2019, for this and the next quote.

20. Sherine Hamdy, *Our Bodies Belong to God: Organ Transplants, Islam, and the Struggle for Human Dignity in Egypt* (Berkeley: University of California Press, 2012); Soha Bayoumi and Sherine Hamdy, "Nationalism, Authoritarianism, and Medical Mobilization in Post-Revolutionary Egypt," *Culture, Medicine, and Psychiatry* 47, no. 1 (2023): 37–61; Rania Kassab Sweis, "Saving Egypt's Village Girls: Humanity, Rights and Gendered Vulnerability in a Global Youth Initiative," *Journal of Middle East Women's Studies* 8, no. 2 (Spring 2012), and "Security and the Traumatized Street Child: How Gender Shapes International Psychiatric Aid, in Cairo," *Medical Anthropology Quarterly* 32, no. 1 (2017): 5–21.

21. The psychiatrist Sally Toma is currently using mostly social media platforms (especially Facebook) to disseminate more awareness about eating disorders. She has more than forty thousand followers.

22. Recent scholarship documents both the alienation of elites in the context of spreading private education and the link between neoliberalism and Islamization under the Mubarak regime: Noha Roushdy, "International Schools and the Production of Elite Non-Belonging in Cairo's Satellite Cities," *Égypte, Soudan, Monde Arabe*, no. 24 (2023): 127–52; Hanya Sobhi, "The De-Facto Privatization of Secondary Education in Egypt: A Study of Private Tutoring in Technical and General Schools," *Compare* 42, no. 1 (2012): 4767, and "Secular Façade, Neoliberal Islamization: Textbook Nationalism from Mubarak to Sisi," *Nations and Nationalism* 21, no. 4 (2010): 805–24. The next quote is from El-Massry, 2019.

23. Rached, *Quatre femmes d'Egypte/Four Women of Egypt*.

24. Badran, *Feminists, Islam and Nation*, 232–50; *Al-Mar'a Al-'Arabiya wa Qadaya al-Falastin*, Proceedings of the Eastern Women's Conference in Defence of Palestine, Cairo, October 15–18, 1938, with an introduction by Sania Sharawi and a foreword by Sherine Elbanhawy (Hildenborough, UK: Rowayat, 2024).

25. Suzan Fayyad, Cairo, June 19, 2019.

26. El-Massry, 2019.

27. Ahmed, *A Quiet Revolution: The Veil's Resurgence, from the Middle East to America*; Fadwa El Guindi, *Veil: Modesty, Privacy and Resistance* (Oxford: Berg, 1999).

28. Asef Bayyat, *Life as Politics* (Stanford, CA: Stanford University Press, 2013).

29. El-Massry, 2019, for this and the next quote (about Khaled Said).

30. Rabab Al-Mahdi, "Enough! Egypt's Quest for Democracy," *Comparative Political Studies* 42, no. 8 (August 2009): 1001–39.

31. El-Massry, 2019.

32. al-Mahdi, "Enough! Egypt's Quest for Democracy," 1019.

33. al-Mahdi, "Enough! Egypt's Quest for Democracy."

34. El-Massry, 2019. For Harman's work, see Chris Harman, *The Prophet and the Proletariat* (London: Socialist Workers Party, 1998).

35. Hossam el-Hamalawy, "Comrades and Brothers," *Middle East Report,* no. 242 (Spring 2007). The next quote is from El-Massry, 2019.

36. El-Hamalawy, "Comrades and Brothers."

37. El-Massry, 2019.

38. See part 3 in this book and Yasmin El-Rifae, *Radius: A Story of Feminist Revolution* (London: Verso Books, 2022).

39. El-Massry, 2019.

40. El-Massry, 2019.

41. Joel Beinin, "Workers and Egypt's January 25 Revolution," *International Labor and Working-Class History* 80, no. 1 (2011): 189–96.

42. Alaa Abd El-Fattah, "Alf Tahia al-'Ummal," June 21, 2007.

43. See also Tara Povey, *Social Movements in Egypt and Iran* (London: Palgrave Macmillan, 2015).

44. Interview with women activists of the independent syndicate of the tax collectors, 'Aish wa Hurriyya Party, Cairo, November 7, 2014. Rasha Elgebali is currently (2024) the head of the union of workers in the real estate taxation authority in Alexandria.

45. Elgebali, 2014.

46. El-Massry, 2019.

47. El-Massry, 2019.

48. El-Massry, 2019.

49. El-Massry, 2019.

50. Mahienour El-Massry, "On the Anniversary of the Assassination of Shaima al-Sabbagh," letter from Qanateer Prison, January 24, 2016, in Collective Antigone, *Imprisoning a Revolution: Writings from Egypt's Incarcerated* (Oakland: University of California Press, 2024), 224–26.

51. Mahienour El-Massry, "Prison Is a Microcosm of Society," translated by Radwa al-Barouni in *Mada Masr,* June 7, 2014, reprinted in Collective Antigone, *Imprisoning a Revolution,* 219–22.

52. Private communication, August 1, 2021.

53. El-Massry, "On the Anniversary of the Assassination of Shaima al-Sabbagh," 226.

CHAPTER NINE

1. Agnes Heller, "Hannah Arendt on Tradition and New Beginnings," in *Hannah Arendt in Jerusalem,* ed. Steven Aschheim (Berkeley: University of California Press, 2001).

2. She founded the Egyptian Democratic Academy, an organization of young Egyptian activists working toward the promotion of democracy, human rights, and

political participation, and the "Free Egyptian Woman, Speak Out" Group (Mesriya Hurra, Etkallemy), which seeks to empower women to participate in social and political activities and hold leadership positions in all fields. Esraa was also a columnist for *al-Masry al-Youm* newspaper, and she had her own talk show program on ONTV Live.

3. For a timeline, see Frontline Defenders, "Timeline about Esra Abdel Fattah's Case."

4. Abdel Hadi, January 18, 2018. Manal's father is Bahey Eldin Hassan, the founder of the Cairo Institute for Human Rights Studies and the Arab Network for Human Rights.

5. Shady Nour, personal communication, New York City, December 2022. Shady Nour, a filmmaker and political activist, is the son of Gameela Ismail and Ayman Nour.

6. Personal communications: Hind Mahmoud, Cairo, June 18, 2023; Hala Shukrallah, Cairo, June 19, 2023; Nawla Darwiche, Cairo, June 20, 2023.

7. "Meet Asmaa Mahfouz and the Vlog that Helped Spark the Revolution," YouTube video, posted February 1, 2011, by Iyad El-Baghdadi, 4 min., 36 sec., www .youtube.com/watch?v=SgjIgMdsEuk.

8. The first country to open the internet was Tunisia in 1992. The internet became generalized in the 1990s and blogging in the early 2000s. The first conglomerate of blogs in the Arabic language was created by the couple Manal Hassan and Alaa Abd El-Fattah (Manalaa, 2005). Four Arab Bloggers Meetings have been sponsored by Heinrich Böll-Global Voices (Beirut 2008 and 2009, Tunis 2011, and Amman 2014).

9. Fieldwork notes and multiple conversations with Egyptian students and young middle-class professionals between 2011 and 2024.

10. The notion of modesty is very important in Muslim cultures, it concerns both women and men, and even if it has evolved over time, it maintains a strong gender connotation. El Guindi, *Veil: Modesty, Privacy and Resistance.*

11. For example, right before the revolution, after the New Year's Eve massacre of twenty-three Coptic worshippers at the Church of the Two Saints in Alexandria, the writer, academic, and public intellectual May Telmissany published three columns in *Rose al-Yusuf* newspaper titled "Al-Dawla" (The State), the third of which was released on January 25, 2011, advocating for full secularism, respect of the rule-of-law and substantial equality between Muslim and Christian citizens. May Telmissany, "Nomadic Citizenship: Reflections on Exile and the Revolution," *Journal of the African Literature Association* 15, no. 3 (2021): 516.

12. Joel Beinin, "Workers' Protest in Egypt: Neoliberalism and Class Struggle in the 21st Century," *Social Movement Studies: Journal of Social, Cultural and Political Protest* 8, no. 4 (2009): 449–54.

13. Baron, *Egypt as a Woman.*

14. Tara Povey, "Voices of Dissent: Social Movements and Political Change in Egypt," in *Muslim Secular Democracy,* ed. Lily Zubaidah Rahim (New York: Palgrave Macmillan, 2013), 233–52.

15. Activist of Bidaya who wishes to remain anonymous, October 12, 2014.

16. Activist of Bidaya who wishes to remain anonymous, October 12, 2014.

17. Pratt, "The Queen Boat Case in Egypt."

18. Sarah Hegazi, "A Year after the Rainbow Flag Controversy," *Mada Masr*, June 15, 2020. The original version, in Arabic, was published by *Mada Masr* in September 2018. Hegazi took her own life on June 14, 2020.

19. Most of these groups are a product of the feminist schools organized across Egypt by Nazra for Feminist Studies after 2011. Until 2013 there were about fifty-five groups across Egypt. Not all of them continued to operate in the following years. Mozn Hassan, Ayat Osman, Tasnim Haggag, and Shaima Tantawi (Nazra for Feminist Studies), Cairo, December 19, 2018. The number of organizations and women's initiatives and collectives that mushroomed in Egypt between 2011 and 2014 is larger. Claudia Ruta, "Gender Politics in Transition: Women's Political Rights after the January 25 Revolution" (master's thesis, American University in Cairo, 2021).

20. Basma Abdel Rahman, December 3, 2011. Basma is a psychiatrist and a literary translator who at the time of the interview was part of the El-Nadeem team. She is also the daughter of two leftist intellectuals, the lawyer Zinat al-Askary and the writer Mohamed El-Mor.

21. Interview with a member of the Popular Committee to Defend the Revolution who wishes to remain anonymous, Cairo, December 5, 2011.

CHAPTER TEN

1. Linda Martín Alcoff, "Experience and Knowledge: The Case of Sexual Abuse Memoires," in *Feminist Metaphysics: Explorations in the Ontology of Sex, Gender and Identity*, ed. Charlotte Witt (New York: Springer, 2011), 222.

2. Linda Martín Alcoff, "Philosophy Matters: A Review of Recent Work in Feminist Philosophy," *Signs: Journal of Women in Culture and Society* 25, no. 3 (2000): 841–82; Uma Narayan, "Essence of Culture and a Sense of History: A Feminist Critique of Cultural Essentialism," *Hypatia* 13, no. 2 (1998): 86–106; Lila Abu-Lughod, *Do Muslim Women Need Saving?* (Cambridge, MA: Harvard University Press, 2013).

3. Lobna Darwish, Cairo, December 4, 2013.

4. Recent sociological research problematizes the notion of both leaders and leaderless revolution. Asef Bayat, *Revolution without Revolutionaries: Making Sense of the Arab Spring* (Stanford, CA: Stanford University Press, 2020); Rusha Latif, *Tahrir's Youth: Leaders of a Leaderless Revolution* (Cairo: American University in Cairo Press, 2022).

5. Lawyer of Al-Nakib Center for Training and Democracy Support, Cairo, December 5, 2011.

6. S.M., young woman activist who wishes to remain anonymous, Cairo, December 3, 2011.

7. Ahdaf Soueif, "Protesters Reclaim the Spirit of Egypt," *BBC News Middle East*, February 13, 2011. In the title one can read a reference to the famous novel by

Tawfiq al-Hakim, *The Return of the Spirit,* a canonical text in Egyptian modern literature, which celebrates the 1919 anticolonial revolution and Egyptian nationalism. A graffiti featuring al-Hakim and the title of his novel was painted in downtown Cairo in 2011.

8. Nawal al-Saadawi, "Egyptian Feminist Nawal El Saadawi in Cairo's Tahrir Square: The City in the Field," *Ms. Magazine,* February 7, 2011, and Democracy Now!, "Leading Egyptian Feminist, Nawal al-Saadawi: 'Women and Girls Are Beside Boys in the Streets,'" January 31, 2011.

9. Darwish, 2013.

10. Darwiche, 2018.

11. Amnesty International, "Egypt Rises: Killings, Detentions and Torture in the '25 January Revolution," May 19, 2011.

12. Activist, Bidaya, October 12, 2014.

13. The regime deployed cameleers and horse riders from Giza to attack the protesters who refused to leave Tahrir after Mubarak's speech on February 1, where he offered not to run for the September 2011 presidential elections and promised to instruct the Parliament to change the presidential electoral law.

14. Hassan, 2018. The Hisham Mubarak Law Center was a human rights organization founded by Ahmed Seif and other human rights lawyers and named in memory of their colleague Hisham Mubarak, who died prematurely in 1998.

15. Darwish, 2013.

16. Today (2024) she works as researcher at the Egyptian Initiative for Personal Rights (EIPR).

17. Nazra for Feminist Studies, "Egypt: Statement from Nazra for Feminist Studies about Mob Sexual Assaults," June 13, 2014; "Testimony from a Survival of Gang Rape on Tahrir Square Vicinity," January 26, 2013, https://nazra.org/en/2013/01/testimony-survival-gang-rape-tahrir-square-vicinity; "Testimonies on the Recent Sexual Assaults on Tahrir Square Vicinity," June 13, 2012, https://nazra.org/en/2012/06/testimonies-recent-sexual-assaults-tahrir-square-vicinity; "Continued Militarization: Increased Violence Against Women Human Rights Defenders during Dispersal of Cabinet Sit-in; Women Activists Beaten, Brutalized and Subjected to Sexual Violence," December 18, 2011, https://nazra.org/en/2011/12/continued-militarization-increased-violence-against-women-human-rights-defenders; "The Mob-Sexual Assaults and Gang Rapes in Tahrir Square during the Celebrations of the Inauguration of the New Egyptian President Is Sufficient Proof for the Inefficiency of the Recent Legal Amendments to Combat These Crimes," June 9, 2014, https://nazra.org/en/2014/06/mob-sexual-assaults-and-gang-rapes-tahrir-square-during-celebrations-inauguration-new.

18. El-Nadeem, "Live Testimonies on Sexual Torture in Tahrir Square and Surrounding Neighborhoods," Cairo, February 1, 2013.

19. El-Nadeem, "Live Testimonies on Sexual Torture in Tahrir Square and Surrounding Neighborhoods."

20. Paul Amar, *The Security Archipelago: Human-Security States, Sexuality Politics, and the End of Neoliberalism* (Durham, NC: Duke University Press, 2013), 200.

21. Lucia Sorbera, "Challenges of Thinking Feminism and Revolution in Egypt between 2011 and 2014," *Postcolonial Studies* 17, no. 1 (2014): 63–75.

22. Raewyn Connell, *Masculinities,* 2nd ed. (Cambridge: Polity Press, 2005).

23. Baron, *Egypt as a Woman.*

24. Baron, *Egypt as a Woman.*

25. Huda Sha'rawi, *Harem Years: The Memoirs of an Egyptian Feminist (1879–1924),* trans. Margot Badran (London: Virago, 1986).

26. Margot Badran, Cairo, January 15, 2018.

27. Lawyer of Al-Nakib,2011.

28. Hala Shukrallah, "Why Does the Counter-Revolution Target Women and Copts?," Ahram Online, March 9, 2011.

29. Facebook posts, March 9, 2011.

30. Darwish, 2013.

31. Amnesty International, "Egypt Rises," 2011.

32. Darwish, 2011.

33. S. M., young woman activist who wishes to remain anonymous, 2011.

34. Heba Afify, "New Witnesses Testify in Favour of Virginity Test Plaintiff," *Egypt Independent,* February 26, 2012.

35. Nazra for Feminist Studies, "We Pledge to Continue the Pursuit of All Involved in This Crime and Attempted Cover-Up: Military 'Virginity Testing' Verdict: Not the Last Battle," National Council for Human Rights, Egypt, Mar. 12, 2012, https://nazra.org/en/2012/03/military-virginity-testing-verdict-not-last-battle.

36. Aliaa Elmahdy, A Rebel's Diary (blog), http://arebelsdiary.blogspot.com/?zx=3ad57624c5588e68.

37. *Suzee in the City* (blog), "Women in Graffiti: A Tribute to the Women of Egypt," January 7, 2013, https://suzeeinthecity.wordpress.com/2013/01/07/women-in-graffiti-a-tribute-to-the-women-of-egypt/.

38. Darwish, 2013.

39. Heba Afify, "'Virginity Test' Doctor Acquittal Reveals Judiciary Shortcomings," *Egypt Independent,* March 8, 2012.

40. Sherine Hafez, "The Revolution Shall Not Pass through Women's Bodies: Egypt, Uprising and Gender Politics," *Journal of North African Studies* 19, no. 2 (2014): 184.

41. Heba, young woman activist who wishes to remain anonymous, November 30, 2011.

42. Association for Freedom of Thought and Expression, "About Muhammad Mahmud and the Conflict about the Story: The Events of Muhammad Mahmud 19–20 November 2011" (in Arabic), Cairo, 2016; Lucy Ryzova, "The Battle of Muhammad Mahmud Street in Cairo: The Poetics and Politics of Urban Violence in Revolutionary Time" *Past and Present* 247, no. 1 (2020): 237–317.

43. Heba, 2011.

44. Heba, 2011.

45. Personal communication by Claudia Ruta, at that time UN Woman officer in Cairo and the author of "Gender Politics in Transition."

46. Ahdaf Soueif, "Image of Unknown Woman Beaten by Egypt's Military Echoes around world," *Guardian* (US edition), December 18, 2011, and *Cairo: My City, Our Revolution.*

47. Badran, *Feminists, Islam, and Nation,* 77.

48. Graffiti emerged at the beginning of 2011 as the art of the revolution. A number of collections have been dedicated to this phenomenon: Sherif Abdel-Megid, *Ard ard (Surface-to-Surface)* (Cairo: Egyptian Association for Books, 2011), and *al-ḥurriyya la budda Gaat: Ultras Graffiti (Freedom Will Come for Sure: The Ultra's Graffiti)* (Cairo: Nahdetmisr, 2012); Sherif Boraïe, ed., *al-Judran Tahtaf: Graffiti al-Thawra al-Misriya (Wall Talk: Graffiti of the Egyptian Revolution)* (Cairo: Zaituna, 2012); Heba Helmy, *Gowaya Chahid* (Martyr Inside Me) (Cairo: Dar Al-Ain, 2013); Mia Gröndhal, *Revolution Graffiti: Street Art of the New Egypt* (Cairo: American University in Cairo Press, 2013); Elisa Pierandrei, *Urban Cairo: La primavera araba dei graffiti* (Milano: Informant, 2012).

49. Bahia Shehab, "A Thousand Times No," presentation at TEDGlobal 2012, June 2012, www.ted.com/talks/bahia_shehab_a_thousand_times_no?subtitle=en.

50. Sally Toma, November 2, 2014.

51. Toma, 2014.

CHAPTER ELEVEN

1. Criminal Chamber of the Court of Cassation in Ruling No. 289 of April 24, 1950. It was amended with Ruling No. 4794 of February 14, 1985, "to add that the assailant must have had mental intent, meaning that it was not accidental. Law No. 11 of 2011 was later added to increase the penalty against attackers of children under the age of 18, under article 269 of the Criminal Code, to three to fifteen years in prison." Reda Lowla, "15 Egyptian Laws, Rulings that Protect, Support, Empower Women," *Egypt Today,* March 3, 2019.

2. Nadia Sonneveld, "Khul' Divorce in Egypt: How Family Courts Are Providing a 'Dialogue' between Husband and Wife," *Anthropology of the Middle East* 5, no. 2 (2010): 100–120.

3. Law 38 of 1972, amended in June 2009. Previous attempts to guarantee women's representation in the lower house were in 1979, when 30 seats out of 360 had been reserved to women in the lower house, but this provision was canceled in 1986.

4. Magda Adly, "Introduction," in *Live testimonies of Sexual Tortures in Tahrir Square and Surrounding Neighborhoods* (Cairo: El-Nadeem, 2013), 2.

5. Egyptian Initiative for Personal Rights (EIPR), "About Nawal Ali and the Black Wednesday," January 29, 2021.

6. EIPR, "About Nawal Ali and the Black Wednesday." In March 2013, eight years after "Black Wednesday," the African Commission on Human and Peoples' Rights issues its decision to condemn the Egyptian government, demanding it reopen investigations into the incidents of Black Wednesday and to prosecute the

accused, and compensate each of the four complainants (the deceased Nawal, Ebir, Shaima, and Eman) on physical and psychological harm, and the government is obliged to report within 180 days on the implementation of the sentence.

7. Manal Hassan, "Masturbate, Masturbate, Masturbate. Wherever You Go!," Manala (blog), October 5, 2005, accessed November 15, 2020, https://manal218.rssing. com/chan-8637685/latest-article3.php?fbclid=IwAR2arcx-AUMRentYBb2 Y2zFY3IndNaRKN2HVoqBl_YAGy8RViinF4CrSDqM.

8. Amar, *Security Archipelago.*

9. Alaa Abd El-Fattah, "Eid: A Festival of Sexual Harassment," October 27, 2006.

10. Aliyya Shoukry, Rasha Mohammad Hassan, and Nehad Abul Komsan, *"Clouds in Egypt's Sky": Sexual Harassment; From Verbal Harassment to Rape; A Sociological Study* (Cairo: Egyptian Centre for Women's Rights [ECWR], 2008).

11. Quoted in Mariam Kirollos, "Sexual Harassment in Egypt: Myths and Realities," Jadaliyya, July 16, 2013.

12. Hend Kheera, Cairo, December 9, 2011.

13. Kirollos, 2013.

14. Darwish, 2011.

15. Darwish, 2013, for this and the next quote.

16. Darwish, 2013.

17. Yasmin El-Rifae, London, June 28, 2018.

18. Darwish, 2013.

19. Opantish Statement, June 29, 2018, document published in Yasmin El-Rifae, *Radius: A Story of Feminist Revolution,* 34.

20. El-Rifae, 2018.

21. El-Rifae, 2018.

22. Interview with an activist of Basma who wishes to remain anonymous, Cairo, October 2014.

23. Darwish, 2013.

24. Darwish, 2013; El-Rifae, 2018.

25. Darwish, 2013.

26. El-Rifae, 2018.

27. El-Rifae, 2018.

28. Dalia Abdel Hamid, Cairo, October 14, 2014.

29. Nazra for Feminist Studies, "Sexual Violence between the Philosophy of Law and the Problems of Application" (in Arabic), May 30, 2018, https://nazra. org/2018/05/.

30. Elham Eidarous, "From Speaking Out to Equity: Nuisance Is Not Enough" (in Arabic), *Mada Masr,* June 14, 2022.

CHAPTER TWELVE

1. FO 141/511/5.

2. Facebook post, January 25, 2011, viewed January 25, 2019, www.facebook.com/ragia.omran.

3. Shukrallah, 2018.

4. Facebook post, February 10, 2019, viewed February 10, 2019.

5. Hala Shukrallah, Cairo, June 19, 2023

6. Collective Antigone, *Imprisoning a Revolution*, 22.

7. Military courts to prosecute political activists were first established in Egypt by the British in 1919, a practice continued by successive governments till the present day. *Times,* July 19, 1919, Gen. Allenby Clemency, where there is a report about the closure of Military Trials and Decipher from General Allenby (Cairo), July 9, (Protocol: 102067, 14 July 1919), Kew, paper 168 Folder Political, Egypt File 24-930 (PP 91796–122443), 1919–20, 3718.

8. Ahdaf Soueif, "Egypt's Revolution Is Stuck in a Rut, but We Still Have the Spirit to See It Through," *Guardian* (UK edition), July 13, 2011.

9. Basma Abdel Rahman, Cairo, December 3, 2011.

10. Darwish, 2011.

11. Darwish, 2013.

12. Darwish, 2013.

13. Toma, 2014; Sally Toma, "Alice in Trauma-Land," *Mada Masr,* October 31, 2014.

14. Yara Sallam, Cairo, June 5, 2018.

15. Egyptian Initiative for Personal Rights, "Statement on International Women's Day," March 8, 2019.

16. Solafa Magdi, "Women's Prisons in Egypt: Testimonies of Cruelty Behind Concrete," Tahrir Institute for Middle East Policy, November 20, 2023.

17. Abdel Fattah al-Sisi, "Draft Statement: The United Nations Summit for the Adoption of the Post-2015 Development Agenda," New York, September 25, 2015.

18. Yara Sallam, "I Lost Track of Time in Every Sense of the Word: On Coping with Prison and Its Aftermath," *Mada Masr,* October 13, 2019.

19. Yara Sallam, Cairo, June 5, 2018.

20. Yara Sallam, "Jan 25, 5 Years On: On the Revolution that I Missed," *Mada Masr*, January 26, 2016. The next quote is from Sallam, 2018.

21. Selma Botman, "The Experience of Women in the Egyptian Communist Movement, 1939–1954," *Women's Studies International Forum* 11, no. 2 (1988): 117–26. The next few quotes are from Sallam, 2018.

22. For a summary and an analysis of the case, see TIMEP, "Brief: Case 173: Egypt's Foreign Funding Case," February 28, 2019.

23. Mohamed Lotfy, personal communication, Cairo, December 2018.

24. See, for instance, Human Rights Watch, "Egypt: Renewed Crackdown on Independent Groups: Government Investigating Human Rights Workers," June 15, 2015.

25. Sallam, 2018, for this and the next few quotes.

26. Joel Beinin, *The Dispersion of Egyptian Jewry: Culture, Politics, and the Formation of a Modern Diaspora* (Berkeley: University of California Press, 1998), 6.

27. Beinin, *The Dispersion of Egyptian Jewry*, 144.

28. Beinin, *The Dispersion of Egyptian Jewry*, 144.

29. Beinin, *The Dispersion of Egyptian Jewry*, 157.

30. Beinin, *The Dispersion of Egyptian Jewry*, 158.

31. Sallam, 2018. Yara's grandmother is in fact named among the women activists of the Communist Party in the 1940s; see Hanan Ramadan, ed., *Al-Mar'a wa al-Haraka al-Shiu'i al-Masri hatta 1965* (*Women and the Egyptian Communist Movement until 1965*) (Cairo: Dar Al-Mahrusa, 1999), 9. The research, funded by the Arab Research Center for the Study and Documentation of the Arab World and Africa, was a very popular oral history project, and the book had two editions: one, the abovementioned, which I consulted in the WMF library; the other published by the Arab Research Center in 2002.

32. Hani Shukrallah, Cairo, January 4, 2018.

33. Gennaro Gervasio, *Da Nasser a Sadat: Il dissenso laico in Egitto* (Roma: Jouvence, 2007).

34. Botman, "The Experience of Women," 121. The next quote is from Sallam, 2018.

35. I found Davis's books in the library of the feminist collective Ikhtiyar and discussed her work with its members during a research seminar in December 2015. The Egyptian sociologist Sarah Salem, at the forefront of the generation of feminist scholars that suggests decolonial approaches in feminist Middle East Studies, wrote about Davis's reception in Egypt. Sara Salem, "On Transnational Feminist Solidarity: The Case of Angela Davis in Egypt," *Signs: Journal of Women's Studies* 43, no. 2 (2018): 245–67. The next quotes are from Sallam, 2018.

36. Yara Sallam, "How We Got Used to the Screams of Those on Death Row," *Mada Masr*, October 10, 2017.

37. Yara Sallam, "Did You See Aya in Qanater Prison?," *Mada Masr*, February 12, 2016. More of her writings are on her blog: https://talkingpersonal.blogspot.com/?view=timeslide. The next quote is from Sallam, 2018.

38. Kandiyoti, "Fear and Fury: Women and Post-Revolutionary Violence."

CONCLUSION

1. Gameela Ismail, personal communication, June 19, 2024.

2. Lina Attalah, personal communication, June 18, 2024.

3. Mai El-Mahdy, personal communication, June 13, 2024.

4. Lina Attallah, at the conference of the Italian Society for Middle East Studies, Naples, June 2022.

5. Joan Sangster, "Telling Our Stories: Feminist Debates and the Use of Oral History," *Women's History Review* 3, no. 1 (1994): 5–28.

BIBLIOGRAPHY

ARCHIVAL COLLECTIONS

Al-Mar'a al-Gadida (New Woman Foundation), Library, Cairo.

American University in Cairo, Rare Books and Special Collections Library, Huda Sha'rawi's Private Collection.

Archivio Centrale di Stato, Roma, Fondo del Consiglio Nazionale delle Donne Italiane.

Bibliothèque Marguerite Durand, Paris.

Dar al-Hilal, Section Maktaba (Library), Cairo.

Dar al-Kutub, Section Dawriyat, Cairo.

Hoda Sha'rawi Association, Library, Cairo.

Hossam el-Hamalawy photo collection, https://url.au.m.mimecastprotect.com/s/8 4xyC2xMQziKVWVoGCnk9vj?domain=3arabawy.substack.com/.

International Archiev Vrouwenbeweging, Amsterdam.

Library of Congress, Washington DC.

National Archives UK (formerly Public Records Office), Foreign Office and Colonial Office Collections.

National Library, Florence.

Rose al-Youssef Archive, Cairo.

SOAS Digital Collection Middle East Women's Activism, https://digital.soas.ac.uk/mewa.

Women and Memory Forum Library and Oral History Archive.

Women's Library, London School of Economics and Political Sciences, London.

ORAL HISTORY INTERVIEWS

Activist of Basma who wishes to remain anonymous, Cairo, December 5, 2015.

Activist of Bidaya who wishes to remain anonymous, Cairo, October 12, 2014.

Activist of the Egyptian Women's Union who wishes to remain anonymous, Cairo, November 30, 2011.

Activist of the Egyptian Youth Federation who wishes to remain anonymous, Cairo, December 1, 2011.

Activist of the Masr al-Qawiyya (Strong Egypt) Party who wishes to remain anonymous, Cairo, November 7, 2014.

Activist of the Popular Committee to Defend the Revolution who wishes to remain anonymous, Cairo, December 5, 2011.

Activist who wishes to remain anonymous, Cairo, December 3, 2011.

Activists of Ganubiyya Hurra, Aswan, December 14, 2019.

Ahlam Gamal, Cairo, June 24, 2019.

Aida Seif El-Dawla, Cairo, January 4, 2018.

Amal Abdel Hadi, Cairo, January 18, 2018.

Amina Shafik, Cairo, January 29, 2020.

Arab Lutfi, Cairo, January 15, 2018.

Azza Matar, Cairo, June 6, 2018.

Azza Soliman, Cairo, December 9, 2018, and follow-up Facetime call, Sydney-Cairo, June 13, 2020.

Basma Abdel Aziz, Cairo, December 18, 2018.

Basma Abdel Rahman, Cairo, December 3, 2011.

Dalia Abdel Hamid, Cairo, October 14, 2014, and November 25, 2015.

Doaa Adbel Aal, Cairo, December 8, 2011, and October 9, 2014.

Eba'a El-Tamami, Cairo, October 28, 2014.

Elham Eidarous, Cairo, November 2, 2014, and December 14, 2017.

Farida al-Naqqash, Cairo, January 14, 2018, and December 16, 2022.

Fatma Fouad, National Council for Human Rights, Cairo, November 2011.

Fatma Imam, December 4, 2011, and November 11, 2018.

Fatma Ramadan, Cairo, September 23, 2014.

Gameela Ismail, Cairo, January 9, 2018.

Hala Shukrallah, Cairo, January 18, 2018, and June 19, 2023.

Hani Shukrallah, January 4, 2018.

Heba, young woman activist who wishes to remain anonymous, November 30, 2011.

Hend Kheera Cairo, December 9, 2011, and September 24, 2014.

Iman Bibars, Cairo, December 7, 2011.

Laila Soliman, Cairo, October 22, 2014.

Laila Soueif, Cairo, December 3, 2015.

Lawyer of Al-Nakib, Center for Training and Democracy Support who wishes to remain anonymous, Cairo, December 5, 2011.

Lobna Darwish, Cairo, December 6, 2011, and December 3, 2013.

Magda Adly, Cairo, December 4, 2011, and January 16, 2017.

Mahienour El-Massry, Cairo, June 23, 2019.

Manal Hassan, Cairo, January 18, 2018.

Margot Badran, Cairo, January 6, 2017, and January 15, 2018.

Mohammad Fouda (National Community for Human Rights and Law), Cairo, September 24, 2014.

Mohammed Metwally, Cairo, December 7, 2011.

Mozn Hassan, Cairo, December 15, 2017.

Mozn Hassan, Ayat Osman, Tasnim Haggag, and Shaima Tantawi (Nazra for Feminist Studies), Cairo, December 19, 2018.

Nada Salah (member of Masr al-Qawiya party), Cairo, November 7, 2014.

Nagwa Abbas, Cairo, June 6, 2018.

Nawal al-Saadawi, Cairo, October 10, 2014.

Nawla Darwiche, Cairo, January 7, 2018, and June 19, 2023.

Nayera Magdy, Cairo, December 5, 2011, and October 9, 2014.

Omar Ahmed, December 6, 2011.

Ragia Omran, Cairo, January 15, 2018.

Rasha Elgebali, Cairo, November 7, 2014.

Rawia Sadek, Cairo, December 15, 2018.

Safinaz Kazem, Cairo, January 18, 2020.

Sally Toma, Cairo, November 2, 2014.

Samia and Lamia Lutfi (NWF), Cairo, December 7, 2011.

Seham Saneya Abd el-Salam, Cairo, December 15, 2022.

Shereen Abouelnaga, Sydney, August 26, 2019.

Soraya (Suzee) Morayef, Cairo, November 29, 2011.

S. M., young woman activist who wishes to remain anonymous, 2011.

Suzan Fayad, Cairo, June 23, 2019.

Wael Iskandar, Cairo, October 15, 2014.

Yara Sallam, Cairo, June 5, 2018.

Yasmin El-Rifae, London, June 28, 2018.

Zinat Al-Askary, Cairo, December 28, 2022.

REFERENCES

Abd El-Salam, Siham. "A Comprehensive Approach for Communication about Female Genital Mutilation in Egypt." In *Female and Male Circumcisions: Medical, Legal, and Ethical Considerations in Pediatric Practice,* edited by George C. Denniston, Frederick M. Hodges, and Marilyn F. Milos. New York: Kluwer Academic and Plenum, 1999.

———. *Female Genital Mutilation: Violation of Human Rights.* Cairo: Cairo Institute for Human Rights Studies, 1995.

———. "Female Sexuality and the Discourse of Power: The Case of Egypt." MA thesis, American University in Cairo, 1998.

———. "Genital Mutilations. History, and Suggestions for Change." Paper presented at the International Meeting on Preventing and Eliminating Female Genital Mutilation, Swedish Parliament, Foreign Ministry, Ministry of Health and Social Affairs, Stockholm, 2003.

Abdel Fadil, Mahmoud. *The Political Economy of Nasserism*. Cambridge: Cambridge University Press, 1980.

Abdelfattah, Alaa. "Alf Tahia al-'Ummal." June 21, 2007. Accessed January 4, 2022. https://web.archive.org/web/20090111224740/http://www.manalaa.net/node/87303.

———. "Eid: A Festival of Sexual Harassment." October 27, 2006. https://web.archive.org/web/20090218231309/http://manalaa.net/taxonomy/term/1134.

Abdel Hadi, Amal. "A Community of Women Empowered: The Story of Deir El Barsha." In Female Circumcision: Multicultural Perspectives, edited by Rogaia M. Abusharaf. Philadelphia: University of Pennsylvania Press, 2006.

———. "Islam, Law, and Reproductive Health in Egypt." In Islam, Reproductive Health, and Women's Rights. Kuala Lumpur: Sisters in Islam, 2000.

Abdel-Megid, Sherif. *al-ḥurriyya la budda Gaat: Ultras Graffiti (Freedom Will Come for Sure: The Ultra's Graffiti)*. Cairo: Nahdetmisr, 2012.

———. *Ard ard (Surface-to-Surface)*. Cairo: Egyptian Association for Books, 2011.

Abdelrahman, Maha. "The Nationalisation of the Human Rights Debate in Egypt." *Nations and Nationalism* 13, no. 2 (2007).

Abdel Wahab Afifi, Nadia, and Amal Abdel Hadi, eds. *The Feminist Movement in the Arab World: Interventions and Studies from Four Countries; Egypt, Palestine, Sudan, Tunisia*. Cairo: Dal El-Mostaqbal al Arabi, 1996.

Abouelnaga, Shereen. *Women in Revolutionary Egypt: Gender and the New Geographics of Identity*. Cairo: American University in Cairo Press, 2019.

Abu-Bakr, Omaima. "Articulating Gender: Muslim Women Intellectuals in the Pre-Modern Period." *Arab Studies Quarterly* 32, no. 3 (2010).

———. "Rings of Memory: 'Writing Muslim Women' and the Question of Authorial Voice." *The Muslim World* 103, no. 3 (2013).

———. "Teaching the Words of the Prophet: Women Instructors of the Hadith (Fourteenth and Fifteenth Centuries)." *Hawwa* 1, no. 3 (2003).

———. *Writing Women's Worlds: Bedouin Stories*. Berkeley: University of California Press, 2008.

Abu-Lughod, Lila. "Against Universals: Dialects of (Women's) Human Rights and Human Capabilities." In *Rethinking the Human,* edited by J. Michelle Molina and Donald K. Swearer. Cambridge, MA: Harvard University Press, 2010.

———. "Dialects of Women's Empowerment: The International Circuitry of the Arab Human Development Report." *International Journal of Middle East Studies* 41, no. 1 (2009): 83–103.

———. *Do Muslim Women Need Saving?* Cambridge, MA: Harvard University Press, 2013.

———, ed. *Remaking Women: Feminism and Modernity in the Middle East*. Princeton Studies in Culture/Power/History. Princeton, NJ: Princeton University Press, 1998.

Abu-Lughod, Lila, Fida J. Adeli, and Frances Hasso. "Overview: Engaging the Arab Human Development Report 2005 on Women." *International Journal of Middle East Women Studies* 41, no. 1 (2009): 59–60.

Abu-Lughod, Lila, and Rabab El Mahdi. "Beyond the 'Woman Question' in the Egyptian Revolution." *Feminist Studies* 37, no. 3 (2011): 683–91.

Acioly, Claudio C. "Can Urban Management Deliver the Sustainable City? Guided Densification in Brazil versus Informal Compactness in Cairo." In *Compact Cities: Sustainable Urban Forms for Developing Countries,* edited by Rod Burgess and Mike Jenks. London: Routledge, 2002.

Adly, Magda. "Introduction." In *Live Testimonies of Sexual Tortures in Tahrir Square and Surrounding Neighborhoods.* Cairo: El-Nadeem, 2013.

Afify, Heba. "New Witnesses Testify in Favor of Virginity Test Plaintiff." *Egypt Independent,* February 26, 2012. https://egyptindependent.com/new-witnesses-testify-favor-virginity-test-plaintiff/.

———. "'Virginity Test' Doctor Acquittal Reveals Judiciary Shortcomings." *Egypt Independent,* March 8, 2012.

Ahmed, Leila. *A Quiet Revolution: The Veil's Resurgence, from the Middle East to America.* New Haven, CT: Yale University Press, 2011.

———. *Women and Gender in Islam: Historical Roots of a Modern Debate.* New Haven, CT: Yale University Press, 1992.

Ahmed, Sara. *Living a Feminist Life.* Durham, NC: Duke University Press, 2017.

Al-Ali, Nadje Sadig. *Iraqi Women: Untold Stories from 1948 to the Present.* London: Zed Books, 2007.

———. *Secularism, Gender and the State in the Middle East: The Egyptian Women's Movement.* Cambridge: Cambridge University Press, 2000.

Al-Ali, Nadje, and Nicola Pratt. *What Kind of Liberation? Women and the Occupation of Iraq.* Berkeley: University of California Press, 2009.

Al-Anani, Khalil. "Egyptian National Dialogue: A Lost Opportunity for National Salvage." Arab Center Washington DC, July 7, 2023.

Alcoff, Linda Martín. "An Epistemology for the Next Revolution." *Transmodernity* 1, no. 2 (2011).

———. "Experience and Knowledge: The Case of Sexual Abuse Memoires." In *Feminist Metaphysics: Explorations in the Ontology of Sex, Gender and Identity,* edited by Charlotte Witt. New York: Springer, 2011.

———. "Philosophy Matters: A Review of Recent Work in Feminist Philosophy." *Signs: Journal of Women in Culture and Society* 25, no. 3 (2000): 841–82.

Ali, Zahra. *Women and Gender in Iraq: Between Nation-Building and Fragmentation.* Cambridge: Cambridge University Press, 2018.

Allam, Nermin. *Women and the Egyptian Revolution: Engagement and Activism during the 2011 Arab Uprisings.* Cambridge: Cambridge University Press, 2018.

Al-Mahdi, Rabab. "Enough! Egypt's Quest for Democracy." *Comparative Political Studies* 42, no. 8 (August 2009): 1001–39.

Al-Mar'a Al-'Arabiya wa Qadaya al-Falastin (The Arab Woman and the Palestinian Issue). Proceedings of the Eastern Women's Conference in Defence of Palestine, Cairo, October 15–18, 1938. With an introduction by Sania Sharawi and a foreword by Sherine Elbanhawy. Hildenborough, UK: Rowayat, 2024.

Al-Masri, Sana'. *Khalfa al-Hijab: Mawaqif al-jama'at al-Iislamiyya min Qadiyyat al-Mar'a*. Cairo: Sina lil-Nasht, 1987.

Al-Naqqash, Farida. *Al-Sijn Wa al-Watan*. Cairo: Dal al-Kalima Lilnashr, 1982.

———. "Barred from Writing in Egypt." Translated by Marilyn Booth. *Index on Censorship* 12, no. 3 (1983): 20–22.

Al-Saadawi, Nawal. *Al-Mar'a wa al-Jins*. Beirut: Al-Nashirun al-'Arab, 1972.

———. "Egyptian Feminist Nawal El Saadawi in Cairo's Tahrir Square: The City in the Field." *Ms. Magazine,* February 7, 2011,

———. *The Hidden Face of Eve: Women in the Arab World*. London: Zed Books, 1980. Original Arabic, *al-Wajha al-'Ari lil-Mar'a al-'arabīyya*, 1977.

———. "How to Fight against the Postmodern Slave System." Atlanta, Georgia, September 11, 2008. In *The Essential Nawal El Saadawi: A Reader,* edited by Adele Newson-Horst, 10–17. London: Zed Books, 2010.

———. "Women and the Poor: The Challenge of Global Justice." Keynote address to the Global '94 Congress, Tampere, Finland, July 3–7, 1994. In *The Essential Nawal El Saadawi: A Reader,* edited by Adele Newson-Horst, 78–89. London: Zed Books, 2010.

Al-Sayyid, Mustapha Kamal. "State, Society and Violations of Human Rights in Egypt." *Cairo Papers in Social Sciences* 17, no. 3 (1994).

Al-Zayyat, Latifa. "Al-Katib Wa-l-Hurriya." *Al-Fusul* 11, no. 3 (n.d.).

Amar, Paul. *The Security Archipelago: Human-Security States, Sexuality Politics, and the End of Neoliberalism*. Durham, NC: Duke University Press, 2013.

Amin, Galal. *Whatever Happened to the Egyptians? Changes in Egyptian Society from 1950 to Present*. Cairo: American University in Cairo Press, 2000.

Amnesty International. "Egypt Rises: Killings, Detentions and Torture in the '25 January Revolution." May 19, 2011. www.amnesty.org/en/documents/mde12/027/2011/en/.

Anzaldúa, Gloria. *Borderlands/La Frontera: The New Mestiza*. 3rd ed. San Francisco: Aunt Lute Books, 2007.

Assaad, Marie Bassili. "Female Circumcision in Egypt: Social Implications, Current Research, and Prospects for Change." *Studies in Family Planning* 11, no. 1 (January 1980): 3–16.

Association for Freedom of Thought and Expression. *'An Mumammad Mahmoud wa al-sir'a hawla al-hikaya (About Muhammad Mahmud and the Conflict about the Story: The Events of Muhammad Mahmud) 19–20 November 2011*. Cairo, 2016.

Attalah, Lina. "Human Rights in Focus." *Mada Masr,* April 16, 2015.

———. "On a Belated Encounter with Gender." In *Our Women on the Ground: Essays by Arab Women Reporting from the Arab World,* 45–56. New York: Penguin Books, 2019.

Badran, Hoda. *The Road to Beijing: Egyptian Women's Journey*. Cairo: UNDP Cairo and Al-Harara Publishing, 1997.

Badran, Margot. "Body Politic(s): Women, Power, and Sexuality in Egypt." In *Feminism and Islam: Secular and Religious Convergences*. London: Oneworld, 2009.

———. "Competing Agendas: Feminists, Islam, and the State in 19th and 20th Century Egypt." In *Women, Islam and the State,* edited by Deniz Kandiyioti. London: Macmillan, 1991.

———. "Dis/Playing Power and the Politics of Patriarchy in Revolutionary Egypt: The Creative Activism of Huda Lutfi." *Postcolonial Studies* 17, no. 1 (2014): 47–62.

———. "Egypt's Revolution and the New Feminism." The Immanent Frame (blog), March 3, 2011.

———. "Egypt's Revolution and the New Feminism." Reset (blog), March 7, 2011. www.resetdoc.org/story/egypts-revolution-and-the-new-feminism/.

———. "Expressing Feminism and Nationalism in Autobiography: The Memoirs of an Egyptian Educator." In *De/Colonizing the Subject: The Politics of Gender in Women's Autobiography,* edited by Sidonie Smith and Julia Watson. Minneapolis: University of Minnesota Press, 1992.

———. *Feminism beyond East and West: New Gender Talk and Practice in Global Islam.* New Delhi: Global Media Publications, 2007.

———. *Feminists, Islam, and Nation: Gender and the Making of Modern Egypt.* Princeton, NJ: Princeton University Press, 1995.

———. "Foreign Bodies: Engendering Them and Us." In *The Concept of the Foreign: An Interdisciplinary Dialogue,* edited by Rebecca Saunders. New York: Lexington Books. 2003.

———. "Gender Activism: Feminists and Islamists in Egypt." In *Identity Politics and Women: Cultural Reassertions and Feminisms in International Perspective,* edited by Valentine M. Moghadam. London: Routledge, 1994.

———. "Huda Sha'rawi and the Liberation of the Egyptian Woman." PhD thesis, Oxford University, 1977.

———. "Independent Women: More than a Century of Feminism in Egypt." In *Arab Women: Old Boundaries, New Frontiers,* edited by Judith Tucker. Bloomington: Indiana University Press, 1993.

———. "The Institutionalization of Middle East Women's Studies in the United States." *Middle East Studies Association Bulletin* 22, no. 1 (1988): 9–18.

———, ed. "Islamic Feminism." *Samyukta: A Journal of Gender and Culture* 2, no. 1 (2017).

———. "Keeping FGM on the Run? Between Resolution and Constitution." Ahram Online, January 10, 2013.

———. "Theorizing Oral History as Autobiography: A Look at the Narrative of a Woman Revolutionary in Egypt." *Journal of Women's History* 25, no. 2 (2013): 161–70.

———. "Towards Islamic Feminisms." In *Hermeneutics and Honor in Islamic/ate Societies.* Harvard Middle East Monograph Series, edited by Asma Afsarrudin. Cambridge, MA: Harvard University Press, 1999.

Badran Margot, and miriam cooke, eds. *Opening the Gates: A Century of Arab Feminist Writing.* Bloomington: Indiana University Press, 1990.

Baron, Beth. *Egypt as a Woman: Nationalism, Gender, and Politics.* Berkeley: University of California Press, 2005.

———. *The Women's Awakening in Egypt: Culture, Society, and the Press.* New Haven, CT: Yale University Press, 1994.

Bayat, Asef. *Life as Politics.* Stanford, CA: Stanford University Press, 2013.

———. *Revolution without Revolutionaries: Making Sense of the Arab Spring.* Stanford, CA: Stanford University Press, 2020.

Bayoumi, Soha, and Sherine Hamdy. "Nationalism, Authoritarianism, and Medical Mobilization in Post-Revolutionary Egypt." *Culture, Medicine, and Psychiatry* 47, no. 1 (2023): 37–61.

Beinin, Joel. *The Dispersion of Egyptian Jewry: Culture, Politics, and the Formation of a Modern Diaspora.* Berkeley: University of California Press, 1998.

———. "Workers and Egypt's January 25 Revolution." *International Labor and Working-Class History* 80, no. 1 (2011): 189–96.

———. *Workers and Peasants in the Modern Middle East.* The Contemporary Middle East 2. Cambridge: Cambridge University Press, 2001.

———. "Workers' Protest in Egypt: Neo-Liberalism and Class Struggle in 21st Century." *Social Movement Studies* 8, no. 4 (2009): 449–54.

Biancani, Francesca. *Sex Work in Colonial Egypt: Women, Modernity and the Global Economy.* London: I. B. Tauris, 2021.

Bier, Laura. *Revolutionary Womanhood: Feminisms, Modernity, and the State in Nasser's Egypt.* Stanford, CA: Stanford University Press, 2011.

Booth, Marilyn. "Before Qasim Amin: Writing Women's History in 1890s Egypt." In *The Long 1890s in Egypt: Colonial Quiescence, Subterranean Resistance,* edited by Marilyn Booth and Anthony Gorman, 365–98. Edinburgh: Edinburgh University Press, 2014.

———. *May Her Likes Be Multiplied: Biography and Gender Politics in Egypt.* Berkeley: University of California Press, 2001.

———. "Women's Prison Memoirs in Egypt and Elsewhere: Prison, Gender, Praxis." *Middle East Report,* no. 149 (1987): 35–41.

———. "Zaynab Fawaz Al-'Amili." In *Essays in Arabic Literary Biography, 1850–1950,* edited by Roger Allen, 93–97. Wiesbaden: Harrassowitz Verlag, 2010.

Boraïe, Sherif, ed. *al-Judran Tahtaf: Graffiti al-Thawra al-Misriya (Wall Talk: Graffiti of the Egyptian Revolution).* Cairo: Zaituna, 2012.

Botman, Selma. "The Experience of Women in the Egyptian Communist Movement, 1939–1954." *Women's Studies International Forum* 11, no. 2 (1988): 117–26.

Boyle, Kevin, and Adel Omar Sherif, eds. *Human Rights and Democracy: The Role of the Supreme Constitutional Court of Egypt.* London: Kluver, 1996.

Bruzzi, Silvia, and Lucia Sorbera. "Pour une histoire à part égale des femmes et du genre dans les sociétés musulmanes." *Genre & Histoire* 25 (2020).

Caine, Barbara. *Biography and History.* 2nd ed. London: Red Globe Press, 2019.

The Care Collective. *The Care Manifesto: The Politics of Interdependence.* London: Verso Books, 2020.

Carlson, Bronwyn, Madi Day, Sandy O'Sullivan, and Tristan Kennedy, eds. *The Routledge Handbook of Australian Indigenous Peoples and Futures.* London: Routledge, 2023.

Carnegie Endowment for International Peace. "A Backgrounder on the Socialist Popular Alliance Party." October 19, 2011.

Cole, Juan Ricardo. *Colonialism and Revolution in the Middle East: Social and Cultural Origins of Egypt's Urabi Movement*. Princeton, NJ: Princeton University Press, 1993.

Collective Antigone. *Imprisoning and Revolution: Writings from Egypt's Incarcerated*. Oakland: University of California Press, 2025.

Comaroff, Jean, and John L. Comaroff. *Theory from the South: Or, How Euro-America Is Evolving toward Africa*. London: Routledge, 2012.

Connell, Raewyn. *Masculinities*. 2nd ed. Cambridge: Polity Press, 2005.

———. *Southern Theory: The Global Dynamics of Knowledge in the Social Sciences*. Crows Nest, NSW: Allen & Unwin, 2007.

cooke, miriam. "Introduction." *Journal of Middle East Women's Studies* 18, no. 1 (March 2022): 147–49.

———. *Nazira Zeineddine: A Pioneer of Islamic Feminism*. Oxford: Oneworld, 2010.

———. "Telling Their Lives. A Hundred Years of Arab Women's Writings." *World Literature Today* 60, no. 2 (1986): 212–16.

———. *War's Other Voices: Women Writers on the Lebanese Civil War*. London: Cambridge University Press, 1988.

———. *Women and the War Story*. Berkeley: University of California Press, 1997.

———. *Women Claim Islam: Creating Islamic Feminism through Literature*. Florence: Routledge, 2001.

Cowman, Krista. "Collective Biography." In *Research Methods for History,* edited by Lucy Faire and Simon Gunn, 85–103. Edinburgh: Edinburgh University Press, 2022.

Crenshaw, Kimberle. "Mapping the Margins: Intersectionality, Identity Politics, and Violence against Women of Color." *Stanford Law Review* 43, no. 6 (1991): 1241–99.

Daly, M. W., ed. *The Cambridge History of Egypt*. Vol. 2, *Modern Egypt, from 1517 to the End of the Twentieth Century*. Cambridge: Cambridge University Press, 1998.

Davis, Angela Y. *Women, Race and Class*. New York: Vintage Books, 1983.

de Lauretis, Teresa. *Figures of Resistance: Essays in Feminist Theory*. Urbana: University of Illinois Press, 2007.

Dellenborg, Lisen, and Maria F. Malmström. "Listening to the Real Agents of Change: Female Circumcision/Cutting, Female Genital Mutilations and Human Rights." In *Female Genital Cutting: Global North and South,* edited by Sara Johnsdotter. Malmö: Center for Sexology and Sexuality Studies, Malmö University, 2020.

Democracy Now! "Leading Egyptian Feminist, Nawal El Saadawi: 'Women and Girls Are Beside Boys in the Streets.'" January 31, 2011. www.democracynow.org /2011/1/31/women_protest_alongside_men_in_egyptian.

Derrida, Jacques. *Specters of Marx: The State of the Debt, the Work of Mourning and the New International*. Routledge Classics. London: Routledge, 2006.

Djebar, Assia. *L'amour, la fantasia: Roman.* Paris: J.-C. Lattès/Enal, 1985.

———, dir. *La nouba des femmes du Mont-Chenoua.* New York: Women Make Movies, 1977.

Dunne, Michele, and Amr Hamzawy. *Egypt's Secular Political Parties: A Struggle for Identity and Independence.* Washington, DC: Carnegie Endowment for International Peace, 2017.

Du Roy, Gaétan. *Les zabbālīn du Muqattam: Ethnohistoire d'une hétérotopie au Caire (979–2021).* Leiden: Brill, 2022.

Egyptian Center for Women's Rights. "ECWR Rejects the Draft Personal Status Law." February 24, 2021. http://ecwronline.org/?p=8470.

Egyptian Centre for Women's Legal Rights (CEWLA). *Honour Crimes: An Analytical Perspective.* Cairo: CEWLA, 2002.

Egyptian Initiative for Personal Rights (EIPR). "About Nawal Ali and the Black Friday." January 29, 2021. www.facebook.com/EIPR.org.

———. Statement on International Women's Day. Press release, March 8, 2019. https://eipr.org/en/press/2019/03/international-womens-day-periods-prison.

Egyptian Organization for Human Rights. *The Situation of Human Rights in Egypt: Annual Report, 2004* (in Arabic). Cairo, 2004.

Egyptian Streets. "Egypt Introduces 20 Years Imprisonment for Female Genital Mutilation." January 21, 2021.

Eidarous, Elham. "From Speaking Out to Equity: Nuisance Is Not Enough" (in Arabic). *Mada Masr,* June 14, 2022.

El Agati, Mohamed, ed. *Youths and Radical Groups from the Perspectives of Youth.* Cairo: Arab Forum for Alternatives and Rosa Luxemburg Foundation, 2015.

El-Dawla, Aida Seif. "The Political and Legal Struggle over Female Genital Mutilation in Egypt: Five Years Since the ICPD." Special issue, *Reproductive Health Matters* 7, no. 13 (May 1999): 128–36.

———. "Reproductive Rights of Egyptian Women: Issues for Debate." *Reproductive Health Matters* 8, no. 16 (2000): 51.

El-Dawla, Aida Seif, Amal Abdel Hadi, and Nadia Abd El Wahab. "Women's Wit over Men's: Tradeoffs and Strategic Accommodations in Egyptian Women's Reproductive Lives." In *Negotiating Reproductive Rights: Women's Perspectives across Countries and Cultures,* edited by Rosalind P. Petchesky and Karen Judd. London: Zed Books, 1998.

El Guindi, Fadwa. *Veil: Modesty, Privacy and Resistance.* Oxford: Berg, 1999.

El Guindi, Nadia. "'Had This Been Your Face, Would You Leave It as Is?' Female Circumcision among the Nubians of Egypt." In *Female Circumcision: Multicultural Perspectives,* edited by Rogaia Mustafa Abusharaf. Philadelphia: University of Pennsylvania Press, 2006.

El-Hamalawy, Hossam. "Comrades and Brothers." *Middle East Report,* no. 242 (Spring 2007).

El Hamamsy, Walid, and Mounira Soliman. *Popular Culture in the Middle East and North Africa: A Postcolonial Outlook.* London: Routledge, 2013.

El-Massry, Mahienour. "Discourse of Acceptance of the Ludovic Trarieux Award." October 31, 2014. www.youtube.com/watch?v=Z-uuBoiGdWM.

———. "On the Anniversary of the Assassination of Shaima al-Sabbagh." Letter from Qanateer Prison, January 24, 2016. In *Collective Antigone, Imprisoning a Revolution: Writings from Egypt's Incarcerated,* 224–26. Oakland: University of California Press, 2025.

———. "Prison Is a Microcosm of Society." Translated by Radwa al-Barouni in *Mada Masr,* June 7, 2014. Reprinted in *Collective Antigone, Imprisoning a Revolution: Writings from Egypt's Incarcerated,* 219–22. Oakland: University of California Press, 2025.

El-Nadeem. "Live Testimonies on Sexual Torture in Tahrir Square and Surrounding Neighborhoods." February 1, 2013. https://elnadeem.org/2013/02/01/70/?lang=en.

———. "Our Reply to the MOH Allegations Regarding Closure of El Nadim." Press release, February 25, 2016. El-Nadeem archive. Accessed January 3, 2019.

El Nossery, Névine. *Arab Women's Revolutionary Art between Singularities and Multitudes.* Cham: Springer International, 2023.

El-Rifae, Yasmin. "The Most Eloquent Speaker at the Climate Summit Is Alaa Abd El Fattah." *New York Times,* November 12, 2022. www.nytimes.com/2022/11/12/opinion/alaa-hunger-strike-egypt-cop.html.

———. *Radius: A Story of Feminist Revolution.* London: Verso Books, 2022.

Elsadda, Hoda. "Challenges, Opportunities, and Methodological Issues in the Creation of Oral History Archives in the Arab World." *Cairo Papers in Social Sciences* 35, no. 1 (2018).

———. "Egypt." In *Arab Women Writers: A Critical Reference Guide, 1873–1999,* edited by Radwa Ashour, Ferial J. Ghazoul, and Hasna Reda-Mekdashi, 98–161. Cairo: American University in Cairo Press, 2008.

———. "Gendered Citizenship: Discourses on Domesticity in the Second Half of the Nineteenth Century." *Hawwa* 4, no. 1 (2006): 1–28.

———. *Gender Studies in the Arab World: An NGO Phenomenon.* World Humanities Report, Consortium of Humanities Centers and Institutes, 2023.

———. "Women and Justice in the Egyptian Constitution: A Reading from Within." *Al-Raida,* no. 143–44 (Fall/Winter 2014): 18–26.

———. "Women and Memory" (interview, in Arabic). *Alif: The Journal of Comparative Poetics* 19 (1999): 210–30.

Elsaman, Radwa. "Egypt: Making Exceptions Doesn't End Discrimination against Women Judges." Enheduanna, a Blog of the Middle East Women's Initiative, May 2, 2021. www.wilsoncenter.org/blog-post/egypt-making-exceptions-doesnt-end-discrimination-against-women-judges.

El-Sisi, Abdel Fattah. "Draft Statement: The United Nations Summit for the Adoption of the Post-2015 Development Agenda." September 25, 2015. Accessed June 20, 2024. https://sustainabledevelopment.un.org/content/documents/20253egypt.pdf.

Eltahawy, Mona. "Why Do They Hate Us?" *Foreign Policy,* April 23, 2012.

El-Zanaty and Associates (Egypt), Ministry of Health and Population (Egypt), and ICF International. *Egypt Health Survey 2015.* Cairo and Rockville, MD, 2015.

Fahmi, Khaled. *All the Pasha's Men: Mehmed Ali, His Army, and the Making of Modern Egypt.* Cambridge: Cambridge University Press, 1997.

———. *Mehmed Ali: From Ottoman Governor to Ruler of Egypt.* Oxford: Oneworld, 2009.

———. "Women, Medicine, and Power in Nineteenth Century Egypt." In *Remaking Women: Feminism and Modernity in the Middle East,* edited by Lila Abu-Lughod. Princeton Studies in Culture/Power/History. Princeton, NJ: Princeton University Press, 1998.

Fawzi, Essam. "Personal Status Law in Egypt. An Historical Overview." In *Women's Rights and Islamic Family Law: Perspectives on Reform,* edited by Lynn Welchman. London Zed Books 2004.

Fenoglio-Abd El Aal, Irene. *Défense et illustration de l'Égyptienne: Aux débuts d'une expression féminine.* Cairo: Center for Economic, Legal, and Social Studies and Documentation, 1988.

Fraisse, Geneviève. *La fabrique du féminisme: Textes et entretiens.* Paris: Éditions le passager clandestine, 2012.

Frontline Defenders. "Timeline about Esra Abdel Fattah's Case." www .frontlinedefenders.org/en/profile/esraa-abdel-fattah. Accessed June 2, 2024.

Geer, Benjamin. "Autonomy and Symbolic Capital in an Academic Social Movement: The March 9 Group in Egypt." *European Journal of Turkish Studies* 17 (2013). https://doi.org/10.4000/ejts.4780.

Gervasio, Gennaro. *Da Nasser a Sadat: Il dissenso laico in Egitto.* Roma: Jouvence, 2007.

Ghazoul, Ferial. "Editorial" (in Arabic). *Alif: The Journal of Comparative Poetics* 19 (1999): 210–30.

Ghiglia, Marianna. "Journalistes en quête d'eux-mêmes: Une socio-histoire des professionnels de l'information en Égypte (1941–nos jours)." Doctoral thesis, Aix-Marseille University, 2020.

Ginat, Rami. "The Egyptian Left and the Roots of Neutralism in the Pre-Nasserite Era." *British Journal of Middle Eastern Studies* 30, no. 1 (2003): 5–24.

Grewal, Inderpal. *Transnational America: Feminisms, Diasporas, Neoliberalisms.* Durham, NC: Duke University Press, 2005.

Gröndhal, Mia. *Revolution Graffiti: Street Art of the New Egypt.* Cairo: American University in Cairo Press, 2013.

Hafez, Sherine. "The Revolution Shall Not Pass through Women's Bodies: Egypt, Uprising and Gender Politics." *Journal of North African Studies* 19, no. 2 (2014): 172–85.

———. *Women of the Midan: The Untold Stories of Egypt's Revolutionaries.* Bloomington: Indiana University Press, 2019.

Hamdy, Sherine. *Our Bodies Belong to God: Organ Transplants, Islam, and the Struggle for Human Dignity in Egypt.* Berkeley: University of California Press, 2012.

Hammad, Hanan. "Arwa Salih's 'The Premature': Gendering the History of the Egyptian Left." *Arab Studies Journal* 24, no. 1 (2016): 118–42.

———. *Industrial Sexuality: Gender, Urbanization, and Social Transformation in Egypt*. Austin: University of Texas Press, 2016.

———. "The Other Extremists: Marxist Feminism in Egypt, 1980–2000." *Journal of International Women's Studies* 12, no. 3 (2011): 217–33.

Hamzeh, Manal. "The Enduring Alliance of Nationalism and Patriarchy in Muslim Personal Status Laws: The Case of Modern Egypt." *Feminist Issues* 6, no.1 (1986): 19–43.

———. *Women Resisting Sexual Violence and the Egyptian Revolution: Arab Feminist Testimonies*. London: Zed Books, 2021.

Harman, Chris. *The Prophet and the Proletariat*. London. Socialist Workers Party, 1998.

Hassan, Manal. "Masturbate, Masturbate, Masturbate. Wherever You Go!." Manala (blog). October 5, 2005. Accessed November 15, 2020. https://manal218.rssing.com/chan-8637685/latest-article3.php?fbclid=IwAR2arcx-AUMRentYBb2YzzFY3IndNaRKN2HVoqBl_YAGy8RViinF4CrSDqM.

Hasso, Frances, "Beyond the Treatment Room: The Psyche-Body-Society Care Politics of Cairo's El-Nadeem." *Signs: Journal of Women in Culture and Society* 49, no. 1 (Autumn 2023): 1–29.

———. "Empowering Governmentalities Rather than Women: The Arab Human Development Report 2005 and Western Development Logics." *International Journal of Middle East Women Studies* 41, no. 1 (2009): 63–82.

Hatem, Mervat Fayez. "Economic and Political Liberation in Egypt and the Demise of State Feminism." *International Journal of Middle East Studies* 24, no. 2 (1992): 231–51.

———. *Literature, Gender, and Nation-Building in Nineteenth Century Egypt: The Life and Works of 'Aisha Taymur*. New York: Palgrave Macmillan, 2011.

Hegazi, Sarah. "A Year after the Rainbow Flag Controversy." *Mada Masr*, June 15, 2020.

Heller, Agnes. "Hannah Arendt on Tradition and New Beginnings." In *Hannah Arendt in Jerusalem*, edited by Steven E. Aschheim. Berkeley: University of California Press, 2001.

Helmy, Heba. *Gowaya Chahid* (*Martyr Inside Me*). Cairo: Dar Al-Ain, 2013.

Heshmat, Dina. "A Journey in the Archives in the Footsteps of Fikriyya Husni" (in Arabic). In *Gendering the Arab Archive* (in Arabic), edited by Laila Dakhli, Hoda Elsadda, Zahra Ali, Lamia Moghnieh, Hana Soliman, and Reem Joudi. Beirut: Arab Council for the Social Sciences, 2024.

———. *Egypt 1919: The Revolution in Literature and Film*. Edinburgh: Edinburgh University Press, 2020.

Hicks, Neil. "Transnational Human Rights Networks and Human Rights in Egypt." In *Human Rights in the Arab World: Independent Voices*, edited by Anthony Tirado Chase and Amr Hamzawy. Philadelphia: University of Pennsylvania Press, 2006.

hooks, bell. *Ain't I a Woman: Black Women and Feminism.* London: Pluto Press, 1987.

Hoyle, Mark S. W. "The Mixed Courts of Egypt, 1875–1885." *Arab Law Quarterly* 1, no. 4 (August 1986).

Human Rights Watch. "Egypt: Margins of Repression; State Limits on Nongovernmental Organization Activism," July 3, 2005. www.hrw.org/report/2005/07/03/egypt-margins-repression/state-limits-nongovernmental-organization-activism.

———. "Egypt: Renewed Crackdown on Independent Groups; Government Investigating Human Rights Workers." June 15, 2015. www.hrw.org/news/2015/06/15/egypt-renewed-crackdown-independent-groups.

Jad, Islah. *Palestinian Women's Activism: Nationalism, Secularism, Islamism.* Syracuse, NY: Syracuse University Press, 2018.

Jakes, Aaron G. *Egypt's Occupation: Colonial Economism and the Crises of Capitalism.* Stanford, CA: Stanford University Press, 2020.

Jan Michiel Otto, ed. *Sharia and National Law: Comparing the Legal Systems of Twelve Islamic Countries.* Cairo: American University in Cairo Press, 2010.

Jayawardena, Kumari. *Feminism and Nationalism in the Third World.* London: Zed Books, 1986. ACLS Humanities Ebook Collection.

Kamel, Nadia. *Al-Mawluda.* Cairo: Karma Publishing, 2018.

———, dir. *Salata baladi = Salade maison.* New York: Women Make Movies, 2007.

Kandiyoti, Deniz. "Disquiet and Despair: The Gender Sub-Texts of the Arab Spring." Open Democracy, June 26, 2012. www.opendemocracy.net/search/?query=Deniz+Kandiyoti. Accessed January 2, 2020.

———. "Promise and Peril: Women and the Arab Spring." Open Democracy, March 8, 2011. www.opendemocracy.net/en/5050/promise-and-peril-women-and-arab-spring/. Accessed January 2, 2020.

———. *Women, Islam, and the State.* Philadelphia: Temple University Press, 1991.

Kandiyoti, Deniz, Nadje Al-Ali, and Kathryn Spellman Poots. *Gender, Governance and Islam.* Edinburgh: Edinburgh University Press, 2019.

Karam, Azza M. *Women, Islamisms and the State: Contemporary Feminisms in Egypt.* Basingstoke: Macmillan Press, 1998.

Kassab Sweis, Rania. "Saving Egypt's Village Girls: Humanity, Rights and Gendered Vulnerability in a Global Youth Initiative." *Journal of Middle East Women's Studies* 8, no. 2 (Spring 2012).

———. "Security and the Traumatized Street Child: How Gender Shapes International Psychiatric Aid, in Cairo." *Medical Anthropology Quarterly* 32, no. 1 (2017): 5–21.

Keddie, Nikki R, and Beth Baron. *Women in Middle Eastern History: Shifting Boundaries in Sex and Gender.* New Haven, CT: Yale University Press, 1992.

Keddie, Nikki R., and Lois Beck. *Women in the Muslim World.* Cambridge, MA: Harvard University Press, 1978.

Khafagi, Fatma. *Honour Crime in Egypt.* United Nations Expert Group Meeting, Violence against Women: Good Practices in Combating and Eliminating Violence against Women. Vienna, May 2005.

Khalil, Andrea. "Gender Paradoxes of the Arab Spring." *Journal of North African Studies* 19, no. 2 (2014): 131–36.

Khodary, Yasmin, Noha Salah, and Nada Mohsen. "Middle Eastern Women between Oppression and Resistance: Case Studies of Iraqi, Palestinian and Kurdish Women of Turkey." *Journal of International Women's Studies* 21, no. 1 (2010): 204–26.

Kienle, Eberhardt. *A Grand Delusion: Democracy and Economic Reform in Egypt.* London: I. B. Tauris, 2001.

Kirollos, Mariam. "Sexual Harassment in Egypt: Myths and Realities." Jadaliyya, July 16, 2013.

Kozma, Liat. *Policing Egyptian Women Sex, Law, and Medicine in Khedival Egypt.* Syracuse, NY: Syracuse University Press, 2011.

Kreil Aimon, Sorbera Lucia, and Serena Tolino. *Sex and Desire in Muslim Cultures: Beyond Norms and Transgression from the Abbasid to the Present Day.* London: I. B. Tauris, 2020.

Latif, Rusha. *Tahrir's Youth: Leaders of a Leaderless Revolution.* Cairo: American University in Cairo Press, 2022.

Lazreg, Marnia. *The Eloquence of Silence: Algerian Women in Question.* London: Routledge, 1994.

———. *Islamic Feminism and the Discourse of Post-Liberation: The Cultural Turn in Algeria.* Abingdon, UK: Routledge, 2021.

Leane, Jeanine. *Guwayu—For All Times: A Collection of First Nations Poems.* Broom, Western Australia: Magabala Books, 2020.

———. *Walk Back Over.* Calton South, Victoria: Corditebooks, 2018.

Lemma, Bonny. "A Million Women's Movements: Reconciling Diverse Conceptions of Feminism." *Harvard International Review* 40, no. 3 (Summer 2019): 14–15.

LeVine, Mark. *Heavy Metal Islam: Rock, Resistance, and the Struggle for the Soul of Islam.* Oakland: University of California Press, 2022.

———. *We'll Play till We Die: Journeys across a Decade of Revolutionary Music in the Muslim World.* Oakland: University of California Press, 2022.

LeVine, Mark, and Lucia Sorbera. "Collaborative Ontologies and the Future of Critical Theory." *Souffles Mondes: A Pan-African Journal and Platform,* no. 3 (2024).

Lindbeck, Monika. "Women Judges in Egypt: Discourse and Practice." In *Women Judges in the Muslim World a Comparative Study of Discourse and Practice,* edited by Nadia Sonneveld and Monika Lindbekk. Leiden: Brill, 2017.

Loewenfeld, Erwin. "The Mixed Courts in Egypt as Part of the System of Capitulations after the Treaty of Montreux." *Transactions of the Grotius Society* 26 (1940): 83–123.

Lowla, Reda. "15 Egyptian Laws, Rulings That Protect, Support, Empower Women." *Egypt Today,* March 3, 2019.

Lugones, María. "Toward a Decolonial Feminism." *Hypatia* 25, no. 4 (2010): 742–59.

Magdy, Solafa. "Women's Prisons in Egypt: Testimonies of Cruelty behind Concrete." Tahrir Institute for Middle East Policy, November 16, 2023.

Mahmoud, Saba. *Politics of Piety: The Islamic Revival and the Feminist Subject.* Princeton, NJ: Princeton University Press, 2005.

Malmström, Maria Frederika. "The Continuous Making of Pure Womanhood among Muslim Women in Cairo: Cooking, Depilating, and Circumcising." In *Gender and Sexuality in Muslim Cultures,* edited by Gul Ozyegin. Farnham, UK: Taylor & Francis, 2016.

———. *The Politics of Female Circumcision in Egypt.* London: I. B. Tauris, 2016.

Malmström, Maria Frederika, and An Van Raemdonck. "'The Clitoris Is in the Head!' Female Circumcision and the Making of a Harmful Cultural Practice in Egypt." In *Interrogating Harmful Cultural Practices: Gender, Culture and Coercion,* edited by Chia Longman and Tasmin Bradley. Farnham, UK: Routledge, 2015.

Masterson, J. M., and J. H. Swanson. *Female Genital Cutting: Breaking the Silence, Enabling Change.* Washington, DC: International Center for Research on Women (ICRW) and the Center for Development and Population Activities (CEDPA), 2000.

McCallum, Pamela. "Questions of Haunting: Jacques Derrida's 'Specters of Marx' and Raymond Williams's 'Modern Tragedy.'" *Mosaic* 40, no. 2 (2007): 231–44.

McGrath, Ann, Laura Rademaker, and Jakelin Troy, eds. *Everywhen: Australia and the Language of Deep History.* Lincoln: University of Nebraska Press, 2023.

Mehrez, Samia. *Egypt's Culture Wars: Politics and Practice.* London: Routledge, 2011.

———. "Huda Lutfi in Context." In *Egypt's Culture Wars.* Cairo: American University in Cairo Press, 2008.

———. "Translation and the Postcolonial Experience: The Francophone North African Text." In *Rethinking Translation: Discourse, Subjectivity, Ideology,* edited by Laurence Venuti. London: Routledge, 1992.

———. "Where Have All the Families Gone: Egyptian Literary Texts of the Nineties." *Arab Studies Journal* 9/10, no. 2/1 (2001): 31–49.

Mehrez, Samia, and Venetia Porter. *Huda Lutfi.* Dubai: Atlas Media, 2010.

Mernissi, Fatima. *Beyond the Veil: Male-Female Dynamics in Modern Muslim Society.* New York: Shenkman, 1975.

Mersal, Iman. *Fi Athar 'Ainat al-Zayyat.* Cairo: al-Kotob Khan, 2019.

Mervat, Hatem. "The Politics of Sexuality and Gender in Segregated Patriarchal Systems: The Case of Eighteenth- and Nineteenth-Century Egypt." *Feminist Studies* 12, no. 2 (1986): 251–74.

Moller Okin, Susan, Azizah Y. Al-Hibri, Sander L. Gilman, Joseph Raz, Saskia Sassen, Cass R. Sunstein, and Yael Tamis. *Is Multiculturalism Bad for Women?* Princeton, NJ: Princeton University Press, 1999.

Moloney, Charley. "Climate Campaigner Greta Thunberg Pleads for Blogger Alaa Abdel Fattah's Freedom." *The Times* (UK), October 31, 2022. www.thetimes.co.uk/article/climate-campaigner-greta-thunberg-pleads-for-blogger-alaa-abd-el-fattahs-freedom-tr5x6wohg. Accessed October 31, 2022.

Mossallam, Alia. *Strikes, Riots and Laughter: Al-Himamiyya Village's Experience of Egypt's 1918 Peasant Insurrection.* LSE Middle East Centre Paper Series, no. 40 (2020).

Moustapha, Tamir. "Got Rights? Public Interest Litigation and the Egyptian Human Rights Movement." In *Human Rights in the Arab World: Independent Voices,* edited by Anthony Tirado Chase and Amr Hamzawy. Philadelphia: University of Pennsylvania Press, 2006.

———. *The Struggle for Constitutional Power: Law, Politics, and Economic Development in Egypt.* Cambridge: Cambridge University Press, 2007.

Mubarak, Salma. *Amina Rachid ou la traversée vers l'autre.* Casablanca: Centre culturel du livre, 2020.

Musa, Nabawiyya. *Al-Mar'a wa al-'Amal (Woman and Work).* Alexandria: Matba' al-Qawmi, 1920.

———. *Tarikhi bi qalami (My Story Written with My Own Pen).* Cairo: Women and Memory Forum, 1999.

Naber, Nadine. "Imperial Feminism, Islamophobia, and the Egyptian Revolution." Jadaliyyah, February 11, 2011. www.jadaliyya.com/pages/index/616/imperial-feminism-islamophobia-andthe-egyptian-revolution.

Narayan, Uma. "Essence of Culture and a Sense of History: A Feminist Critique of Cultural Essentialism." *Hypatia* 13, no. 2 (1998): 86–106.

National Council for Human Rights, Egypt. Council Sessions. Accessed June 29, 2024. https://nchr.eg/en/Connciel-Sessions.

Nazra for Feminist Studies. "Continued Militarization: Increased Violence Against Women Human Rights Defenders during Dispersal of Cabinet Sit-in; Women Activists Beaten, Brutalized and Subjected to Sexual Violence." December 18, 2011. https://nazra.org/en/2011/12/continued-militarization-increased-violence-against-women-human-rights-defenders.

———. "Egypt: Statement from Nazra for Feminist Studies about Mob Sexual Assaults." June 13, 2014.

———. "The Mob-Sexual Assaults and Gang Rapes in Tahrir Square during the Celebrations of the Inauguration of the New Egyptian President Is Sufficient Proof for the Inefficiency of the Recent Legal Amendments to Combat These Crimes."June9,2014.https://nazra.org/en/2014/06/mob-sexual-assaults-and-gang-rapes-tahrir-square-during-celebrations-inauguration-new.

———. "Sexual Violence between the Philosophy of Law and the Problems of Application" (in Arabic). May 30, 2018. https://nazra.org/2018/05/.

———. "Testimonies on the Recent Sexual Assaults on Tahrir Square Vicinity," June 13, 2012. https://nazra.org/en/2012/06/testimonies-recent-sexual-assaults-tahrir-square-vicinity

———. "Testimony from a Survival of Gang Rape on Tahrir Square Vicinity."January26,2013.https://nazra.org/en/2013/01/testimony-survival-gang-rape-tahrir-square-vicinity.

———. "We Pledge to Continue the Pursuit of All Involved in This Crime and Attempted Cover-Up: Military 'Virginity Testing' Verdict: Not the Last Battle."

March 12, 2012. National Council for Human Rights, Egypt. https://nazra.org/en/2012/03/military-virginity-testing-verdict-not-last-battle.

Nelson, Cynthia. *Doria Shafik, Egyptian Feminist: A Woman Apart.* Gainesville: University Press of Florida, 1996.

Nye, Joseph S., Jr. "What New World Order?" *Foreign Affairs,* Spring 1992.

O'Grady, Siobhán. "As Egypt Hosts COP27, Its Most Famous Political Prisoner May Die, Family Warns." *Washington Post,* November 3, 2022. www.washingtonpost.com/world/2022/11/03/alaa-prisoner-egypt-cop27/.

Paniconi, Maria Elena. *Bildungsroman and the Arab Novel: Egyptian Intersections.* Abingdon, UK: Routledge, 2023.

Passerini, Luisa. *Autobiography of a Generation: Italy, 1968.* Hanover, NH: University Press of New England, 1996.

———. *Europe in Love, Love in Europe: Imagination and Politics between the Wars.* New York: New York University Press, 1999.

———. *Fascism in Popular Memory: The Cultural Experience of the Turin Working Class.* Cambridge: Cambridge University Press, 1987.

———. *Memory and Utopia: The Primacy of Intersubjectivity.* London: Equinox, 2007.

Pierandrei, Elisa. *Urban Cairo: La primavera araba dei graffiti.* Milano: Informant, 2012.

Povey, Tara. *Social Movements in Egypt and Iran.* London: Palgrave Macmillan, 2015.

———. "Voices of Dissent: Social Movements and Political Change in Egypt." In *Muslim Secular Democracy,* edited by Lily Zubaidah Rahim, 233–52. New York: Palgrave Macmillan, 2013.

Pratt, Nicola. *Embodying Geopolitics: Generations of Women's Activism in Egypt, Jordan, and Lebanon.* Oakland: University of California Press, 2020.

———. "Human Rights NGOs and the 'Foreign Funding Debate' in Egypt." In *Human Rights in the Arab World: Independent Voices,* edited by Anthony Tirado Chase and Amr Hamzawy. Philadelphia: University of Pennsylvania Press, 2013.

———. "The Queen Boat Case in Egypt: Sexuality, National Security and State Sovereignty." *Review of International Studies* 33, no. 1 (2007): 129–44.

Qassim, Tal'at Fu'ad, interview with Hisham Mubarak. "What Does the Gam'a al-Islamiyya Want?" In *Political Islam: Essays from the Middle East Report,* edited by Joel Beinin and Joe Stork, 314–26. Berkeley: University of California Press, 1987.

Rached, Tahani, dir. *Quatre femmes d'Egypte/Four Women of Egypt.* DVD. Montreal: National Film Board of Canada, 1997.

Rachid, Amina. "Dans notre société masculine, je me sentais descendante d'une race féminine." *Al-Hilal,* April 2002.

Ramadan, Hanan. *Al-Mar'a wa al-Haraka al-Shiu'i al-Masri hatta 1965 (Women and the Egyptian Communist Movement until 1965).* Cairo: Dar Al-Mahrusa, 1999.

Rauf Ezzat, Heba. "Women and Ijtihad: Toward a New Islamic Discourse" (in Arabic). *Alif: The Journal of Comparative Poetics* 19 (1999).

Reynolds, Dwight F., ed. *Interpreting the Self: Autobiography in the Arabic Literary Tradition.* Reprint, 2020. Berkeley: University of California Press, 2001.

Ribeiro, Djamila. *Il luogo della parola.* Alessandria: Capovolte, 2021.

Rothstein, Jed, dir. *Before the Spring after the Fall.* 2013.

Roushdy, Noha. "International Schools and the Production of Elite Non-belonging in Cairo's Satellite Cities." *Égypte, Soudan, Monde Arabe,* no. 24 (2023): 127–52.

Rowbotham, Sheila. *Women, Resistance and Revolution.* London: Allen Lane, 1972.

———. *Women's Liberation and Revolution: A Bibliography.* 2nd ed. Bristol: Falling Wall Press, 1973.

Ruta, Claudia. "Gender Politics in Transition: Women's Political Rights after the January 25 Revolution." Thesis, American University in Cairo, 2021.

Ryzova, Lucy. "The Battle of Muhammad Mahmud Street in Cairo: The Poetics and Politics of Urban Violence in Revolutionary Time." *Past and Present* 247, no. 1 (2020): 237–317.

Sadiq, Reza. "Endless Emergency: The Case of Egypt." *New Criminal Law Review* 10, no. 4 (Fall 2007): 532–53.

Saleh, Arwa, and Samah Selim. *The Stillborn: Notebooks of a Woman from the Student-Movement Generation in Egypt.* Chicago: Chicago University Press, 2017.

Salem, Sara. "On Transnational Feminist Solidarity: The Case of Angela Davis in Egypt." *Signs: Journal of Women's Studies* 43, no. 2 (2018): 245–67.

Salime, Zakia, and Frances Hasso. *Freedom without Permission: Space and Bodies in the Arab Revolutions.* Durham, NC: Duke University Press, 2016.

Sallam, Yara. "Did You See Aya in Qanater Prison?" *Mada Masr,* February 12, 2016. https://madamasr.com/en/2016/02/12/opinion/u/blog-did-you-see-aya-in-qanater-prison/.

———. "How We Got Used to the Screams of Those on Death Row." *Mada Masr,* October 10, 2017. https://madamasr.com/en/2017/10/10/opinion/u/blog-how-we-got-used-to-the-screams-of-those-on-death-row/.

———. "I Lost Track of Time in Every Sense of the Word: On Coping with Prison and Its Aftermath." *Mada Masr,* October 13, 2019. https://madamasr.com/en/2019/10/13/opinion/u/i-lost-track-of-time-in-every-sense-of-the-word/.

———. "Jan 25, 5 Years On: On the Revolution That I Missed." *Mada Masr,* January 26, 2016. https://madamasr.com/en/2016/01/26/opinion/u/jan-25-5-years-on-on-the-revolution-that-i-missed/.

———. "Talking Personal." https://talkingpersonal.blogspot.com/?view=timeslide. Accessed January 2, 2020.

Sami, Aziza. "Republished: Marie Assaad—Egypt's Gentle Warrior." Ahram Online, March 11, 2021. http://english.ahram.org.eg/NewsContent/32/1168/198001/Folk/Inspiring-Women/Marie-Assaad-Egypts-Gentle-Warrior.aspx.

Sangster, Joan. "Telling Our Stories: Feminist Debates and the Use of Oral History." *Women's History Review* 3, no. 1 (1994): 5–28.

Sardar Ali, Shahheen. "Women's Rights, CEDAW and International Human Rights Debates: Toward Empowerment?" In *Rethinking Empowerment,* edited by Jane L. Parpart, Shirin M. Rai, and Kathleen A. Staudt. New York: Routledge, 2002.

Schwedler, Jillian, and J. Clark. "Islamist-Leftist Cooperation in the Arab World." *ISIM Review* 18 (Autumn 2006): 10–11.

Seif, Sanaa. "Press Conference of Global Campaign to Demand Climate Justice." Sharm El-Sheikh, German Pavilion, November 8, 2022.

Sergent, Lidya. *Women and Revolution: A Discussion of the Unhappy Marriage of Marxism and Feminism.* Montreal: Black Rose Books, 1981.

Shafik, Doria. *La femme nouvelle.* Cairo: E&R Schindler, 1944.

Sharabi, Hisham. *Neopatriarchy: A Theory of Distorted Change in Arab Society.* New York: Oxford University Press, 1988.

Sharafeldin, Marwa. "Challenges of Islamic Feminism in Personal Status Law Reform: Women's NGOs in Egypt between Islamic Law and International Human Rights." In *Feminist and Islamic Perspectives: New Horizons of Knowledge and Reform,* edited by Omaima Abu Bakr. Cairo: Women and Memory Forum, 2013.

———. "Islamic Law Meets Human Rights: Reformulating Qiwamah and Wilayah for Personal Status Law Reform Advocacy in Egypt." *Men in Charge* (2015): 163–96.

Shaʿrawi Huda. *Harem Years: The Memoirs of an Egyptian Feminist (1879–1924).* Translated by Margot Badran. London: Virago, 1986.

Sharoni, Simona. "Women and Gender in Middle East Studies: Trends, Prospects and Challenges." *Middle East Report,* no. 205 (1997): 27–29.

Shehab, Bahia. "A Thousand Times No." Presentation at TEDGlobal 2012, June 2012. www.ted.com/talks/bahia_shehab_a_thousand_times_no?subtitle=en.

Shoukry, Aliya, Rasha Mohammad Hassan, and Nehad Abul Komsan. "Clouds in Egypt's Sky": Sexual Harassment; From Verbal Harassment to Rape; A Sociological Study. Cairo: Egyptian Centre for Women's Rights (ECWR), 2008.

Shukr, Abdul Ghaffar. *The Socialist Youth Organization: An Egyptian Experience in Leadership Preparation 1963–1976.* Beirut: Center For Arab Unity Studies, 2004.

Shukrallah, Hala. "Why Does the Counter-Revolution Target Women and Copts?" Ahram Online, March 9, 2011.

Sobhi, Hanya. "The De-Facto Privatization of Secondary Education In Egypt: A Study of Private Tutoring in Technical and General Schools." *Compare: A Journal of Comparative and International Education* 42, no. 1 (2012): 47–67.

———. "Secular Façade, Neoliberal Islamization: Textbook Nationalism from Mubarak to Sisi." *Nations and Nationalism* 21, no. 4 (2010): 805–24.

Soliman, Azza. "Opening Ceremony of the International Film Festival on Human Rights." March 9, 2018, Geneva, Switzerland. Accessed January 2, 2020. http://prixmartineanstett.org/En-Prix2018.html.

Sonneveld, Nadia. "Khulʿ Divorce in Egypt: How Family Courts Are Providing a 'Dialogue' between Husband and Wife." *Anthropology of the Middle East* 5, no. 2 (2010): 100–120.

———. "Women's Access to Legal Education and Their Appointment to the Judiciary: The Dutch, Egyptian, and Indonesian Cases Compared." In *Women Judges in the Muslim World: A Comparative Study of Discourse and Practice,* edited by Nadia Sonneveld and Monika Lindbekk. Leiden: Brill, 2017.

Sonneveld, Nadia, and Monika Lindbekk, eds. *Women Judges in the Muslim World: A Comparative Study of Discourse and Practice.* Leiden: Brill, 2017.

Sorbera, Lucia. "Challenges of Thinking Feminism and Revolution in Egypt between 2011 and 2014." *Postcolonial Studies* 17, no. 1 (2014): 63–75.

———. "Egyptian Feminist Union at the 9th Congress of International Women Suffrage Alliance (Rome, 1923)." In *Egitto oggi,* edited by Elisabetta Bartuli. Bologna: Il Ponte, 2005.

———. "An Invisible and Enduring Presence: Women in Egyptian Politics." In *Informal Power in the Greater Middle East,* edited by Luca Anceschi, Andrea Teti, and Gennaro Gervasio, 159–74. London: Routledge, 2014.

———. "Gli esordi del femminismo egiziano: Costruzione e superamento di uno spazio nazionale femminile." *Genesis: Rivista della Società Italiana delle Storiche* Vol. 6, no. 1 (2007): 115–36.

———. "Narrare il sé, raccontare la modernità: Ambienti, temi e forme della scrittura femminile in epoca moderna." In Lorenzo Casini, Maria Elena Paniconi, and Lucia Sorbera, *Modernità arabe: Nazione, narrazione e nuovi soggetti nel romanzo egiziano,* 245–352. Messina: Mesogea, 2012.

———. "Viaggiare e svelarsi alle origini del femminismo egiziano." In *Margini e confini: Studi sulla cultura delle donne nell'età contemporanea,* edited by Anna Rosa Scrittori. Venezia: Cafoscarina, 2006.

———. "Writing Revolution: New Inspirations, New Questions." *Postcolonial Studies* 17, no. 1 (2014): 104–8.

Soueif, Ahdaf. *Cairo: My City, Our Revolution.* London: Springer, 2012.

———. "Egypt's Revolution Is Stuck in a Rut, but We Still Have the Spirit to See It Through." *Guardian* (UK edition), July 13, 2011.

———. "Image of Unknown Woman Beaten by Egypt's Military Echoes around World." *Guardian* (US edition), December 18, 2011

———. "Protesters Reclaim the Spirit of Egypt." *BBC News Middle East,* February 13, 2011.

Spivak, Gayatri Chakravorty. "'Woman' as Theatre: United Nations Conference on Women, Beijing 1995." *Radical Philosophy,* no. 75 (1996).

Stabili, Maria Rosaria. *Il sentimento aristocratico: Élites cilene allo specchio (1860–1960).* Lecce: Congedo, 1996.

Suzee in the City (blog). "Women in Graffiti: A Tribute to the Women of Egypt," January 7, 2013. https://suzeeinthecity.wordpress.com/2013/01/07/women-in-graffiti-a-tribute-to-the-women-of-egypt/.

Tadros, Mariz. "Mutilating Bodies: The Muslim Brotherhood's Gift to Egyptian Women." Open Democracy, May 24, 2012.

Telmissany, May. "Nomadic Citizenship: Reflections on Exile and the Revolution." *Journal of the African Literature Association* 15, no. 3 (2021): 509–23.

Thabit, Munirah. *Thawra fi-l-Burj al-'Aji: Mudhakkirati fi 'Ashrin 'Aman 'an Ma'rakat Huquq al-Mar'a al-Siyasiya (A Revolution in the Ivory Tower: My Memoirs of Twenty Years of Struggle for Women's Political Rights).* Cairo: Dar al-Ma'arif, 1946.

Thompson, Elizabeth. *Colonial Citizens: Republican Rights, Paternal Privilege, and Gender in French Syria and Lebanon.* New York: Columbia University Press, 2000.

TIMEP. "Brief: Case 173: Egypt's Foreign Funding Case." February 28, 2019. https://timep.org/reports-briefings/timep-brief-case-173-egypts-foreign-funding-case/.

Toledano, Ehud. "Social and Economic Change in the 'Long Nineteenth Century.'" In *The Cambridge History of Egypt,* edited by M. W. Daly. Cambridge: Cambridge University Press, 1998.

Tolino, Serena. "Gender Equality in the Egyptian Constitution: From 1923 to 2014." *Oriente Moderno,* no. 2 (2018): 140–65.

Toma, Sally. "Alice in Trauma-Land." *Mada Masr,* October 31, 2014.

Toubia, Nahid. "Challenges Facing the Arab Women at the End of the 20th Century." In *Opening the Gates: A Century of Arab Feminist Writing,* edited by Margot Badran and miriam cooke. Bloomington: Indiana University Press, 1990.

———. *Women of the Arab World: The Coming Challenge.* London: Zed Books, 1988.

Tucker, Judith E. "Decline of the Family Economy in Mid-Nineteenth Century Egypt." *Arab Studies Quarterly* 1, no. 3 (1979): 245–71.

———. *In the House of the Law: Gender and Islamic Law in Ottoman Syria and Palestine.* Berkeley: University of California Press, 1998.

———. "Rescued from Obscurity: Contributions and Challenges in Writing the History of Gender in the Middle East and North Africa." In *A Companion to Gender History,* edited by Teresa A. Meade and Merry E. Wiesner-Hanks, 393–412. Malden, MA: Blackwell, 2004.

———. *Women in Nineteenth-Century Egypt.* Cambridge: Cambridge University Press, 1985.

Van Nieuwkerk, Karin. "'Repentant' Artists in Egypt: Debating Gender, Performing Arts and Religion." *Contemporary Islam* 2, no. 3 (2008): 191–210.

Van Raemdonck, An. "Egyptian Activism against Female Genital Cutting as Catachrestic Claiming." *Religion and Gender* 3, 2, 2013: 235–37.

Wahba, Dina. "My Revolution!" In *Women Rising: In and Beyond the Arab Spring,* edited by Rita Stephan and Mounira M. Charrad, 318–20. New York: New York University Press, 2020.

Wallach Scott, Joan. *The Politics of the Veil.* Princeton, NJ: Princeton University Press, 2007.

Warnock, Fernea Elizabeth, and Basima Qattan Berzigan. *Middle Eastern Muslim Women Speak.* Austin: University of Texas Press, 1977.

Waterbury, John. *The Egypt of Nasser and Sadat: The Political Economy of Two Regimes.* Princeton, NJ: Princeton University Press, 1983.

Winter, Bronwyn. *Hijab and the Republic: Uncovering the French Headscarf Debate.* Syracuse, NY: Syracuse University Press, 2008.

Women's International Democratic Federation. *Congrès international des femmes: Compte rendu des travaux du congrès qui s'est tenu à Paris du 26 novembre au 1er décembre 1945.* Paris: Fédération démocratique internationale des femmes, 1946.

Wright, Alexis. *Tracker: Stories of Tracker Tilmouth*. Artarmon, NSW: Giramondo Publishing, 2017.

Youssef, Lubna, and Salwa Kamel, eds. *Proceedings of the 11th International Symposium on Comparative Literature: Creativity and Revolution, 13–15 November 2012*. Department of English Language and Literature, Faculty of Arts, Cairo University, Giza, Egypt, 2014.

Zayyat, Latifa. *The Search: Personal Papers*. London: Quartet Books, 1996.

Zulfikar, Mona, ed., and the Communication Group for the Enhancement of the Status of Women in Egypt. *Legal Rights of Egyptian Women in Theory and in Practice*. Cairo: Dar Al-Kutub, 1992.

INDEX

1919 Revolution, 27, 28, 29, 210, 226, 234; anti-British, 20, 30, 90, 104, 201; memory of, 27; events of, 28

1967 War, 39, 40, 104

2011 Revolution, 2, 6, 9, 14, 18, 21, 99, 120, 190, 209, 189, 223, 252, 257; eighteen days, 3, 9, 10, 22, 105, 134, 154, 169, 190, 193–99, 202, 221, 224, 237; naming of, 3; women activists in, 9, 130, 135, 187, 192, 219, 226, 242

Abaza, Mona, 209

'Abbas, 104, 105

Abbas, Kamal, 99

Abbas, Nagwa, 270n45

'Abd Allah, 112

'Abd al-Radi, Thuraya, 97

'Abd al-Rahman, 'Aisha (Bint Shati), 32

Abdel Aziz, Basma, 7

Abd El-Fattah, Alaa, 13, 28, 29, 171, 197, 218, 231, 233, 236, 284n42, 287n8, 292n9

Abdel Fattah, Esraam, 182–85

Abdel Fattah, Wael, 143

Abdel Hadi, Amal, 40, 58, 63, 78, 81, *92fig.*, 104, 129, 130, 183, 270n45

Abdel-Meguid Radwan, Zeinab, 87

Abd El Nasser, Gamal, 16, 36, 37, 38, 39, 40, 44, 107, 112, 145, 202, 209, 241, 245, 246, 247

Abdel Rahman, Basma, 237, 288n20

Abdelrahman, Maha, 87

Abdel Razik, Hussein, 39

Abd el-Salam, Seham Saneya, 45, 52, 53, 55, 58, 59, 270n45

Abdelwahab, Hoda, 239

Abd El-Wahab, Nadia, 58

Abouelnaga, Shereen, 83–85

Abu-Aita, Kamal, 172

Abubakr, Omaima, 71

Abu Khair, Shaima, 216. *See also* Black Wednesday

Abu Khomsa, Nehad, 120

Abul Ghar, Mohamed, *166fig.*

Abu-Lughod, Lila, 70

Abu Sa'da, Hafez, 91

Abu Teeg, Mervat, *127fig.*

Abu Zeid, Jihan, 97

activism: across Arab world and Middle East, 1; attacks against women's, 255; communist women's, 16, 246; dilemmas of women's, 146; Egyptian women's in solidarity with Palestine, 163, 253, 254; and family relationships, 3, 43, 95; feminist in Egypt, 5, 6, 124, 236; Gameela Ismail's, 137, 144, 154; gender, 12, 63, 189, 190; genealogies of, 28, 29, 183, 245; human rights, 12, 113; leading women, 50; *longue durée* of women's, 2–4, 9, 11, 79, 215, 136, 256; Nawal al-Saadawi's, 74; NGOs, 132, 160, 258; post-ideological, 157, 165–68, 185; pro-democracy, 142, 182; repression of, 156; student political activism, 125; transnational, 55, 171; of women and foreign funding, 77; of women and the government, 77; of women during the *nahda*, 31; of women in 1970s student movement,

activism *(continued)*
46–49; of women in 1980s, 55; of women
in 1990s, 71; of women in 2011 Revolution, 2, 3, 7, 9–11, 190; of women in
late-1940s to early 1950s, 33, 36; of
women supporting political prisoners,
236; of women under Nasser regime, 37;
and women's friendship, 15, *16fig.*; women
and human rights movement, 90, 94;
women environmental and human
rights, 12; women's health, 57; women's
memories of, 104; youth, 177, 184
'adala ijtima'iyya (social justice), 185. *See
also under* justice
Adham, Soraya, *92fig.*
Adly, Magda, 22, 47, 103–17, 199, 215,
270n45
Afghanistan: 2001 war against, 69; jihad-
ists moving to, 159
Afify, Heba, 205
Aflatun, Inji, 32–36, 241
Africa, 58, 71, 73; historiography of feminism in, 2; railway in, 30; feminism/
feminists in, 55; women in, 72, 73
African Commission on Human and
People's Rights (ACHPR, Banjul,
Gambia), 216, 241, 291n6
Ahmed, Leila, 15
Ahmed, Sara, 5, 184
Ain Shams: Hospital, 111; University,
40, 44
Airport Hospital, 112
'Aish wa Hurriyya (Bread and Freedom)
Political Party, 150, 171
al-Ahaly (newspaper), 39
al-Akhbar (newspaper), 39
al-'Arish (village), 88, 89
al-Askary, Zinat, 44, 270n45, 288n20
al-Ayyubi, Na'imah, 119
al-Azhar, 52, 60, 93, 105, 125, 272n18
al-Badari (village), 105
al-Badiya, Bahithat (pen name of Malak
Hifni Nasif), 33, 108
al-Bahhat, Saniyya, 97
Alcoff, Linda Martín, 17, 193
al-Dawla, 'Ismat Saif, 105
Alexandria, 6, 13, 153, 155, 157, 158, 162, 165,
166, *166fig.*, 169, *176fig.*; April 6 move-

ment in, 171; Criminal Court, 156, 176;
Sidi Ghaber in, 225; syndicate in, 171;
union of workers in real estate taxation
authority, 286n44; Two Saints Church,
287n11; University, 163; women strikers
in, 171; Muslim Brotherhood attack
against young woman from Tamarod
movement, 224–25
al-Fajr al-Jadid (magazine), 246
al-Gebali, Tahani, *92fig.*, 119, 215
Algeria, 1, 39, 43; civil war, 69, 159; feminist
scholars in, 128; Liberation Front, 39;
novelists in, 14
al-Ghad Party, 142, 165, 167
al-Ghazali, Zeinab, 269n36
al-Gindi, Aida, *92fig.*, 97
al-Guindi, Yussuf, 105
Al-Guindy, Abir, 216. *See also* Black
Wednesday
al-Hilal (journal), 38
al-Hilali, Nabil, 93, 94
Ali, Khaled, 150
'Ali, Muhammad (Pasha), 30
Ali, Nawal, 216, 217. *See also* Black
Wednesday
al-Islam, Ahmed Seif, 94
al-Ittihad al-Nisa' al-Misri (Egyptian
Feminist Union [EFU]), 10, 15, 31, 234
alimony, 127
al-Jumhuriyya (newspaper), 39
al-Kosheh (village), 91
al-Lababidi, Laila, 97
Allard Prize for International Integrity, 118
Alliance of Arab Women, 97
Alliance of the Continuing Revolution
(Tahalluf al-thawra mustamirra), 208
Alliance of Women's Organizations, 206
al-Mahdi, Rabab, 167, 236
al-Mahdiyya, Munira, 29
al-Mansheya (district), 156
al-Mar'a wa al-'Amal (Woman and Work),
32
al-Mar'a wa al-Jins (Woman and Sex), 44,
218
al-Masri, Sana', 155–77
al-Masriyya, Na'ima, 29
al-Masry al-Youm (newspaper), 264n31,
287n2

al-Mohandessin (neighborhood), 40
al-Moudjahid (newspaper), 39
al-Mubtasirun (The Stillborn), 48, 227
al-Musawwar (newspaper), 202
al-Nahda Square, 228
al-Naqqash, Amina, 38
al-Naqqash, Farida, 37, 38, 39, 42, 270n46
al-Qadiseen (Two Saints Church), 165,
　287n11
al-Qaida, 159
al-Rif al-Misr (The Egyptian Countryside), 32
al-Saadawi, Nawal, 10, 14, 42, 44, 55, 57, 59,
　67, 71, 72, *73fig.*, 75, 97, 109, 126, 159, 195,
　239, 241, 270n44
al-Sabbagh, Shaima', 131, 133, 172, 175, 176,
　255
al-Said, Amina, 55
al-Sayyed Sa'id, Muhammad, 94
al-Sha'ab (newspaper), 39
al-Sheikh, Rania, 242
al-Sherif, Nahed, 242
al-Tahan, Hanan, 242
al-Tantawi, Ahmed, 153
al-Tantawi, Muhammad Sayyid, 53
al-Wafd Daily (newspaper), 142
al-Wayli (neighborhood), 110
al-Zayyat, Enayat (*Fi Athar Enayat al-
　Zayyat [Traces of Enayat]*), 16
al-Zayyat, Latifa, 34, 36, 39, 43, 164, 247
Amer, Khoulud Said, 239
American University in Cairo (AUC), 50,
　52, 70, 140, 189
Amin, Galal, 69
Amin, Nasser, 94
Amin, Shahira, 205
Amnesty International, 114, 118, 196, 204
anti-imperialism, 36
Anzaldúa, Gloria, 17, 84, 189
April 6 protests, 182. *See also* April 6 Youth
　Movement
April 6 Youth Movement, 172, 182, 185, 243
Arab Democratic Nasserist Party, 167
Arab League, 95
Arab Organization for Human Rights, 94
Arab Socialist Union, 38
Arab Spring, 9
Arab Women Solidarity Association
　(AWSA), 55, 74, 97

Arab world, 14, 18, 55, 69, 73, 103, 145, 185, 234
Arab-Israeli War (1948), 246
Arafa, Marwa. 239
archives, 18, 19, 210; alternative, 256; audio-
　visual, 139; British Foreign Office, 234;
　counter-archive, 28; ephemeral, 210; of
　feelings, 201, 204, 205, 213; for the future,
　256; living, 256; of Islamic courts in
　Egypt, 15; of *L'Egyptienne*, 108; my own,
　234; National Archives (Egypt), 256;
　official, 213; private, 202; unauthorized,
　256; Women and Memory Forum, 51
Arman, Farida, 138
army: British, 31; Egyptian, 32, 40, 228, 237
Artists for Change, 167
'*ashawiyya* (informal urban settlements, or
　slum), 113, 121, 122
Ashour, Radwa, 36, 67
Assaad, Marie Bassili, 50–52, *51fig.*, 57,
　59–60, *92fig.*, 129
assault: "immoral," 229; police, *174fig.*;
　sexual, 191, 192, 198, 199, 205, 206, 214,
　216, 219, 222, 223, 225, 226, 227, 230, 238,
　289; street, 217; women's, 231. *See also*
　harassment; Quwwa dud al-Taharrush
　(Operation Anti-Sexual Harassment
　[Opantish]); rape
Association for Health Education, 73
Aswan, 6, 13, 53, 251
Asyut (governorate), 105
Attalah, Lina, 3, 12, 254, 255
authoritarianism: authoritarian policy, 203;
　authoritarian state, 85, 87, 108, 129, 133;
　intersectionality of, 146; military or
　authoritarian states, 129; modern
　project of development and women,
　230; and patriarchy, 136, 151, 253; postco-
　lonial, 71, 146. *See also* capitalism;
　Islamism/Islamists
authorities: British colonial, 186; Islamic
　Egyptian, 60
autobiography, 18, 268n26
Awraq Ishtirakiya (Socialist Papers), 170
'Azza, Rasha, 237, 245

Badran, Hoda, 10
Badran, Margot, 14, 18, 28, 53, 70, 119, 129,
　210

INDEX · 321

Baheira (village), 188

Bahrain, 68

baltagiya (state-sponsored thugs), 147, 169, 202

Banat Masarwa (Daughters of the Egyptians), 189

Bangladesh, 128

Barah (Safe Space), 188

Baron, Beth, 15, 186, 201

Battle of the Camels, 197

Bayt al-Ummah (House of the Nation), 27

Bayyat, Asef, 164

BBC Arabic, 125

Bedouin women, 89

Beijing Declaration and Platform for Action, 83

Beinin, Joel, 170, 245, 246

Berlin Wall, fall of, 69

Bier, Laura, 16, 41

bin Laden, Osama, 159

Bint al-Ard Association (Jam'at Bint al-Ard), 97, 284

biography, 2, 5, 16, 17, 22, 77, 138; collective biography, 5, 6, 14, 18, 21, 22, 256; genre of, 4; political biography, 22, 104, 132, 156, 157, 236; of women, 16. See also *tarjama*

biopolitics, 109

Black Wednesday, 148, 149, 216, 217, 218, 241, 291n6. *See also* Al-Guindy, Abir; Ali, Nawal; Egyptian Initiative for Personal Rights (EIPR); harassment; rape

blogs: Arabic blogosphere, 183; bloggers, 171, 182, 183, 184, 197, 206, 217, 282n34; 287n8. *See also* Abd El-Fattah, Alaa; Abdel Fattah, Esraa; Hassan, Manal; Nejm, Nawara

blue-bra incident, 209, 210, 211. *See also* harassment

Board of the World Council of Churches, 52

borders, 13, 71, 85, 153, 192; Egyptian, 72, 155; Gaza, 252; Kuwait-Iraq, 68; national, 82; violence of, 84

Bosnia (genocide of Muslims in), 69

Botman, Selma, 247

Boutros-Ghali, Boutros, 88

Bulaq el-Dakhrur, 121–24

Bush, George H. W., 67

Bussy (Look), 189

Cabinet: clashes, 242, 244; sit-in, 208, 211, 289

Café Groppi, 205

Café Riche, 134

Cairo: *678* (film), 218; American College for Girls, 51; criminal court, 156; fires, 36; Opera House, 134; University, 15, 29, 35, 39, 70, 71, 83, 88, 129, 138, 140, 241, 281n32

Cairo Institute for Human Rights Studies (CIHRS), 58, 78, 113

capitalism: and authoritarianism, 146; colonial, 29; economy, 45; and fundamentalism, 72–75; global, 76; neoliberal, 69, 71, 72, 146; postmodern, 72; structures, 30; system, 30

care: in 2011 Revolution, 194; feminist theory, 140, 144, 154, 182; radical care, 239

Case 1567/2024 (joining a terrorist group and organizing a demonstration), 255

Case 173/2011 (NGO "foreign funding" case), 131

Catholics, 123, 128

censorship, 38, 75, 80, 255, 256

Center for Development and Population Activities, 58

Center for Egyptian Women's Legal Assistance (CEWLA), 11, 121

Center for Gender Studies (AUC), 71

Center for Human Rights Legal Aid, 113

Center for Social Research at the American University in Cairo, 52

Center for Socialist Studies, 169

Center for Trade Union Services, 99

Central Agency of Public Mobilization and Statistics, 79

Channel Three, 140

Chechnya, genocide of Muslims in, 69

Christians, 52, 128

churches, 123, 125, 130, 149, 150, 185, 287n11; Two Saints in Alexandria, 165

Civil Movement for Democracy, 137, 152, 153

civil society, 12, 44, 58, 60, 68, 69, 90–93, 112, 191, 243, 281n30, 282n5

Civil Society Popular Committee, 207

civil war: in Syria, Yemen, Libya, 1; American, 30; in Algeria, 69

clashes: Muhammad Mahmoud, November 2011, *8fig.*, 195, 135, 208, 220; Cabinet, December 2011, 242, 244; Alexandria Criminal Court, December 2012, 156

Cliff, Tony, 169

Clinton, Hillary, 83

clitoridectomy, 52

clitoris, 52, 251

Clouds in Egypt's Sky, 218

Coalition for Women's Issues, 58

Cold War, 49, 68, 191; post-Cold War, 68, 69, 70, 144

colonialism: and coloniality of gender, 256; and colonized society (Egyptian women in), 119; and colonized territory, 275n16; European, 19; gendered nature of, 2; heritage, 237; and matrix of power, 253; and violence of borders, 85

Committee for Working Women's Affairs, 57

Committee to Defend the Revolution, 205

Communist Party of Egypt, 246

conformism, 164

Connell, Raewyn, 11, 263n25

Constitution: Egyptian, 7, 8, 132

Convention on the Elimination of All Forms of Discrimination against Women (CEDAW), 86, 277n1

COP27 conference at Sharm el-Sheikh, 12, 13

Copenhagen: 1939 International Women Suffrage Alliance Conference, 163, 253; 1982 UN World Conference on Women, 82

Coptic Christians, 51, 89, 106, 123, 149, 203, 220, 234; Coptic Orthodox, 51, 279n3; minority, 123; Two Saints Church, 165, 287n11

Coptic Evangelical Organization for Social Services, 63

"the corridor" (*al-mamarr*) (theory), 41, 44, 88, 246

Council for Motherhood and Childhood, 54

counterrevolution, 1, 21, 58, 188, 207, 213, 243; forces, 6, 199, 241; narratives about, 257

coup, Egypt 2013, 1, 11, 76, 143, 228, 262n5, 282n4, 282n5

courts: Constitutional Court, 93, 119, 215, 284n4; consular, 119; Islamic, 15; mixed, 119, 289n4

COVID-19 crisis, 236, 255

culture: Egyptian, 56–58, 169; Egyptian artistic scene, 15, 17; Egyptian sphere, 15, 35; folk, 131, 175; and imaginary, 27, 31; modernization of, 62

Curiel, Henri, 246

Cynthia Nelson Center for Gender Studies at AUC, 71

Darwiche, Nawla, 47, 82, *92fig.*, 104, *127fig.*, 184, 270n45

Darwiche, Yusef, 246

Darwish, Lobna, 194, 198, 205, 207, 238

Davis, Angela, 248, 294n35

Deir El-Barsha (village), 63

de Lauretis, Teresa, 17

democracy, 87, 107, 203; activists for, 135; conditions for, 144; democratization, 34, 37, 181, 281n26; promotion of, 167, 286n2; real, 150; third wave of, 68, 69

demonstrations: 1919 women's anti-British, 31, 200, 201, 210; 1967 Egypt's defeat, 7, 106; 1982 against Israeli invasion of Lebanon, 93; 2003 Police Day, 184; 2003 solidarity with Iraq, 3, 163; 2005 Kefaya, 127, 149, 166, 167, 217, 281n26; al-Aqsa Intifada solidarity, 114; anti-Brotherhood, 222; April 6 movement, 172; assassination of Shaima' al-Sabbagh at a, 255; blaming women participating in, 199; blue-bra, 209; emergency law prohibiting, 90; independent trade union, *200fig.*; initiatives against violence against women during, 10; January 2011, 221; January 25, 2011, 186; January 2015, 131; June 2011, 241; June 30, 2013, 262n5; Mahalla, 99–99; March 8 women's, 202, 203; November 2011, 135; October 2023, 153, 253; violence against women during, 192, 195, 217, 219, 220, 222, 231, 242; women in, 20. *See also entries for revolutions*

Deom, Nada, 12

Desert Storm, 67
desire, 64, 65
detention of women, 239; pretrial, 145, 236, 182
development: 1980s neoliberal policies and strategies, 76, 252; developmentalist organizations, 53; economic, 40, 53, 240; Egyptian government developmentalist nationalist ideology and agenda, 106, 124, 230; Egypt's right to development, 86; global, 83; government policies on, 55; UN International Conference on Population and Development (ICPD), 55; UN Women's Decade and development, 275n28
diaspora, Egyptian, 231
disability, as feminist concern, 161
dissent: repression of, 236; transgenerational transmission of, 6, 39; and women, 80, 254
divorce, 73, 118, 120, 124, 216; civil, 123; law, 62; lawful, 215; provisions for, 66. See also *khul'*
Djebar, Assia, 14
Doctors for Change, 167
Dostour Party, 89, 137, 152, 153, 182, 234, 282n4, 282n6
Douek, Rymond, 246
Duke University, 74
Durik (Your Role), 188
dystopia, 193–94

Eastern Women Conference in Defense of Palestine, 163, 253
Economic Restructuring and Stabilization Program (IMF), 170
Economics and Political Science (Faculty of), 71
economy: Egyptian, 29; global political, 146; political economy (of Egypt), 251
education: feminist, 247; equal, 36
Egypt: citizens and people, 6, 34, 40, 114, 151, 177, 184, 185; civil society, 12, 91; contemporary, 137; economic growth, 126; government, 55, 67, 78, 83, 140, 214, 215, 257; government attack on LGBTQ, 188; government policies, 52, 81; participation in Iraq war coalition, 74; protest

culture, 4; public sphere, 137, 168; regional position of, 67; republican age and history in, 16, 38; rural, 58, 121; spirit of, 195. *See also* activism; elections; demonstrations; *and specific events, people, places, and organizations*
Egyptian Association to Combat Torture, 92
Egyptian Center for Economic and Social Rights, 243
Egyptian Center for Women's Legal Aid, 113
Egyptian Center for Women's Rights (ECWR), 120, 217, 218
Egyptian Centre for Culture and Arts–Makan, 27
Egyptian Commission for Rights and Freedoms, 243
Egyptian Council for Women, 202
Egyptian Demographic Health Survey (1999), 57
Egyptian Emergency State Security Courts, 116
Egyptian Federation of Trade Unions, *200fig.*
Egyptian Feminist Union (EFU), 10, 15, 31, 234
Egyptian Initiative for Personal Rights (EIPR), 213, 216, 239, 240
Egyptian Ministry of Health, 57; Egyptian Health Issue Survey (2015), 62
Egyptian Movement for Change, Kefaya, 166
Egyptian Organization for Human Rights (EOHR), 91, 94, 111, 112, 124, 125
Egyptian Social Democratic Party, 153
Egyptian Trade Federation, 170
Egyptian Women's Union, 74
Egyptian Workers and Peasants Communist Party (Hezb al-'Ummal wa al-Fallahin ash-Shiu'i al-Masri), 40, 46, 47, 246
Egyptian Youth Federation, 135
Egypt Independent (newspaper), 12
'Eid: 2006, sexual mobs, 217, 218; 2008, sexual mobs, 217; they are celebrating 'Eid in prison, 240
Eidarous, Elham, 230
El-Baqer, Mohamed, 236

ElBaradei, Mohamed, 282n4
el-Borai, Nagel, 113
El-Dawla, Aida Seif, 92, 103–17, *115fig.*, 129, *233fig.*, 270n45, 279nn5,8
elections: in late-1980s, 110; early 2000s students union elections, 168; in 2005, 87, 142, 20; 2011 under military rule, 131, 135, 192, 203, 208, 209, 222; Gameela Ismail runs for, 145–50, 152; Mubarak speech on 2011 presidential, 289n13; Nawal al-Saadawi elected at board of Medical Doctors Union, 73; women's right to run for, 145
Elgebaly, Rasha, 171
El Guindi, Fadwa, 62
el-Hamalawy, Hossam, 168, 171
elite, Circassian, 30
El-Khoffash, Rima, *92fig.*
Elmahdy, Aliaa, 206
El-Mahdy, Mai, 254
El-Massry, Mahienour, 22, 155–77, *166fig.*
El-Massry, Waffa, 166
El-Nadeem Center for the Psychological Treatment and Rehabilitation of Victims of Violence and Torture, 11, 22, 46, 103, 104, 109, 111–17, 163, 199, 214, 215, 229, 239, 278n3, 288n20
El-Rifae, Yasmin, 231
Elsadda, Hoda, 51, 70, 71, 88, *92fig.*
Elsaman, Radwa, 132
El-Shaer, Ismail, 216
El-Sisi, Abdel Fattah, 8, 11, 13, 131, 143, 152, 156, 199, 204, 240, 242, 244, 254, 282n5
Eltahawy, Mona, 9
Eman (Farida Arman's sister and Gameela Ismail's aunt), 139
emancipation: working-class, 31; women's, 31, 76
Engels, Friedrich, 169
environment and environmentalism, 12, 50
epistemologies: decolonial and Indigenous, 2, 17, 19, 71, 111, 159, 189, 193, 294n35; Queer feminist, 17, 189, 192, 196
equality, 7, 9, 17, 30, 46, 47, 79, 82, 120, 129, 132, 145, 150, 164, 169, 187, 189, 215, 221, 236, 247, 248, 257, 287n11
exile, 10–12, 27, 28, 74, 96, 151, 188, 206, 231, 239, 243, 255

experience: Beijing, 84, 85; as episteme, 193, 204; feminist, 6, 80, 129; of human rights violations, 114; international, 126; and memorialization, 217, 231, 234, 236
Ezbet Khairallah (settlement), 13
Ezmatis, 105

Fahmi, Aida, *92fig.*
Family Planning Association (Egypt), 58
family: and care, 141; feminist, 183, 247; history and memory, 104, 105, 245, 247; and law, 80, 118–29; and patriarchy, 108, 253; of political activists, 93, 94, 95, 104, 108, 113, 114, 124, 125, 130, 137–43, 148, 152, 153, 158, 159, 160, 164, 176, 177, 183, 184, 216, 233, 240, 250, 255; women and honor, 64, 106; and women's work, 98
Fanon, Frantz, 41
Farag, Fatemah, 12
Fatah, 69
Fathi, Amal, 243
Fayad, Suzan, 22, 46, 47, 103–17, 163, 270n45
female circumcision, 11, 52, 54–56, *61fig.*, 63, 121, 126. *See also* female genital cutting or mutilation (FGM)
female genital cutting or mutilation (FGM), 50, 52–60, 62, 65, 66, 110, 109, 273n25; FGM Free Village Model, 60; FGM Task Force, 22, 45, 50–66, 126
femicide, 123
Femi-hub, 189
femininity: construction of, 63, 70; normative, 186; storytelling about, 189
feminism: Arab, 109, 248; associations and organizations, 10, 31, 37, 48, 50, 55, 56, 60, 76, 78, 97, 121, 184, 216, 218, 219, 234; discourses, Egyptian, 181, 248; in Egypt, 14, 15, 19, 21, 52, 54, 64–66, 68, 73, 74, 76, 79–82, 99, 104, 109, 122, 124, 118, 129, 132, 133, 141, 161, 187, 189, 190, 192, 202, 205, 218, 236, 247; Egyptian anthropologists, 63; feminist century, in Egypt, 28, 163, 259; feminist literary consciousness, 30; feminist lives, 5, 39, 100, 183, 184; feminist networks, 137, 282n34; feminist schools, 188, 288n19; genealogies of Egyptian, 29; herme-

INDEX · 325

feminism *(continued)*
neutics and exegesis, 29; historians, in Egypt, 9, 17; historiography, 2, 13, 234; ideas, theory, and political thought, 6, 17, 108, 181, 198, 205, 263n25; initiatives, 12, 60, 219; Islamic, 128, 129, 257, 281n31; institutionalization of, 126; journalists, 31, 55, 160; Muslim Women, 129; praxis, 83; transnational, 132. *See also specific organizations and people*

feudalism, 34

fiqh (Islamic jurisprudence), 123, 129

First Nations, 19

Ford Foundation Cairo Office, 60

foreign funding: issue, 78, 97, 112, 116, 258; Case 173/211, 131, 182

Foreign Office, British, 234

Fouda, Farag, 75, 92, 94, 112, 159

Four Women of Egypt (documentary), 15, *16fig.*, 40

Fraisse, Geneviève, 9

France, 30, 150, 245

Free Egyptian Woman, Speak Out (group), 287n2

freedom: individual, 164; of choice, 130

Friday of Rage, 4

fundamentalism, 72, 75, 129

Gaber, Mahmud, 94, 113

Gabr, Naila (Ambassador), 86

Gama'at al-dirasat al-'Arabiya (Association of Arab Studies), 125

Gama'a al-Islamiyya (Islamic Society), 88, 93, 158, 159

Ganubiyya Hurra (Free South), 187, 188

gay men, 188. *See also* LGBTQ; Queen Boat

Gaza, 69, 153, 163, 252, 253

gender: analytical category, 4, 70; in Arabic, 70; and colonialism, 2; coloniality of, 256; controversies about, 6; equality, 9, 17, 82, 129, 164; and family memories, 105; gap, 80, 136; and heteropatriarchy, 204; history, 17; and inequalities, 30, 35, 248; intersectionality of, 247, 257, 258; mainstream, 126; and Marxism, 46, 48; and representations, 21, 63, 213, 256; and political economy, 78; and power, 5, 20, 21, 49, 54, 55, 56, 62, 65, 75, 80, 83, 128,

145, 151, 160, 181, 215; and prisons, 239; and ratification of UN Conventions in Egypt, 86; and religion, 133; and Revolutionary Socialists, 168, 169; and Sarah Hegazi's writing, 188; and sexuality, 1, 32, 227, 231; and 2011 Revolution, 186, 187, 190, 192, 194, 219; and violence, 199, 209, 210

genealogy/ies, 4, 11, 28, 29, 49, 104, 108, 132, 138, 144, 245, 257

General Agreement on Tariffs and Trade, 76

General Assembly of the United Nations (Paris), 86

General Authority for Egyptian Cultural Palaces, 202

generation (millennial), 191

Geneva, 51

German Technical Cooperation Agency, 121

Gezi Park (protest), 1

Gharbiyya (governorate), 105

Ghazoul, Ferial, 70

Gheith, Rabee, 55

Ghozlan, Engy, 218

Giza (governorate), 122, 169

global financial crisis (1873), 30

Global South, 68, 69, 214

Gomaa, Faten, *92fig.*

governance, transnational, 82

Grand Mufti, 53

Grewal, Inderpal, 83

Group for Democratic Development, 113

Group of Seven (Group of Women Concerned with the Affairs of the Egyptian Woman), 120

The Guardian, 195

Hafez, Sherine, 207

Hamas, 1, 69, 252

Hamawi, Dina, 245

Hamilton, Omar Robert, *196fig.*

Hammad, Hanan, 16, 30

harakat al-ummat (movement of the mothers), 235

Harakat Ansar al-Salam (Partisans of Peace Movement, 1950), 35, 269n35

harassment: anti-sexual harassment groups, 186, 220, *224figs.*; of human rights defenders, 243; juridical, 182; march

326 · INDEX

against, 223; sexual, 98, 116, 142, 187, 195–98, 203, 210–30, 241–43; of women in Egypt, 98, 116, 142, 147. *See also* assault; Quwwa dud al-Taharrush (Operation Anti-Sexual Harassment [Opantish]); rape

Harem Politique: Le Prophete et le Femmes, 65

Harman, Chris, 168, 169

Harrassmap, 218

Hashim, Labiba, 32

Hassan, Bahey Eldin, 94, 112, 243, 287n4

Hassan, Manalm, 171, 183, 184, 197, 217, 287n8

Hassan, Mozn, 279n5

Hasso, Frances, 109

Hawa al-Horreya (Whims of Freedom), 27

Hawwa (Eve) (journal), 55

headscarf, 184, 185

health: mental, 73; minister of, 56; of political prisoners, 232; public, 56; public services for, 56, 65, 110, 247, 257; sexual and reproductive, 54, 55, 56, 110; women's, 20, 50, 57, 58, 77, 110, 121, 123; women's holistic approach to, 12, 66, 123, 161, 229; women's mental, 73, 56

Hegazi, Sarah, 188

Hegazy, Aya, 249

Hekayyat Gameela (Gameela's Talks), 143

Helwan (strike), 11, 114, *174fig.*

Helwan Community Services Center, Bashayir, 96

Heshmat, Dina, 28

Hetata, Sherif, 159

Hezb al-Nisa' (The Women's Party) (1945), 33

Hezb al-Tagammu' al-Watani al-Taqadomi al-Wahdawi (National Progressive Unionist Party), 38, 39, 44, 89, 126, 167, 278n15

Hezb al-'Ummal (Workers' Party), 160, 285n18

hijab, 97, 130, 159, 160, 164, 208

Hisham, Neama, 236

Hisham Mubarak Law Center, 243, 289n14

historians, of Egypt, 256

history: contemporary, 5, 6, 17, 18, 27, 76, 77; Egyptian, 20, 182; oral, 88, 96, 247,

253, 257, 294n31; political, 3, 39, 140, 182; social, 140

Hollande, François, 150

hooks, bell, 32, 184

"honor crime" (murder of a female family member), 121, 124

human rights: activists (Egyptian), 12; agenda in Egypt, 86, 188; community in Egypt, 93, 155; crisis, 12; Egyptian organizations, 199, 244; movement in Egypt, 14, 21, 85, 93, 94, 97, 100, 104, 141, 183, 191, 252, 257; organizations in Egypt, 113, 218, 236; violation of in Egypt, 13, 191

Human Rights and Social Development Desk, 86

Human Rights Centre for the Assistance of Prisoners, 113

human rights defenders: in Egypt, 93, 104; Egyptian feminist, 89

Hussein, Aziza, 57, 59, *92fig.*, 129

Hussein, Saddam, 67

Husain Mosque, 31

Ibn Khaldun Center for Development Studies, 94, 116

Ibrahim, Saad Eddin, 94, 116

Ibrahim, Samar, 242

Ibrahim, Samira, 205, 206

Ibrahim, Somaya, *92fig.*, *127fig.*

identity, normative, 188

Ikhtiyar for a Feminist Choice, 187, 188

Ikhwan (Muslim Brotherhood). See Muslim Brotherhood (Ikhwan)

Imam, Fatma, 129

Iman Mersal, 16, 97

imprisonment, 10, 23, 43, 75, 156, 176, 185, 191, 234, 236, 238, 240, 244, 255

incest, 123

independence, of Egypt, 27, 28. *See also* 1919 Revolution

independent syndicate (in Egypt), 171, 172; of tax collectors, 171

Indian Embassy, 36

Indigenous: language, 120; people, 85, 275n16; theories, 189

industry: industrial action, 171; industrial culture, 31; industrial workforce, 30; textile, 30

Infitah (opening), 69

inheritance, 118

injustice, social, 35, 69, 162

integrity, bodily, 161, 236. *See also* female genital cutting or mutilation (FGM)

intellectuals: Egyptian, 255; feminist Muslim, 128; public, 30, 92, 94, 100, 134, 164, 287n11; secular, 159

intelligence, British, 28, 31

international forums, 49, 126

International Monetary Fund (IMF), 75–77, 170, 252

International Planned Parenthood Federation, 57

International Women Suffrage Alliance (IWSA), 163, 253

International Women's Day, 89, *127fig.*, 202, 203, 220, 254

intersubjectivity, 2, 5, 18

Intifada, 95; Al Aqsa, 1, 114; Second, 163; Palestinian, 79

invasion, Arab-Islamic, of Egypt, 159

Iran: 1979 Revolution, 9; 2009 Iran Green Wave, 1; Iraq-Iran war, 67; Islamic feminism in, 128

Iraq: Iraq-Iran war, 67; Gulf War (1990–91), 67, 68, 69, 74; Egyptian people's solidarity with, 181, 254; US invasion of (2003), 163

Ireland, 33

Islamism/Islamists, 7, 22, 34, 36, 72, 76, 112, 129, 164; activists, 169; disagreements with the Marxists, 165, 243; discourse about women, 160; feminists against, 76; and FGM, 53, 57, 62, 65; and gender, 160, 281n30; and human rights, 89; ideology, 105, 158, 159; militants, 88; and Nawal al-Saadawi, 74, 75; political prisoners 1990s, 113; radical, 93, 158, 159

Ismail, Amira, 138

Ismail, Gameela, 22, 116, 134–54, *136fig.*

Ismailia, 35, 130, 139

Isma'il, Hala, 97

Israel, 36, 40, 41, 45, 67, 74, 84, 89, 104, 113, 160, 246, 252; invasion of Lebanon, 93

Istikmal al-thawra (Completion of the Revolution), 208

Ittihad al-Nisa' al-Qawmi (National Feminist Union), 36

Ittihad Bint al-Nil (Union of the Daughter of the Nile), 33; journal, 30

Jihadism, 75, 158, 159

Jihan Law, 120

jil al-tis'inat (generation of the nineties), 17

Jordan, 54, 131

Journalists for Change, 167

Judaism and Jewish people: Egyptian, 16; families, 15, 246, 247; fundamentalism, 75; laws, 279n3

jurisprudence, 123, 129

justice, 12, 17, 29, 66, 89, 123, 125, 129, 137, 141, 143, 155, 156, 167, 177, 182, 185, 194, 198, 203, 207, 217, 230, 234, 240, 257; social justice, 12, 29, 167, 177, 182, 185, 194, 203, 240, 252

Justice and Freedom Party, 131

Kadhibun (Liars), 211

Kamal, Hala, 71

Kamel, Nadia, 15

Kamel, Nayela, 16

Kamel, Saad, 16

Kandiyoti, Deniz, 15, 250

Karam, Azza, 120

karama (dignity), 185

Karama Party, 143, 165, 167, 282

Kazem, Safinaz, 15, *16fig.*, 42, 270n44

Keddie, Nikkie, 15

Kefaya, 147, 149, 166, 167, 182, 216, 217, 254; *kefaya* (enough), 185

Kellini, Georgette Sobhi Abdou, 87

khafd (reduction), 52

Khaled, Amru, 164

Khalil, Hamidah, 31

Khalil, Hisham Mustafa, 149

Khalil, Kamal, 111

Khayatt, Albert, 232

Khedive Isma'il, 30

Kheera, Hend, 8, 219

khitan (cutting), 22, 50, 52, 53, 55, 57, 60, 62–65, 74, 110, 114. *See also* female genital cutting or mutilation (FGM)

khul' (divorce) law, 62, 120, 126, 215. *See also* divorce

328 · INDEX

King Fu'ad University, 38
Kozma, Liat, 30
Kutla al Mesriya (political bloc), 149
Kuwait, Emirate of, 67, 68, 84, 158
kwashiorkor (children's disease), 45

Labor Organization, 99
Labor Party (Egyptian), 167
laicism, 128
Lajnat al-Nisa'i lil Muqawama al-Sha'biyya
   (Women's Committee for Popular
   Resistance), 35
Lajnat al-Wafd al-Markaziyah lil-Sayyidat
   (Wafdist Women's Central Committee
   [WWCC]), 31
Land Center for Human Rights, 113
law: anti-demonstration, 230; anti-terrorism (Law 97/1992), 90; association (Law
   32/1964 and Law 84/2002), 90, 91, 243;
   Concerning the Regulation and Organ-
   ization of Journalism and Press Func-
   tions, 113; Egyptian, 79, 121; electoral,
   excluding women from suffrage (1923),
   34; emergency (Law 162/1958) 90; Law
   1/2000, 119; Mubarak offers to emend
   electoral law (in 2011), 289n13; Personal
   Status Law (PSL), 8, 22, 44, 58, 80, 118,
   119, 120, 123, 132, 133, 136, 181; Protest
   Law (Law 107/2013), 156; Islamic,
   86, 118
Lazreg, Marnia, 15
League of Women University and College
   Students (1945), 33
Leane, Jeanine, 19, 20
Lebanon, Israeli invasion of, 93
the Left/leftist activists, 157, 160, 162, 167,
   156, 170, 242, 247; family, 250; feminist,
   194, 244; new, 108, 168; post-2011, 171;
   Shaima' al-Sabbagh, 175; young women,
   164
legal charges: debauchery, 116, 188; defamation, 182, 216; misuse of social media,
   182; organizing a demonstration, 255;
   spreading of false news, 18. See also law
L'Egyptienne (magazine), 34, 108, 119
Lenin/Leninist, 41, 47, 168, 169, 285n18
LGBTQ: demands, 188; community and
   groups, 187, 188; rights, 187, 188, 190, 223

Liberal Constitutional Party (Wafd). See
   Wafd Party
liberalism: and activists in Egypt, 7, 112,
   187, 189; and democratic thought, 93;
   and the economic liberal turn, 74; and
   feminists, 36, 125, 133, 248, 257; and
   human rights activists, 112; party, 165,
   167, 282n4; political visions, 158, 164,
   165; and women, 21, 22, 36, 77, 135, 150.
   See also Wafd Party
liberation: intersectionality of, 110; of
   political prisoners, 13, 37; women's, 5, 14,
   17, 36, 37, 194, 254, 257
Libya, 1, 105
Logan, Laura, 206
Lord Allenby (Field Marshal), 232
Lorde, Audre, 184
Lotfy, Mohamed, 243
Ludovic Trarieux International Human
   Rights Prize, 155
Lutfi, Huda, 17
Luxemburg, Rosa, 169

Maadi (neighborhood), 13, 187, 254
Mada Masr, 3, 12, 155, 156, 190, 252, 262n5
Magdi, Solafa, 239
Magdy, Zeinab, 28
Mahalla al-Kubra (district), 98, 170
Mahfouz, Asmaa, 184–86
Mahfouz, Naguib, 141, 159
Mahmoud, Abdul Majeed (Attorney
   General), 216
Mahmoud, Amal, 92fig.
Mahmoud, Hind, 184
Majlis al-Sha'b (lower house of Parliament),
   215
Majmu'at an-nisa wal dustur (Group of
   Women and the Constitution), 10
Maktab Shabab al-Quwa al-Wataniya (Office
   of the National Youth Group), 165
Manala (blog), 171, 287n8
Mandela, Nelson, 155
manhood, 185. See also masculinity
Manshiyyat Nasir, 59
Mansour, Hala, 92fig.
Mansoura, 97, 160
Maoism, 108
Marai, Afaf, 58

INDEX · 329

marasmus (children's disease), 45, 46

March 8: in 1977, 202; in 2011, 202. *See also* International Women's Day

March 9 Movement for the Independence of the Universities, 29, *166fig.*

March 14, 1919, 31

marriage, 56, 64, 106, 118, 119, 120, 123, 188, 279n7; marriage contract, 120. *See also* divorce

Martine Anstett Award for Human Rights, 118

Marxist-Leninist Egyptian Communist Workers Party (ECWP), 47

Marx/Marxism, 15, 22, 29, 36, 43, 44, 46, 47, 48, 49, 50, 76, 78, 93, 99, 104, 105, 108, 109, 112, 133, 157, 159, 160, 161, 164, 165, 167, 168, 169, 189, 241, 247, 250, 257, 285n18

masculinity: construction of, 70, 226; and gender, 189; hegemonic, 11, 201; normative, 186; studies, 263n25

Maspero state TV building, 139; demonstrations, 220; October 2011 massacre, 241

Masriyyn al-Ahrar (Free Egyptians Party), 149

Matar, Azza, 270n45

Mauritius, Tanzania, 128

McGrath, Ann, 19

media and newspapers, Egyptian, 95, 238, 252; attacking women political activists, 142. *See also specific newspapers and outlets*

Medical Doctors Union, 73

Medinaportal, 143–44

Mehrez, Salwa, 242

Mehrez, Samia, 67

memories: episteme of, 193, 196; family, personal and political, 20, 38, 39, 42, 59, 85, 96, 104, 105, 111, 150, 162, 246, 247; feminist, 5, 175, 202; historical, 27, 74, 76, 193; Memory of Writing (book series), 202; of prison, 74, 240, 244, 245, 247, 248, 250; transgenerational and collective, 27, 28, 29, 48, 161, 191, 193, 198, 247, 257; traumatic, 130, 131, 231; of 2011 Revolution, 190, 191, 194, 195, 202, 210, 212, 213, 241, 242, 256, 258; of violence, 191, 194, 199, 204, 205, 206,

217, 229, 230, 251; women's, 3, 5, 49, 58, 94, 201, 216, 237. *See also* Women and Memory Forum (WMF)

Meqlad, Shahenda, 15, *16fig.*, *92fig.*, 163

Mernissi, Fatima, 14, 65, 129, 248

Mervat, Hatem, 15, 37

#MeToo (in Egypt), 214, 255

Metwally, Hussein, 216

middle class, Egyptian, 32, 33, 40, 51, 58, 162, 164, 165, 167, 171, 221, 251, 287n9

migrants, 72, 75

Milner Commission, 28

Minister of Foreign Affairs, 86

ministries: Ministry of Foreign Affairs, 86; Ministry of Health, 57, 62, 103, 196; Ministry of Health and Population, 196; Ministry of Information, 142; Ministry of Justice, 91; Ministry of Social Affairs, 81, 91, 188

minorities: *mutamassirun* (minorities), 246; sexual, 258

Minya, Upper Egypt, 158

Misr Spinning and Weaving Company Ghazl al-Mahalla, 178. *See also* Mahalla al-Kubra (district)

Mitri, Soad, *97fig.*

Mitri, Wedad, 15, *16fig.*, *92fig.*

mobs: sexual, 220. *See also* assault; harrassment; Quwwa dud al-Taharrush (Operation Anti-Sexual Harassment [Opant-ish]); rape

modernity/modernization, in Egypt, 29, 31, 62, 83, 118

Mohamed, Nanda, 28

Mohamed, Noha, 224

Monazzamat al-Shabab al-Ishtiraki (Social-ist Youth Organization), 40, 41

Morayef, Heba, 205

Morocco, 1, 68, 128

Morsi, Mohammed, 76, 222, 224

Mosallam, Alia, 28, 29

Mosireen (collective), 194, 221, 222, 238

Mousa, Fatma, 39

movements: 1968 global student, 9; civil rights, 9; cross-ideological social, 157; for democracy in, 167, 203; Egyptian Communist, 246, 247; Egyptian nationalism/nationalist, 28; feminist,

52, 150, 154, 186, 206, 249, 257, 259; for human rights, 254; liberal, 282n6; pious, 70, 128, 281n30; post-Islamist pious, 70; radical, 158–59; repression of, 74, 89, 90, 93, 284n11; social, 157, 158, 163, 166, 169, 175, 182, 183, 186; student, 3, 14, 22, 32, 33, 38, 40–50, 53, 64, 68, 94–96, 99, 103, 104, 160–64, 168, 183, 187, 235, 257, 282; women in labor movement, 97; women in 1970s student movement, 43, 45, 48, 134, 148, 190, 215, 234, 250, 282n2; women's, 28, 74, 81, 186; workers, 170. *See also* activism; *harakat al-ummat* (movement of the mothers); Harakat Ansar al-Salam (Partisans of Peace Movement, 1950); human rights; Kefaya; *and other specific movements*

Mu'assasa al-Mar'a al-Gadida (New Woman Foundation [NWF]), 11, 47, 58, 78, 79, 81, 82, 89, 92, 96–99, 108, 150, 160, 183, 184, 194, 214

Mubarak, Gamal, 87, 93, 195

Mubarak, Hisham, 94

Mubarak, Hosni, 142, 158, 159, 160, 167, 172, 196, 199, 202, 203, 208, 209, 212, 224, 282n7; fall of, 143; gender politics, 215; regime, 8, 54, 60, 75, 125, 150, 165, 166, 182, 185, 222, 285n22

Mubarak, Suzanne, 60, 77, 82, 83, 215, 276n38

Muhammad Mahmoud Street, 134, 135, 208, 220

mukhtafeen (disappeared), 12

Multaqa al-Mar'a wa al-Dhakira (Women and Memory Forum), 17, 71, 129

Muntada al-Shabbat (youth forum of NWF), 184

Musa, Nabawiyya, 32, 108, 268n26

Musawah, 129, 131

museums: Egyptian, 204, 207; Museum of Modern Art in Cairo, 36

Muslim Brotherhood (Ikhwan), 42, 62, 75, 76, 88, 93, 97, 131, 149, 163, 165, 167, 168, 199, 212, 224, 228, 242, 245, 262n5, 269n35

Muslim majority countries, 14, 86, 122

Muslim world, 124, 128

Mustafa, Malek, 171

Nabarawi, Saiza, 14, 35, 108

Nafea', Hend, 244

nahda (nineteenth-century Arab Renaissance), 15, 268n18

Nairobi (UN Conference on Women, 1985), 47, *73fig.*, 82, 120, 276n28

Napoleonic Penal Code, 121

Nasif, Kawkab Hifni (Bahithat al-Badiya's younger sister), 33

Nasif, Malak Hifni (pen name Bahithat al-Badiya), 33, 108

Nasserists, 105, 112, 125, 126, 159, 166, 167

National Council for Childhood and Motherhood, 50, 60, 87

National Council for Human Rights, 87, 88

National Council for Students and Workers, 34

National Council for Women, 54, 77, 87, 126, 215, 217

National Democratic Party (NDP), 87, 145, 167, 203

National Dialogue (2023), 137, 152, 282n5

nationalism, 2, 287n7; Egyptian, 186; heteronormative anticolonial, 189; and Marxism in Egypt, 247

nationality (Egyptian), 72

National NGO Commission for Population and Development, 60

National Police Day, 182

National Population Committee, 57

National Progressive Unionist Party (NPUF), 38, 159

National Women's Empowerment Strategy (2017–30), 8

Nawfal, Hind, 128

Nazra for Feminist Studies, 11, 184, 187, 188, 199, 213, 229, 230, 242, 288n19

Nejm, Nawara, 184

neoliberalism: Egyptian agenda, 55; international agenda, 55

Neplantera, 189

New Mestiza, 189

Newsweek (Cairo bureau), 190

New World Order, 54, 68

NGOs (nongovernmental organizations), 17, 22, 49, 57; campaigns to fight violence against women, 126; feminist

NGOs *(continued)*
debates, 57, 62, 78, 249; "foreign funding" case, 131, 243; human rights, 88, 112; independent, 58; and International Conference on Population and Development (ICPD) preparation, 58, 60; Islamist, 92; legislation about, 81, 90, 91, 243, 244, 255; post-2011 critics of liberal feminism and, 188, 191; professionals, 240; and UN conferences on women, 82, 83, 84; women's, 121, 229

Nishan al-Kamal award (Order of the Virtues), 202

Nobel Peace Prize, 182

North Sinai Governorate of Egypt, 88

No to Military Trials for Civilians (NMTC), 237, 238, 240

No to the Capital Punishment, 155

Nour, Ayman (Senator), 87, 142, 167, 238, 278n15, 287n5

Nour, Noor Ayman, 138, 282

Nour, Shady, 138

November 2011 demonstrations, 206, 209, 242

Nubia, 188

Nun (magazine), 97

Obama, Barack, 142

occupations of factories, 186

October 2023, 1, 253

October 7, 2004, 88

officials: conservative religious, 124

Oman, 68

Omran, Ragia, 58, 232

Opantish (Quwwa dud al-Taharrush [Operation Anti-Sexual Harassment]), 220–31, 238

oppression: category of, 21; colonial and gender, 256; discursive, 48; homosexuality, 70, 116, 117; imprisonment and, 176; multiple layers of, 65, 77, 89; patriarchal, 64; sexual, 73

Orientalism, 15, 248

Ottoman Empire, 30, 267n11

Pakistan, 128, 159

Palestine: anticolonial revolts, 253; dehumanization of, 253; Egyptian women's solidarity with, 163, 168, 249, 253, 254; genocide, 252; hospital, 111, 113; people, 181; refugees from, 251; Nakba, 252. *See also* Intifada

pan-Arabism, 247

Paris: Peace Conference, 27; the Rome Group, 246; UN General Assembly, 86; Women's International Democratic Federation Congress, 34

Parliament (Egyptian) (Shura Council), 90, 120, 142, 145

Passerini, Luisa, 18, 266n57

patriarchy: in Egypt, 10, 15, 18, 21, 186, 189; heteronormative colonial, 189; indigenous, 71; intersectionality of, 89; Nawal al-Saadawi on, 72; Raewyn Connell on, 263n25. *See also* authoritarianism; family; gender

Peace Treaty (Egypt-Israel, 1979), 67

Personal Status Law (PSL), 8, 22, 44, 58, 80, 118, 119, 120, 123, 132, 133, 136, 181

"the place of speech" *(lugar de fala)*, 17

Planning Association in Egypt, 58

pleasure, sexual, 56, 110, 111

police stations, Egyptian, 113

Policies Secretariat of the National Democratic Party, 87

politics: Egyptian field, 22, 38, 86, 136, 137, 168; of everyday, 44, 164; of intimacy, 4, 94; parties in Egypt, 136; street, 168

Port Said, 6

positive deviance approach, 126

postcolonial: age, 124; Egypt, 184; feminist critique, 85, 191; nation-state construction, 106; political project, 246; spaces, 192; world, 78

Pratt, Nicola, 88, 266n56

presidency (of Egypt), 167, 215. *See also* names of presidents

Press Syndicate, 148, *166fig.*, 203, 215, 245

Prince, Mona, 7

prisoners, political, 7, 12, 13, 23, 28, 42, 94, 113, 138, 142, 151, 176, 177, 197, 206, 232, 234–36, 237–40, 242, 244, 249, 250, 252, 254, 284n6. *See also* Human Rights Centre for the Assistance of Prisoners

prisons, 227, 231, 232–45, 248, 249–50, 255; al-Wahat, 107; Damanhour, women's,

177, 188; Qanater, 42, 43, 239, 241, 249;
  Tora, 233
prosecutor, Egyptian, 131
Protestants, 128
psychiatry, in Egypt, 109
Public Debt Fund (Caisse de la Dette
  Publique) (1876), 30
Pulcini, Elena, 140

Qale't el-Kabsh slum, *173figs.*
Qanater (prison), 42, 43, 239, 241, 249
Qasr el-Nil bridge, 135, 242
Qasr el-Nil Street, 131, 145, 149
Qatar, 68
Qena (village in Upper Egypt), 139
Queen Boat, 70, 116, 188
Queer activists, 188; Queer-friendly café, 7.
  See also LGBTQ
Quwwa dud al-Taharrush (Operation
  Anti-Sexual Harassment [Opantish]),
  220–31, 238

Rabaa al-Adawiya Square, 228
Rached, Tahani, 15, 163
Rachid, Amina, 15, *15fig.*, 35, 36, 43, 162, 164
Rademaker, Laura, 19
Radio Banat Offline, 189
Rafah (Egypt), 113, 163, 252
Ragab, Mohamed, 145
rainbow flag, 188
Ramadan, Fatma, 79, 99
Ramallah, 51
Ramsis Street, 51
rape, 146, 169, 191, 196, 198, 199, 205, 211,
  213, 217, 218, 219, 220, 223, 226, 227, 229,
  231; in 1919, 29; in 2011 Revolution, 28;
  gang rapes, 241, 242, 250; marital rape,
  66; Nawal al-Saadawi on, 75. *See also*
  assault; harrassment; Quwwa dud
  al-Taharrush (Operation Anti-Sexual
  Harassment [Opantish])
Rashid, Fatma, 33
Ratib, 'Aisha, 128
Rauf Ezzat, Heba, 70
Red Sea, 88, 156
Refa'i, Om, *173fig.*
refugees, 13, 39, 72, 251
Refugees Solidarity Movement, 155

regimes: Arab, 71, 275n17; Egyptian, 4;
  military, 68, 153
relationality, 5, 48
renaissance, Arab, 15. *See also nahda*
repression: political, 6, 11, 30, 42, 69, 75, 77,
  87, 89, 90, 93, 94, 104, 116, 131, 143, 155,
  156, 158, 169, 168, 172, 188, 202, 245, 256;
  sexual, 20, 188
revival: Islamic, 128
revolt: in history, 9, 30, 32, 69; Palestinian,
  153; women's, 46, 151
revolution: 1789 French, 9; 1848 uprisings,
  9; 1917 Bolshevik, 9; 1919 and women,
  201, 210, 226; 1919 anti-British, 20, 27,
  28, 29, 31, 90, 104, 105, 134, 237; 1979
  Iranian, 9; 2005 Lebanon (Cedar), 1;
  decade of the, 2, 22, 207, 213, 214, 224,
  236; as a process, 21, 157, 160; as a space,
  6, 187, 190; theory of the Arab, 105. *See
  also* 1919 Revolution; 2011 Revolution;
  Alliance of the Continuing Revolution
  (Tahalluf al-thawra mustamirra); Arab
  Spring; Committee to Defend the
  Revolution; Istikmal al-thawra (Completion of the Revolution); counterrevolution; Thawrat el-Banat (The Girls
  Revolution); Thawra Misri
Revolutionary Socialists, 135, 155, 160, 165,
  166fig., 165, 167–70, *173figs.*, 182, 185
Ribeiro, Djamila, 17
rights: bodily, 239, 249; sexual and repro-
  ductive, 66, 80, 83, 99, 117, 146, 236,
  249; women's, 77, 81, 83, 97, 114, 118,
  126–28, 136, 172, 189, 191–92, 256, 257;
  women's reproductive, 65; workers', 97,
  171, 181, 186, 194
Rosaria Stabili, Maria, 18
Rosenthal, Mary Ely, 15
Rushdi, Noha, 218
Russia, 9, 67

Sa'ad, Ahmad Sadiq, 245–46
Saad, Reem, *92fig.*
Sabra and Shatila, 93
Sabri, Siham, 47
Sadat, Anwar, 41, 16, 37, 96, 107, 112, 120,
  145, 158–59
Sadat, Jihan, 119

Sadek, Rawia, 243, 270n45
Said, Khaled, 165, 241; mother of, 219; We
    Are All Khaled Said, 182, 185
Sa'id, Muhammad al-Sayyed, 94
Said, Mustafa, 28
Said, Salma, 244
Salafi Party, 135, 212
Saleh, Arwa, 47, 48, 227
Salem, Amir, 94, 111
Sallam, Yara, 236, 239, 240–50, 294n31
Saniyya School, 32
Saudi Arabia, 156, 158
Sawiris, Naguib, 149
Sawsan Othman, 97
scholars and scholarship: in Egypt, 17, 18,
    122; Egyptian, 52; Middle East Studies,
    15; feminist, 9, 12, 14, 18, 65, 82, 84, 123,
    128, 161, 184; Southwest Asia and North
    Africa (SWANA), 2, 17
security: apparatus, 185, 220; Central
    Security Conscripts, 210; Egyptian, 89;
    Egyptian Emergency State Security
    Court, 116; Israeli, 89; personnel, 202,
    233, 243; Security Directorate, 176; state
    security forces/national, 10, 80, 81, 91,
    95, 103, 115, 135, 147, 148, 168, 169, 172,
    176, 212, 215, 254, 255, 284n1; UN Secu-
    rity Council Resolution, 67
Seif, Mona, 13, 205, 233, 237, 244
Seif, Sana, 13
self-determination, women's, 65, 86
Seliman, Sarah, 230
sex, 72, 146, 187; ignorance about, 65;
    intercourse, 214; relationships, 196;
    workers, 248
sexism, 75, 110, 161, 168, 206
sexuality, 64, 207, 231, 243, 256, 258; issues,
    121, 161; normative discourse about, 187;
    perception of, 192; reconceptualization
    of, 188; women's, 65
Shabab min Agl el-Tagheer (Youth for
    Change), 167
Shafik, Amina, 270n44
Shafik, Doria, 31–32, 33, 37; house arrest, 36
Shaima Tantawi, 288n19
Sharafeldin, Marwa, 129, 282n33
Sha'rawi, Huda, 31, 35, 36, 108, 202, 234, 253
shari'a, 86, 118, 121

Sharif, Amal, 58
Shehab, Bahia, 8, 209, 210
Shukrallah, Alaa, 94
Shukrallah, Hala, 79, 89, *92fig.*, 94, 95, 98,
    104, 184, 203, 233, 234
Shukrallah, Hani, 46, 94, 104, 108, 247
Shura Council (Egyptian Parliament), 90,
    120, 142, 145
*Sidewalk Stories: Women in Cairo's Public
    Spaces* (exhibition), 230
Sidi Gaber (Alexandria neighborhood), 225
Sidqi, Isma'il, 35
Sidqi-Bevin treaty, 35
socialism, 87, 168
Socialist Labor Party, 159
Socialist Popular Alliance Party, 10, 282n6
social media, 7, 152, 153, 177, 182, 185, 203,
    204, 230, 234, 239, 244, 285n21
social work, 36, 50, 132
Soliman, Azza, 22, 113, 118–33, *127fig.*
Soliman, Laila, 27, 209, 256
Sorbonne, 33
Soueif, Ahdaf, 7, 195, *196fig.*, 209, 234, 236
Soueif, Laila, 29, 47, 104, *115fig.*, 236, 238
Spivak, Gayatri Chakravorty, 82, 276n28
Stalinism, 108, 168
state: building, 76; Egyptian, 15, 83, 86, 140,
    159, 236, 257; feminism, 37; postcolonial,
    184; modern, 127, 201; postcolonial
    republican, 106; television, 135, 139, 142,
    143, 154
storytelling, 20, 175, 189
strikes, 170; in 1990s, 99; in 2008, 186; in
    2011, 208; and emergency law, 90; in
    Helwan (1989), 111, 114; hunger, 36, 231,
    237, 238; women leading, 171, 172, 182
struggle: class, 36, 44; workers', 170
Sudan, 157, 251
Suez Canal, 30, 38
suffrage, 33, 36, 55, 145, 155. *See also* Interna-
    tional Women Suffrage Alliance
    (IWSA)
Suleiman, Omar, 209
Supreme Council of the Armed Forces
    (SCAF), 135, 206, *212fig.*
survivors, 103, 109, 114, 190, 193, 198, 199,
    205, 213, 217, 226, 227, 229
Syria, 1, 13, 15, 68, 105, 251

Taba, 88
Tadros, Marilyn, 58
Tagammuʿ Party, 38, 39, 44, 89, 126, 167, 278n15
Taha, Eman, 216. *See also* Black Wednesday
tahara (purity), 52, 53
Tahrir Bodyguard, 220, 223
Tahrir Square, 2, 30, 74, 130, 131, 134, 154, 163, 169, 175, 182, 186, 187, 190, 194–95, *196fig.*, 197–98, 199, 203, 204, 208, 210, 220, 221, 223, 242, 252
Talʿat Harb, 175
Tallawi, Mervat (Minister for Social Affairs), 91
Tamarod, 224, 225
tarjama (translation/biography), 5. *See also* biography
Task Force against Sexual Harassment, 218
tax collectors sit-in, 170, 171
Tekla, Lila Ibrahim, 88
Tel Aviv, 40
Telmissany, May, 7, 287n11
terrorists, 218; Wasat Party, 167; woman MP, 273n25; young activists in 2011, 135
testimonies, 10, 11, 18, 21, 51, 53, 75, 83, 89, 94, 121, 131, 135, 139, 184, 193–95, 199, 202–5, 216, 217, 222, 227, 237, 234, 236, 239, 240, 241, 243, 249, 257; as episteme, 193
Thabit, Munira, 33
Thawra Misri (Egyptian Revolution), 159
Thawrat el-Banat (The Girls Revolution), 189
"the third square," 224, 228
Thunberg, Greta, 13
Tiananmen Square, 69
Tinar and Sanafr, 156
Toma, Sally, 211, 238, 285n21
Toson sit-in, 171
transgender, 187, 249
transmission, 160, 161, 247, 256, 78trauma: of assault/rape/sexual attack, 216, 226; collective, 205; Doria Shafik, 37; exile, 188; experience of, 20, 113, 130, 133, 191, 198, 220; generational, 231; human rights community traumatized, 92, 112; after imprisonment, 238, 112, 115; memories of 2011 Revolution, 231; protection from, 59; after Rabaa, 228; silencing and

perpetuation of, 195; traumatic events, 18, 131; traumatic memory, 131; violence, 193, 217, 220, 257. *See also* memories
travel ban, 11, 50, 103, 182, 239, 255, 263n27
tripartite aggression (1956), 35
Trotskyists, 105, 168
Troy, Jakelin, 19
Tucker, Judith, 15
Tunisia, 1, 54, 78, 287n8
Turkish Ukrainian, 15

Umm al-Misriyyin (Mother of the Egyptians), 28
underground metal scene, 138
United Nations (UN): Cairo office, 154; development and Egyptian feminist critique of it, 82; global agenda on development, 55; International Conference on Population and Development (ICPD), 55; Security Council Resolution 678, 67; Summit for the Adoption of the Post-2015 Development Agenda, 240; Universal Declaration of Human Rights, 86; UN Women, 254; UN Women's Committee, 57; UN Women's Decade, 275n28; women and development, 126, 191; World Conferences on Women (Mexico City 1975, Copenhagen 1980, Nairobi 1985, Beijing 1995), *73fig.*, 75, 77, 78, 82, 83, 126, 214, 275n28
universities: in Egypt, 40, 191. *See also specific universities*
Untha (Female), 188
Upper Egypt, 62, 63, 104, 139, 158, 205, 206. *See also* Nubia
uprisings: 1848 uprisings, 9; 1919 anticolonial, 28, 31, 90; anti-British, 104; Arab Spring, 9; popular, in March 1919, 27; Palestinian, 163, 253. *See also specific uprisings and revolutions*
ʿUrabi, Ahmed (Colonel), 30. *See also* ʿUrabi revolt
ʿUrabi revolt, 30, 32
utopia, 2, 193, 195

veil, 70, 72, 150, 164, 205, 210
victims, 1, 7, 9, 11, 96, 112, 113, 114, 146, 190, 199, 204, 213, 219, 227, 243, 249

INDEX · 335

violence: domestic, 47, 84, 115, 121, 123, 188; in Egyptian society, 206; Egyptian state, 85, 114, 209, 213, 218, 231; sexual, 23, 151, 181, 184, 189, 190, 192, 193, 195, 198, 201, 205, 210, 212, 213, 214, 215, 216, 217, 218, 219, 220, 222, 226, 227, 228, 229, 230, 236, 241, 249, 250. *See also* assault; borders; colonialism; demonstrations; El-Nadeem; harrassment; memories; rape; trauma

virginity test, 204–6, 220, 238

Wafd Party, 27, 105, 167, 269n35, 278n15; Wafdist meeting, 28; Women's Central Committee, 31

Wahba, Dina, 10

wali (the guardian), 120

war: American Civil War, 30; in Algeria, 69; of attrition (Egypt-Israel), 84; civil wars in Syria, Yemen, Libya, 1

Wasif Bey Ghali, Madame, 232

West Bank, 69

White House (US), 142

Wiradjuri, 19

women: academics, 17; artists and writers, 17, 212; bodies of, 17, 54, 106, 150, 190, 215, 273n28; and development, 19, 126; education of, 32, 33, 106; Egyptian, 21, 22, 54, 57, 69, 72, 78, 80, 209; European residents in Egypt, 119; experiences of, 3, 14, 28, 80, 88, 89, 106, 109–11, 114, 116, 193, 198, 210, 212, 217, 234; feminist intellectuals, 71, 81, 95, 127, 131, 132, 133, 145, 165, 186, 203, 209, 211, 239, 253, 257, 259; freedom of, 72, 164; and Gender Studies (WGS), 71; history of, 33; intellectuals, 2, 4, 14, 16, 21, 67, 69, 70; issues of, 44, 46, 58, 71, 74, 75, 78, 80, 81, 114, 123, 126, 127, 138, 189, 227; journalists, 79, 138; lawyers, 119, 123; liberation of, 17, 36, 257; Muslim, 14, 15, 106, 125, 186, 215; nationalists, 186; organizations in Egypt, 246; parliamentarians, 144; perspectives of, 17; poverty, 77, 182; representation of Arab, 1; revolution and revolutionaries, 10, 150, 169, 190, 191, 198, 226; Sudanese, 154; three generations of, *92fig.*; trafficking of, 72; transgenerational solidarity and transmission, 133, 137, 141, 248, 250; university students, 44; writing, 79. *See also names of specific people and organizations*

Women and Memory Forum (WMF), 17, 71, 129

Women's International Democratic Federation (WIDF) and Women's International Democratic Federation Congress, 34, 35

Women's Party, 33, 36

Words of Women from the Egyptian Revolution, 213

Workers for Change, 167

working class, Egyptian, 28

World Bank, 76, 78, 252

World War I, 28

World War II, 32, 33, 35, 67

Year of Women (2017), 8

Yemen, 1, 274n2

young Egyptians, 104, 197

Youssef, Ranya, 155

Youth Women's Christian Association (YWCA), 51, 57

Yugoslavia (Socialist Federal Republic), 69

Zaghlul, Sa'd, 27–28, 215

Zaghlul, Safiyya, 28

Zahran, Farid, 153

Zaki, Nadera, *92fig.*

Zamalek, 36, 51, 156, 253

Zarei, Mohamed, 94, 113

Zifta, 105

Zulfikar, Mona, 87, 88, 127

Founded in 1893,
UNIVERSITY OF CALIFORNIA PRESS
publishes bold, progressive books and journals
on topics in the arts, humanities, social sciences,
and natural sciences—with a focus on social
justice issues—that inspire thought and action
among readers worldwide.

The UC PRESS FOUNDATION
raises funds to uphold the press's vital role
as an independent, nonprofit publisher, and
receives philanthropic support from a wide
range of individuals and institutions—and from
committed readers like you. To learn more, visit
ucpress.edu/supportus.

www.ingramcontent.com/pod-product-compliance
Ingram Content Group UK Ltd.
Pitfield, Milton Keynes, MK11 3LW, UK
UKHW010051020625
459173UK00001BB/3